D1223499

Leadership in Recreation and Leisure Services

Timothy S. O'Connell, PhD
Brock University

Brent Cuthbertson, PhD
Lakehead University

Terilyn J. Goins, PhD
Regent University

Editors

Human Kinetics

Library of Congress Cataloging-in-Publication Data

Leadership in recreation and leisure services / Timothy O'Connell, Brent Cuthbertson, Terilyn J. Goins, [editors].
    pages cm
    Includes bibliographical references and index.
    1. Leisure industry--Textbooks. 2. Recreation--Textbooks. 3. Tourism--Textbooks. 4. Leadership--Textbooks. 5. Recreational leadership--Textbooks. I. O'Connell, Timothy S., 1968- II. Cuthbertson, Brent, 1961- III. Goins, Terilyn J.
    GV188.L43 2014
    790.06'9--dc23
    2013013581

ISBN: 978-0-7360-9531-0

Parts of chapter 4, "Facilitating Group Experiences," have been adapted from *Team-Building Activities for the Digital Age: Using Technology to Develop Effective Groups* by Brent D. Wolfe and Colbey Penton Sparkman, Human Kinetics, 2010.

The web addresses cited in this text were current as of March 11, 2014, unless otherwise noted.

Acquisitions Editor: Gayle Kassing, PhD; **Developmental Editor:** Jacqueline Eaton Blakley; **Assistant Editors:** Anne Rumery, Casey A. Gentis, and Elizabeth Evans; **Copyeditor:** Patsy Fortney; **Indexer:** Katy Balcer; **Permissions Manager:** Dalene Reeder; **Graphic Designer:** Joe Buck; **Graphic Artist:** Denise Lowry; **Cover Designer:** Keith Blomberg; **Photographs (interior):** © Human Kinetics, unless otherwise noted; Chapter opener 1 © Fai Nan I Dreamstime.com (p. 2); Chapter 2 Brand X Pictures (p. 18); Chapter opener 4 © Oren Gelbendorf I Dreamstime.com (p. 50); Chapter opener 5 Jim West (p. 68); Chapter 6 Copyright SWP, Incorporated 2004 (p. 96); Chapter opener 8 © Winzworks I Dreamstime.com (p. 140); Chapter opener 9 © Hill Street Studios/E/ Blend Images RM/age footstock (p. 154); Chapter 10 tholi75 (p. 182); Chapter opener 11 © Vinciber I Dreamstime.com (p. 208); Chapter 12 © Corbis. All right reserved (p. 236); Chapter opener 13 © Jim West/age footstock (p. 256); Chapter opener 14 Joselito Briones (p. 276); **Photo Asset Manager:** Laura Fitch; **Photo Production Manager:** Jason Allen; **Art Manager:** Kelly Hendren; **Associate Art Manager**: Alan L. Wilborn; **Printer:** Sheridan Books

Printed in the United States of America   10   9   8   7   6   5   4   3   2   1

The paper in this book is certified under a sustainable forestry program.

Human Kinetics
Website: www.HumanKinetics.com

United States: Human Kinetics, P.O. Box 5076, Champaign, IL 61825-5076
800-747-4457
e-mail: humank@hkusa.com

Canada: Human Kinetics, 475 Devonshire Road Unit 100, Windsor, ON N8Y 2L5
800-465-7301 (in Canada only)
e-mail: info@hkcanada.com

Europe: Human Kinetics, 107 Bradford Road, Stanningley, Leeds LS28 6AT, United Kingdom
+44 (0) 113 255 5665
e-mail: hk@hkeurope.com

Australia: Human Kinetics, 57A Price Avenue, Lower Mitcham, South Australia 5062
08 8372 0999
e-mail: info@hkaustralia.com

New Zealand: Human Kinetics, P.O. Box 80, Torrens Park, South Australia 5062
0800 222 062
e-mail: info@hknewzealand.com

E5181

Contents

Preface   vii

Acknowledgments   viii

Preface

There are many examples of good leaders throughout history. When we are asked to think of exemplary leaders, people such as Abraham Lincoln, Indira Gandhi, Winston Churchill, Pierre Trudeau, and Vince Lombardi may come to mind. Among others, U.S. President Barack Obama has focused new attention on what it is to be a leader in the 21st century. The new millennium has brought rapid change that demands that recreation and leisure studies professionals be on the cutting edge of new insights in leadership and leadership development. Social, economic, cultural, political, and technological developments in the last 10 years require recreation and leisure services professionals to not only understand new perspectives on leadership, but also be able to apply this knowledge with increasingly diverse groups of people.

The purpose of this book is to bring the study of leadership in the field of recreation and leisure services into the 21st century by combining classic leadership information and theory with hot new topics. The first six chapters that make up part I help students examine their own values, attitudes, and beliefs, which shape how they approach leadership, and provide information on the theory and practice of leadership. Classic leadership theory, interpersonal communication skills, and the ethical considerations of leading others are addressed in a format that integrates theory and practice. This information sets the stage for part II, in which students learn about working with others in a professional way. Topics such as group dynamics, the unique requirements of leading in recreation and leisure settings, and managing risk are considered. Part III examines leadership from an organizational perspective. These three chapters look at leadership from both an internal and external perspective, and consider what it means to lead in the recreation and leisure services profession as a whole. The progression of content is designed to help students understand the myriad roles of leaders in the field of recreation and leisure services. All chapters present material in an engaging, practical format that facilitates the understanding and application of leadership theory.

This book takes into account recent developments in leadership theory and integrates them into the practices of the recreation and leisure services profession. Information is presented in a way that encourages discussion and promotes individual reflection on how to put leadership principles into practice. As an edited text, it draws from the expertise of a number of authorities in the field of leadership in the leisure services field. In addition to foundational information about leadership, this book also addresses topics such as leading generational—and even intergenerational—groups, risk management, leading interorganizational collaborative efforts, and leading for change to broaden students' understanding of leading in the 21st century. It will serve as a reference for students as they move into their professional lives and face real-world issues as emerging leaders.

Each chapter in this book includes a discussion of the integration of leadership theory and practice (in addition to a foundational chapter). Additionally, each chapter features an opening scenario, learning outcomes, a profile of a leader in the industry, examples of best practices from the field, a summary, discussion questions, key terms, and a bibliography list of sources that are cited in the text or may be of interest to the reader.

This book goes beyond a simple examination of traditional leadership models by helping students become effective leaders in the exciting field of leisure services in the 21st century.

eBook
available at
HumanKinetics.com

Acknowledgments

We would like to recognize some people who made the book possible. Gayle Kassing brought us the original idea for the text and was instrumental in developing the initial proposal. Thank you for your vision. Jackie Blakley has an unerring eye for detail and she has persevered during the life of the project, making suggestions and generally keeping us all on track. Every single chapter has benefitted from her input. Perhaps as all manuscripts should, this book has changed from its first configuration. Features have been added, altered, dropped, reconceived, redesigned, and finally refined. Our contributing authors have patiently worked with us and endured multiple requests for revisions and even new material. We salute the willingness and tenacity of our authors in seeing this book to its conclusion. Those people in our personal lives who allowed us to disappear from time to time to write, edit and manage endless correspondence in order to meet evolving deadlines deserve more than our thanks. That you love us and understand us is support that simply cannot be measured. Finally, the people with whom we've worked over the years who have helped us hone our knowledge and practice of leadership are both significant and legion. You are our mentors, our students, our colleagues and our trip participants. Thank you all.

Part I

Personal Leadership

Before stepping into a leadership role, people must begin the journey toward self-discovery. They must engage in an inner pursuit to discover who they are, what they care about, what motivates them, and what qualities they embody that will prepare them for what lies ahead. In essence, leadership is a personal quest that begins on the inside and works its way out. This is of particular significance to leaders in the field of leisure services and recreation, whose job is to guide others in understanding their own roles within the groups they serve and the community at large. The first part of this text focuses on the process of self-development in relation to leadership growth and potential.

Chapter 1 opens with a discussion of the demands leaders face within the recreation and leisure services field. Tim O'Connell explores trends that influence leadership within this field, as well as opportunities available to those interested in the profession. Because recreation and leisure services is an ever-changing discipline, leaders have an opportunity to be creative in their conceptualization and style of leadership, while exploring alternate perspectives. Whatever those perspectives might be, a "person-first" approach that puts human growth at the forefront will likely be the most productive and rewarding.

In chapter 2, Brent Cuthbertson begins the demanding task of defining and describing the leadership process and what it means to discover facets of the self that might contribute to leadership development. Tools available to those seeking greater self-awareness include personality assessments, measurements of self-esteem and confidence, assessments of one's governing values and beliefs, and evaluations of emotional intelligence. Cuthbertson describes the connection between understanding one's self and growing into a capable leader.

Chapter 3 moves beyond the self into the relational realm in which leaders must examine their leadership styles as revealed in their communications with others. Terilyn Goins discusses the roles various facets of communication play in leadership success, with an emphasis on the visual, vocal, and verbal components of the communication process. Goins addresses face-to-face versus virtual communication encounters and discusses the unique challenges leaders may face in the virtual environment. The chapter ends with an introduction to an interpersonal leadership model that may be adapted to any leadership situation.

In chapter 4, Brent Wolfe introduces the facilitation process and discusses what it means to be a facilitator and the unique roles a facilitator plays, including that of an unobtrusive observer who indirectly guides the group process while leading the group forward. Facilitators are guides, managers, and negotiators whose job is to challenge group participants while managing risk and sustaining a safe environment in which people are free to express their perspectives as they strive to reach their goals.

Inevitably, when people come together, issues of cultural diversity must be addressed. In chapter 5, Lynn Anderson explains diversity and considers strategies leaders can use to include all people regardless of background. Anderson introduces ways leaders can foster diversity and appreciate and benefit from the unique qualities and perspectives people of diverse backgrounds bring to recreation and leisure situations. She provides insights into inclusive leadership at the micro, meso, and macro levels and demonstrates how communities and agencies flourish when leaders embrace and implement an inclusive philosophy.

In chapter 6, Mary Breunig offers a hearty discussion of leadership theories and styles, ethical theories, decision-making methods, and a model for ethical decision making. Breunig introduces some of the classical theories of leadership, such as trait theory, the great man theory, charismatic and heroic leadership theories, and situational leadership theory. She intertwines this with a discussion of the leader values and ethics that operate at the core of leader action. The chapter concludes with a discussion of the variables in the decision-making process and a demonstration of the essence of ethical decision making for leaders dealing with issues within the practice of the recreation and leisure services profession.

Chapter 1

Introduction to 21st-Century Leadership in Leisure Services

Tim O'Connell

" *Innovation distinguishes between a leader and a follower.* "

—Steve Jobs

J uanita, the director of the department of recreation for a large town in North America, has called a stakeholder meeting to begin planning for a new multipurpose recreation center and library. The town's economy is based largely on agriculture since the manufacturing industry that was once a mainstay in the community closed as a result of global competition. Many of the town's citizens are retired, and most young people move away after finishing high school. Juanita consulted with her staff to figure out whom to invite to the meeting. The final list included members of local sport and recreation leagues, leaders from the migrant farmworker community, the director of the chamber of commerce, a social worker from the regional health and human services agency, the president of the mayor's youth council, the head librarian, and the chair of the senior citizen center's advocacy group as well as individual community members who had expressed interest in being involved. After struggling to find a date for the group to meet in person, Roger (the assistant director of recreation) suggested setting up an electronic meeting for those who couldn't be there in person. Juanita thought this sounded like a great idea, until she discovered that some of the people who couldn't make it didn't have access to a computer or didn't know how to use the technology to log in to the meeting. She is under a tight time line to get the planning underway, because the consulting company hired to conduct a needs assessment needs to get started in the next couple of weeks. Juanita is left scratching her head about how to proceed.

Learning Outcomes

At the conclusion of this chapter, students will be able to:

▶ Describe the role of leisure services leaders in an increasingly globalized society.

▶ Explain the social, cultural, technological, and political trends affecting leadership in leisure services.

▶ Appreciate the range of leadership opportunities available to leisure services professionals.

The leisure services profession has gone through a number of exciting changes in recent years. Given the ever-evolving social, cultural, technological, and political environments of the 21st century, it is imperative that new leisure service professionals be adequately prepared to lead in the new millennium. Having a solid understanding of leadership theory and an in-depth knowledge of how to lead and follow others is essential to being a competent leisure services professional. This chapter discusses how the demands of the 21st century are revolutionizing the way leisure services professionals go about working with others at the individual, group, agency, and professional level. It helps students contextualize and situate leadership in the provision of modern leisure services. Students will gain an understanding of how the knowledge and practice of leadership has advanced within the last century.

What Is Leadership?

Leaders today often operate in intense conditions that are radically different from those of only 10 years ago. The very nature of leading, and those being led, has morphed from a top-down, leader-focused approach to more collaborative, individualized frameworks of leadership. Although various models and theories of leadership are discussed throughout this book, we approach **leadership** as the process of navigating change that enables leaders and followers to reach higher levels of accomplishment and self-actualization. Leadership (and leaders) in the 21st century are characterized by the following:

- An interactional approach in which the roles of leader and followers are often blurred by the context and conditions present at a specific moment in time

- An understanding that the perceptions of both the leader and followers influences how individuals, and subsequently groups, comprehend a situation

- The recognition that the context of leadership is multifaceted, ambiguous, and dynamic and that this is the product of complex social relationships and environmental, political, and economic conditions

- A move away from a rigid approach to leadership, in which certain behaviors and actions are prescribed, to a fluid model in which current factors are considered and responded to in unique ways (i.e., the context of leadership is unpredictable from situation to situation)

Recreation and Leisure Services Leaders in the 21st Century

The world has clearly undergone a massive transformation in the last decade. As such, recreation and leisure leaders must be aware of the scale and speed of change on a global scale and be ready to respond. Communication systems, technology, social trends, and the political landscape have affected how recreation and leisure leaders go about their day-to-day responsibilities of working with clients, program participants, and citizens. Figure 1.1 shows some of the factors influencing recreation and leisure services in the 21st century.

Although transformations at the regional or national level may take some time to filter down to local recreation and leisure organizations, leaders in the field can expect powerful bursts of change at unexpected times, which will happen faster and faster as society (and the world) becomes more sophisticated (Pinnow, 2011). Change is something recreation and leisure leaders can't afford to ignore. They must be ready to respond in two ways—by helping their organizations acclimate to changing social and cultural conditions, and by recognizing how changing conditions affect their own responsibilities as facilitators, mentors, and administrators. Leaders have to carefully address the effects of change on themselves and their organizations while also addressing the needs of those they serve who are being influenced by global trends, fads, and immediate access to information (Pinnow, 2011).

Global economic trends have moved from a reliance on agriculture to industry to service-oriented professions. Recreation and leisure services leaders must also be aware of how knowledge has become a fourth pillar of the economy, and how knowledge creation affects the practice of leadership. Although many recreation and leisure organizations operate from a service model of program provision, leaders should not overlook how knowledge creation spurs the speed and scope of change. Traditionally, many recreation and leisure organizations have offered programs and activities such as sports leagues, after-school programs, swimming lessons,

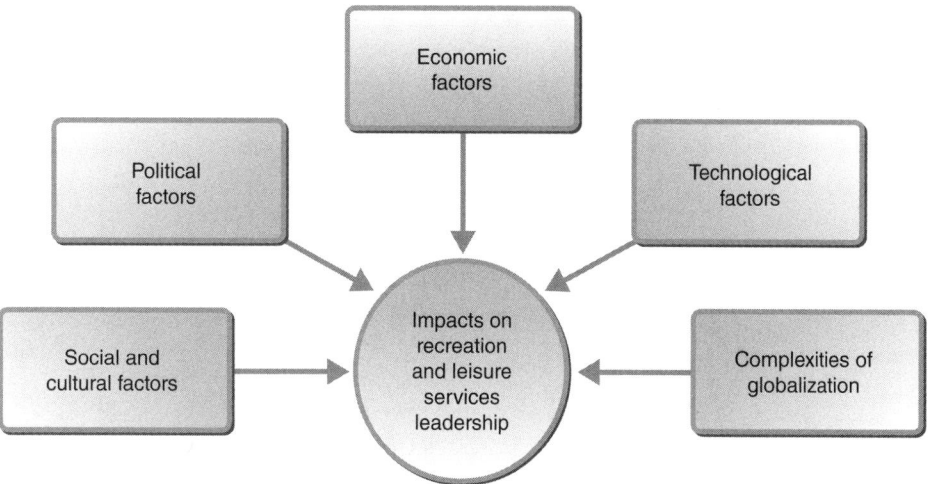

Figure 1.1 Factors affecting recreation and leisure services leadership.

and therapeutic activities. However, an increase in the privatization of recreation and leisure services has resulted in many traditional departments' becoming clearinghouses of information for their constituents. As processes that used to be done in-house by recreation and leisure leaders, such as the design and planning of recreation and leisure programs and facilities, are outsourced to consultants, knowledge creation and information sharing have taken more of a central role in many leaders' day-to-day work.

Impacts of an Increasingly Complex World

Technology and the speed of access to information have shortened the time needed for leaders, and the people they work with, to respond to the challenges and issues faced by their organizations. Quick responses with inventive answers are expected. However, it takes time to develop novel approaches to these problems.

Because of ready access to information through the Internet, television, and cell phones, recreation and leisure leaders now multitask to a much greater extent than in the past. Processes that used to be carried out step by step must now happen all at once. These sequential processes allowed recreation and leisure leaders to establish goals and objectives before the next step began. With the blurring of these boundaries, leaders often struggle with getting a clear picture of whether all aspects of a program or activity are in place. This

situation requires that they become more adept at communicating with those with whom they work, as well as at delegating decision making, program design, and program delivery to others. Leaders who want control over all aspects of a task will find themselves challenged to move projects forward.

One study indicated that many leaders were lacking in four important aspects of leadership—leading people, strategic planning, inspiring commitment, and managing change (Leslie, 2009). Because of the pressure to respond to challenges in a timely and innovative manner, recreation and leisure leaders must be able to trust others who are involved in the process—in other words, to work within a flattened organizational structure, or one in which there is relatively no "middle management" and front-line workers are directly involved in the decision-making process. This is particularly important in public agencies, which increasingly rely on nonpaid volunteers and community members. Moreover, contemporary leaders are finding that those with whom they work are less motivated by traditional styles of leadership (to be discussed in more detail in chapter 6) and more motivated by transformational and interactive approaches to leading (Winkler, 2010).

Social and Cultural Impacts

Social and cultural trends have certainly affected how recreation and leisure services leaders go about the business of leading and providing recreation and leisure opportunities to their clients and constituents. These include an unstable global economy, social isolation, an aging population, and increasing cultural and ethnic diversity.

The Unstable Global Economy

One of the biggest issues in society today is the unstable global economy. Figure 1.2 indicates unemployment rate percentages in the month of January from various countries in 2010, 2011, and 2012.

Unstable unemployment affects recreation and leisure leadership and service provision in a number of ways. First, as more and more people struggle to find jobs, recreation and leisure organizations may experience increased participation rates because people have more free time. However, these people have limited means to pay for these opportunities, which creates challenges for leaders. Additionally, those with fewer financial resources increasingly look for recreation and leisure opportunities closer to home to decrease transportation costs. Similarly, short-term activities and programs become more attractive for people who cannot afford to participate in long-term activities.

Second, leaders working in public agencies that rely on taxes for a majority of their operating funds may have to look for alternative sources of funding for their programs. They may also have difficulty replacing recreation staff or securing goods and materials for their programs. This creates the need for creative leadership solutions including partnering with other organizations such as private firms, schools, and corporations. Although many public recreation and leisure services organizations have struggled with reductions in funding, the number of private agencies offering recreation and leisure services has increased. Usually driven by profit, these agencies have benefited from people's willingness to pay for services, which is a relatively new trend in a field in which services were often free or offered for a nominal fee.

Third, in an interesting paradox, people value time and money in different ways. For instance, for some people time is more important than money, whereas for others money is more important than time. Pinnow (2011) wrote: "Time is a scarce commodity. . . . The issue of money also plays a role in this paradox. Some spend money in order to save time, while others invest time to save money" (p. 12). Recreation and leisure leaders will have to be aware of the various ways clients or participants view time and money and lead accordingly.

Fourth, as the Occupy Wall Street movement in late 2011 demonstrated, more people are becoming disenchanted by the widening gap between the "haves" and "have nots." A simple Internet search yields plenty of evidence that the people with the greatest amount of wealth are continually earning increasingly greater percentages of a country's income than those with less wealth. Twenty-first-century recreation and leisure services leaders will have to consider how this disparity affects how they go about their work. For example, people with easier access to disposable income (and thus a greater ability to pay for specialized programs) may demand that recreation and leisure services programs be offered at specific times, in certain

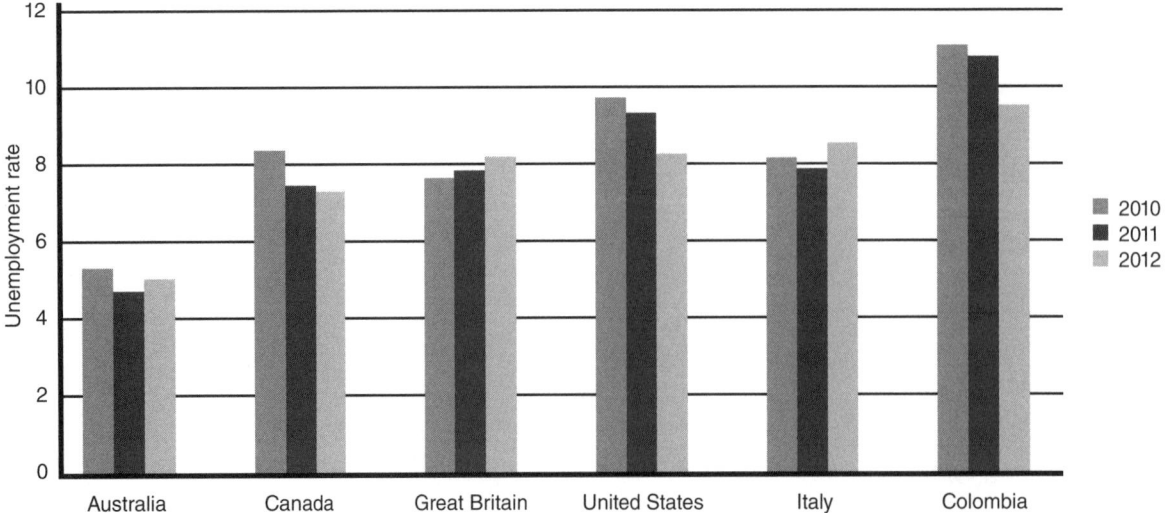

Figure 1.2 Three-year unemployment rates for selected countries.

locations, or with expensive equipment. This could raise the costs of these activities and quickly price out people with less disposable income. Taking heed of the **gentrification** of neighborhoods in large cities or the displacement of downhill ski industry employees in Aspen, Colorado, to other nearby towns (because they can't afford the rent in the town of Aspen itself), recreation and leisure leaders should be aware of similar influences on their programs and make appropriate decisions.

Finally, people have placed higher or lower values on work or leisure at various points during the past several decades. When economic conditions decline and work becomes scarce, people place more value on work and less on recreation and leisure. This may be particularly true with the recent turn to a knowledge-based economy. As Pinnow (2011) pointed out: "This highly skilled, educated, mobile, cosmopolitan, communicative, immensely intellectually flexible, and committed knowledge generation no longer lives to work, but works to live. Nevertheless the motto of the successful firm Gore (makers of 'Gore-Tex') is: 'Make money and have fun.' More and more companies offer their employees the opportunity for joint leisure time, essentially becoming a substitute family of sorts" (p. 5). Additionally, in some countries, such as Canada, recent legislative action has done away with mandatory retirement. As a result, many people are choosing to continue to work past the typical retirement ages of 62 to 65. However, in an interesting counter-trend known as the slow movement, other people have moved toward less work and more leisure time through practices such as job sharing, early retirement, and less expenditures on material goods.

Social Isolation

Another social and cultural impact affecting recreation and leisure services leadership is the decline of traditional social security systems such as community service organizations, churches, clubs, and extended families. This phenomenon is perhaps best described in the book *Bowling Alone: The Collapse and Revival of American Community* (Putnam, 2000), in which the author cites a number of alarming trends indicating that people are losing **social capital** by not connecting with others the way they did in the 20th century. For example, he reports a 58 percent decrease in participating

in club meetings, a 35 percent decrease in friends dropping in, and a 43 percent decline in families having dinner together. This may affect how recreation and leisure services leaders develop and facilitate programs. For example, programs may be focused on individual recreation activities rather group recreation activities. This can also affect how people interact with each other in a group setting. For example, people may be more concerned with their own experience and satisfaction than that of the group as a whole.

Another trend in North America has been toward individualism and away from egalitarianism (Pinnow, 2011). Recreation and leisure services leaders should be aware of the positive and negative effects of this trend on their roles. People who are more focused on themselves as individuals tend to be more knowledgeable and confident and have a broader range of skills than those who operate more from an egalitarian framework. Recreation and leisure leaders can use this to their advantage by giving these people more decision-making and planning responsibilities. Although it may seem counterintuitive, people who operate from an individualistic viewpoint, when properly led, can be creative and committed to a group or task. This is particularly true when leaders help them develop and implement the knowledge, skills, and dispositions that are important to them. In essence, people who understand that engagement in something can help them develop and reach their goals will respect and appreciate the opportunity to do so.

However, an individualistic framework may also contribute to a decrease in social capital and investment in community, and an increased focus on individual career advancement and identification with the self instead of with the democratic principles that better society and culture as a whole. As a result, leadership styles, programs, and services that were once designed for homogeneous groups of people will no longer be appropriate. Recreation and leisure services leaders will have to focus on individual and small group needs instead of using a "one size fits all" approach. This will require that they be flexible and able to lead in a number of contexts, some of which may require that they wear multiple hats at one time. Moreover, because of the easy access to information, people with an individualistic bent will be more knowledgeable and able to make informed choices in an instant.

Leisure Leaders

Jessica Duliban

MY PREPARATION

- BRLS in recreation and leisure studies with a major in community recreation—Brock University, St. Catharines, ON
- Scholastic Achievement Award, Rotary Club of Oshawa, Ontario

MY CAREER

I work for the City of Welland, Ontario, in the Welland Community Wellness Complex. Formerly the Rose City Seniors Activity Centre, the Welland Community Wellness Complex opened its doors on September 9, 2011, after undergoing a $9 million renovation sponsored by the municipality, the Province of Ontario, and the federal government of Canada. The facility is now for people of all ages and has almost doubled in size. It includes office areas, meeting rooms, a library, a billiards room, a woodshop, a 400-seat theater, a therapeutic pool and hot tub, an exercise room, a computer lab, a multipurpose activity room, a gymnasium, and an atrium that overlooks the Welland Canal. Located on the banks of the Welland Recreational Waterway, the Welland Community Wellness Complex is situated in the heart of Welland. It offers over 80 programs for people of all ages and abilities. It also offers drop-in programs that anyone may participate in with a Wellness Pass. Over 1,500 pass holders visit the Complex regularly and participate in both the annual and new special events that encourage everyone to get involved and, most important, have fun.

The mission of the Welland Community Wellness Complex is to deliver high-quality programs, services, and activities that encourage people of all ages and abilities to engage in healthy and active lifestyles.

Pass holders have lunch, enjoy both the drop-in and paid programs, and participate in special events. Some come strictly to socialize and be involved in the community center. As a part of City Hall, the Complex has 10 full-time and 6 part-time staff members.

As arts and culture coordinator for the city of Welland, I am responsible for coordinating and

Photo courtesy of Ryanne Hale.

implementing arts and culture programming in the city. The core functions of my job are developing arts and culture opportunities in the community; advocating the benefits of arts and culture by promoting community outreach and participation; developing programs, activities, and special events; and monitoring arts and culture trends in light of community sociocultural and economic factors to create relevant programs and services. I am very busy at my job; there is never a dull moment or break, which keeps me on my toes. I have an opportunity to connect with the community, get others involved, and create a sense of pride in what Welland has to offer in the Niagara Region.

I started at Brock University having no idea what I wanted to do as a career. I went into recreation and leisure studies because I have a passion for recreation and community involvement. In my fourth year, I started my placement with the City of Welland, which at the time was hosting a celebration for the Olympic Torch Relay. Students were needed to coordinate the volunteers and oversee the event. I became very passionate about this event and wanted it to be a huge success for the city. The result was so rewarding. Thousands showed up, and it ran so successfully with all of our hard work. City workers and the mayor were also very pleased. It was then that I thought, Hey, I could do this as a living! I worked over the limit of hours for placement (100 hours) and started asking for additional projects and work to be more involved with the city.

The staff at City Hall appreciated my dedication, and it did not go unnoticed. For my final project I was asked to evaluate the city's recreation and culture master plan. My insights and feedback were brought to the city council and other departments. As a result, I was offered a part-time job after graduating in April of 2010. I already knew most of the staff from my placement, so the transition was easy, and this time I was getting paid! I worked part-time from April to August and landed a full-time job in the Development Services Department in September. After working in that department for a year and learning all aspects of the job, I was ready for something new. The arts and culture position was posted, and I applied. This brought me back to my roots, and I was able to use my degree more directly. I have been in this position for one year now and enjoy every minute of it.

I enjoy creating programs and events that excite people. I really enjoy working with the community and bringing the public to the events that we host on a regular basis. Creating events and partnerships is very rewarding because I get to see projects come to fruition and my hard work pay off. When I see familiar faces at events, I figure I must be doing something right. I do wish that arts and culture had been addressed in my classes at Brock University. Because arts and culture have become prominent in today's community planning, it would help to be exposed to it in today's curriculum. For my part, I had to take the time to learn what art and culture means in the context of community because we never discussed it in class. I believe that it is just a matter of time before arts and culture becomes an integral part of every city's planning.

My philosophy of leadership affects my day-to-day work because I have made it a part of my lifestyle. If I believe that a program or event isn't good enough for me, then it isn't good enough for the community. I have created many programs and activities that have needed to be changed to meet the needs of others. I have also made successful programs larger and better. Whether and how to change a program depends on what people expect and what I expect from the community. I also want to set a daily example and be a role model. I aspire to have the courage, confidence, and commitment to connect with and inspire others to achieve extraordinary results through teamwork. Because I work different hours every day, I need to stay in communication with coworkers to ensure that we work as a unit and achieve our outcomes. I try to treat others as I want to be treated, with fairness and respect. A big part of my philosophy is to strive for excellence and keep a positive attitude. I pursue excellence (not perfection), and I expect others to do the same. Challenges will come, but with the right attitude, I believe that we can overcome them all.

MY ADVICE TO YOU

The adage "hard work pays off" applies to everyone who strives for success. The best plan is to set both personal and professional goals that will help you succeed. Make connections and partnerships with people, organizations, and teachers so that they remember you. Being remembered by a leader will help you become one as well. Don't forget to celebrate wins, no matter how small. Little victories are the stepping-stones to great accomplishments. Continue to grow as a leader every day. Do not settle for anything. Motivate yourself to be better.

Working in the recreation and leisure field is both challenging and rewarding because I can see my hard work affect others in the community. I have had the pleasure of starting my career in recreation and leisure early, while my ideas are fresh and the adrenaline is going. I have the opportunity to make change and create. Recreation, leisure, and arts and culture have such a large impact on people, and the benefits extend to those of all ages—children, youth, young adults, families, and seniors. Community recreation also promotes ethnic and cultural harmony. Giving people satisfaction and improving their quality of life is what I strive to do every day.

In this new era of individualism, employees and other recreation and leisure professionals with whom a leader works require individualized leadership. Leaders can no longer afford to assume that a particular approach to working with others will always be appropriate; a supportive approach that supplies individuals with the information and tools they need to get the job done is required. In the past, employees could be encouraged to do what they were supposed to be doing by coercion or pressure. Recreation and leisure services leaders in the 21st century will be required to question the traditional management structures and leadership techniques that have been institutionalized in many organizations and create conditions that promote self-directed work and address emotional intelligence, action, and creativity (Pinnow, 2011).

Recreation and leisure services leaders in the 21st century have the good fortune of having the opportunity to develop their own styles of leadership as traditional leadership models and methods become obsolete. This humanistic approach to leadership will allow them to focus on developing leadership skills that are meaningful, contextual, and fulfilling. By adopting a "person-first" perspective on leadership (i.e., putting the client or participant, employee, and self at the forefront of leading), recreation and leisure services leaders can approach leadership from a sustainable perspective. This is important because "a leader spends three quarters of his or her (active) life on work, i.e., on a very energy-consuming activity that requires his or her complete energy. That is why work has to give leaders something back, be it positive energy, motivation and a sense of achievement, recognition, fulfillment, joy or growth" (Pinnow, 2011, p. 5). An approach to leadership that focuses on individual growth and

Best Practices From the Field

Tim Arnold, the outreach director for the Southridge Shelter in St. Catharines, Ontario, Canada, operates a unique recreation and leisure program for people who are homeless and staying at the shelter. Tim, who has a background in corporate training and development, helped initiate this program when he first joined the shelter staff five years ago. The purposes behind the daily recreational programming offered at Southridge are not only to engage residents in a healthy, active lifestyle, but also to provide an opportunity for connections to develop between program volunteers and shelter residents. Long-lasting friendships are often developed out of a shared love for the recreation and leisure programs, which provide a strong basis for relationships.

Southridge offers a wide variety of recreation and leisure programs, which is somewhat of an anomaly in the world of homeless shelters. For example, the highly popular Team Sports Night provides residents and volunteers with a great way to stay active and have fun. An assortment of sports, including basketball, volleyball, ultimate Frisbee, and the shelter favorite, ball hockey, are offered on a regular basis. Shelter staff combine teamwork and friendly competition to create an exciting and encouraging atmosphere in which people can succeed, have fun, and make friends.

Southridge also partners with a local indoor rock climbing gym to offer another recreational activity for those seeking fun, challenge, and adventure. Residents and volunteers work together and encourage each other to climb high and set goals. Southridge Shelter also offers a photography program that allows residents to express themselves visually, as well as to travel away from the shelter on field trips around the local area for photo shoots. Participants take pictures and learn how to electronically edit them while making connections with each other and with program volunteers. The shelter also has a more traditional games and movie night.

When asked what makes the recreation programs at Southridge so special, Tim commented, "In our shelter, we've found that life change happens best in relationships, and for most of our homeless friends, healthy and committed relationships are few and far between. Our recreational programs are the very best catalyst for these relationships to happen. Once volunteers and homeless residents are engaged in an activity they both enjoy, the feeling of 'us and them' quickly disappears and they very quickly become friends that are just hanging out together. We constantly see this result in very unlikely, but life-changing friendships."

The recreation programming at the Southridge Shelter is a great example of a best practice of leadership in recreation and leisure services for the 21st century.

development can create conditions for leaders to get these rewards. By doing justice to themselves, recreation and leisure services leaders will be better positioned to help others.

Aging Population

Certain demographic changes are affecting leadership in the field of recreation and leisure services in the 21st century. For example, in North America the average age of the general population is increasing. In 1950, the percentage of people aged 65 and older in the United States was 8.1 percent. That increased to 12.8 percent in 2009, and is projected to reach over 20 percent by 2050 (Shrestha & Heisler, 2011). By 2050, one in five people in the United States will be age 65 or over. While over the past 60 years the population of the United States has been aging, a relatively stagnant birth rate has leveled off in the last 10 years to approximately 13.8 births per 1,000 people (Shrestha & Heisler, 2011). As seen in figure 1.3, an aging population (with a subsequently higher death rate) coupled with a flat birth rate is projected to negatively affect population growth in the United States.

Another potential impact on the provision of recreation and leisure services is the higher cost of health care for this aging population. Many publically funded agencies are finding their resources funneled to hospitals and preventative care instead of to recreation and leisure programming. Finally, level (or decreasing) population growth rates mean

fewer consumers of recreation and leisure services. Recreation and leisure services leaders must be prepared to deal with this reality.

Despite the trend of many people working past normal retirement age mentioned earlier, there will be a large influx of older people (particularly men) showing a preference for leisure over work. Many of these people are retiring with enough money to participate in recreation and leisure activities of their choosing. The explosion of the cruise industry, casinos, and educational travel such as Elderhostel, and an increase in overall interest in healthy living are signs of this trend. Recreation and leisure services leaders in the 21st century will be working more with people who are older because growth in this age group has outpaced that in any other age group. Leaders have to be in tune with the needs and expectations of older people who are informed and have desire for and the financial wherewithal to participate in active recreation and leisure programs.

Cultural and Ethnic Diversity in North America

Another demographic trend of which recreation and leisure services leaders in the 21st century need to be aware is the increasing diversity of the population in North America (Shrestha & Heisler, 2011). This has been influenced by two factors. First, although immigration policies favor the entry of younger people, they also allow for the entry of extended family members such as parents and

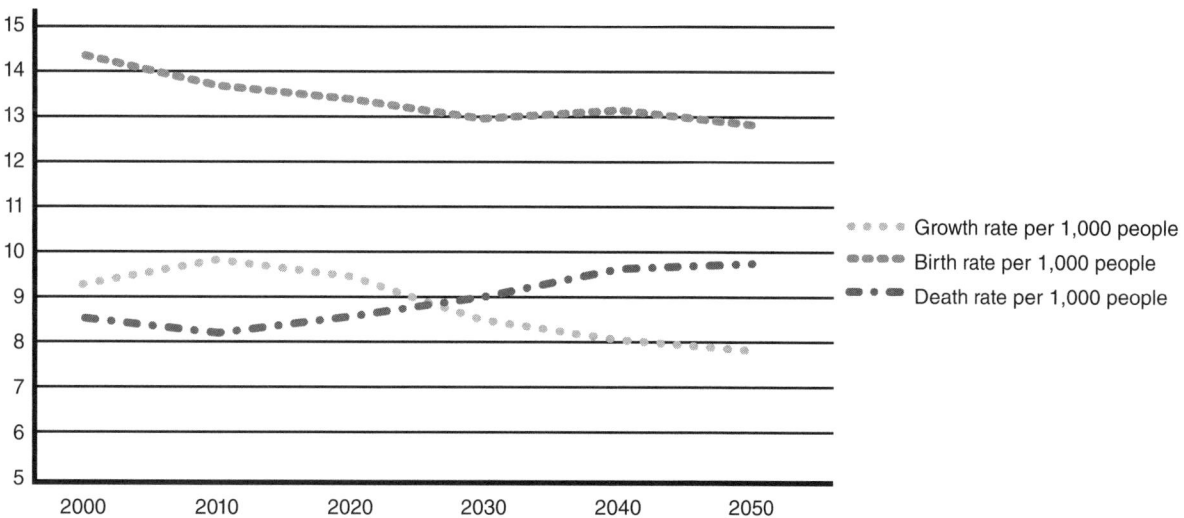

Figure 1.3 Population growth in the United States.

grandparents (Shrestha & Heisler, 2011). Second, cultural and ethnic groups age, have children, and die at different rates.

Figure 1.4 indicates the percentage of the population in the United States by race in 2009. It is projected that the percentage of the population of whites (approximately 75 percent) and blacks, or African Americans (13 percent), will stay relatively stable through 2050 (Shrestha & Heisler, 2011). The racial group expected to have the strongest growth rate is Asians, reaching 7.8 percent of the population in 2050, which would be up from 3.8 percent in 2000. The Hispanic population is determined differently from the populations of whites and blacks because people can report whether they are of Hispanic or non-Hispanic origin, regardless of other race. Nevertheless, it is projected that people of Hispanic origin will comprise 30 percent of the population in the United States by 2050, up from 12.5 percent in 2000 (Shrestha & Heisler, 2011). In general, the Hispanic population was reported by the National Research Council (2006) as being young, having a lower level of education, and working disproportionately in lower-wage jobs.

Twenty-first-century recreation and leisure services leaders will have to be aware of, and respond to, people based on their racial and cultural heritages. For example, someone from a culture that values hierarchical work structures may be best led using more traditional styles of leadership.

One result of a more diverse population is increased pride among minority groups (Russell,

2005). With this increased pride will come the demand for more individualized and equitable services. As previously mentioned, 21st-century leaders will have to be adept at leading on an individualized level. They will have to consider not only the goals and objectives but also the social and cultural context of the people with whom they are working. Leaders will have to be cognizant of an individual's racial and cultural background, sexual orientation, affiliation with religious groups, and disability.

Technological Impacts

As previously mentioned, technology has changed daily life around the world and particularly in developed countries such as those in North America. The pace of communication, driven by the Internet, wireless technology, and cell phones, is a double-edged sword for recreation and leisure services leaders. The quickness and ease of communication allows for an effortless exchange of information and strategy and helps in decision making and the day-to-day practice of leadership. However, it also means that leaders must be prepared to respond quickly to any issues or challenges that arise. Technology also allows leaders to develop connections with their organizations' clients or participants, cooperating organizations, government officials, business partners, and suppliers of goods and services. These connections certainly facilitate the provision of quality recreation and leisure opportunities.

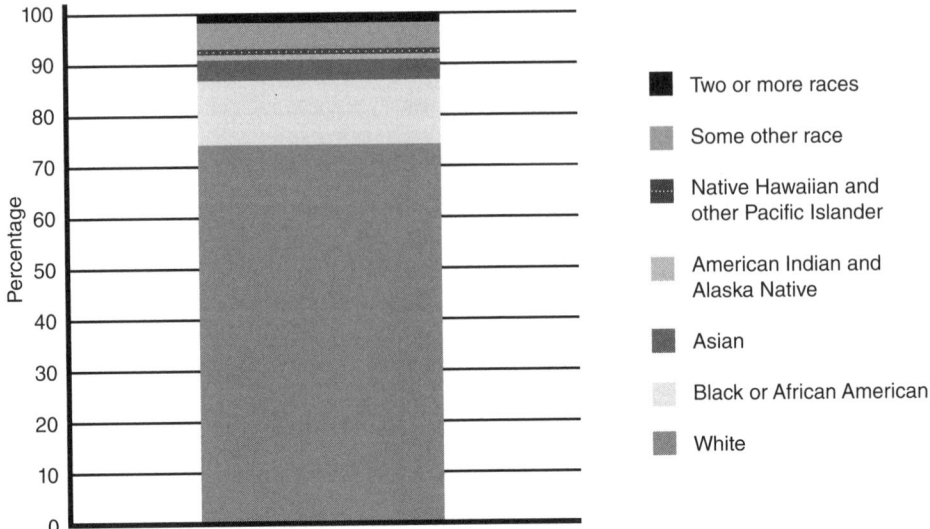

Figure 1.4   Percentage of U.S. population by race in 2009.

Recreation and leisure services leaders have a wealth of knowledge available at their fingertips for planning, designing, delivering, evaluating, and leading recreation programs. They are certainly at the center of the knowledge economy in this regard! As already mentioned, responding to change has become more of a focal point for leaders in the 21st century. This requires that they be constantly learning through reading, attending training and development seminars, and putting their knowledge and skills into practice. Leaders in the 21st century must have a grasp of both information and communication technology because it will result in optimal conditions for success.

Like leaders, clients, participants, and employees can also access information quickly through enhanced technology. As a result, they are more informed, most likely have clearer expectations about what a recreation or leisure experience will entail, have done some comparison shopping among similar opportunities available to them, and have the ability to access information "on the fly" during their experience in a program. In fact, many recreation and leisure services leaders are incorporating information technology into the fabric of their programs because it is so firmly established in people's everyday lives. Although some may argue that this is counter to the true essence of a recreation or leisure experience, recreation and leisure leaders in the 21st century must be prepared to address it. In the same manner, employees and others with whom a leader works will also have (and expect) access to information through communications technology. Not only does it help people do their jobs more effectively (for the most part), but technology also appeals to the needs of contemporary workers, helping them feel more self-directed and creatively engaged in their work. In essence, workers no longer rely on leaders for information. Technology enables them to get what they need to do their jobs in a way that suits their particular styles. This is not to say that leaders can't or shouldn't shape the development of a project or product, but rather that technology can complement the process.

The rapid pace at which technology is developing also creates exciting possibilities for recreation and leisure services leaders. New technology is emerging at an exponential rate, and adopting these technologies is an attractive option for many leaders. However, they must carefully balance new technology with other factors such as resource availability (e.g., financial, personnel, environmental) and the viability of the technology over the long term. For example, recreation and leisure services leaders may be faced with the choice of upgrading expensive fitness machines to those with enhanced features on a yearly basis. Alternately, some may choose to keep older fitness equipment, or even stay completely "old school" and go solely with free weights.

As a result of the impacts of technology and communication, 21st-century recreation and leisure services leaders must be well versed in a wide array of topics, be knowledgeable in the use and application of technology in the workplace for both employees and clients or participants, and be aware of global developments in technology that will directly affect their practice as leaders. However, although technology and communication

Photo courtesy of Bill Mitchell.

Modern rock climbing equipment is an example of how technology has changed the nature of recreation.

have influenced modern society, the nature of what leaders do remains relatively unchanged. They provide recreation and leisure opportunities to clients and participants to the best of their abilities.

Political Impacts

Politics can certainly affect leaders in the field of recreation and leisure services. Political boundaries between countries are minimized as the world quickly becomes a much smaller place as a result of advances in technology and communication. Recreation and leisure services leaders will be pushed to provide opportunities not only for people in their local and regional communities, but also for global clients or participants. Consider the fact that people in the European Union can move relatively freely from country to country with little problem. They can thus participate in a wide variety of recreation and leisure opportunities without having to worry about political boundaries or processes such as customs and immigration checks.

Recreation and leisure leaders in the 21st century, particularly those working for public agencies, must be prepared to attend to politics. For example, recreation and leisure service provision may be affected by the dominant ideologies of a political party in power. Leaders will be increasingly pressured to structure their programs to fit the thinking of particular political parties. This pressure may come as direct requests to convey a certain type of information or provide (or not provide) certain programs, or less directly as reductions in funding or resourcing or a lack of inclusion in important meetings. Leaders in the field may also be seen by the people with whom they work as political conduits. They may be asked to not only represent the views of a particular political party, but also to advocate for the politics of those they serve. In this regard, leaders will increasingly find themselves working as political go-betweens, especially because contemporary frameworks of leadership favor team-oriented approaches over autocratic models of leadership. Leaders may find themselves having to navigate competing political viewpoints on an increasingly regular basis.

With the rise of individualism and less concern for the good of the masses, recreation and leisure services leaders may find themselves confronting increased challenges to operating procedures, building new facilities, and creating new programs. These challenges often come from **NIMBYs**, or people whose stance toward issues is "Not In My BackYard!" For example, leaders may find themselves and their organizations challenged by individuals or small groups who oppose new facility construction in their neighborhood or who oppose the implementation of a new program because of the type of clientele it may serve.

On the other hand, recreation and leisure leaders in the 21st century have the opportunity to work with individuals and groups of people who are increasingly volunteering their time for programs or issues. These individuals and groups often emerge as friends groups that are focused on advocacy. For example, just outside St. Catharines, Ontario, Canada, is a small day-use provincial park. The Friends of Short Hills is "a community-based organization dedicated to preserving the cultural and natural integrity of Short Hills Provincial Park through liaison with Ontario Parks, volunteer work, public education and fund raising activities" (Friends of Short Hills Park, 2011). From a political standpoint, recreation and leisure services leaders will find themselves continuously working with NIMBYs and friends groups alike. Navigating political waters is often best learned through experience.

Friends groups advocate for many recreation and leisure resources, such as the Short Hills Provincial Park in Ontario, Canada.

Finally, recreation and leisure services leaders in the 21st century, like their predecessors in years past, will have to deal with the internal politics of the groups of people with whom they work. The rise and speed of social media outlets such as Facebook, Twitter, and LinkedIn are both a boon and a bane to leaders. If used wisely by a leader and followers, these outlets can certainly add to the strength and richness of a group and help accomplish the task at hand. However, if not managed properly, they can disrupt the politics of a group and contribute to poor group dynamics. Recreation and leisure services leaders in the 21st century no longer have to worry just about the conversations around the water cooler; they have to be aware of, and respond to, discussions and exchanges in cyberspace as well. As mentioned earlier, this will require that they be adept at using technology and advances in communication.

Setting the Stage for Leading in 21st-Century Recreation and Leisure Services

Although the potential impacts of social, cultural, economic, technological, and political trends on recreation and leisure services leaders may seem daunting, there are plenty of opportunities available to assist new and developing leaders in the 21st century. Many of these are discussed throughout this book. However, a brief overview of some of these ideas for leading in the 21st century is provided here.

• Learning about leadership and how to lead is an ongoing process. In the past, a single workshop or course on leadership was the extent of leaders' training; the rest was learned on the fly. Twenty-first-century leadership development may take months or years as many organizations provide emerging leaders with mentors and ongoing training, and require involvement in professional development programs both inside and outside their organizations.

• Individual leadership development doesn't happen in a vacuum. As discussed throughout this chapter, as the contemporary practice of leadership has moved away from a leader-centered approach to a team focus, so has the way leaders learn about leading. Increasingly, this is happening in a group context.

• Practical and experiential learning is moving to the forefront of leadership training and development programs. It is no longer enough for leaders to attend lectures or read about new models and frameworks for leadership; applied practice in the work setting is increasingly crucial for success. Support from the organization and a supervisor prior to and after these training experiences is important as well.

• As many organizational budgets for training and development are affected by the global economy, on-the-job training and development opportunities are becoming more important. Peers, colleagues, and teams will use the workplace as a learning laboratory while also going about their daily jobs.

• Working with a mentor is becoming increasingly important to the development of emerging leaders. Through this process, leaders receive personalized training from seasoned leaders who are familiar with the context in which they are working. In turn, emerging leaders become mentors, which, in and of itself, is a form of continuing leadership development.

• Organizations are increasingly turning away from "off the shelf" leadership training and development opportunities and toward custom-designed learning experiences. Many organizations are developing partnerships with consulting agencies or other service providers to offer long-term training and development opportunities that provide continuity in the experiences provided. If the organization for which an emerging leader works doesn't follow this practice, the leader may be able to find professional development opportunities that are affordable and that enable her to develop relationships that will meet her specific needs over time.

• There is an increasing recognition of the importance of the spiritual aspects of leadership. The term *spiritual,* in this sense, does not relate to a particular religion or religious beliefs, but to the inner core of the leader (Fairholm & Fairholm, 2009). A leader who has recognized, has developed, and is satisfied with his inner core will be able to inspire others and help them flourish. Spiritual leadership, in this regard, relates to a more humanistic, whole-person approach to leading and following. Twenty-first-century leaders in recreation and leisure services should be cognizant of this opportunity for growth as a leader.

These opportunities are only the tip of the iceberg. The possibilities for learning and practicing the intricacies of leadership are endless. Twenty-first-century leaders do need to keep an open mind and continually critically examine their own leadership in light of their workplace, who they are working with, and their own needs.

Summary

Leadership, particularly as the 21st century continues to unfold, has increasingly focused on confronting change while at the same time working to enable followers (and the leaders themselves) to reach their full potential. A wide range of social, cultural, technological, economic, and political trends have shaped, and will continue to influence, the theory and practice of leadership. As society continues to embrace ever-faster forms of technology and communication, and the notion of supporting individuals as unique beings becomes more firmly entrenched in the fabric of Western culture, 21st-century recreation and leisure services leaders will find themselves operating in an increasingly smaller and more globalized world. Traditional limitations, including economic, political, and cultural boundaries, will remain blurred

and present challenges and exciting opportunities to contemporary leaders. Emerging leaders who strive to keep learning and refining their practice and knowledge of leadership will be best positioned to help their clients, participants, and followers to succeed. As Pinnow (2011) concludes:

The ideal manager does not exist.

Leadership begins with yourself.

Leadership is primarily self-management and relationship management.

Leadership is a constant learning process.

Leadership means loving people.

Leadership can be learned, but certain leadership traits are prerequisites—especially initiative and empathy.

Leadership requires the integration of individual needs and organizational objectives.

Leadership is the combination of management and guidance.

Leadership can—to a limited extent—be measured.

Leadership is an issue for our millennium. (p. 238)

Questions for Reflection and Discussion

1. What are some of the factors that Juanita is facing in the opening scenario of this chapter? What do you suggest she do about the meeting?

2. With a group of four or five others, share your most recent leadership experience. What influenced how you acted as a leader in that situation?

3. If you were to predict what recreation and

leisure leaders are going to be doing in 10 years, what would it be? How about in 20 years?

4. With the class, brainstorm strategies that recreation and leisure leaders can use to confront the challenges of leading in the 21st century.

5. List five ways technology influences your own recreation and leisure.

Key Terms and Definitions

gentrification—The process by which one group of people, usually those of lower socioeconomic class or minority groups, are gradually displaced from one location to another by the influx of middle-class or nonminority groups looking for lower-cost housing.

leadership—The process of navigating change that enables leaders and followers to reach

higher levels of accomplishment and self-actualization.

NIMBY—An acronym for people who challenge local development close to their homes or residences. NIMBY stands for Not In My Back Yard.

social capital—Benefits gained from belonging to a group or produced through maintaining social relationships.

Bibliography

Bledow, R., Frese, M., & Mueller, V. (2011). Ambidextrous leadership for innovation: The influence of culture. *Advances in Global Leadership, 6,* 41-69.

Center for Creative Leadership: www.ccl.org

Center for Leader Development: www.centerforleaderdevelopment.com

Fairholm, M.R., & Fairholm, G.W. (2009). *Understanding leadership perspectives: Theoretical and practical approaches.* New York: Springer Science & Business Media.

Friends of Short Hills Park. (2011, December 14). Friends of Short Hills Park. Retrieved from www.friendsofshort-hillspark.ca/page/home.

Leslie, J.B. (2009). *The leadership gap: What you need, and don't have, when it comes to leadership talent.* Center for Creative Leadership. www.ccl.org.

National Recreation and Park Association, Professional Development: www.nrpa.org/education-certification

National Research Council. (2006). Multiple origins, uncertain destinies: Hispanics and the American future. M. Tienda & F. Mitchell (Eds.), *Panel on Hispanics in the United States—Committee on Population, Division of Behavioral and Social Sciences and Education.* Washington, DC: The National Academies Press.

Pinnow, D.F. (2011). *Leadership—What really matters: A handbook on systemic leadership.* Berlin, Germany: Springer.

Putnam, R. (2000). *Bowling alone: The collapse and revival of American community.* New York: Simon & Schuster.

Russell, R. (2005). *Leadership in recreation* (3rd ed.). New York: McGraw-Hill.

Shrestha, L.B., & Heisler, E.J. (2011). *The changing demographic profile of the United States.* (Congressional Research Service Report RL32701). Retrieved from the Federation of American Scientists website: *www.fas.org/sgp/crs/misc/RL32701.pdf.*

Winkler, I. (2010). *Contemporary leadership theories: Enhancing the understanding of the complexity, subjectivity and dynamic of leadership.* Berlin, Germany: Springer.

Chapter 2

Self-Leadership

Brent Cuthbertson

" There is nothing noble about being superior to some other person. The true nobility is in being superior to your previous self.

"

—Hindustani Proverb

From as far back as she could remember, Elise had been inspired by some wonderfully strong female role models. She was impressed by her mother, a single parent who had raised her and her two brothers while working full-time and finishing a university degree. Elise definitely admired her mother's work ethic and her dedication to family. A camp counselor Elise had when she was 13 years old showed her that she could be skilled and physically capable in all sorts of outdoor activities. A favorite heroine in novels she read as a girl was a no-nonsense and tough-minded female police officer who struggled against a few narrow-minded male colleagues, outsmarted criminals, and eventually won the trust of her partner on the force.

In her career with her city's parks and recreation department, Elise was recently promoted, and her new responsibilities included training and supervising all summer youth programs coordinators. Psychologically, the full weight of the position seemed immense, but Elise was determined to be successful. She vowed to have the most efficient summer crew in department memory.

Modeling herself after the women she admired, Elise worked hard to develop a week of training that was thorough, structured, and full of useful and relevant information. Sensing that something was missing, however, Elise asked if she could share her plan with her supervisor. He agreed, listened patiently, and then made only one comment: "Elise, there is nothing wrong with what you have planned; it sounds like a great training week. Just make sure that they all learn how to care for kids the way you always have."

In what she could only describe as one of life's "aha" moments, Elise realized that she needed to understand her own leadership better, capitalize on her own strengths, and, while honoring her mentors, not try to *be* them.

Learning Outcomes

At the conclusion of this chapter, students will be able to:

▶ Define or describe leadership and self-leadership.

▶ Articulate why understanding one's self is an important part of becoming an effective leader.

▶ Demonstrate an understanding of personality development and identify selected personality types and associated tests.

▶ Identify some personal beliefs and values and how they play a role in their own leadership.

In some ways, the title of this chapter can be a little confusing. Self-leadership is not about how to coach yourself, or how to imagine you are both leader and follower to practice being a better leader. It's not about leading yourself in some kind of literal sense. But it still has a lot to do with leadership, and in particular, your own leadership.

So what exactly *is* self-leadership? It's about understanding yourself in the context of leadership. It's about taking stock of yourself as a person and analyzing yourself honestly without modesty or conceit to gain an accurate picture of who you are. It's about personal growth to help you build on your strengths and improve where you need to. However, to take those steps, you must put in the time and effort to gain a clear and accurate picture of who you are.

Leadership is not easily defined or described, and the conditions are constantly shifting in leadership situations. Making the right decisions at the right time is much more complicated than simply following some set of leadership rules. Being an effective leader sometimes feels more like an art than a science; in truth, it's a bit of both. Good leadership is a dynamic process in which personal values, feelings, and judgment are at least as important as any objective set of rules that may apply to the leadership roles in which you find yourself.

Given the unstable nature of the landscape of leadership, and the fact that the ground under your decisions keeps shifting, you will be a much better leader for having done some self-analysis. This will keep you grounded when you need it most. It is quite likely that the leaders you have respected most in your life have been highly self-reflective. They may not have shown it on the outside, but virtually all leaders worth their salt question themselves. They ask themselves: How does this fit with my values? What impact will my decision and my behavior have on my follower(s)? Is this decision just and ethical? Will it help achieve the goals I have for myself and for my group? Are there alternatives?

To be fair, some situations are clear-cut, with answers that are mostly obvious. For example, in many situations involving a significant threat to mind or body, immediately eliminating or reducing that threat is usually the right course of action. Pulling someone back from the brink of a cliff—literally or metaphorically—is always appropriate. Exciting in the moment, those decisions are often straightforward and, from a leadership perspective,

almost boring! The real excitement in leadership occurs with the more subtle, everyday decisions that you make. Becoming an excellent leader requires considering the many shades of gray that make up human interactions. This means not only assessing the situation, but also knowing how you fit with it, how you can best interact with those shades of gray to achieve a positive outcome.

Toward a Definition of Leadership

Exactly what leadership means has been debated for a very long time. Early in our attempts to understand it, we defined leaders in terms of their personal and physical characteristics. In other words, leaders were believed to be born rather than made. We have tried to understand leadership in terms of the effectiveness of the style of leadership displayed (e.g., autocratic, democratic, and laissez-faire styles), and we have attempted to convince leaders to alternate their styles depending on the makeup of the group and the situations they face. Some theories have also made a case for matching leaders with group members in terms of characteristics.

It is probably safe to say that no leadership theory has been able to adequately define leadership or explain how a leader can be effective 100 percent of the time. There are simply too many considerations that go with each decision, let alone each group! Human beings simply do not behave like mathematics equations or subatomic particles; we are infinitely more unpredictable. Perhaps all we can hope for, then, is to strive for the best understanding possible of ourselves and those who might look to us for leadership.

Despite the fact that leadership is a complex concept with no consensus on a definition, it is still important to gain a sense of how some of the significant thinkers on the subject have described it. Table 2.1 offers interesting quotes by leaders as well as researchers who have investigated the phenomenon. It is not an exhaustive list of definitions, but it represents the main currents in how leadership has been, and is currently, conceived.

Most current thinking seems to revolve around a leader's influence within a group, with broad interpretations of what constitutes influence and how it is achieved. It could come from exerting direct influence, as in the case of a recognized leader, or it could surface indirectly from one of

Leisure Leaders

Luc Cousineau

MY PREPARATION

- HBOR in outdoor recreation; HBA in women's studies; and BSc in natural science (biology)—Lakehead University, Thunder Bay, ON
- Canadian Millennium Laureate—Class A; Lakehead University President's Award; Lakehead University Robert Poulin Award for Outstanding Citizenship; Leonard Foundation Award; Datatel Award
- Ontario Camps Association board of directors
- Outdoor Council of Canada Leadership Instructor; NCCP 1; CSIA II; CSCF 1; NLS; LNT Trainer

MY CAREER

I am currently employed with the YMCA-YWCA of Guelph, Ontario, a community benefit organization open to everyone. Starting with a focus on healthy child, youth, and young adult development, we excel in delivering lifelong opportunities for health and personal growth. The YMCA-YWCA serves the Guelph area, employs over 250 people, and serves a member and nonmember population of over 7,500 on an ongoing basis.

As director of Camp Nagiwa, a residential summer camp operated by the YMCA-YWCA of Guelph, my duties include planning and implementing camp programming, developing and implementing a marketing strategy, hiring and maintaining a staff during camp operations, managing program operations at the non-Guelph camp area, hiring and managing a staff team, preparing and maintaining the program budget, writing and maintaining policy, and ensuring adherence to camp and government standards. The breadth of responsibilities keeps my job fresh, even though I repeat some tasks year to year.

Given the changing landscape of this competitive field in terms of regulations and practices, continual change and reinvention is required to remain relevant and viable. I came to summer

Photo courtesy of Luc Cousineau.

camping as a camper myself and grew to understand the great value of camp experiences to both individuals and communities. My leadership style involves giving my staff a great deal of freedom within larger limits with the hope of pushing them to extend themselves creatively and develop into adept leaders, thinkers, and employees.

MY ADVICE TO YOU

Remember that there is a plethora of jobs out there beyond guiding and working as a contract program facilitator. Although program facilitation is excellent work, and extremely valuable, your leadership education is diverse, pertinent, and often real-world, and places you in a great position to be a leader in many spheres. Do not be afraid to challenge yourself and the convention by applying for jobs outside of your comfort zone. You may surprise yourself.

This field can be challenging, but also extremely rewarding. Take the time to learn from those who lead you, even if you don't like them. The bosses you don't get along with are perhaps the ones who will teach you the most.

Table 2.1 Leadership Quotes and Definitions

John K. Hemphill and Alvin Coons	Leadership is the behaviour of an individual when he is directing the activities of a group toward a shared goal.
Warren Bennis	Leadership is the capacity to translate vision into reality.
Edwin P. Hollander	Leadership is a process of influence between a leader and those who are followers.
Peter Drucker	Effective leadership is not about making speeches or being liked; leadership is defined by results not attributes.
Dwight Eisenhower	Leadership is the art of getting someone else to do something you want done because he wants to do it.
Stephen Covey	Management is efficiency in climbing the ladder of success; leadership determines whether the ladder is leaning against the right wall.
John Kenneth Galbraith	All of the great leaders have had one characteristic in common: it was the willingness to confront unequivocally the major anxiety of their people in their time. This, and not much else, is the essence of leadership.
Lao Tzu	A leader is best when people barely know he exists, when his work is done, his aim fulfilled, they will say: we did it ourselves.
Nelson Mandela	It is better to lead from behind and to put others in front, especially when you celebrate victory when nice things occur. You take the front line when there is danger. Then people will appreciate your leadership.
Ivan Illich	Leadership does not depend on being right.
John C. Maxwell	All leadership is influence.
John F. Kennedy	Leadership and learning are indispensible to each other.

the members of the group. In the latter case, simply making a suggestion that is adopted by the group could be interpreted as leadership. Suffice to say that, although more direct forms of influence are still important, the idea that leadership can come from anywhere at any time is more accepted than it used to be. This means that leadership moments happen all around us, influencing us constantly. If you want to participate in your group's direction, and if you want to influence the direction and outcome of your group's efforts, you need to understand a little more of yourself, what is important to you, and the strengths and weaknesses of your style of engaging others.

Understanding Your Self

Exactly who—or what—is this "you" that you need to be more familiar with to be a better leader? Using the language of psychologists and social psychologists who have done much of the work in this area, we'll refer to this fascinating concept as the **self**. In these terms, the self refers to the essential qualities that distinguish us as individuals. Although it easy enough to see how you are both similar to and different from others in your physical appearance, it is more difficult to understand the fullness of your self regarding less tangible qualities. For example, the roles that gender and sexuality, race, spirituality or fundamental values, personal relationships, and many more components of self play in every person's life interact to create a multilayered, incredibly complex, and unique person. Your reflections on these components form the basis of how you see yourself in the world, how you construct your own identity. And so we arrive at what is known as self-identity, or self-concept. The reflective process is necessary in any development of self-concept for the simple reason that self-concepts are based on assessments of these many elements or characteristics of the self. For example, if you say you are a quick learner, you are making an assessment of, among other things, your intelligence. It is part of how you define yourself and then present yourself to others.

Knowing your self—being aware of the various components that make up your whole self—is one thing, but it is virtually impossible for you to possess that knowledge without deciding whether you like what you know of yourself. It is a very short step, then, from self-identity to self-esteem, sometimes called self-worth. Self-esteem involves placing a moral judgment on your knowledge of your self. Simply put, **self-esteem** is the degree to which you like and value the person you believe yourself to be. Carl Rogers, a well-known American psychologist, believed that people generally have two self-concepts: who they are, and who they would like to become. The latter self-concept, the ideal self, is the person you envision yourself to be, based on the values you hold about the components that make up your self.

For example, if you really value having a positive outlook, it becomes embedded in what you see as your ideal self. If you also see yourself as a generally positive person, you closely match your ideal self, at least for that component of your self-identity. The closer a person's actual self-identity matches the ideal self on a variety of characteristics, the happier that person tends to be. A person whose self-identity closely matches his ideal self can be said to have high self-esteem.

High self-esteem is a real benefit to your leadership. As you become more competent, you also become more confident. As you gain more life skills and grow personally, you have more experience at your disposal for making good decisions. As you face challenges and then resolve long-standing issues, you tend to gain empathy for others in their own struggles. And as you become more comfortable with yourself, you can make room for the expertise of others; you will feel less threatened in your leadership, and you will be able to consult with others when appropriate to make better decisions that are more likely to be accepted by the members of the group. These are just a few of the positive outcomes of becoming more like the person you want to be; there are many more.

With that said, you should also be a little cautious in your plan for self-improvement. Make sure your ideal self is an enhancement of you, and not someone entirely different. In other words, avoid the temptation to try to reach perfection or to mentally flog yourself if you have traits that are seemingly impossible to change. You must be realistic. In addition, because you can't work on everything, you may want to target specific areas as priorities. Develop strategies that include action plans or steps to follow. Identify where you can find information on the characteristic you would like to address, and speak to mentors who you

Photo courtesy of Gregg Badger.

There are many positive outcomes to becoming more like the person you want to be.

believe embody those characteristics. However, before you get to that point, there are other things you need to know.

Personality

Let's take a look at what we mean when we talk about personality, how you can assess your own personality, and how you can plan for personal development. **Personality** refers to the particular patterns of thought, behaviors, and emotions that are expressed by an individual. The patterns and their underlying psychological causes can be conscious or unconscious, but they are generally consistent and enduring.

Although people may share certain personality patterns, personalities are thought to be unique. You do not have the same personality as anyone else. Having different experiences; brain chemistry; genetic structures; physical, social, and cultural environments; and a host of other influences guarantees that you are unique in your personality.

Even though you are unequalled by another living soul, you do share some general tendencies with others that can be classified. For instance, if you are stubborn, you may know others who share that characteristic. There will be differences in degree and perception, but you share with those people a recognizable personality trait. You may have a friend who is also stubborn, but she may be even more stubborn than you, and she might prefer to call herself "persistent."

A variety of personality tests have been devised by researchers and psychologists to assist people in learning about the characteristics they possess. In these tests, people answer questions that are then often grouped or categorized to formulate typologies to provide general descriptions of their personalities. Here we'll discuss three of the most common tests.

Myers-Briggs Type Indicator (MBTI)

Working with research conducted by Carl Jung, Katharine Briggs and her daughter, Isabel Myers, developed a personality test that asks questions on four opposite pairings, or dichotomies (Myers, 1998).

▶ **Extraversion (E) and Introversion (I).** Extraverts prefer action; introverts prefer thought and reflection. Myers-Briggs recognizes that people can operate in either category, but prefer to operate in one or the other. Extraverts feel recharged by action-oriented experiences, whereas introverts need time alone in reflection to renew themselves.

▶ **Sensing (S) and Intuition (N).** These two characteristics indicate preferences for how to gather information. People oriented toward sensing tend to trust their senses and distrust unexplained insight. They like their information to be concrete and verifiable. Those preferring intuition like and trust abstract ideas and theories.

▶ **Thinking (T) and Feeling (F).** Once information is gathered, decisions are made. This dichotomy explains people's preferences for how to make decisions. Those oriented toward thinking prefer to look at a situation from a logical and rational standpoint. Those who prefer a feeling approach like to be emotionally connected to their decisions; sympathizing or empathizing with others involved becomes important.

▶ **Judgment (J) and Perception (P).** This pair describes how one relates to the outside world. Judgment people tend to prefer structure and having matters resolved. Perception people enjoy flexibility and adapting to changing situations.

Respondents make choices on statements that reflect the differences between the pairs, resulting in a preference for one or the other in each dichotomy. The preference within one pair is coordinated with the preferences in the other pairs to create a four-letter designation for each respondent. For example, if you identify preferences for Extraversion, Intuition, Feeling, and Judgment, your designation would be ENFJ. There are 16 possible combinations.

For further reading and options on taking the MBTI test, visit www.myersbriggs.org/my-mbti-personality-type/mbti-basics.

Keirsey Temperament Sorter

David Keirsey developed a 16-type personality test that is both similar to and different from the MBTI (Keirsey, 1998). Similarities exist in the pairings of opposite personality concepts and in the identification of 16 combinations describing people's dominant personality orientations. The combinations in Keirsey's Temperament Sorter are further categorized into four clusters, which he named according to the major behavior displays that they indicate.

▶ **Guardians (SJ).** This group is described as security seeking. They like to feel part of something and are generally organized.

▶ **Artisans (SP).** Combining preferences in sensing and perceiving, Artisans seek stimulation and like to create.

▶ **Rationals.** People in this group seek knowledge and information. Logical tasks tend to be a strength of Rationals.

▶ **Idealists.** Idealists seek meaning and are very concerned with personal growth. Those who love teaching and counseling often fall into this group.

For further reading and options on taking the Keirsey Temperament Sorter, visit www.keirsey.com.

True Colors Test

Building on Keirsey's work, Don Lowry developed a test that attempts to capture the same constructs of personality in descriptions of four color groupings. The True Colors Test designates primary and secondary colors with accompanying descriptions. The descriptions are contained in table 2.2. For further reading and options on taking the True Colors Test, visit www.true-colors.com/.

Table 2.2 True Colors Personality Test: Color Descriptions

Color	Personality type description
Orange	People with a primary orientation toward the color Orange are described as energetic. Seizing the moment, being full of intensity, and seeking excitement are Orange characteristics. Those in this category concentrate on achieving results and winning. "I want to live life to the full and I want to do it now!"
Gold	Gold people look for stability and assurance in life. A solid work ethic, punctuality, and being organized and dependable are all characteristics of those whose primary color is Gold. Family and maintaining cultural traditions are important to these folks. "He's reliable enough to set your watch by."
Blue	Blue is calm. Blue is tranquil. Blue is loyal. Blue people make great friends. They have a calming influence, and they do whatever they can in another's hour of need. A sense of belonging, great capacity for empathy, and balance and harmony are hallmarks of blue personalities. "She will walk a mile over broken glass to help her friends."
Green	Green people are so intellectually critical that they may find flaws in their own test results! Oriented to the logical, Greens seek information and look for mental stimulation. They often value mind over emotion. They feel drawn to philosophical argument and value the knowledge gained through science. "Nowhere am I so desperately needed as among a shipload of illogical humans." —Mr. Spock (*Star Trek*)

Other tests have been developed, including the Minnesota Multiphasic Personality Inventory and the famous Rorschach Test, which involves interpreting ink blots. These tests have primarily been applied in clinical settings, but have also been used for corporate decisions (e.g., which applicant will be hired or who will be promoted) and in court cases, especially during child custody hearings. Criticisms have been leveled at all personality tests, but their popularity and use remain consistent in North America. It is important to note that most of these tests rely heavily on self-reporting, which means that the results are dependent on the respondent being truthful. It is possible that someone may answer in a way that is not entirely accurate, or even that the choices offered do not represent clear distinctions in someone's preferences. Some research has shown that respondents have been given a different typology when they have taken the test a second time. Each developer or rights holder of the content of these tests maintains that the tests should be administered and interpreted professionally, and most of them have also developed proprietary training courses for such purposes.

An important consideration is the fact that access to these tests is controlled, and most are delivered on a pay-for-service basis. Because of the complex and sensitive nature of personality testing, as well as commercial considerations, such controls are unavoidable, but this also has the unfortunate consequence that not everyone will be able to pursue this line of insight into their personalities. There is, however, nothing to stop you from pursuing a more informal approach in which you conduct some honest self-analysis. You may even solicit the help of trusted friends and family members.

Values, Beliefs, and Emotional Intelligence

If it is not clear yet in this chapter, let me be unequivocal now. Leadership—your leadership—is about you. Your ability to be the best leader you can be does not depend on your attempts to copy others or emulate great historical figures. Rather, it has everything to do with knowing who you are and understanding what you need to do to become a better version of you. It is all about you. Of course, that doesn't mean that you can't learn from others, but you need to evaluate how what you learn from others will fit in with your own leadership style. In your ongoing efforts to know and improve your leadership, it is also important to recognize that your beliefs and values have a significant role to play.

Beliefs are the ideas and concepts that we hold to be true, even without complete knowledge or evidence. Many people, for instance, have religious beliefs that they hold dearly. People can believe in ghosts, in the existence of life on other worlds, or that they have a soul mate. Beliefs are generally not provable (at least for the time being; they may be proved or disproved later on), but they are important nonetheless because they form the basis

Anton

Leadership—your leadership—is about you.

for our values systems. **Values**, then, are ideas that we hold to be important. They tend to form directives for us to follow. As we weave together values we choose to live by, we create a values system, a coherent and internally consistent set of related values.

Values are outgrowths of our beliefs. We can believe a great many things, and those beliefs that have a moral imperative will potentially lead us to make some sort of value statement—or statements—that are dependent on the beliefs we hold. It is not always the case that a stated value is accompanied by a stated belief. The underlying belief may be unstated or implied, but it is present regardless. To understand the relationship between beliefs and values, consider the Three Laws of Robotics in Isaac Asimov's collection of science fiction short stories, *I, Robot* (1950):

▶ A robot may not injure a human being or, through inaction, allow a human being to come to harm.

▶ A robot must obey the orders given to it by human beings, except where such orders would conflict with the First Law.

▶ A robot must protect its own existence as long as such protection does not conflict with the First or Second Laws.

These laws described by Asimov are correctly thought of as values. They give direction for how robots should behave and how humans can expect robots to behave. They describe what is important in robot–human relationships. What is left unsaid is the foundation on which these values rest. Two beliefs that might inform the Three Laws of Robotics could be expressed like this:

▶ Human beings are more important than robots.

▶ The purpose of robots is to serve human beings.

People must believe these two statements to be true to hold the values set out by the Three Laws.

We all have beliefs and values that guide our actions. Depending on the amount of work and thought we have put into reflecting on them, our systems of beliefs and values will have varying degrees of consistency. In other words, if you have not spent any time thinking about the things that matter to you and the ideas you believe to be true, you likely either have a hodgepodge of beliefs and values that often conflict, or have simply adopted the beliefs and values of someone else, who has essentially done the work for you. In the first case, life may be more confusing than you would like it to be, whereas in the second case, you may not actually believe or value some of the things set out for you, which can cause internal conflict. The result is also confusion because you may feel compelled to act against your true values or ignore the values you claim to hold.

The ancient Greek philosopher Socrates was so convinced that personal growth was the highest purpose for humans that he said, "The unexamined life is not worth living." Although some may consider his statement extreme, research does show that critical reflection of one's beliefs and values tends to lead to personal growth and more consistent, more effective leadership. In their research on the subject, Kouzes and Posner (2006) found that "Clarity of personal values matters greatly to our feeling motivated, creative, and committed to our workplaces. When we're clear

Best Practices From the Field

There is a reason that the National Outdoor Leadership School (NOLS) is one of the premier organizations offering leadership training in wilderness environments. Founded in 1965 and headquartered in Lander, Wyoming, USA, NOLS conducts wilderness leadership education courses across the globe. According to NOLS, the goal of every course it offers is "to give you the tools to lead your own expeditions" (www.nols.edu/about/values.shtml). At the core of its identity, then, is the development of people as leaders, both in backcountry settings and everyday life.

Although the organization takes pride in all of its staff, volunteers, and trustees, central to the delivery of the values-laden curriculum are the more than 500 full-time and seasonal instructors who have direct contact with students on the courses. The school's philosophy on quality instruction is that excellent instructors create excellent courses, and NOLS creates a work culture and opportunities in which leadership development can thrive. For example, subsidized workshops are offered to help active instructional staff expand their experience as well as their opportunities within NOLS. Senior faculty in NOLS conduct professional development seminars in a wide array of course content for others out of the belief that a diversity of experiences yields a mutual benefit for the individual and the organization. Well-rounded instructors tend to display more maturity and greater depth of judgment. Learning new skills also reminds instructors what it is like to be a student, strengthening their empathy with and connections to their own students.

NOLS is aware of the need for continued personal growth and actively encourages new challenges for its staff. A fair and transparent internal hiring mechanism when positions become vacant recognizes the benefits of professional renewal and avoids the kind of stagnation that can develop when people are urged to stay in one job simply because they are good at it. Outlets for expression include publication in the NOLS alumni magazine *The Leader* and staff newsletter. Further challenges can be pursued through an active publication house and research programs.

NOLS is recognized by many as the leader in wilderness leadership education. One of the reasons the organization has gained such an enviable reputation is its commitment to a work culture that advocates continuous leadership development among its own people. In this way it is a fitting example of best practices in 21st-century leadership.

about our personal values, we feel empowered, ready and prepared to take action. Ready to be a leader" (p. 96).

As Kouzes and Posner maintain, a solid, well-thought-out system of beliefs and values is essential for developing authenticity in your leadership, the kind of leadership that demonstrates self-confidence and earns the respect of others. The question is: How do you go about examining your beliefs and values?

Like personality constructs, beliefs and values are complex and not easily pinpointed. You will also find that no values system is perfectly consistent. In addition, as a naturally flawed human being, you will never be able to live up to all of your values all of the time. Your values, and even your beliefs, will likely change with time as you learn new things and as some of your beliefs become refined or even refuted. Keeping an open mind and being willing to grow can also be important in the development of your values.

Many online sources offer lists of values that you can review and then choose as priorities. However, you can also develop your own list of values that may be more meaningful than those in lists provided by others. This way, you can be more specific and even create descriptive values statements rather than single words.

Beliefs and values are subjective. Even though logic and rationality can be applied to these subjective components, objective rules are of limited value in governing our communications. Have you ever been surprised by someone's reaction to something you've done or said—or something they thought you *should have* done or said? Have you found yourself feeling upset or elated without fully understanding what is making you feel that way? These common experiences are just two examples of the complexity of human emotions and interactions, and we have all had our share of miscommunication and misunderstanding. However, perhaps you also know people who seem really in touch with their own emotions, who appear to easily read others' emotional states, and always say the right thing. Such people display a high level of what has been called **emotional intelligence**.

Salovey and Mayer (1990) developed a framework for emotional intelligence (EI), describing it as "the subset of social intelligence that involves the ability to monitor one's own and others' feelings and emotions, to discriminate among them and to use this information to guide one's thinking and actions" (p. 189). Social intelligence is the degree to which we can understand the motivations and behaviors of others and adapt our own responses to work and communicate effectively with them. It's no surprise, then, that Salovey and Mayer (1990) saw EI as a set of skills. Like any other set of skills that relates to working with others, emotional intelligence has a lot to say about our effectiveness as leaders.

Goleman (2011) believes that EI and leadership are intimately linked. In fact, he maintains that most models attempting to explain leadership at its most complex are, in their majority, EI-based, with four basic components: self-awareness, self-management, social awareness, and relationship management. Self-awareness speaks to your knowledge of your own emotional states. Recognizing emotions as they surface, acknowledging the feelings associated with recurrent emotions, and understanding how emotions drive your thoughts and behavior all inform self-awareness.

Self-management is about engaging your emotions in a way that is positive or at least productive. You can choose to modify impulsive emotions; for example, delaying immediate gratification for a bigger gain later on is a form of managing a potentially destructive emotion. Once you have a handle on how you react emotionally to situations (emotional self-awareness), you can adapt and consciously select actions and even thoughts that would create more positive outcomes for you. If a new smartphone has just been released that you would really like to have, would you rush out to buy one, even though your old phone works just fine and a new one will cost you a lot of money? Or, knowing that your current network provider will allow you to upgrade three months from now, could you wait, get the phone for free, and save the money?

In social awareness, empathy—the ability to understand and connect with others—is an important characteristic. If you have had the privilege to be part of or witness a group in which all the members respect each other, take time to really hear and understand each other, and communicate honestly, you have no doubt witnessed the effectiveness that characterizes such groups as well. On the other hand, one or more individuals who are rude in their communication, lack respect for others and their ideas, display contempt, or try to intimidate people in order to push their own agendas can place a group and their productivity in jeopardy. In the latter situation, the motivation to work to your potential can be compromised, and groups full of competent people often fail or do not achieve what they could otherwise.

This understanding of others, and the associated benefits of acting on a heightened social intelligence, is an important asset for leaders. Researchers have found that people can be pro-

People can be profoundly affected by the emotional tone set in a group, especially by its leader.

© Human Kinetics

foundly affected by the emotional tone set in a group, especially by its leader. The brain state that results in each individual from emotional comfort, emotional detachment, or even anxiety will inevitably influence the way they relate to others and ultimately the outcomes of the group as a whole. In this way, it's easy to see how the emotional well-being of the members in the group should be of great concern for leaders.

Relationship management, the final component of four in Goleman's framework of emotional intelligence, requires that one have a firm grasp of the other three (self-awareness, self-management, and social awareness). From a leadership perspective, this final goal of leading others effectively depends heavily on knowing yourself well, being in control of your own reactions to situations, and understanding others and their motivations. Relationship management involves inspiring others, focusing on teamwork and collaboration, and managing conflict (Goleman, 2011). While these themes are picked up in later chapters with more detail, and are less germane to the topic of self-leadership, perhaps one thing that should be said here is that emotional intelligence is another field of study that makes it clear that successful leadership is contingent on knowing yourself.

Summary

An understanding of the self is important for effective leadership and for growth as a leader. This chapter explored the concepts of self-leadership as it relates to personal growth. Personality and personality types were discussed, as were major personality assessment tests such as the Myers-Briggs Type Indicator, Keirsey Temperament Sorter, and True Colors Test. Beliefs, values, and emotional intelligence were introduced as a final component of self-understanding and improving your own leadership.

Questions for Reflection and Discussion

1. With a partner or in a small group, discuss the following:
   - Is high self-esteem the same as being arrogant or conceited?
   - Can you have high self-esteem and still be humble?
   - What would it feel like to have high self-esteem?
   - What are some benefits of high self-esteem to leadership?

2. Set aside some time to reflect on your own personality. You can keep in mind the categories and descriptions used by the tests outlined in this chapter, but you may not want to speak to them directly. Here are some strategies to help you:
   - Begin by reminding yourself what a personality is (i.e., create a definition).
   - Develop a list of personal characteristics you would like to focus on (e.g., extraversion/introversion, creativity, organization and logistics, importance of emotion and feeling, importance of relationship development and maintenance). These represent only a few, so spend a decent amount of time thinking of more.
   - Develop questions that address your relationship with each of the categories. For example, in considering whether you are extraverted or introverted, you may already have a good feeling for your orientation, but ask yourself some specific questions that deal with typical situations you find yourself in. For example, Do I prefer to relate to people one on one or in groups? At social gatherings, do I circulate, or do I wait for people to come and talk to me? Do others seem to be intimidated by me, or am I intimidated by others?
   - Answer the questions honestly and with some depth. Don't avoid any areas you think of. It may even help to answer the questions out loud. Write out your answers or record them in some way for later reference.
   - Using all of your answers, write a description of yourself, er . . . your "self."
   - Ask someone or a small group of people you trust to set aside some time to give

you feedback. You may want to give them some background (e.g., what you mean by personality) and instructions on how the session will work.

- Read them the description of yourself and ask for feedback. The feedback should be honest, but respectful of you, and should include where they agree and disagree with you, things they think you have missed in your assessment, and further questions for you to consider.

- Be open and have some fun. Remember that if you have chosen your feedback candidates well, their input will remind you why you trust them.

- With feedback on your description, you should now be armed with very good information about your personality—your actual self. Compare this to your ideal self.

- Identify characteristics of your actual self that you would like to work on, and then set out a plan for doing so (if you have not done this before, you may want to start with minor characteristics).

- Celebrate your strengths (those characteristics in your actual self that are closely aligned with your ideal self), and consider how you can use them to your advantage.

3. Perform a values assessment by developing a list of values that are most important to you (try to keep the list relatively short; perhaps 5 to 10 values statements). Study the list and attempt to identify the beliefs that form the foundation for your values. Ask yourself the following questions:

- Are all of your beliefs and values supportive of each other, or are there conflicts?

- Where do your values and beliefs come from? What experiences in your life may have contributed to you adopting them (i.e., why did you choose these beliefs and values)?

Try to come up with another short list of values that are next in line of importance to those in the list you already created. Are they caused by the same beliefs you identified in the preceding steps, or do you need to identify more beliefs to explain them?

As your list grows, do you see any potential conflicts, or is everything still consistent? If conflicts exist, how would you resolve a conflict that arose between two or more of your values? What event or information could you imagine that might change your mind about anything on your list? Is there any information that would help make your beliefs stronger and your values more consistent? If so, how would you obtain that information?

How will knowing more about your beliefs and values affect the decisions you make as a leader? Be as specific as you can.

Key Terms and Definitions

beliefs—The ideas and concepts that people hold to be true, even without complete knowledge or evidence.

emotional intelligence—The degree to which an individual understands their own feelings and emotions, can control and positively engage their own emotions, understands the emotional signals and motivations for behavior in others, and can successfully adapt to the emotionally driven behavior of others to help create positive outcomes.

personality—The particular patterns of thought, behaviors, and emotions that are expressed by an individual.

self—The essential qualities that distinguish people as individuals.

self-esteem—The degree to which people like and value who they believe themselves to be.

values—Ideas that we view as important to how we conduct ourselves that tend to be outgrowths of our beliefs.

Bibliography

Asimov, I. (1950). *I, robot.* Garden City, NY: Doubleday.

Goleman, D. (2011). *Leadership: The power of emotional intelligence – selected writings.* Northampton, MA: More Than Sound.

Keirsey, D. (1998). *Please understand me II: Temperament, character, intelligence.* Del Mar, CA: Prometheus Nemesis Book Company.

Kouzes, J.M. & Posner, B.Z. (2006). *A leader's legacy.* San Francisco: Jossey-Bass.

Kouzes, J.M., & Posner, B.Z. (2008). We lead from the inside out. *Journal of Values Based Leadership, 1* (1). Retrieved online from www.valuesbasedleadershipjournal.com/issues/vol1issue1/kouzes_posner.php.

Myers, Isabel Briggs. (1998). *Introduction to type: A guide to understanding your results on the Myers-Briggs Type Indicator.* Mountain View, CA: CPP.

Salovey, P., & Mayer, J. (1990). Emotional intelligence. *Imagination, Cognition, and Personality, 9* (3) 185-211.

Chapter 3

Interpersonal Communication Skills

Terilyn Goins

" *The art of communication is the language of leadership.*

—James Humes

Marilyn, an enthusiastic entrepreneur, is excited about her company start-up, Getting Connected, a business designed to pull together people from various levels of employment (e.g., self, collaborative, cooperative, traditional) into locally established social networking hubs. Her objective is to create an environment that fosters creativity and innovation, bringing together some of the greatest and brightest minds in the community to inspire and empower them to grow personally and professionally. Having worked for a small organization for many years, Marilyn is familiar with traditional ways of doing business, regular face-to-face board meetings, communication via e-mail as necessary based on the workday, and a clear organizational hierarchy in which employees understand and are comfortable with their positions within the company. Marilyn knows, however, that her new venture will stretch the boundaries of the traditional workplace, introducing a virtual environment that restructures and, in some instances, redefines the communication experience and its potential impact on leadership.

Learning Outcomes

At the conclusion of this chapter, students will be able to:

▶ Describe the nature of interpersonal communication and identify seminal works.

▶ Understand the roles of listening, perception, and communication competence in the communication process.

▶ Describe the relationship between communication and leadership, including the challenges and advantages of face-to-face and virtual communication.

▶ Explain the three Ps of leadership (an interpersonal leadership model).

Communication and leadership are so intricately intertwined that it is often difficult to separate the two. Although communication does not define the leadership process, it is virtually impossible to lead effectively without the ability to clearly articulate your message to others. Hackman and Johnson (2009) noted, "Leadership is human (symbolic) communication which modifies the attitudes and behaviors of others in order to meet shared group goals and needs" (p. 11). Because leaders are typically responsible for communicating their vision to followers, they must possess in-depth knowledge and understanding of the communication process, a multifaceted, multilayered endeavor that requires a great deal of thought and reflection. It is through communication that leaders create reality; transmit information about the past, present, and future; and move people toward goal achievement (Hackman & Johnson, 2009, p. 6).

The Nature of Interpersonal Communication

Being connected with others is one of the greatest needs human beings experience; through communication, we establish and sustain relationships with others, mutually attempting to meet each other's physical, emotional, psychological, and spiritual needs. The communication process is quite sophisticated and multifarious with interdependent components that allow for an exchange of messages between two people or among many people. It is dynamic and transactional, involving a simultaneous, continuous transmission of information from one person to another in an attempt to create meaning for those involved in the interaction (Wood, 2009).

As figure 3.1 illustrates, the communication process is endless, and as people interact, their knowledge about and connections with each other expand (Dance & Larson, 1976; Dance & Zak-Dance, 1986). The helical model represents the totality of a person's communication, from birth to the present moment. "The communication process, like the helix, is constantly moving forward and yet is always to some degree dependent upon the past, which informs the present and the future" (Dance, 1967, p. 296). All people possess their own communication spirals, and whenever spirals meet, messages are transmitted. The potential exists to

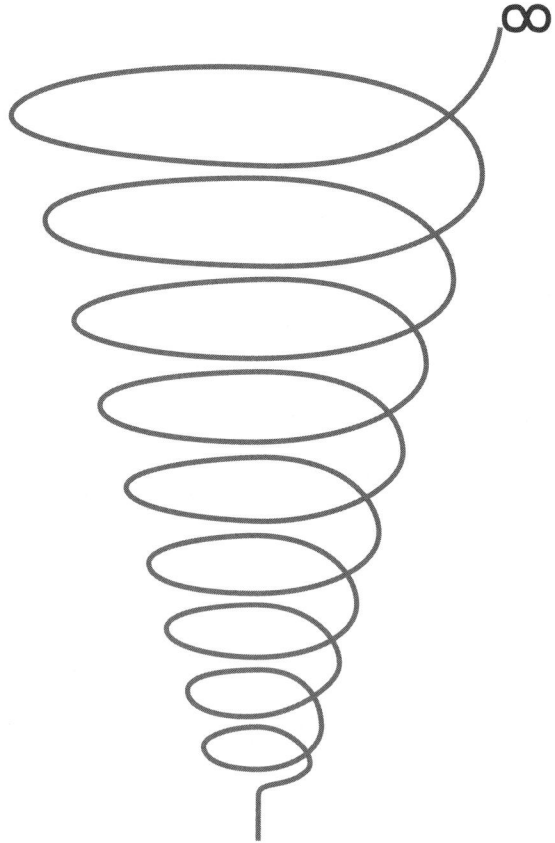

Figure 3.1 Helical communication model.
Reprinted, by permission, from F.E.X. Dance, 1967, Toward a theory of human communication. In *Human communication theory*, edited by F.E.X. Dance (New York: F.E.X. Dance).

substantially intertwine with another helix, to make contact at specific times and on specific areas of content, to touch at a single moment in time, or to never engage at all (Gamble & Gamble, 2013).

Face-to-face interactions involve three channels: visual, vocal, and verbal. The visual and vocal elements of communication encompass the nonverbal quality of our interactive experiences (e.g., facial expression, eye contact, body orientation, vocal cues), whereas the verbal aspect of communication is the words we speak as we try to bridge the gap of understanding and meaning (Argyle, 1988; Knapp & Hall, 2002).

Visual Channel

The visual channel of communication represents everything visible during the communication transmission, including things such as facial expression; body language; eye contact; the use of touch, time, and space; and overall physical appearance. These visual components can support or contradict the words we speak. For example, imagine that you've scheduled an hour-long meeting with your supervisor to address some concerns you have about a special event you are organizing for local youth. In the middle of the meeting, your supervisor's cell phone rings, interrupting the conversational flow. She glances at her phone to see who's calling and comments, "I'll catch up with him later," allowing the call to go to voice mail. Thinking that the interruption is over, you continue with the conversation. After a couple of minutes, just enough time for the caller to leave a voice mail, your supervisor picks up her phone and begins pushing buttons, apparently checking for the voice mail. Sensing that the call may actually be important to her, you offer to step out of the office and give her time to return the call. Upon your offer, she insists that it can wait and apologizes for the interruption. Because of the disparity between the words spoken and the accompanying nonverbal behavior, you quickly wrap up the meeting even though you're still unclear about some of the things the two of you discussed. Obviously, it is essential that the words we speak match the visual behaviors we display; if they don't, the intended message will be compromised.

Vocal Channel

The vocal channel of communication represents how we say what we say, including characteristics such as tone, pitch, rate, volume, emphasis, articulation, pronunciation, accent, and dialect. The vocal medium frequently serves as our "emotional tell," revealing to others our genuine emotional state, often without our knowledge. For instance, how many times in any given day does someone ask you, "How are you?" And, how many times, in response to that question, do you say, "I'm fine, thank you"? The words are always the same, but the "emotional tell" gives the message recipient insight into how you're really doing, as displayed through, for example, a lower voice pitch, a slower rate of speaking, or a quieter volume. Although it may be possible to mask our true emotional state by exercising control over our bodily reactions (e.g., smiling, leaning in, nodding at precisely the right time), the subtle changes in our emotional state typically sneak into the intricacies of our vocal display (Lewis, 1998). It is those subtle vocal changes that may prompt you to follow up on your

initial question, asking, "Are you sure you're OK?" or "How are you *really* doing?"

Verbal Channel

The verbal channel of communication represents the words we say, including our specific word choice and use of vocabulary. As we engage in communication with another person, we are constantly sending and receiving messages, interpreting everything that is happening nonverbally and verbally, to create and sustain interpersonal relationships. Interestingly, whenever verbal and nonverbal messages conflict, and we must choose which one to believe, the nonverbal messages carry more weight and often drive our interpretative assessment and ensuing response (Knapp, 1972; Malandro & Barker, 1983; Mehrabian, 1971, 1981).

Listening and the Perception Process

Within the communication process, listening contributes significantly to the success or failure of an interaction. As people receive messages, they must decipher the information, frame it within their world of understanding, and interpret the intended meaning. Accordingly, listening is a specific component of the perception process that contributes to our understanding of self and others (Goss, 1982).

Content Versus the Relational Dimension of Meaning

Every message we communicate contains content and a relational dimension of meaning. The content dimension is simply the topic of conversation. The relational dimension, on the other hand, is much more complicated and is often an unspoken facet of the interaction that makes statements about the quality of the relationship; that is, how people feel about those with whom they are engaged (Bavelas, 2011). It is through the relational dimension of meaning that we communicate feelings of affinity, inclusion, respect, and control (Mehrabian, 1981). Whereas the content dimension is objective and cognitive, the relational dimension is subjective and emotive.

Consider a debate between local county supervisors and residents regarding how to pay for a newly constructed sports complex, in which the people involved disagree on the appropriateness of the recommended funding. The supervisors advocate raising real estate taxes for all 65,000 county residents, whereas the residents suggest it would make more sense to outsource services, cut staff overhead, reduce costs, and use the money saved to fund the complex. In the midst of the debate, tempers flare, name calling ensues, and the overall tone of the exchange turns hostile; many residents storm out of the meeting. Within a short time frame, the supervisors make a unilateral decision to move forward with their plan, leaving the residents feeling angry and powerless. In this situation, the content of the discussion is the funding options the two groups are exploring. The relational dimension, however, as observed primarily through the visual and vocal elements of the interaction, points to issues related to respect, inclusion, and control.

Active Listening

Because miscommunication and conflict are so much a part of day-to-day interactions, it is essential to find ways to recognize and deal with them. Often, leaders assume that speaking clearly is the most essential component of the communication process, overlooking the tremendous significance of the listening process. Although the objective of speaking is to be understood, it is through listen-

Listening facilitates understanding.

© Human Kinetics

ing that we understand (Covey, 2004). Through active listening, we can allay many of the interactive faux pas we endure. You can listen actively by doing one or all of the following: (1) clarify by paraphrasing the speaker's message, (2) interject subtle prompts, and (3) ask questions (Wood, 1999, p. 204).

Although passive listening is appropriate at times (e.g., listening for entertainment purposes), most interactive experiences demand greater listening attentiveness. To listen actively to another person, you must be consciously engaged in the process, attuned to even the most subtle nuances that may be packaged in the transmitted message. Sometimes messages are straightforward and easy to comprehend and act on, whereas at other times, layers of meaning exist that can only be unraveled via active listening. Even the simplest of messages can stump the most sophisticated communicators. The following communication scenarios demonstrate ways to use active listening to improve an encounter:

> *You're going to meet your friend for dinner at a local restaurant the two of you frequent. The area in which you live has two franchises of the same restaurant on different sides of town. When setting up the event, the communication goes something like this:*
>
> *You: I'm available for dinner tonight. Why don't we get together?*
>
> *Friend: Sounds great! Where would you like to eat?*
>
> *You: How about our favorite Italian place?*
>
> *Friend: That sounds awesome! Seven o'clock?*
>
> *You: Perfect! See you there.*

On the surface, this encounter seems straightforward. Unfortunately, because neither of you has engaged in active listening, you end up at different restaurant locations, waiting for the other to arrive, finally leaving angry and frustrated. The fiasco could have been avoided through active listening. Consider the same interaction a little differently:

> *You: I'm available for dinner tonight. Why don't we get together?*
>
> *Friend: Sounds great! Where would you like to eat?*
>
> *You: How about our favorite Italian place?*
>
> *Friend: Which location—my side of town or yours?*

You: You came over here last time, so I'll come out your way.

Friend: Okay. Seven o'clock?

You: Perfect!

Friend: Looking forward to it; I'll see you at the Italian place on my side of town at seven o'clock tonight?

You: Exactly. See you there.

Consider another example.

You're a financial administrator in charge of handling all expense accounts for your department. You pride yourself on being well organized and detail oriented. Unfortunately, you quickly discover that not everyone possesses these qualities, and you end up badgering one particular employee, Andrew, to get the receipts necessary for a timely turnaround on expense reimbursement. On one occasion, Andrew storms into your office and, in an accusatory tone, complains, "It's been over a month since my training session in California, and I've yet to be reimbursed for gas mileage, hotel expenses, and meals; that's a bit unreasonable, don't you think?" Because of the emotionally charged nature of this interaction, it is vital that you employ all three steps of the active listening process:

1. *Paraphrase: "I understand that you're upset because a lot of time has passed since your trip and you're still waiting for reimbursement."*

2. *Interject subtle prompts: "I'm not really clear about what happened in this situation. Typically, the reimbursement process is more efficient than that."*

3. *Ask questions: "To whom did you submit your report? Is it possible that your receipts for that trip have been misplaced? Were you able to complete all of the appropriate paperwork, including attaching your receipts, when you submitted your expense report?"*

The preceding scenario about meeting a friend at a restaurant is simple enough that paraphrasing alone sufficed to clarify the message. In this scenario, which is more emotionally sensitive, you should use all three steps to fully comprehend what's going on and to maintain a positive relationship.

Perception Checking

In addition to active listening, you can reduce miscommunication through perception checking, a process that helps ensure that people are sharing the same reality. Perception checking involves three steps:

1. Identify the behavior you've observed in the other person(s).

2. Offer two possible interpretations of the behavior.

3. Seek clarification of the behavior. (Adler & Proctor II, 2011, p. 105)

Although it is normal to make assumptions about other people's behaviors, assumptions left unchecked can create flawed perspectives that ultimately damage and inhibit growth of the relationship. For example, consider how Alex, a highly motivated, self-starter employee might view a micromanagement style of leadership. Given Alex's goal-driven initiative, he might feel stifled by the micromanager and question her faith in him to do his job well. If Alex blindly accepts his assumption as truth, he may build a defensive wall around himself, thereby hindering his ability to interact effectively with his supervisor, which may, in turn, diminish his workplace success. If, however, Alex understands the importance of aligning perceptions, he can use the perception checking strategy to determine whether a disparity exists between his perspective and reality. Here is how he might do this:

1. *Identify the behavior he has observed from his supervisor:* "I've noticed several times this week that you've come up behind me to check my work."

2. *Offer two interpretations:* "Are you concerned about my ability to complete the assignment to your standards?" *Or:* "Is there some aspect of the assignment that you would like to go over with me?"

3. *Seek clarification:* "Am I just being paranoid, or is something else going on?"

Perception checks and active listening can greatly minimize frustration in communication encounters. Often, we assume that the knowledge we have in our heads is the same knowledge our communication partner possesses. Unfortunately, that small error in thinking can be the impetus for

Leisure Leaders

Heather Stilwell

MY PREPARATION

- BA in cinema and broadcasting arts— Azusa Pacific University, Azusa, CA
- MA in broadcast journalism—Syracuse University, Syracuse, NY
- Communications Student of the Year, Radio—Azusa Pacific University, May 2004
- Who's Who Among American College Students, 2004
- Who's Who Among American High School Students, 2000
- Member, Society of Professional Journalists (SPJ)
- Member, National Communication Association (NCA)
- Member, American Copy Editors Society (ACES)
- Member, Broadcast Education Association (BEA)

MY CAREER

Building a college radio station from scratch is challenging and exhilarating. Biola University was, historically, no stranger to broadcast media; however, its airwaves had been dead for years when I was brought on staff. After three years of gradually purchasing equipment, outfitting the studios with proper furniture, and recruiting and training students as staff members and talk-show hosts, music DJs, sports announcers, and news reporters and anchors, Biola radio was reborn. The station, known as the Torch, is an online-streaming station that seeks to serve the Biola community consisting of students, faculty, staff, and alumni. In its first year of 24/7 broadcasting, the station averaged near 1,000 listeners a month.

As faculty adviser of the Torch, I am responsible for ensuring the station is not violating its

Photo courtesy of Heather Stilwell.

legal responsibilities concerning broadcast regulations and music royalties. I hire and train a handful of students who are leadership staff for the station; these students in turn train other students who are interested in having an on-air shift or being involved with the station in a more minor role. Additionally, I oversee the finances of the station, and I work with the station engineer to ensure the studios are outfitted with properly working equipment.

As a student, I was the sports director for my campus radio station, and I admired the impact my faculty adviser had on the radio staff. After obtaining a bachelor's degree, I taught high school English and multimedia for two years before returning to graduate school. While attending Syracuse University for my master's degree, I began working at the local radio station as a news reporter and weekend anchor. This job eventually led to other job offers in the radio and television news business. Because of family medical concerns, I left the field for a time and taught and trained students as the faculty adviser of the Torch. This job allowed me to share my passion for the broadcasting field while having a more flexible schedule.

Leadership is twofold. First, it is about service. Leaders will not be effective unless they demonstrate that they are willing to do the job required of others. This breeds respect of those under a leader. The second aspect is that strong leadership creates a team mentality that instills ownership of tasks. If staff members truly feel valued, the quality of the work increases. Students put in far more time than what is required of their positions because they love seeing the awareness and popularity of the radio station grow in the Biola community.

MY ADVICE TO YOU

Be a moral adult: Choose the high road when it comes to gray areas. Always consider the image and reputation your actions could portray. If there is a possibility that something could shed a negative light, you are most likely better off choosing a different option.

Have a vision and don't give up. Leading others requires moving yourself and others toward a goal. Yet you cannot lead others if you do not have a sense of where you are headed. Be a visionary, dream, and remind yourself of those dreams when setbacks hit. There will be struggles, but a steadfast and positive spirit is key

to ensuring those under you continue to have faith in your goals.

Affirm those under you. Encouraging words that let those you lead know they are valued will help tremendously when disagreements, controversy, and the need for discipline arise. When people know you believe in them, they will perform to a higher standard and do so voluntarily.

Work in the name of fun can seem surreal at times! It is fun. However, in the moments when struggles happen or the more mundane and menial tasks require attention, remember why you love what you are doing.

---

very large gaps between meaning conveyed and meaning received. Consequently, it is essential that we make use of the tools available to facilitate a meeting of the minds.

Communication Competence and Leadership

Leadership success depends on developing interpersonal communication skills and using them to achieve established goals (Hackman & Johnson, 2009). Through communication, we connect with other human beings, regulating our own and others' behaviors (Dance & Larson, 1976). To lead effectively, however, we must do more than understand the communication process; we must prove ourselves to be communication competent, using the most effective and appropriate communication behavior in any given situation, while maintaining established relationships on terms acceptable to all involved (Adler & Proctor II, 2011; McCroskey, 1982). Competent communicators exhibit a wide range of styles and behaviors, possess the cognitive ability to accurately assess a situation, and display the skill and commitment necessary for acting appropriately. Leaders are considered competent if they possess the "knowledge and the skills to effectively communicate, and they also have the motivation or willingness to demonstrate these abilities" (Macik-Frey, 2007, p. 25). To be effective, leaders must create a

sense of community and vibrancy within which to communicate a unified vision and accomplish established goals.

Good leaders use communication as a means to an end. Whether they intend to enact a vision, motivate followers to action, change people's minds, or manage impressions, effective leaders understand what is required of them and know how to use communication to accomplish their goals. Hackman and Johnson (2009) identified the following three clusters of communication skills leaders must possess:

1. Linking skills, which include observing the interactive environment and building a trusting climate in which participants can function

2. Envisioning skills, which involve creating and establishing strategies or visions from the status quo

3. Regulating skills, which help leaders influence and motivate others

In addition to establishing and reaching tangible goals, leaders must also connect to individuals and build relationships.

To create a holistic model of leadership, Kouzes and Posner (1987, 2002) interviewed people in leadership positions to discover the behaviors that typify successful leaders. Their research yielded five practices that allow leaders to excel, as shown in figure 3.2.

A close examination of Kouzes and Posner's five leadership practices reveals that effective

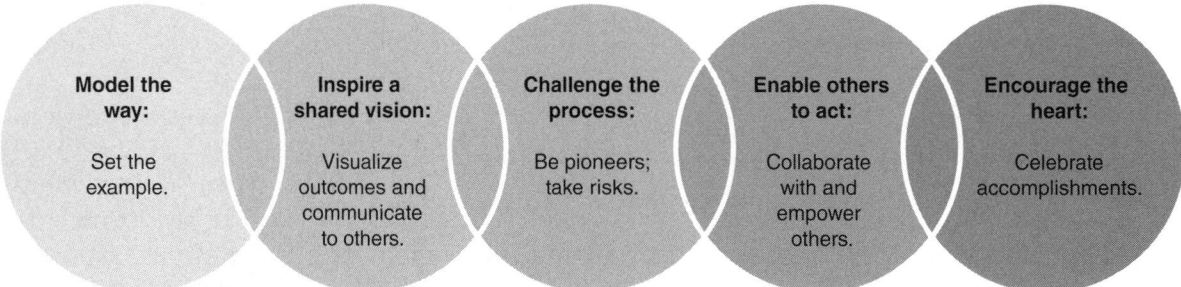

Figure 3.2 Kouzes and Posner's five practices of leadership.
Based on Kouzes and Posner 2002.

communication skills are at the core of each practice. Through both verbal (spoken and written) and nonverbal messages, exemplary leaders engage their followers, setting the example, articulating the vision, innovating change, and empowering others by recognizing their individual gifts and talents.

Task- Versus Relations-Oriented Leadership

Quality leaders take into account both task and relationship components when considering what leadership strategy best fits any given situation. At one end of the spectrum is a concern for productivity and task completion, and at the other end is interpersonal connectedness with a focus on process and people skills. Task-oriented leaders focus on establishing goals and defining and managing assigned tasks and roles, whereas relations-oriented leaders concentrate on establishing connections between people, encouraging team development, collaborating, and creating collective ventures.

The differences between task- and relations-oriented leadership are similar to those between content and relational dimensions of meaning. Although both are vital to leadership and communication success, it is important to recognize the value of each, and to understand the origin of problems that arise. Often, problems in the workplace manifest as people issues rather than task issues. Feelings of disrespect, disempowerment,

Best Practices From the Field

A local consulting firm recently underwent significant restructuring, and as a result of economic downturns, was forced to consolidate jobs and lay off some of its long-standing contractors. Unfortunately, word spread of the impending layoffs, and before the company could exercise damage control, the remaining contractors decided to jump ship rather than face the same fate as their colleagues. By the time the powers that be figured out what was happening, it was too late; they had lost many of their best and most loyal partners. Although there are no quick fixes in situations such as this, organizational leaders can employ strategies to help them not only avert such negative outcomes, but also maintain company integrity.

- *Increase communication within the company.* Provide as much information to all involved as is feasible in the situation. In the absence of information, people typically make it up themselves, which often does not fare well for the organization.

- *Be honest.* Although this may seem like a cliché, honesty is among the most important communicative strategies to use in stressful, uncomfortable situations. Hiding or misconstruing the truth can result in loyalty and trust issues that will later impede company progress.

- *Involve the affected people as much as possible.* Many case studies on this issue reveal that involving essential personnel in decisions can reduce anxiety, enhance company relations, and reveal options that may not be obvious to those making the decisions.

- *Put relationships ahead of the bottom line.* Regardless of the actions taken, it is essential that everyone involved feel valued in the process. Leaders need to demonstrate affinity, inclusion, and respect.

disliking, or noninclusiveness then carry over into work performance. As the saying goes, People quit people; they don't quit jobs. Consequently, if leaders want their followers to produce for them, they must attend to the way they solicit productivity. The bottom line is, if we want results, we have to communicate appreciation and respect for those from whom we seek those results, both personally and professionally.

Traditional Face-to-Face Versus E-Leadership

In the technology-rich environment in which we live, our key interpersonal and professional encounters are not likely to be solely face-to-face or virtual. Rather, our relationships exist on a continuum between more or less virtual. Some of us believe that virtual encounters, via Facebook, MySpace, Skype, FaceTime, and the like, enhance our already established relationships. **On the other hand,** Instagram and Twitter are encounters experienced almost exclusively online, such as IT specialists who contract their services to institutions and perform the majority of their work within the online environment. In exclusively online encounters, face-to-face interactions are supplemental and secondary to the online experience.

As the world grows smaller through technology-driven globalization, questions emerge about the effectiveness of traditional face-to-face leadership models within the virtual environment. In face-to-face interactions, participants enjoy a complete communication experience, along with an immediacy that gives them a chance to reflect, seek feedback, and respond based on the information obtained. Furthermore, the immediacy of face-to-face encounters fosters a sense of aliveness and community that has to be manipulated and created in situations in which people are separated by time, culture, and distance (Kerfoot, 2010). E-leaders, in contrast to traditional leaders, enact their leadership roles in virtual networks such as e-mail, instant messages, videoconferences, webinars, FaceTime, Google Hangout, and Skype. Although such technologies provide quick access to a lot of information and a vast array of communication venues, they can also create feelings of anxiety as a result of information overload (Avolio & Kahai, 2003; Belanger & Watson-Manheim, 2006).

Because of the apparent interpersonal disconnectedness the virtual environment affords, it is natural for e-leaders to focus more time on tasks than relationships. This, of course, is a grave error because rapport, cohesion, and trust are essential to virtual team success. An absence of relational connection can result in increased interpersonal conflict, which inhibits productivity (Bergiel, Bergiel, & Balsmeier, 2008; Hertel, Geister, & Konradt, 2005; Rosen, Furst, & Blackburn, 2007). Unfortunately, the nature of the virtual environment makes it difficult for leaders to recognize such conflict and address it in a timely fashion. Because of factors such as culture, time, and space differences, along with divergent levels of technological expertise, e-leaders also have difficulty succinctly articulating a vision, a mission, and objectives to virtual participants (Dewar, 2006), which, in turn, potentially squelches feelings of unity and enthusiasm.

Although some leadership behaviors are equally important in face-to-face and virtual settings, evidence suggests that certain actions are more important than others depending on the degree of virtualness. For example, in highly virtual environments, participants believe it is important for leaders to establish a clear and common understanding of tasks, "focusing on outcomes and deliverables rather than on team members' activities" (Zimmerman, Wit, & Gill, 2008, pp. 328-329). Additionally, they suggest that leaders establish and maintain relationships in a time-efficient manner, avert misunderstandings, ensure that everyone feels a part of the team, be sensitive to cultural diversity, and emphasize shared values among team members (Walvoord et al., 2008).

Consider the job of educators offering courses that are administered entirely online. To accomplish similar goals online to those achieved in face-to-face classes, instructors must meticulously measure their words, communicate more frequently, read between the lines students write, engage each student individually rather than as a part of the class, and constantly reassure students that they can succeed in the course. In essence, because there are limited opportunities to engage students as a group within the virtual environment, instructors must work much harder to reach a goal that's comparatively simple to attain in person. Additionally, when a misunderstanding, miscommunication, or conflict occurs in the virtual environment, it takes significant time and effort to repair the damage, and sometimes it's not even possible to do so.

Because people in a virtual setting often have little to no firmly established interpersonal connection to those who lead them, it is all too easy to assign negative or dishonest motives when things go awry. Quashing those attitudes, once in motion, can be quite the feat for even the most experienced leaders.

Leadership Within a Virtual Environment

Without question, leading in online environments presents greater challenges than leading in face-to-face environments. Computer-mediated communication is here to stay; thus, it is essential to consider strategies to enhance the online leadership process. It should be obvious by now that the area in need of the most work within the virtual environment is the interpersonal, relationship dimension of the communication process. When people feel valued, they produce, regardless of the communication medium. Following are some suggestions for improving performance and satisfaction in computer-mediated situations:

1. Establish a clear set of rules regarding communication behaviors—how frequent, how much, and to what extent (Lin, Standing, & Liu, 2008).

2. Set consistent meeting times for the group as a whole, and connect via other media whenever possible, such as FaceTime, telephone, Skype, and chat sessions (Cascio, 2000).

3. Create an easily accessible central databank of information for participants (Hertel, Geister, & Konradt, 2005; Powell, Piccoli, & Ives, 2004).

Also, if at all feasible, as early as possible in the process, virtual participants should meet face-to-face, even if it is only once. When virtual groups meet face-to-face, they more readily establish essential interpersonal connections and develop the rapport, respect, and trust they need to carry them through the assigned project(s). Because the focus within the virtual encounter tends to be task oriented, face-to-face meetings should concentrate on relational development among participants and ironing out any existent or potential misunderstandings or conflict issues (Hertel, Geister, & Konradt, 2005; Lantz, 2001; Powell, Piccoli, & Ives, 2004).

Leadership Within a Hybrid Environment (Both Face-to-Face and Virtual)

Although computer-mediated communication is best suited for certain tasks, such as passive, informational, and nonsocial tasks (e.g., brainstorming), the optimum situation in which to lead is a combination of virtual and face-to-face encounters. When both are used, the task and interpersonal demands can be met with greater ease, thereby enhancing overall productivity. For instance, instructors of hybrid courses that combine virtual and face-to-face instruction do not have to scrutinize every word, nor do they need to expend as much effort to meet every student's need. Face-to-face instruction enables them to cover a topic or address an issue once rather than have to repeat it a number of times, depending on the number of student inquiries. Additionally, impressions of e-leaders tend to be more accurate when interpersonal connectedness is established in the face-to-face encounters. As figure 3.3 illustrates, relational depth tends to function on a continuum of least intimate to most intimate based on degree of face-to-face encounters.

Advantages of Face-to-Face Communication

For a number of reasons, face-to-face communication may be superior to mediated communication. Face-to-face communication is more nonverbally substantive; and the communication experience is more comprehensive. It presents a stronger social, emotional, and cultural context and is generally less stressful than computer-mediated communication (Daft & Lengel, 1984; Hancock, 2004; Short, Williams, & Christie, 1976; Sproull & Kiesler, 1986; Thompson & Coovert, 2003; Walther, 1993). Additionally, when the other person doesn't respond in a virtual environment, you can never be totally certain of whether the person received the message or is simply ignoring you. Unfortunately, this phenomenon often elicits a number of not-so-positive assumptions that can later backfire (Bergiel, Bergiel, & Balsmeier, 2008; Dewar, 2006).

Imagine a situation in which a coworker attempts to contact you via e-mail to discuss an important issue and you don't receive the message. In the absence of a response, your coworker

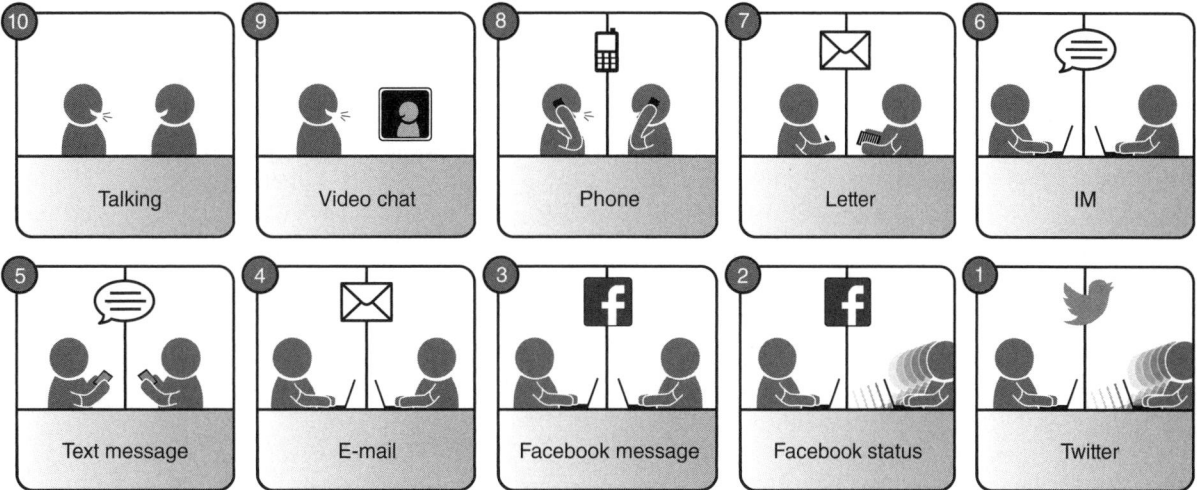

Figure 3.3 Ten dimensions of intimacy in today's communication.
Reprinted, by permission, from J. Lee.

assumes that you are ignoring the message and complains to your boss. The boss subsequently calls you into her office to address your apparent apathy. You're completely taken by surprise because you never received the e-mail, which you tell your boss. The misunderstanding is resolved and the meeting is scheduled. The incident would never have happened had your coworker simply followed up with a telephone call or office visit.

It is possible to avoid such unnecessary communication mishaps by adhering to a few simple e-mail etiquette rules:

▶ Never use e-mail to address emotionally charged or sensitive issues that are better communicated face-to-face. E-mail should primarily be reserved for exchange of information.

▶ E-mail the person back within 24 hours of the time the message was sent to you.

▶ Stay away from flashy colored and patterned backgrounds because they can distract from the message conveyed.

▶ Avoid using all caps in your e-mail response because it can come across as yelling.

▶ After a couple of responses on an issue, you need to change the subject of your e-mail. Don't have 20 e-mails referencing an issue that was resolved 15 e-mails back.

▶ Run a spell-check and then read through your response thoroughly to ensure that it doesn't contain major grammatical errors. If you write *Susan went to there house,* the spell-checker

will not catch this error because the word *there* is spelled correctly (the correct word is *their).*

▶ If you haven't heard back from the person in 72 hours, send a follow-up e-mail to check the status of your original e-mail. If you still receive no response, you may have to resort to picking up the telephone. This will alleviate any unnecessary, and probably inaccurate, assessments about why the person has not responded to your e-mail.

The immediacy of face-to-face encounters creates a strong sense of community and vibrancy that is often difficult to negotiate in computer-mediated environments.

Advantages of Virtual Communication

Although mediated communication introduces chellenges that can typically be avoided in face-to-face encounters, it is not without advantages. We can now interact with people across the globe, which introduces cultural exposure beyond what we could ever have imagined. We can reconnect on Facebook with people we haven't seen or heard from in years; we can have virtual, face-to-face encounters, via FaceTime, Skype, or Google Hangout, with friends and family who live across the globe or across the street; we can play games with complete strangers; we can even meet and court people we've met only over the Internet.

Many people report that the virtual communication experience has actually improved the quantity and quality of their relationships with others, resulting in more regularly scheduled and substantive contact time (Boase et al., 2006; Dainton & Aylor, 2002; Wellman et al., 2008). Moreover, the absence of the visual component in many virtual encounters tends to create an equalizing effect and openness among participants that may not exist in face-to-face encounters. Visual cues available face-to-face tend to highlight features we use to discriminate against one another, such as sex, race, attractiveness, body size, age, and physical limitations. The virtual environment, on the other hand, diminishes such power plays, encouraging inclusiveness, respect, and affinity. Put another way, computer-mediated communication focuses more on the content dimension of the interaction and less on the relationship dimension, or at the very least redefines it. In virtual communication, absent the visual display, there is no race, sex, ethnicity, religion, and social or cultural status. It is pure, unadulterated human-to-human contact. See figure 3.4 for a visual depiction of the advantages of face-to-face and virtual communication.

Whether face-to-face or virtual, the communication process is complex. For it to succeed, all

participants must fully commit to the experience. In face-to-face interactions, it is necessary to confront issues as they emerge, which doesn't always allow for sufficient processing time before forging ahead. Virtual communication, on the other hand, gives participants a chance to step away from the situation, reflect on what's happening, and carefully respond after thinking things through. In any case, it is essential to consider the purpose of the interaction and select the medium of communication that best suits that purpose and can accomplish established goals.

Interpersonal Leadership Model

Author Warren Bennis said, "The process of becoming a leader is much the same as becoming an integrated human being" (Bennis and Goldsmith, 1997, p, 8). It is not enough for leaders to merely communicate a message; they must connect interpersonally with their followers, creating an atmosphere of mutual trust and respect. The interpersonal leadership model represented in figure 3.5 identifies three qualities of successful leaders: principle, purpose, and passion, otherwise known as the three Ps of leadership. As the model reveals, each quality is defined by specific attitudes and intentions that must be communicated both verbally and nonverbally to followers. These collective characteristics combine to create a well-rounded, interpersonally competent leader who understands the importance of living a principled life, enacting a purposeful vision, and displaying a passionate desire to move forward and evoke change.

Principled Leaders

When my oldest son was in first grade, his teacher told me that he was a person of great character because, in her words, "he stands up for what is right when others choose to do wrong." Needless to say, that comment probably tops the list as one of the best "mom moments" I've ever had. More important, however, it demonstrated what it means to be a person of principle, doing what is right regardless of circumstance.

Principled leaders are characterized by three distinct qualities. First, they are *transparent*; they possess no hidden agendas, are forthright in their communication with others, and are willing to be vulnerable if that's what it takes to get the job done. There's something truly magnetic about "real"

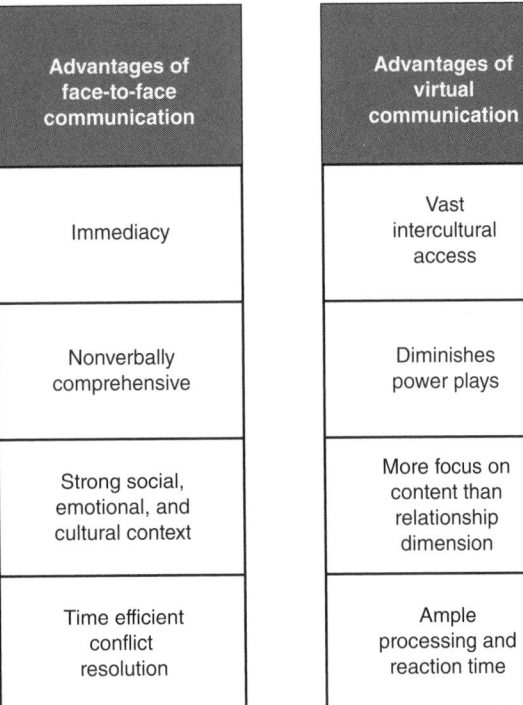

Figure 3.4 Advantages of face-to-face and virtual communication.

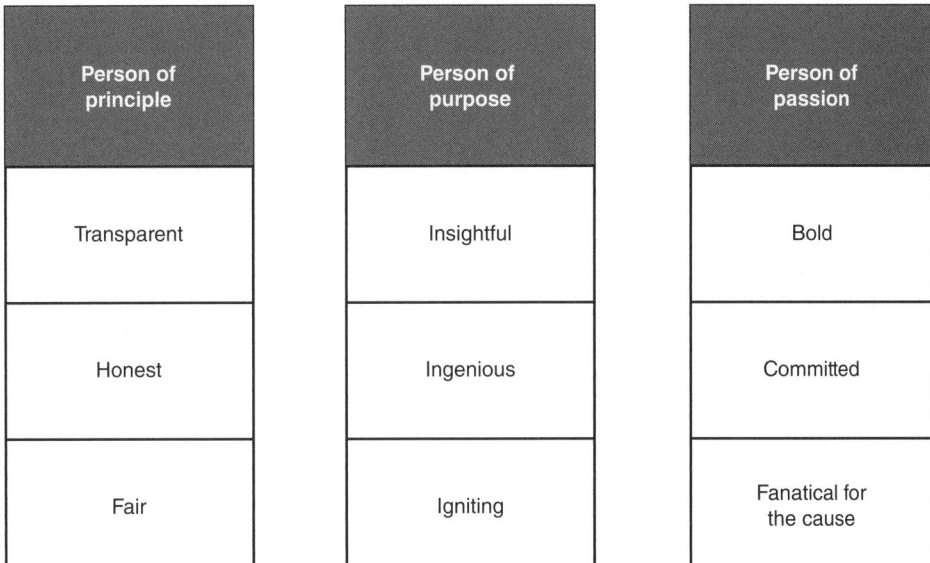

Person of principle	Person of purpose	Person of passion
Transparent	Insightful	Bold
Honest	Ingenious	Committed
Fair	Igniting	Fanatical for the cause

Figure 3.5 Interpersonal leadership model.

people. This concept resonates with the authentic leadership style in which leaders are true to themselves, acting with great character and integrity rather than trying to be all things to all people (Avolio & Gardner, 2005; Gardner et al., 2005; George, 2007; Ilies, Morgeson, & Nahrgang, 2005; Sparrowe, 2005).

Second, principled leaders are *honest*; they do not sit back and take credit for something they didn't do. Additionally, they communicate their honest thoughts, beliefs, and opinions in a way that is palatable and "other oriented," thinking through what needs to be said and articulating it so as to guard the valuable relationships they've formulated.

Third, principled leaders are *fair*; they realize that regardless of our stations in life, we are all equals deserving of the same rights and privileges. Their influence stems from simply acknowledging others and genuinely caring about people as individuals. "Transforming leaders define public values that embrace the supreme and enduring principles of a people" (Burns, 2003, p. 29).

Purposeful Leaders

Most of us are innately drawn to authentic people, but we are also attracted to those who display confidence, as they speak their convictions. Even if we disagree with them, we find appealing those who are assertive, enthusiastic, and alluring. To lead effectively, people must be purposeful in their crafting and articulation of the group's vision; they must possess the three i-factors. Purposeful lead-

ers are, first, *insightful*; they can see what others cannot—beyond the obvious. For instance, early in his career, Walt Disney was fired from a newspaper for his lack of ideas (Rosner, 2005); he later transformed his ideas into a multi-billion-dollar empire.

Second, purposeful leaders are *ingenious*; they think and act outside the box (some don't even realize there is a box). One year, for my birthday, my son gave me a most unusual gift: a small, colorful peacock figurine. I thought the gift was kind of odd because I don't collect any type of figurines. I asked him why he had gotten me that particular gift, and he said, "I wanted to get you something that matched your personality, something colorful." "Creative leadership begins when a person imagines a state of affairs not presently existing" (Burns, 2003, p. 153). When my son bought me the peacock figurine, he stepped out of bounds and imagined something different from what he had previously known and experienced.

Third, purposeful leaders are *igniting*. They not only see what should and could be but also make it a reality. Through their insight and their ingenuity, they pass their vision on to others. These leaders, whom we sometimes refer to as charismatics or visionaries, exude confidence, competence, and trustworthiness (Hackman & Johnson, 2009).

Passionate Leaders

You can have the greatest message in the world, but words have little meaning without the enthusiasm and passion to articulate your ideas. Passionate leaders are *bold*; they communicate their vision with unbridled enthusiasm, unashamed and unafraid of repercussions. Passionate leaders engage and empower followers with zealous fervor. They are *committed* to the vision and strive to fulfill it despite any obstacles, all the while preserving leader–follower relationships. Finally, passionate leaders are *fanatics for their cause*; they take whatever calculated risks are necessary for propelling the group forward, using their personal passion and enthusiasm to motivate others to perform at their highest potential (Hackman & Johnson, 2009).

Leaders who stand for what's right, commit to a worthwhile vision, and go the distance regardless of cost can accomplish things far beyond what the mind imagines. Truly transformational leaders possess the following qualities (among others):

▶ Idealized influence or charisma (parallels principled and passionate leadership); they inspire a sense of vision and mission through strong values and ideals, while garnering trust and respect from followers.

▶ Inspirational motivation (parallels passionate leadership); they lead the way through clear communication of high expectations, while empowering behaviors that enhance goal achievement.

▶ Intellectual stimulation (parallels purposeful leadership); they encourage followers to think outside the box, seeking and enacting innovative strategies for problem resolutions.

▶ Individualized consideration (parallels principled leadership); they ensure that followers have a supportive climate within which to operate, meeting individual needs through coaching, advising, and mentoring (Bass, 1985, 1990; Bass & Avolio, 1994). Moreover, transformational leaders are typically people of principled values and ideals, skilled at motivating others to strive for the greater good rather than being driven by self-interests (Kuhnert, 1994).

"Through effective communication, leaders lead. Good communication skills enable, foster, and create the understanding and trust necessary to encourage others to follow a leader" (Barrett, 2006, p. 385). Leaders desiring to influence others' lives in positive ways are necessarily concerned with what they communicate to their followers. Through principle, purpose, and passion, they demonstrate their deep-seated values and integrity as they articulate their vision, mission, and objectives in such a way that stimulates the mind, stirs the heart, and stabilizes relationships.

Summary

Leaders communicate via visual, vocal, and verbal channels. When they do, they must realize the importance of listening actively to their communication partners. Because of perceptual differences, it's relatively easy to misunderstand someone's motivations or misconstrue the intended meaning. By regularly practicing active listening, leaders can greatly reduce the simple communication mishaps that result in confusion and conflict. As the Greek sage Epictetus once said, "We have two ears and one mouth so that we can listen twice as much as we speak." Additionally, recognizing the difference between the content and the relationship dimension of meaning can assist leaders in identifying the root of communication problems and resolving issues quickly.

Technological advances have expanded communication well beyond face-to-face encounters, allowing for diverse experiences in the virtual environment. Unfortunately, resolving miscommunication within the virtual environment is generally more difficult than it is face-to-face. The lack of visual and vocal cues in many virtual communication modes increases the possibility of misunderstandings. Consequently, in this environment leaders must establish ground rules, including how communication problems will be addressed, when and how the group will conduct business, and where participants can access the information they need to manage their assigned tasks.

Reflecting on the opening scenario of Marilyn and her start-up company, Getting Connected, it is clear that Marilyn's success in this entrepreneurial endeavor resides in her ability to meet her employees' needs, in both online and face-to-face environments. At the end of the day, each person must perceive Marilyn as a competent communicator, verbally and nonverbally, and one who understands not only what it takes to get the job done, but also the most task-efficient and relationship-appropriate way to accomplish the goals at hand. With the understanding that quality leadership and communication are necessarily linked, what strategies might Marilyn employ to ensure her success as a leader and entrepreneur?

Clearly, leaders face different challenges in virtual environments than they do face-to-face. Using communication to create and sustain relational connections is essential in both environments; thus, it makes good sense for leaders to discover ways to combine the best of both worlds to find that happy medium between virtual and face-to-face encounters. Leadership within both the face-to-face and virtual environments must include strong interpersonal communication skills that exhibit clearly established principles; the purposeful articulation of a vision, a mission, and objectives; and a genuine passion to make a difference in the lives of others. In the words of James C. Humes, "Every time you have to speak, you are auditioning for leadership" (1991, p. 13).

Questions for Reflection and Discussion

1. Describe a miscommunication or conflict you have experienced that was rooted in the relationship dimension as opposed to the content dimension of the communication encounter. How did you resolve the issue?

2. What challenges do you think a virtual learning environment would create compared to a face-to-face learning environment?

3. Explain how communication is linked to a person's ability to lead. What specific communication qualities must a leader possess to be successful?

4. How do a person's listening skills contribute to or detract from communication effec-

tiveness? Describe a time in your life when poor listening habits resulted in a conflict, misunderstanding, or other communication mishap. What would you do differently if you could experience the interaction again?

5. Describe a communication incident (e.g., at work, with family, with a team) in which you were at your best or worst as a communicator. Who was involved? Where were you? What made it your best or worst communication event? How did others react? What was the result? If it was your worst communication event, what could you have done to create a different outcome?

Key Terms and Definitions

active listening—Clarification of messages received through paraphrasing, prompts, and questions.

communication—Dynamic and transactional process involving a simultaneous, continuous transmission of information from one person to another in an attempt to create meaning for those involved in the interaction.

communication competence—Using the most effective and appropriate communication behavior in any given situation while maintaining established relationships on terms acceptable to all involved.

content dimension—Topic of conversation.

e-leadership—Leadership accomplished primarily through technology, operating outside of typical time, space, and organizational boundaries.

helical model of communication—Represents the totality of a person's communication, from birth to the present moment.

hybrid—Style of communication that blends face-to-face and virtual communication.

leadership—Symbolic communication that modifies the attitudes and behaviors of others in order to meet shared group goals and needs.

passive listening—Mechanical and effortless listening.

perception checking—Process that helps ensure that people are sharing the same reality.

relational dimension—Makes statements about the quality of a relationship; that is, how people feel about those with whom they are engaged.

relation-oriented leadership—Leadership focused on establishing connections between people, encouraging team development, collaborating, and creating collective ventures.

task-oriented leadership—Leadership focused on establishing goals and defining and managing assigned tasks and roles.

verbal channel of communication—Represents the words we say, including our specific word choices.

virtual communication—Communication and behaviors mediated by information technologies.

visual channel of communication—Represents everything visible during the communication transmission, including things such as facial expression; body language; eye contact; the use of touch, time, and space; and overall physical appearance.

vocal channel of communication—Represents how we say what we say, including characteristics such as tone, pitch, rate, volume, emphasis, articulation, pronunciation, accent, and dialect.

Bibliography

Adler, R.B. & Proctor II, R.F. (2011). *Looking Out Looking In* (13th ed.). Boston: Wadsworth Cengage Learning.

Argyle, M. (1988). *Bodily communication* (2nd ed.). New York: Methuen.

Avolio, B.J., & Gardner, W.L. (2005). Authentic leadership development: Getting to the root of positive forms of leadership. *Leadership Quarterly, 16*, 315-338.

Avolio, B., & Kahai, S. (2003). Adding the 'E' to E-leadership: How it may impact your leadership. *Organizational Dynamics, 31* (4), 325-338.

Bamlund, D.C. (1962). Toward a meaning-centered philosophy of communication. *Journal of Communication, 12*, 197-211.

Barrett, D.J. (2006). Strong communication skills a must for today's leaders. *Handbook of Business Strategy, 7* (1), 385-390.

Bass, B.M. (1985). *Leadership and performance beyond expectations.* New York: Free Press.

Bass, B.M. (1990). From transactional to transformational leadership: Learning to share the vision. *Organizational Dynamics, 18*, 19-31.

Bass, B.M., & Avolio, B.J. (1994). *Improving organizational effectiveness through transformational leadership.* Thousand Oaks, CA: Sage.

Belanger, F., & Watson-Manheim, M.B. (2006). Virtual teams and multiple media: Structuring media use to attain strategic goals. *Group Decision and Negotiation, 15*, 299-321.

Bennis, W. & Goldsmith. (1997). *Learning to Lead.* London: Nicholas Brealey Publishing.

Bergiel, B.J., Bergiel, E.B., & Balsmeier, P.W. (2008). Nature of virtual teams: A summary of their advantages and disadvantages. *Management Research News, 31* (2), 99-110.

Boase, J., Horrigan, J.B., Wellman, B., & Rainie, L. (2006). *The Strength of Internet ties.* Washington, DC: Pew Internet & American Life Project.

Bower, D.J., Hinks, J., Wright, H., Hardcastle, C., & Cuckow, H. (2001). ICTs, videoconferencing and the construction industry: Opportunity or threat? *Construction Innovation, 1* (2), 129-144.

Brown, W.K. (2009). Listen Up. *Professional Safety, 54* (4), 8.

Burns, J.M. (2003). *Transforming Leadership.* New York: Grove Press.

Cascio, W.F. (2000). Managing a virtual workplace. *Academy of Management Executive, 14* (3), 81-90.

Covey, S.R. (2004). *The 7 habits of highly effective people: Restoring the character ethic.* New York: Free Press.

Curtis, D.B., Winsor, J.L., & Stephens, R.D. (1989). National preferences in business and communication education. *Communication Education, 38* (1), 6-14.

Daft, R.L., & Lengel, R.H. (1984). Information richness: A new approach to managerial behavior and organizational design. *Research in Organizational Behavior, 6*, 191-233.

Dainton, M., & Aylor, B. (2002). Patterns of communication channel use in the maintenance of long distance relationships. *Communication Research Reports, 19*, 118-129.

Dance, Frank E.X. (1967). Toward a theory of human communication: Original essays. In Frank E.X. Dance (Ed.), *Human communication theory*, pp. 288-309. New York: Holt, Rinehart, and Winston.

Dance, F.E.X., & Larson, C. (1976). *The functions of human communication: A theoretical approach.* New York: Holt, Rinehart and Winston.

Dance, F.E.X., & Zak-Dance, C. (1986). *Public speaking.* New York: Harper & Row.

Dewar, T. (2006). Virtual teams—Virtually impossible? *Performance Improvement, 45* (5), 22-25.

Face to face—Power to change: A conversation with Bernard M. Bass. *Leadership in Action, 23* (2), 9-11.

Gamble, T.K., & Gamble, M. (2013). *Communication works.* New York: McGraw-Hill.

Gardner, W.L., Avolio, B.J., Luthans, F., May, D.R., & Walumbwa, F. (2005). "Can you see the real me?" A self-based model of authentic leader and follower development. *Leadership Quarterly, 16*, 343-372.

George, B. (2007). Authentic leaders: They inspire and empower others. *Leadership Excellence, 24* (9), 16-17.

Goss, B. (1982). Listening as information processing. *Communication Quarterly, 30* (4), 304-307.

Hackman, M.Z., & Johnson, C.E. (2009). *Leadership: A communication perspective* (5th ed.). Long Grove, IL: Waveland Press.

Hancock, J.T. (2004). Verbal irony use in face-to-face and computer-mediated conversations. *Journal of Language and Social Psychology, 23*, 447-463.

Hertel, G., Geister, S., & Konradt, O. (2005). Managing virtual teams: A review of current empirical research. *Human Resource Management Review, 15,* 69-95.

Humes, J.C. (1991). *The Sir Winston Method: Five Secrets of Speaking the Language of Leadership.* New York: Morrow.

Ilies, R., Morgeson, F.P., & Nahrgang, J.D. (2005). Authentic leadership and eudaemonic well-being: Understanding leader-follower outcomes. *Leadership Quarterly, 16,* 373-394.

Kerfoot, K.M. (2010). Listening to see: The key to virtual leadership. *Nursing Economics, 28* (2), 114-116.

Knapp, M.L. (1972). *Nonverbal communication in human interaction.* New York: Holt, Rinehart and Winston.

Knapp, M.L., & Hall, J.A. (2002). *Nonverbal communication in human interaction.* Crawfordsville, IN: Thomson Learning.

Kouzes, J.M., & Posner, B.Z. (1987). *The leadership challenge: How to get extraordinary things done in organizations.* San Francisco: Jossey-Bass.

Kouzes, J.M., & Posner, B.Z. (2002). *The leadership challenge* (3rd ed.). San Francisco: Jossey-Bass.

Kuhnert, K.W. (1994). Transforming leadership: Developing people through delegation. In B.M. Bass & B.J. Avolio (Eds.), *Improving organizational effectiveness through transformational leadership* (pp. 10-25). Thousand Oaks, CA: Sage.

Lantz, A. (2001). Meetings in a distributed group of experts: Comparing face-to-face, chat, and collaborative virtual environments. *Behaviour and Information Technology, 20(2),* 111-117.

Larson, C.E., Backlund, P.M., Redmond, M.K., & Barbour, A. (1978). *Assessing communicative competence.* Falls Church, VA: Speech Communication Association and ERIC.

Lewis, H. (1998). *Body language: A guide for professionals.* Thousand Oaks, CA: Sage.

Lin, C., Standing, C., & Liu, Y. (2008). A model to develop effective virtual teams. *Decision Support Systems, 45* (4), 1031-1045.

Macik-Frey, M. (2007). *Communication-centered approach to leadership: The relationship of interpersonal communication competence to transformational leadership and emotional intelligence.* Unpublished doctoral dissertation. The University of Texas at Arlington.

Malandro, L.A. & Barker, L. (1983). *Nonverbal communication.* Reading, MA: Addison-Wesley.

McCroskey, J.C. (1982). Communication competence and performance: A research and pedagogical perspective. *Communication Education, 31,* 1-7.

Mehrabian, A. (1971). *Silent messages.* Belmont, CA: Wadsworth.

Mehrabian, A. (1981). *Silent messages: Implicit communication of emotion and attitudes* (2nd ed.). Belmont, CA: Wadsworth.

Neff, T.J., & Citrin, J.M. (1999). *Lessons from the top: The search for America's best business leaders.* New York: Currency/ Doubleday.

Powell, A., Piccoli, G., & Ives, B. (2004). Virtual teams: A review of current literature and directions for future research. *Data Base, 35* (1), 6.

Richmond, V.P., & McCroskey, J.C. (2004). *Nonverbal behavior in interpersonal relations.* Boston: Allyn and Bacon/ Pearson Education.

Rosen, B., Furst, S., & Blackburn, R. (2007). Overcoming barriers to knowledge sharing in virtual teams. *Organizational Dynamics, 36* (3), 259-273.

Rosner, B. (2005, Feb. 25). Working wounded: Getting pink-slipped. ABC News.

Short, J., Williams, E., & Christie, B. (1976). *The social psychology of telecommunications.* New York: Wiley & Sons.

Sparrowe, R.T. (2005). Authentic leadership and the narrative self. *Leadership Quarterly, 16,* 419-439.

Sproull, L., & Kiesler, S. (1986). Reducing social context cues: Electronic mail in organizational communication. *Management Science, 32,* 1492–1512.

Stech, E.L. (1983). *Leadership communication.* Chicago: Nelson-Hall.

Thompson, L.F., & Coovert, M.D. (2003). Teamwork online: The effects of computer conferencing on perceived confusion, satisfaction, and post discussion accuracy. *Group Dynamics: Theory, Research, and Practice, 7,* 135-151.

Walther, J.B. (1993). Impression development in computer-mediated interaction. *Western Journal of Communication, 57,* 381-398.

Walvoord, A., Redden, E., Elliott, L., & Coovert, M. (2008). Empowering followers in virtual teams: Guiding principles from theory and practice. *Computers in Human Behavior, 24* (5), 1884-1906.

Watzlawick, P., & Bavelas, J.B. (2011). Some tentative axioms of communication. In *Pragmatics of human communication: A study of interactional patterns, pathologies, and paradoxes* (pp. 29-52). New York: W. W. Norton.

Wellman, B., Smith, A., Wells, A., & Kennedy, T. (2008). *Networked families.* Washington, DC: Pew Internet & American Life Project.

Wood, J.T. (1999). *Interpersonal communication: Everyday encounters.* Belmont, CA: Wadsworth.

Wood, J.T. (2009). *Communication in our lives* (4th ed.). Belmont, CA: Thomson-Wadsworth.

Yukl, G. (2002) *Leadership in organizations* (5th ed.). Upper Saddle River, NJ: Prentice Hall.

Zimmerman, P., Wit, A., & Gill, R. (2008). The relative importance of leadership behaviours in virtual and face-to-face communication settings. *Leadership, 4,* 321-337.

Chapter 4

Facilitating Group Experiences

Brent Wolfe

" I hear and I forget
I see and I remember
I do and I understand "

—Confucius

"Welcome to the GSU challenge course! My name is Brent, and I am your facilitator for today. From talking with your group, it sounds like you are just starting to get to know one another and you are looking for an experience that will allow you to learn more about each other and start to learn how to work together as a cohesive group. Based on this information, let me tell you a little about our plan for today. First, I will provide you with lots of fun activities that will allow you to learn through doing—a process we call experiential education. Rather than just sit and try to memorize everyone's names and talk about how you think you could work more effectively together, you are going to get a chance to learn through doing! As we go through the activities today, I hope that you start to move from strangers to at least acquaintances, if not friends. I want you to start thinking as 'we' and develop a sense of cohesiveness. I'll be honest: there are some risks in these activities, both physical and emotional. Those risks will be very real, but they will differ from person to person. Part of my job as facilitator is to help provide a safe atmosphere for you today; so although there will be risk involved, safety will be an absolute priority. A lot of what you see me do today will be to provide you with a task or problem that I want you to complete or solve. When you're done with each task, we'll sit down and talk about what we just did. You might be thinking that this talking part could be boring, but you will learn a lot about each other during this time. So, get ready to work, play, and learn today! Now, with all that said, are there any questions for me?"

"I have one. You said that you are a facilitator. What is a facilitator, and what do you do?"

Learning Outcomes

At the conclusion of this chapter, students will be able to:

▶ Explain the three foundational definitions important to the facilitation process.

▶ Facilitate

▶ Facilitator

▶ Servant leadership

▶ Discuss the five roles of a facilitator.

▶ Guide a group through the stages of group development.

▶ Manage real and perceived risks.

▶ Maintain a safe environment.

▶ Negotiate the experiential learning cycle.

▶ Debrief provided experiences.

Although you may be familiar with the quote at the opening of this chapter, comprehending and putting it into practice can be extremely difficult. You may recognize that lessons learned through experience can be more lasting and meaningful than those people merely hear about, but do you know how to integrate such experiences into the learning environment? Can you work with people to provide them with experiences that facilitate comprehension and content application?

Foundational Definitions

To begin to understand what it means to facilitate in 21st-century leisure services, we must revisit the past and examine the definitions of the terms *facilitate* and *facilitator*. An exploration of the intent of these terms will lay the foundation for the remainder of the discussion on facilitation.

Facilitate

To **facilitate** means to make a process easier or to empower people to accomplish a task. Several synonyms are *ease, grease, loosen, smooth,* and *unclog.* This suggests one concept that may be lost or forgotten when considering leading or working with groups—that the facilitator is supposed to bring about movement or change by making things easier. Consider all that is involved in facilitating a meeting. According to the definition, the job of the facilitator is to make the meeting run smoothly and encourage conversations and decisions when appropriate. From a leisure services perspective, this might mean helping to bring summer camp volunteers with different viewpoints to a consensus regarding a particular decision, or leading a group of people through multiple elements on a challenge course. Ultimately, the facilitator attempts to make things easier. As leisure service providers, this definition should not be lost in our practice.

Facilitator

Having briefly explored what it means to facilitate, it is worth considering the definition of the word **facilitator**. It may be easy to make the leap from the verb form to the noun form and say that a facilitator simply makes things easy, but there is an additional, unique concept to consider. Although a facilitator does empower others, this work is done in an unobtrusive, unassuming, and indirect manner. The key words that immediately jump out from this explanation are *indirect* and *unobtrusive.* Although facilitators certainly bring about progress or change by helping to make things easier, they should do so unobtrusively and indirectly. What an incredibly difficult task this is! Expounding on the preceding example, facilitating a meeting of camp volunteers with multiple perspectives should be done without a heavy hand and possibly without the volunteers even knowing that the facilitator is directing the conversation and working to achieve consensus. A challenge course facilitator should attempt to bring about individual or group change by making the experience easy for participants in such a way that they hardly recognize the facilitator's presence.

Although being a facilitator does mean that you should help bring about progress and change by making things easier, the word *indirect* clearly implies that you do not do the work for participants. Ask questions and guide, but do not solve problems or reach conclusions independent of others or the group.

This perspective of the definitions of *facilitate* and *facilitator* in leisure settings may run contrary to many traditional ideas of leadership and even human nature. Perhaps a pithy saying will help to reinforce the concepts of making things easier while being unobtrusive and indirect: Be a guide on the side rather than a sage on the stage.

A sage on the stage does not facilitate and is not a facilitator. A sage on the stage provides information to listeners who are expected to hear, comprehend, and apply the wisdom presented. There

The facilitator should empower participants to accomplish their own objectives.

is not necessarily an attempt to make things easier or to help with understanding. There is simply the dropping of bread that others should be pleased to receive and digest. In contrast to this image is the guide on the side. This person embraces the ideas of aiding others and does so without drawing unnecessary or undue attention to himself. The guide on the side walks alongside a group of people, experiencing what they experience, feeling what they feel, and learning what they learn, much like a shepherd who works from the sides to ensure that all of the sheep remain together. Facilitators should be guides on the side, seeking to encourage understanding and to make situations easier, but do so in a way that attracts minimal attention and recognition.

Servant Leadership

Many similarities exist between the concept of an effective facilitator and the style of leadership known as **servant leadership**. Robert Greenleaf (1991), who coined the term *servant leadership,* suggested that "the servant-leader *is* servant first. . . . It begins with the natural feeling that one wants to serve, to serve *first*" (p. 7). Kent Keith (2008), past CEO of the Greenleaf Center for Servant Leadership, echoed these thoughts: "Servant leadership starts with the desire to serve—a natural, moral desire that is recognized as important by the world's great religions and many great thinkers" (p. 5). One of the 10 characteristics of servant leadership, as identified by Larry Spears (2010), senior advisory editor for the *International Journal of Servant-Leadership,* is a commitment to the growth of people, an excellent description of what a facilitator should be. In the language of servant leadership, facilitators should serve those they work with, helping them to feel important while themselves remaining unobtrusive.

Roles of a Facilitator

Facilitation involves guiding a group through the stages of group development. It also involves managing real and perceived risks, maintaining a safe environment, negotiating the experiential learning cycle, and debriefing provided experiences.

Guiding Group Development

As people in a group get to know one another, relationships change. Some people are naturally drawn closer to others, whereas others establish fewer connections. Regardless of the leisure service or situation, groups typically have to navigate through five stages of development (forming, storming, norming, performing, and adjourning) as they meet, get to know one another, and interact. The job of a facilitator is to understand and guide the group through these five stages as first conceptualized by Bruce Tuckman in 1965.

Forming

Tuckman suggested that as people gather to create a group, they enter into the first stage of group development—**forming**. During this stage, people are less likely to show their true colors than they will be later. Group members are trying to get to know one another and discover more about the people with whom they will be working. At this time, group members are typically polite and patient with each other and, in many cases, willing to give one another the benefit of the doubt. During this stage of the group's development, facilitators should attempt to help break the ice and create a comfortable and safe environment in which people are excited to interact and learn more. The group will typically look more to the facilitator in this stage, so facilitators should encourage group members to begin to look to one another for ideas and suggestions.

Consider the first day of summer camp. Campers are typically excited to be there, but may also have an underlying sense of insecurity or anxiety as they meet other campers for the first time. The facilitator should work to try to reduce these feelings of anxiety in a way that makes the participants feel as though they are reducing their own anxiety. She may initiate an ice breaker activity in which the campers learn more about each other (and may even elect to participate), but should fade into the background to let the group lead and direct the conversations. The facilitator may move the conversation forward when it stalls or provide a new direction when needed, but should never dominate the discussion.

Storming

As naturally happens in relationships of all types, when people get to know one another better, the likelihood for conflict increases. Conflict typically does not arise until people are comfortable enough to disagree with one another. As Tuckman suggested, after a group has progressed through the

Leisure Leaders

Dan Mathews

MY PREPARATION

- BS in therapeutic recreation—Georgia Southern University, Statesboro
- MEd in administration of leisure resources—University of Georgia, Athens, GA
- Certified therapeutic recreation specialist
- Distinguished Service Award, American Camp Association, 2012
- Alumni Award for Distinguished Professional Service, RLST department, UGA, 2005
- Member, External Advisory Board of Clemson University's parks, tourism, and recreation management department
- Faculty member, ACA's E-Institute

Photo courtesy of Josh Cagliani.

MY CAREER

I am the director of camping services for Camp Twin Lakes, which partners with nearly 60 nonprofit youth-serving organizations in the state of Georgia to provide camping opportunities for kids who wouldn't otherwise be able to attend because of serious illnesses, disabilities, and life challenges. Camp Twin Lakes has extensive programming and operates three campsites. I am a certified recreation therapist and I manage camp operations, partner relations, food service, medical oversight, and site and facilities. In 2013 Camp Twin Lakes served more than 3,500 kids in weeklong summer camp experiences and more than 9,000 campers and family members throughout the year at our three camps and in day camps offered at children's hospitals throughout Georgia. I lead 20 full-time staff and nearly 125 seasonal and part-time staff. I also manage an annual budget exceeding $3.5 million.

My job is to manage and extend the impact of our organization on the lives of individuals with serious illnesses, disabilities, and significant life challenges and their families. I work with our staff and volunteer leadership (our board of directors) to ensure safe and high-quality transformative experiences for our targeted populations. I spend a great deal of my time developing relationships to create new programs and opportunities for

Camp Twin Lakes. I also spend much time in management of policies, procedures, budgets, and staff supervision.

I began volunteering in high school with a camp for children with developmental disabilities. It was directed by a recreation therapist. This experience led me to study recreation therapy in college. I then directed the same program, which was a partner of Camp Twin Lakes. My first full-time job was in municipal recreation, directing the therapeutic recreation program for the city of Savannah, Georgia. I realized that a master's degree was necessary for advancement to a leadership position in an organization, so I attended the University of Georgia. I still directed the one-week camp every summer at Camp Twin Lakes. After graduate school, Camp Twin Lakes created a program coordinator position for me, and I have been here ever since.

I have always loved to see the impact that we have on our campers. As I have gotten older, seeing the change in the volunteers and staff really gets me excited. I love to see how the strength and perseverance of the campers we serve inspire our staff, volunteers, and even donors to greater heights professionally and personally. As my job has changed over the years, I do miss the direct interaction with campers and families. There are days when the conference calls and bureaucracy get me down!

My philosophy of leadership is that of servant leadership. I serve to support, inspire, and challenge the staff who in turn support, inspire, and challenge our campers. There are times that I have to manage (i.e., make sure that policies and procedures are enforced), but I have the greatest potential to make the biggest impact on the campers we serve when the staff I lead are inspired and supported by me and our organization.

MY ADVICE TO YOU

I was first attracted to working in recreation and leisure while I was in high school and volunteer-

ing for a one-week overnight camp for children with developmental disabilities. It was the first time I had given to something bigger than myself, and I saw the power of serving others. I realized that no matter how hard I worked, how much I gave, I always, without exception, received more back from those I served. Each summer, I watch children and staff learn from each other. They learn friendship, resilience, independence, and, most important, the life-changing power of serving others.

Understand your own philosophy on why what you do is important. If you are not making a difference in someone's life, change directions. Also, if you do what you love, the money will follow. Find your passion, and maintain high standards.

---

forming stage and members have become comfortable with one another, conflicts may begin to arise. This can be a sign that the group is moving into the **storming** stage of development. At this time, people begin to share information they may have been reticent to share upon first meeting. If a level of comfort and safety has been achieved in the forming stage, group members will feel that they can safely share thoughts and ideas that may run contrary to the norm or those of other group members. At this point personalities, attitudes, beliefs, and values may begin to clash and significant conflict may emerge. In other words, the honeymoon is over and it is time for the real work to begin.

During the storming stage, the facilitator should continue to provide a safe and supportive environment and encourage participants to work through their conflicts to arrive at amicable conclusions. Conflict is not a bad thing. In fact, working through conflicts is a natural occurrence that leads the group into the next stage of development—norming.

Norming

The **norming** stage is marked by the resolution of conflicts and an increased level of understanding and sensitivity. As group members express conflicts and successfully navigate through them, a feeling of mutual respect and cohesiveness can develop. It is important to note here that the conflicts that arise in the storming stage are necessary

for the group to achieve this level of understanding and cohesiveness. Participants have started to learn that they can share their true thoughts and feelings, and although everyone might not agree with them, they will respect them. To help the group move into the norming stage, facilitators should facilitate, rather than avoid, the conflicts that arise.

In the norming stage, the facilitator should provide opportunities for the group to develop a sense of "we-ness." Although the group may not yet be working at the height of efficiency and effectiveness, members are learning to work together during this stage. They are learning one another's strengths and weaknesses. A facilitator could provide opportunities (possibly in the form of initiative activities) to encourage the group to work together and experience success. For example, a parks and recreation director might gather a group of employees to complete a problem-solving activity, such as turnstile, in which each group member must cross through a spinning jump rope without touching the rope. The concept is to provide an experience that will continue to encourage unification and allow members to work with one another.

Performing

As group members continue to work closely with one another in group-specific or contrived tasks that the facilitator provides, they learn how to work with one another while increasing productivity. According to Tuckman, this stage of group development is known as **performing**. As the group

© Brent Wolfe

In the norming stage, people in a group are learning to work together.

progresses through the stages, the facilitator should be moving further to the side. In the performing stage, the facilitator should be further to the side than at any other time during the group process. This is not to say that he leaves the group on its own; rather, he recognizes that he has guided the group to a point at which it can be productive and possesses the necessary skills, abilities, and understanding to function independently (Cain, Cummings, & Stanchfield, 2005).

Adjourning

Tuckman did not articulate the final stage of group development until 1984, when, through further examination of numerous studies, he identified that groups experience one final stage during their life span—**adjourning**. This stage is easily overlooked, but it is vital for helping group members move from their shared experience and go their separate ways.

An example from therapeutic recreation might help to emphasize the importance of the adjourning stage. Consider a facility in which adolescents must receive a court order to be admitted and discharged. Certified Therapeutic Recreation Specialists (CTRS) work with clients throughout treatment, which includes discharge planning. If the client is discharged without planning and preparation,

the results would likely not be good. The client must be prepared for the challenges and struggles ahead and be reminded of the treatment received and progress made.

The adjourning stage in any leisure setting is as important as it is in a therapeutic setting. Facilitators should provide opportunities for group members to look back at all of the shared experiences of the group. Highlights (and lowlights) should be reviewed and discussed. In addition to reviewing shared experiences, group members should also have the opportunity to look into the future and think about how their shared experiences may influence them as they go about the rest of their lives.

During the adjourning stage, the facilitator helps group members transfer their experiences and lessons safely out of the group and into the next phase of their lives. One potential activity for this stage, called mountaintops, involves group members creating written lists of all activities they participated in during the life of the group (both positive and negative). The facilitator might offer a couple of suggestions, but each member should develop a personal list. Once the group members have completed their lists, they draw a representation of a mountain range with multiple peaks and valleys on another piece of paper. They then place all of their experiences on their mountain ranges (more enjoyable events at or near the peaks, and less enjoyable or traumatic events at or near the valleys). After all members have created and labeled their mountain ranges, they may share their drawings with the rest of the group. This simple activity provides opportunities for people to look back at their experiences, look forward to the future, and safely move out of their group experience.

Movement through the stages of group development can happen organically (i.e., without the help or intervention of a facilitator). However, facilitators can unobtrusively pave the way for the group to maneuver through the stages. In doing so, they should keep three things in mind. First, there is no set time for how long it will take a group to move through the stages. Groups progress at their own pace and shouldn't be rushed. Second, groups can certainly regress to earlier stages. This is not a strictly forward-moving process. Facilitators need to be patient with their groups when they appear to move backward and simply try to serve as a guide on the side to help them progress and become more unified. Finally, the lines between stages can be blurred. There can certainly be a difference in opinion about which stage a group is in; it is not an exact science. This said, recognizing group members' behaviors and expectations in the various stages can help facilitators continue to help the group develop.

Managing Real and Perceived Risks

During the progression through the stages of group development, group members are likely to experience varying levels of risk and anxiety. Although risk and anxiety are likely to be present throughout the life of a group, they are typically most prevalent during the earlier stages of development. Facilitators should understand the types of risk that participants might experience. Although real risk is vital to program existence and survival,

perceived risk has not received as much attention. The first type—**real risk**—involves risks identified as a result of a technical assessment of the likelihood of a possible event. Insurance actuaries can inform us of the risks involved in many events we face in life and can assign a particular dollar amount to a given event. A white-water rafting guide, for instance, must understand the real risks associated with the particular river she guides. Perceived risk, on the other hand, is not as quantifiable and receives significantly less attention in both writings and practice. However, it should be just as salient to facilitators.

Perceived risk involves a person's perception of how dangerous a given activity might be. Although an activity's perceived risk is not always founded on the real risk that may be involved, because the person perceives the risk to be high, it is very real to that person. For example, many recreation activities can involve limited (or controlled) actual risk that a person could get physically injured; as a result, safety might appear to be a relatively minor concern. Consider, however, a participant with skin blemishes; for this person, the perceived risk that others might make fun of the skin condition is very real and can make participation difficult. Table 4.1 compares the characteristics of real and perceived risks.

Perceived risks are different for every person, and are potentially debilitating. Davis-Berman and Berman (2002) suggested that people's experiences (personal or vicarious) and media exposure may heighten the sense of perceived risks. For example, group members who have had (or know someone who has had) a less-than-positive experience with team-building activities may approach challenge or ropes courses with skepticism and even a perception of risk. In addition, team-building activities are not always cast in a positive light in the popular media. Television commercials, for example, often satirize team-building activities in an office environment as unnecessary at best and often as simply a joke.

Table 4.1   Real Versus Perceived Risk

Real risk	Perceived risk
Technical assessment	Individual perception of risk
Compares data over time	Differs from person to person
Statistical likelihood of an event occurrence	Real for the individual

The facilitator's job is not to eliminate perceived risks but to identify them and help participants recognize and work with them. Acknowledging that participants may fear sharing about themselves with the group because of something hurtful in the past establishes a caring environment that encourages safe sharing of information.

Maintaining a Safe Environment

Facilitators who understand the risks participants face are in a good position to provide a safe environment. Safety is not simply keeping physical bodies safe. Facilitators should also actively engage in methods that provide a safe emotional environment by developing a full value contract and by practicing challenge by choice.

Full Value Contract

One way to provide an emotionally safe environment that limits both real and perceived risk is to use **full value contracts** (FVCs). FVCs originated in adventure-based counseling and have been shown to create supportive environments. An FVC provides a list of group rules or guidelines that everyone in the group agrees to abide by for the duration of the activity.

The power of an FVC lies in the fact that the group members generate and agree to the selected guidelines. These are not ideas the facilitator generates; the group develops them. Of course, the facilitator can offer suggestions, but the group should feel empowered to add, remove, or adapt any suggested FVC content. The more ownership and input the group invests in the FVC, the more effective it will be. Here are some guidelines commonly included in an FVC:

▶ Respect others and their opinions.

▶ Agree to disagree.

▶ What's said here stays here.

▶ Share honestly.

▶ Listen before speaking.

▶ Only one person talks at a time.

The most effective FVCs reflect the values of the group. A facilitator can start the process by explaining the FVC concept and emphasizing the importance of creating a welcoming and open environment. The facilitator can then ask group members what values they would like to include in the FVC. Remember, the power of the FVC depends on having participants select the values themselves, which means that the facilitator must allow them to do so. As participants suggest values, the facilitator writes them down; once the list has been generated, the facilitator reviews it and asks the group to consider whether to make any changes or additions. When the contract is finalized, it is typed up and posted in a highly visible place so group members can see their selected values each time they participate in the activity. The facilitator might also review the contract with the group each time a new session begins and whenever new members join the group.

Challenge by Choice

In addition to helping the group draw up an FVC, facilitators should introduce Rohnke's (1989) challenge by choice, which includes these four components:

1. The chance to try a potentially difficult or frightening challenge in a supportive and caring atmosphere

2. The opportunity to back off when performance pressures or self-doubt become too strong

3. The chance to try difficult tasks in an environment in which the attempt is more significant than performance

4. Respect for individual ideas and choices (p. 14)

Since Rohnke first articulated those components of challenge by choice, other authors have attempted to develop the concept further. Carlson and Evans (2001) reframed Rohnke's four concepts into three core values. The two concepts of challenge by choice are listed in table 4.2.

In Carlson and Evans' model, participants establish their own goals and create their own definitions of success. For example, on the pamper pole, a common high ropes course element, some participants might feel successful only if they actually jump for the trapeze, whereas others might be satisfied with simply grasping the trapeze as it moves toward them.

The second value in the Carlson and Evans' challenge by choice model is that participants determine how much of an activity or element they want to complete. This closely aligns with the first value of establishing personal goals, but it emphasizes the need for facilitators to honor participants' decisions to complete only a portion of the intended activity. Although some participants might follow an activity from its intended inception

Table 4.2 Comparison of Challenge by Choice

Rohnke (1989)	Carlson and Evans (2001)
The chance to try a potentially difficult or frightening challenge in a supportive and caring atmosphere	The opportunity to establish one's own goals and create one's own definitions of success
The opportunity to back off when performance pressures or self-doubt become too strong	Permission to determine how much of an activity to complete
The chance to try difficult tasks in an environment in which the attempt is more significant than the performance	The chance to make informed decisions based on a full understanding of what an activity will entail
Respect for individual ideas and choices	

to its intended completion, others might decide to stop at an earlier point in the activity.

Finally, participants make informed choices based on a full understanding of the activity, as provided by the facilitator. It is important to recognize that Carlson and Evans' three core values of challenge by choice do not run contrary to Rohnke's original components; rather, they condense and synthesize the original concept.

To keep group members safe, facilitators should provide opportunities for choice. Two qualities that will help them truly embrace and practice the idea of challenge by choice are honesty and respect. Facilitators must be honest with themselves and with participants when providing choices. *They should provide a choice only if they are willing to accept the participant's decision—even if it runs contrary to their own beliefs about how the situation should be handled.* Having choices is very empowering to group members; being given the opportunity to make a choice and then having that choice ignored is debilitating. Also, facilitators need to respect whatever decisions group members make. This is especially important on a challenge course.

If a group member has been given the opportunity to choose how much of an element to complete and has made the choice to complete only half of the element, the facilitator must respect that choice.

Negotiating the Experiential Learning Cycle

The stages of group development describe the process that a group goes through as members meet, get to know one another, and become more functional. While the group is experiencing the stages of group development, there is work to be done and there are activities to facilitate. A facilitator's task is to provide an experience (e.g., planning meeting, baseball game, rafting trip, initiative activity), encourage participants to reflect on that experience, allow them to make generalizations from their experiences and reflections, and encourage them to apply what they have learned to their lives. Organizational psychologist David Kolb (1984) called these four steps (experiencing, reflecting, generalizing, and applying) the **experiential learning cycle** (see figure 4.1).

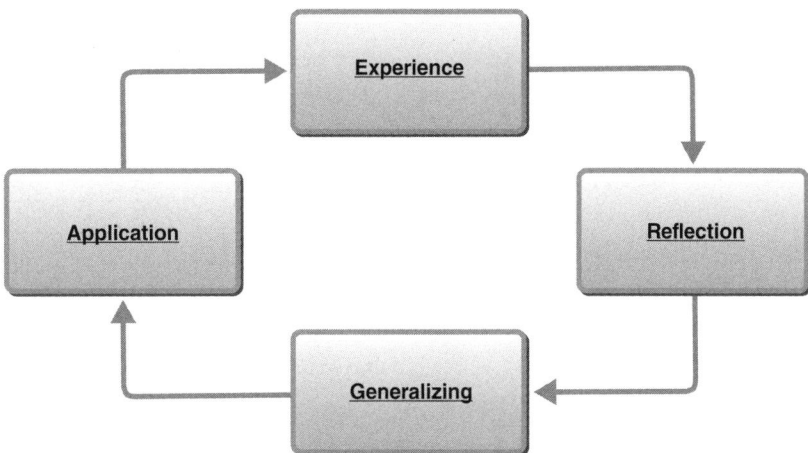

Figure 4.1 Kolb's four-stage model of the experiential learning cycle.

Experiencing

The experiencing step may be most familiar, but may need some re-envisioning. Experiences that can be facilitated include budget meetings, strategic planning meetings, treatment team meetings, sporting events, and adventure experiences. Ultimately, the facilitator can use anything that happens to a group (i.e., the experience) to help the group learn. Unfortunately, in many cases this is where the process ends: you facilitate an activity, people seem to enjoy themselves, problems get solved, no one is hurt or injured, and you call it a success. Regrettably, this approach leaves learning to chance and leaves you unsure of the lessons group members are taking away from the experience. It is even possible that participants will leave the experience having learned the exact opposite of what you intended. Consider, for instance, a planning meeting in which a five-year strategic plan is developed. What if one person was constantly ignored? What if one person had ideas others scoffed at? These people may leave the meeting feeling more disconnected from the group than connected to it. This type of risk is the reason for not stopping at simply providing an experience; facilitators must then lead the group in a period of reflection.

Reflecting

During reflection, group members are encouraged to look back at the activity they just completed and verbalize what they thought and felt, both as individuals and as a group. For this time to be effective, the facilitator must help group members establish a sense of comfort and safety with one another. As previously discussed, one way to accomplish this is through the use of a full value contract (FVC). During the period of reflection, participants should be encouraged to think about what they just did and take time to mentally relive the experience. The time of reflection could begin with smaller breakout groups reflecting on their experiences and then sharing their thoughts with the larger group. In addition, during any reflection period, all participants should be encouraged to share their reflections, even if they differ from those of others in the group. The reflection phase helps group members dig deeper into what they have learned.

Generalizing

During the generalizing step, facilitators should encourage group members to begin thinking about what they have learned through the experience and how they might apply it in their daily lives. Some experiences are contrived situations that people are not likely to encounter in everyday life. Consider, for example, an environmental stewardship activity in which each small group is given an egg, four straws, two sheets of newspaper, and 4 feet (1.2 m) of tape. Groups must construct an encasement for their egg that will prevent it from breaking when dropped onto concrete from a height of 10 feet (3 m). Although participants are not likely to encounter this situation in their lives, they can be encouraged to consider how they might generalize and transfer the principles of stewardship and caring for the environment to their lives. During this time of generalization, the facilitator's job is to help participants recognize similarities between the contrived situation of the activity and situations they may encounter outside the group experience. This analysis might involve identifying patterns, considering how reactions during the experience mimic those in life, or exploring how what they learned during the experience is similar to or different from personal experiences they have had.

Applying

The best evidence that participants have learned something useful is to see them applying it. The applying step is the time for participants to put what they have learned into action in ways that are practical and meaningful to them. Because application implies action, this step must nearly always come after the other three stages—experiencing, reflecting, generalizing—that is, participants must have future opportunities to put what they have learned into practice.

In some cases, a time gap may be necessary so participants can individually process what they experienced without the pressure of a facilitator or other group members. In such cases, facilitators should encourage participants to apply the lessons they have learned to situations and experiences in their lives away from the group. Whatever the specifics of the group's situation, the facilitator should formally discuss the process of intentionally applying lessons learned to new situations and, where possible, provide opportunities for participants to do so.

The application step serves two purposes. First, it enables participants to achieve closure as they conclude the process. After they have had an experience, reflected on it, and drawn generalizations from it, applying what they have learned offers a sense of completion. Second, application offers the opportunity to put what was learned into practice during future experiences, both with and without the group. Accordingly, the four steps are cyclical, and the concluding stage (application) becomes the first stage of a new experience. An example of how this process can work is found in figure 4.2.

By facilitating opportunities for participants to experience, reflect, generalize, and apply the lesson, you create opportunities for them to learn. Having learned the four steps of the experiential learning cycle, a natural question to ask yourself is, How can I facilitate participants' progression through each of the steps?

Debriefing Experiences

Debriefing is a technique used to help groups move through the experiential learning cycle. It involves encouraging participants to relive the experience, articulate what they learned through the experience, and apply what they learned to their lives. The debriefing process, which mirrors the experiential learning cycle, is based in the art of asking questions (see figure 4.3).

It may be natural at this stage to wonder exactly what, in practical terms, a facilitator might do after the experience has been provided to help the group work through the experiential learning cycle (and to a degree move through the stages

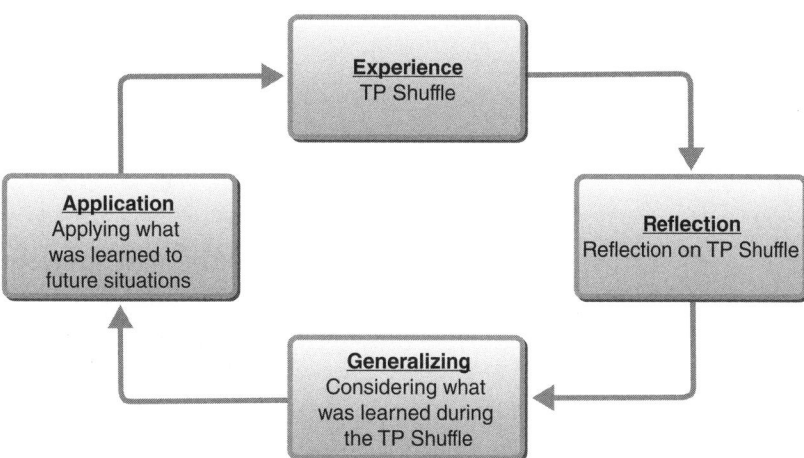

Figure 4.2 Experiential learning cycle example.

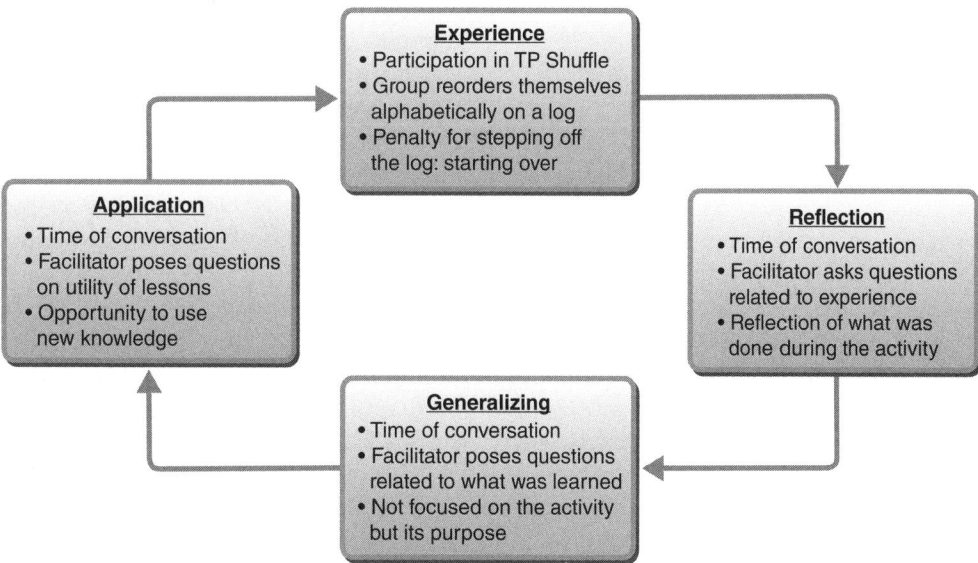

Figure 4.3 Debriefing and the experiential learning cycle.

of group development). This is where debriefing comes into play. This technique enables facilitators to help participants move from the experience itself into a time of reflection, then into a period of generalization, and finally into taking action based on what they have learned. In its simplest form, debriefing simply involves asking questions to highlight behaviors, actions, and comments from participants. The key to conducting an effective debriefing is to ask questions—lots of them. If the debriefing is successful, the facilitator's voice will not be strained at the end because participants will have done most of the talking. During a debriefing, the facilitator's job is to guide the conversation in a positive direction and help group members discover the purpose behind the activity and how they can apply it in their lives or use what they have learned in the future. Following are three categories in which to pose questions:

- ▶ Reliving the experience
- ▶ Exploring the purpose
- ▶ Applying lessons learned to life

By asking questions in each of these categories, facilitators help participants move from simply having a nice experience to having an educational or productive experience that can benefit them in future situations. Be creative in developing questions that make sense to you and are meaningful to the group. Although the prospect of posing questions to the group may seem daunting at first, your comfort level will improve as you become more familiar with the process.

Reliving the Experience

One of the first steps in debriefing is reliving the experience so group members can reflect on the experience they have just had. Facilitators should ask questions that will help participants, in effect, watch a mental replay of what they have just done. During many experiences, it is impossible for one person to see and hear everything that goes on, and talking about what happened can help everyone develop a sense of shared context. In addition, some experiences occur over long time periods; in this case, concerted reflection helps participants remember aspects of the experience they may have forgotten. For example, the facilitator might ask a group that just completed a 20-mile backpacking trip, "What was the most difficult part of the hike for you?" Asking this question allows them to craft

their own responses related to their unique experiences. Another benefit of this question is that there are no right or wrong answers; people share their personal perceptions of the experience.

During this time of reliving the experience, facilitators can help participants engage in two levels of reflection: macro and micro. When asking participants to relive the macro experience, facilitators are asking them to relive the entire experience. This is a natural place to begin, and it also leads nicely into the micro level. At the micro level, the facilitator's role is to help group members relive a particular moment that occurred during the activity—one instance that was particularly poignant or noticeable (e.g., an argument or an unexpected twist). Regardless of the type of moment, the micro level of reliving the experience is akin to using the pause or slow motion feature on a video player to focus on a particular moment.

Exploring the Purpose

By asking questions designed to help group members explore an activity's purpose, we are assuming that there was an intended purpose in the first place. In reality, however, some facilitators fail to establish a clear purpose. Don't let this be the case with your group. Know your group, know what your group members need, and provide experiences that are appropriate for them *where they are*. As you help your group explore the purpose of an activity, you can approach the subject directly by simply asking, "Why do you think we just did this activity?" or "What was the point of this activity?" Such questions can help them understand their particular experiences.

Even though as a facilitator you may have a clearly identified purpose, your group may generate other reasons for participating in an activity. For example, you may be facilitating an arts and crafts activity for children during a summer camp with the purpose of campers designing a creative and unique art project. However, when you ask the campers about the purpose of the experience, they may say that they learned how to work with and share resources with others. The challenge is to be grounded, yet flexible; understand why you are leading the activity and be prepared to help the group see that purpose, but also be willing to explore alternative purposes that group members present. In many cases, participants' insights can greatly expand the range of lessons that can be learned from a given activity.

A personal example may help to illustrate this point. While I was facilitating an activity with the purpose of developing an initial understanding and respect for other group members, conversation among the participants shifted to a focus on the mistakes they had made in their lives. The conversation turned away from the intended focus and moved in an organic fashion toward issues the participants wanted to discuss. The new discussion, although not what I initially intended, was tremendously meaningful for the participants.

Applying Lessons Learned to Life

If participants have relived their experience, come to understand why they engaged in the activity, and have identified lessons learned, they should be prepared to apply their experience to similar future experiences. In the debriefing participants consolidate what they have learned and make statements about how they can apply these lessons in their lives.

To ask good questions about how participants might apply what they have learned to their lives, facilitators need to have an accurate understanding of their lives. If they already have this understanding, this may not be difficult. Facilitators may know where they work, where they live, where they go to school, and projects in which they are involved. They can use this information to ask

specific questions that will help them apply their experiences to their lives.

Facilitators should encourage participants to be as concrete as possible about how they might apply their learning. "I will . . ." statements may be more helpful than broad generalizations. For example, in a group bonding experience with employees of a convention and visitors bureau, a facilitator might ask the question, "How can we show that we value something or someone?" The answer "I can tell someone that I care about him or her" is so broad that it does not readily lend itself to action. A participant encouraged to be more specific might end up with a statement such as: "The next time a coworker takes a stand, I will tell her that I appreciate her willingness to stand up for what she believes." This statement frames the point as an action that the participant is committed to taking ("I will . . .") and identifies the context in which the person will take the action. The more participants are encouraged to apply what they have learned to their lives, rather than offer suggestions to or criticisms of others in their group, the more effective the lessons will be. The application of a lesson is always more powerful when participants conceptualize both a behavior and a context for that behavior.

Remember also that the key to application is action. When participants are asked how they will

© lunamarina - Fotolia.com

As a facilitator, you might have a clearly identified purpose for an activity, but participants might find their own purpose, as well.

apply what they have learned, many are overly ambitious in their comments and ideas. One way to avoid this pitfall is to give the group opportunities to participate in several experiences in which they might be required to practice what they are learning. After the first experience, they can be given the opportunity to apply what they have just learned in a second activity. The debriefing for the second activity could then begin with a discussion of how well group members did in applying the lessons learned from doing the first activity. A very natural example of this is a challenge course experience. Typically, groups participate in several initiative activities, low elements, and high elements; in other words, multiple activities. In this case, it would be important to remind participants of previous "I will…" statements. Additionally, a facilitator could encourage them to apply what they learned from one activity or element to the next. Consider the earlier illustration presented in figures 4.2 and 4.3 involving the TP shuffle. What they learned in the TP shuffle (i.e., the importance of having one person speak at a time) could be directly applied to the next activity—whale watch.

Facilitation Techniques

In addition to using the experiential learning cycle and debriefing questions, facilitators can also use specific techniques to develop their ability to ask useful questions to help participants learn from their experiences. Five techniques to aid you in your role as facilitator are questions, silence, echoes, comparisons, and observations.

These techniques will assist with the debriefing process, but it is important to remember that they form basic guidelines rather than an exact recipe to follow. You can use them to facilitate conversations among participants, and we encourage you to develop your own techniques as well.

Questions

Most leaders and facilitators like to talk! Although this is not a bad thing in itself, it is important when acting as a facilitator that most of your talking come in the form of questions. At the completion of an activity, you may have some amazing insights you are eager to share with your group, and it is easy to think that, as the facilitator, you should go ahead and share your knowledge. However, attempt to temper your desire to offer lengthy insights. Instead, ask questions that help your

group members develop their own insights. This is the art of facilitation! If participants are allowed to develop their own thoughts and ideas and come to their own conclusions, they are more likely to remember what they have learned. One mark of an effective debriefing session is that you have done nothing but ask questions. As the proverb goes, Give me a fish and I eat for a day; teach me to fish and I eat for a lifetime. You want to teach your participants how to fish for their own ideas.

You may also find that questions are particularly helpful when you are working with a group whose members are having difficulty during an experience. Rather than telling a group what to do—how to solve a problem or how to approach a particularly difficult task—ask the participants questions that lead them to develop their own solutions. It is better to gently nudge your group through the use of questions than to simply tell them the answers so they can move forward. Telling the group the answers does not allow them to search for them on their own or to grow from the search process.

Silence

Another very important technique is simply to remain quiet, a major feat that can be difficult to accomplish. As much as is humanly possible, attempt to limit your talking during and after each group experiences. For example, during an activity, you might see a very clear solution or have an insight that would make the group's task much easier. Allow participants to discover it on their own! Even if they don't discover the easy way you observed, they will still have discovered their own way that works for them. Also, in many cases, your suggestion might make perfect sense to you but not to the group; it might even make the group's task more difficult. Similarly, during the debriefing process, limit your speaking to simply asking questions. As mentioned earlier, at the end of an activity, your voice should not feel tired; your participants should have done the bulk of the talking.

Echoes

You can also help your group members learn from an activity by reflecting their questions back to them. Throughout the life of your group and their experiences, group members are going to ask you questions—how to complete a task, how to solve a problem, how other groups have completed an activity. They may even ask you to complete the task or solve the problem for them. Resist the urge to answer any of these questions! Reflect the question back to your participants and encourage them to develop their own techniques and solutions. For example, while facilitating the initiative activity warp speed, a group may ask you how fast other groups have accomplished the task. Rather than say "10 seconds," you could respond by asking how fast they think their group can accomplish the task. This response keeps the focus on the group and its task rather than on other groups and their performance. Although you could provide a direct answer or simply answer yes or no, it is better to ask group members what they think. In other words, rather than giving them the answer, encourage them to develop their own solutions. This ability to reflect participant questions back to them improves with practice, but the lessons participants learn will be much more influential and long-lasting if they develop their own thoughts, ideas, and solutions.

Comparisons

A good facilitator also encourages participants to create comparisons. Thinking about how their experience during an activity compares with experiences in their personal lives can help participants make concrete connections that stick with them rather than broad generalizations with little to no practical meaning. It is particularly helpful to use similes and metaphors to help participants connect an activity to their own lives. A simile or metaphor participants create will hold meaning for them that will enhance the application of lessons learned.

Consider, for example, facilitating an adventure orientation program for incoming college freshmen that involves canoeing. Canoeing requires a partnership between two people who likely don't know each other and may have very different personalities; still, they must figure out a way to move the boat down the river and avoid the pitfalls and obstacles in their way. You could create a connection between the experience of avoiding pitfalls on the river and avoiding pitfalls of drinking, distraction, and drama during the students' first semester at college.

With certain groups similes and metaphors are not particularly useful (e.g., young children or people with cognitive impairments); in these cases, you can help participants apply lessons learned by making more direct comparisons between the staged activity and their lives. For example, in the college freshmen situation, you might draw comparisons between getting along with your canoe partner and getting along with a roommate. The more direct the comparison is, the easier it will be to understand.

Observations

Finally, you may find it helpful to engage in intentional observation during an experience. If you are facilitating an experience but are not involved in completing it or solving the problem it poses, you may be tempted to tune out rather than pay close attention to the participants' actions and the task at hand. It is important, however, that group members see their facilitator invested in the activity, and this means that you may have to train yourself to pay attention even though you are not directly involved. Attempt to pay close attention to what your participants say and do during each activity you lead. By engaging in close observation,

Best Practices From the Field

When Matt McBride accepted the position of challenge course director at Georgia Southern University, he knew he would need to make some changes to the training and development program for the facilitators, but he was more than up for the task. McBride developed a three-level training program to teach student employees how to become facilitators. Level 1 training provides basic knowledge such as spotting, safety, and emergency techniques and procedures. In level 2, facilitators learn from experts in the field how to structure challenge course programs, complete scenario-based problems, and practice debriefing activities. Level 3 training involves shadowing head facilitators and receiving formal written evaluations from them.

Completion of these three levels of training provides facilitators with multiple levels of information and gives them opportunities to practice their skills before working with participants. According to McBride, this training program is invaluable to the development of challenge course facilitators.

you not only show your group members that you are involved, but you also prepare yourself to ask good questions at the micro level. For example, if you overhear a distinctive comment during the experience, you can ask a question about it during the debriefing time.

Careful observation will help you tailor debriefing questions to your group's unique experience and, thus, greatly increase the chance that participants will learn something truly useful. Consider the game of kickball. It might be tempting to be all-time pitcher, to play on one team, or to simply tune out while the game is in progress. With all three of these options, there is the potential to miss critical interactions or verbalizations between participants. You need to remain focused on all group members and attempt to hear and see everything. Although this may seem like a nearly impossible task, observations at this level will allow you to hear comments (both positive and negative) that can be addressed when debriefing the experience.

Summary

Providing indirect and unobtrusive guidance as you help to make an experience easier is the essence of facilitation. The ideas outlined in this chapter are not necessarily easy to follow. This is why you will not become a facilitator overnight; it is a process of becoming and growing as opposed to a destination. Facilitating means guiding a group or team through the stages of group development. As the group progresses from forming to storming to norming to performing and finally adjourning, the facilitator unobtrusively protects group members and makes the path smooth. An effective facilitator also understands that protecting group members requires an appreciation of real and perceived risks, and uses techniques such as a full value contract and challenge by choice to ensure the safety of all group members.

In addition to serving as the guide on the side through the stages of group development and ensuring both physical and emotional safety, facilitators guide groups through the experiential learning cycle. They provide experiences, opportunities to reflect on the experiences, time for generalization and transference, and most important, a chance for group members to apply what they have learned through their experiences. Finally, facilitators ask questions rather than give answers. They ask questions in three categories (reliving the experience, exploring the purpose, and applying the experience to real life) to promote movement through the experiential learning cycle. Several techniques can help facilitators ask questions that encourage growth and application to real life: questions, silence, echoes, comparisons, and observations.

Revisiting the quote from Confucius, the facilitator's job is to provide experiences so group members can truly understand.

Questions for Reflection and Discussion

1. Based on the information provided in this chapter, how would you answer the questions asked by the participant in the opening scenario?

2. What items do you see as vital to include in a full value contract?

3. Do you agree that a facilitator should be a servant leader? Why or why not?

4. Do you believe there is really a difference between real and perceived risk? Is so, how would you define it? If not, why create the distinction?

5. Create a list of activities that you would feel are appropriate for each stage of the group development process.

6. Consider how you would handle the following situation: To extend choices to your group members, you say that anyone who does not want to participate in the prepared activity does not have to. In response to this offer, the entire group elects to sit and do nothing.

Key Terms and Definitions

adjourning—The final stage of group development in which group members must reflect on their experiences and look forward to the future; it is important that the facilitator encourage emotionally safe movement out of the group.

debriefing—A technique that allows facilitators to move a group through the experiential learning cycle. It includes questions in the following categories: reliving the experience, exploring the purpose, and applying lessons learned to life.

experiential learning cycle—A process for encouraging participants to reflect on, generalize, and apply what they have learned from an experience.

facilitate—To make a process easier or to empower people to accomplish a task.

facilitator—Someone who empowers others in an unobtrusive, unassuming, and indirect manner.

forming—The first stage of group development in which group members experience insecurity and apprehension. It is the responsibility of the facilitator to break the ice and promote safe admission into the group.

full value contract—A list of rules or guidelines that everyone in the group agrees to abide by for the duration of the activity.

norming—The third stage of group development in which group members begin to resolve conflict, develop sensitivity, and become more cohesive.

perceived risk—A person's perception of how dangerous an activity might be.

performing—The fourth stage of group development in which group members have developed an increased level of trust and are able to become productive and functional.

real risk—Risk identified as a result of a technical assessment of the likelihood of a possible event.

servant leadership—A form of leadership in which leaders see themselves primarily as servants.

storming—The second stage of group development in which group members typically experience conflict and frustration as a result of clashes in personalities, beliefs, or values.

Bibliography

Association for Challenge Course Technology: http://acctinfo.org

Cain, J., Cummings, M., & Stanchfield, J. (2005). *A teachable moment: A facilitator's guide to activities for processing, debriefing, reviewing, and reflection.* Dubuque, IA: Kendall/Hunt.

Carlson, J.A., & Evans, K. (2001). Whose choice is it? Contemplating challenge-by-choice and diverse-abilities. *Journal of Experiential Education, 24*, 58-63.

Davis-Berman, J., & Berman, D. (2002). Risk and anxiety in adventure programming. *Journal of Experiential Education, 2*, 305-310.

Greenleaf, R. (1991). *The servant as leader.* Indianapolis, IN: Robert K. Greenleaf Center.

Keith, K.M. (2008). *The case for servant leadership.* Westfield, IN: Robert K. Greenleaf Center.

Kolb, D.A. (1984). *Experiential learning: Experience as the source of learning and development.* Englewood Cliffs, NJ: Prentice Hall.

Luckner, J.L., & Nadler, R.S. (1995). *Processing the experience: Strategies to enhance and generalize learning.* Dubuque, IA: Kendall/Hunt.

Neill, J.T. (2008). http://www.wilderdom.com.

Professional Ropes Course Association: www.prcainfo.org

Rohnke, K. (1984). *Silver bullets: A guide to initiative problems, adventure games, and trust activities.* Dubuque, IA: Kendall/Hunt.

Rohnke, K. (1989). *Cowstails and cobras II: A guide to games, initiatives, ropes courses, and adventure curriculum.* Dubuque, IA: Kendall/Hunt.

Rohnke, K., Wall, J.B., Tait, C.M., & Rogers, D. (2003). *The complete ropes course manual* (3rd ed.). Dubuque, IA: Kendall/Hunt.

Spears, L.C. (2010). Character and servant leadership: Ten characteristics of effective, caring leaders. *Journal of Virtues and Leadership, 1*, 25-30.

Tuckman, B. (1965). Developmental sequence in small groups. *Psychology Bulletin, 6*, 384-399.

Chapter **5**

Leadership, Diversity, and Inclusion

Lynn Anderson

" If we are to achieve a richer culture, rich in contrasting values, we must recognize the whole gamut of human potentialities, and so weave a less arbitrary social fabric, one in which each diverse gift will find a fitting place. "

—Margaret Mead, *Sex and Temperament in Three Primitive Societies* (1935)

Latisha, the director of the municipal parks, recreation, and youth services department in a small city, is holding a public meeting to gain input into the redesign of a well-used but aging community center. Even though the community center is located on the outskirts of the city, it is used heavily by community members from across the city during the day when public transportation is running. It is the only multipurpose facility owned by the department and serves a wide range of ages through programs and amenities, from youth soccer to child care to aquatic therapy for older adults. Latisha advertises the public meeting through the department's website and via public service announcements on cable television and in the newspaper. The meeting is being held on a Wednesday night at 8 p.m. at the community center.

The night of the meeting, Latisha scans the room prior to starting and notes that the audience is primarily white, middle-aged, middle-class males. There are no people with disabilities, no people who are poor, few people of color, just a handful of women, and very few young people. Why? What could Latisha have done differently to include all constituents in the planning of the community center renovation? What did she miss?

Learning Outcomes

At the conclusion of this chapter, students will be able to:

▶ Explain the meaning and benefits of diversity and gain insight into a new way of thinking about diversity as natural variations in the human condition.

▶ Appreciate the role inclusion plays in building and strengthening diversity.

▶ Understand inclusive leadership skills at the micro, meso, and macro levels and how they foster diversity in leisure services, including the use of an analytic tool called the inclusion lens.

▶ Describe the new norm and how leaders can help make the mainstream a wide stream with room for all people.

▶ Appreciate the inclusion competencies that leaders can learn and practice to further their professional development.

It is an exciting time to be a leader in leisure services. In the 21st century, the world has become increasingly diverse, creating a cultural vibrancy we have not previously experienced. Leisure services professionals are called on to work in communities, agencies, and settings with high variability in the people served and cultures represented. Whether it is age, ability level, gender, race, ethnicity, socioeconomic status, sexual orientation, religious beliefs, or languages, leaders must be sensitive and aware of the diversity of the people they serve and have the skills and knowledge to facilitate inclusive leisure experiences. Leaders need to be prepared and competent to help weave a social fabric in which all human potentialities are included and celebrated.

This chapter describes several key concepts that are important to understand on the path to becoming a culturally competent leader. We will explore what diversity is and why it is important; a new way of thinking about diversity and inclusion; what inclusive leadership strategies and tools can be used to achieve diversity; and key professional development areas for inclusive leaders. Inclusion is a process that can be facilitated by skilled leaders, and diversity can be the outcome of that process. The chapter also includes some best practices from the field, including a snapshot of two inclusive leaders in parks and recreation who are creating more diverse organizations by their actions.

Diversity Defined

We have used *diversity* as a catch-all buzzword since the early 1960s when civil rights legislation was a strong focus. The word has been used as a goal for communities, institutions, and agencies. It has taken on the form of an ideal and ideology in some organizations. And it has also developed a negative image in some agencies where employees talk disparagingly about "the D word" and the diversity training they are required to take. Aside from the rhetoric that permeates our culture, what do we really mean by the term *diversity*? Surprisingly, this is a difficult question to answer.

What Is Diversity?

The dictionary definition of diversity is as follows:

The condition of having or being composed of differing elements: *variety; especially, the inclusion of different types of people (as people of different races or cultures) in a group or organization; an instance of being composed of differing elements or qualities. (Merriam-Webster, 2012)*

The root of the word *diversity* is from Old French, *diversité,* which means "difference, unique feature, oddness," or from the Latin, meaning "to divert, to turn away" (Harper, 2012). Thus, the basic definition of diversity is focused on difference and even separation, and is insufficient to capture what it means in our culture today.

One current approach to defining diversity does frame it in the context of difference. Smith (2009) defined diversity in relation to identity—those human variations from ability level to gender to race. She asserted that we cannot adequately understand diversity without acknowledging differences in human dimensions that have been or are salient in our society in terms of access, power, and privilege. In the recreation profession, Allison and Schneider (2008), based on the work of Loden and Rosener (1990), identified differences in core and secondary dimensions of human identity as critical to understanding diversity. These dimensions have an impact on the opportunities people have access to and the level of power or control needed for capitalizing on those opportunities. Thus, in this approach, diversity is defined as differences in the human condition that affect our place and role in society.

A second approach to defining diversity frames it in the context of ideals, principles, or outcomes. Although differences are acknowledged as a fundamental concept of identity, the definition goes further and makes explicit what must be in place for diversity to be functional and positive. For example, many agencies have developed definitions of diversity such as the following:

The concept of diversity encompasses acceptance and respect. It means understanding that each individual is unique, recognizing our individual differences. . . . It is the exploration of these differences in a safe, positive, and nurturing environment. It is about understanding each other and moving beyond simple tolerance to embracing and celebrating the rich dimensions of diversity contained within each individual. (Oregon Office of Equity and Inclusion, 2012)

Photo courtesy of Brandi Crowe.

Considering diversity to encompass both difference and similarity can help us appreciate the complexity of each individual.

A third approach to defining diversity is a more macro view of variation (Thomas, 1996). In this view, diversity encompasses not just differences but similarities as well. Diversity is about the collective mix and variation of those similarities and differences along any given dimension in a group. This definition allows us to see more complexity in each human being with whom we interact, and how that complexity enriches the collective mix.

Some would argue, however, that such a broad definition of diversity (the mix of all of our similarities and differences) makes the concept meaningless to those who have experienced dis-

advantage or inequality as a result of a particular difference such as race or ability. If an organization's definition of diversity is too ambiguous or too broad, "people may construe diversity in a manner consistent with their social motivations" (Unzueta, Knowles, & Ho, 2012, p. 303), particularly if they are members of a dominant and privileged social group, such as white people, men, or people without disabilities. Because tension often exists between the idealized notion of diversity and the complicated everyday realities of living with differences, people have difficulty talking about social inequalities in the context of discussions about diversity. "The language of diversity both constructs difference as natural *and* disavows its negative impact on the lives of those who are so constructed" (Bell & Hartmann, 2007, p. 910).

Considering the varying concepts of diversity and the limitations associated with each, I offer the following definition for use in the remainder of this chapter, and for you to consider in leadership roles in the leisure services profession:

> **Diversity** *is the collective mix of humans who interact positively and equitably in a social sphere (e.g., communities, neighborhoods, recreation programs, workplaces), all of whom vary on a continuum across salient dimensions such as race, ethnicity, age, gender, ability, sexual orientation, class, and spiritual beliefs. Diversity honors and embraces the differences we have, but recognizes that those same differences have provided varying levels of privilege, dominance, access, and power. Diversity then must also embrace the active pursuit of social justice and equity.*

How Diverse Are We?

Diversity is here now. Trends across the world are rapidly changing the diversity of our communities and those we serve. Some of the most significant trends related to leadership in leisure services are demographic shifts, the social model of ability, globalization, and technology. Each of these trends has had a profound impact on the composition and function of communities; the day-to-day existence of people within them; and the knowledge, awareness, and competencies needed by 21st-century leaders.

The shift in demographics is perhaps the most noticeable trend. The United States and Canada have become increasingly diverse in terms of race and ethnicity. One-third of Canada's residents will be racial or ethnic minorities and one-fourth will be born in a different country by the year 2031 (Tapia, 2010). In the United States, the same trend is evident; the U.S. Census Bureau (2010) predicts that by 2050, people of color will be the majority. Much of this diversity will be based on immigration, and along with racial and ethnic diversity will come diversity in religious beliefs, languages, and other cultural patterns. As well, both the United States and Canada have an increasingly older population as the baby boom generation ages (Statistics Canada, 2010; U.S. Census Bureau, 2010). Associated with the increase in the aging population is an increase in the number of people with disabilities. The U.S. Census Bureau (2010) informs us that people with disabilities are the largest minority group in the United States, and many within that group are older adults. The role of women in society has changed dramatically in the last several decades with a loosening of sex role stereotypes and, with it, a change in our social structures. People who are gay or lesbian can now legally marry in some regions, changing the face of the "traditional" family. Across the salient dimensions of being human, variation has increased and, with it, diversity. As Smith (2009) stated, "Today, diversity is no longer a projection, it is a reality" (p. vii).

Another trend affecting diversity in our communities is a shifting paradigm, or way of thinking, about differences in ability level. Whereas in the past, many people with disabilities, illness, or frailty lived in institutional settings, such as state facilities, nursing homes, and hospitals, today they are living in their homes and receiving services in the community. People with varying ability, age, and health levels are attending school, shopping, working, residing, and playing alongside others, pushing our systems and our neighborhoods to be more accessible, inclusive, and responsive. Called the **social model of disability**, this paradigm shift sees ability level as a variation in the human condition and a function of the environment as much as it is the impairment or disability (Anderson & Heyne, 2012; Rioux & Carbert, 2003). When we make changes in the environment so a person

with a disability or an older person can function in it, we are using a social model of disability versus a medical model, in which we assume that changes need to be made on the part of the individual. The social model of disability is embraced by the World Health Organization (2003) and the United Nations (2008).

Globalization is a key trend that affects diversity. Media, entertainment, ease of travel, the Internet—all have made national boundaries seem less meaningful and have shrunk the world. Today, we can watch a television program in multiple languages through our cable service; we can eat at restaurants in our communities that feature foods from around the world; and we can participate in nearly any world religion we choose. Globalization has connected people across cultures and fostered an ease in the interchange of ideas, beliefs, and ways of living.

Related to globalization is the tremendous speed with which technology is evolving and becoming integrated into our lives. The World Wide Web and the cellular network allow us to connect and share information with virtually anyone in the world, even in developing countries where communication has historically been nearly impossible. In fact, a recent study revealed that nearly 6 billion of the world's 7 billion people have mobile broadband subscriptions (Whitney, 2012). Technology opens doors for people with varying ability levels, providing assistive devices that allow for mobility, communication, and more. Technology opens avenues of communication never before possible, with online language translators, online sign language interpreters, automated closed-captioning services, and videoconferencing, to name just a few examples. Technology is a driving force in fostering diversity through communication; access to information; and support for learning, functioning, and health.

Diversity is here, fueled by trends on a global scale. Scholars often talk about the value of diversity to individuals and to society. What are those benefits? What do we know about the outcomes of diversity when it is working well?

Benefits of Diversity

Diverse groups, communities, or societies are more resilient, more creative, more interesting, and have more ways to solve problems than those that are less diverse. The benefits of diversity can be felt at all levels of society. In his groundbreaking book, *The Rise of the Creative Class,* Richard Florida (2012) tells us that communities that are the most thriving, vibrant, and creative are those that have high diversity, high levels of tolerance, and inclusiveness. Those same communities have the strongest economic growth as well.

At the agency level, the benefits of diversity include strengthening cultural values within the organization, enhancing agency reputation, attracting and retaining talented people, improving the motivation and efficiency of staff, and improving innovation and creativity among employees (Keil et al., 2007). Socially diverse groups do more than simply introduce new viewpoints or approaches; they outperform more homogeneous groups not because of an influx of new ideas, but because diversity triggers more careful information processing that is absent in homogeneous groups (Phillips, Liljenquist, & Neale, 2009). The mere presence of diversity in a group creates awkwardness, and the need to diffuse this tension leads to better group problem solving.

At the small group and individual levels, many benefits to diversity have been cited in the literature, including increased levels of appreciation for other human beings, greater perspective taking, higher levels of patience, an increased sense of self-worth, and increased empathy and caring (Anderson & Heyne, 2012; Anderson et al., 1997). When people function in small groups that are diverse, their experience is enriched.

When diversity is working well, benefits abound. What does it take to accrue the benefits of diversity? What must be in place for an agency or community to experience diversity in a positive way?

How Can Diversity Be Strengthened?

Smith (2009) stated:

Our challenge is to achieve the benefits of diversity for our institutions and for society. Simply acknowledging diversity will not be sufficient. We can see the difficulties inherent in creating truly diverse communities that work well. Fortunately, a reasonably robust body of knowledge from research and practice now exists and can help illuminate the conditions under which diversity works. (p. viii)

Much of that robust work is in the area of inclusion, the facilitation of which scholars, policy makers, and leaders have been exploring for years. Inclusion is a process; diversity is an outcome. Shifting the focus to the facilitation of inclusion, equity, and excellence can help achieve the benefits of diversity. According to Coffey (2012), "Diversity *and* inclusion must be the complementary cornerstones of our strategy *and* our processes. Diversity without inclusion *will not work"* (p. 3).

The evolution from focusing on diversity to focusing on inclusion has been slow but tangible, and has included these stages:

▶ The "melting pot" assimilation approach, from the 1960s to the mid-1970s, with social movements such as civil rights, affirmative action, and equal opportunity employment

▶ The "salad bowl" multiculturalism approach, from the mid-1970s to the 1990s, with diversity training initiatives in abundance

▶ The inclusion approach, from the mid-1990s to today, with a focus on process and performance, managing diversity, and creating inclusive environments (Coffey, 2012)

Inclusion is a far-reaching concept with subtle implications for how people relate to each other. According to some experts in inclusive recreation (Anderson & Kress, 2003; Anderson, Penny McGee, & Wilkins, 2010; Dattilo, 2002; Heyne, Schleien, & McAvoy, 1993; Schleien, Ray, & Green, 1997), inclusion has the following connotations:

▶ Everyone has the same choices and opportunities for recreation participation.

▶ People participate with others who share their interests, not necessarily their salient differences.

▶ People are invited, welcomed, appreciated, and accepted for who they are.

▶ Participants have the supports and accommodations they need to participate in recreation as fully as possible.

▶ Opportunities exist to interact socially and make friends with people with varying differences and similarities.

Leisure Leaders

Raul "Rocci" Aguirre

MY PREPARATION

- MS in resource management and conservation—Antioch University New England, Keene, NH

- BA in history and BS in recreation and leisure studies—State University of New York at Cortland

- Jonathan Daniels Scholarship; Harlan "Gold" Metcalf Award; SUNY Cortland Recreation Department Alumni Advisory Committee

MY CAREER

The Adirondack Council is the largest citizen environmental organization in New York State, focusing its work on the 6-million-acre Adirondack Park. Started in 1975, the Council's core mission is to ensure the ecological integrity and wild character of the park. The Council also envisions an Adirondack Park with clean air and water and large wilderness areas surrounded by working farms and forests and vibrant communities. With members in all 50 states, the Council currently has 13 staff members in two offices: 9 staff members work in Elizabethtown in the park, and 4 work in the Albany/Capital District office. The Council has a $1.5 million annual budget and is funded by private individuals and foundations; it accepts no government funds.

As director of conservation, I oversee the agenda and strategy for the Council's conservation work throughout the Adirondack region. This includes doing direct advocacy work on behalf of the Council with state and regional officials, responding to specific resource-related issues, managing staff, and overseeing a major internship program.

My early career was spent working as a ranger in federal land management agencies such as the National Park Service and the US Forest Service. I then transitioned to the conservation nonprofit world and focused on habitat restoration work with Trout Unlimited for a couple of years. Prior to coming to the Council, most of my recent work had been in the land conservation world working for regional land trusts.

Photo courtesy of Emily Eisman.

Advocacy work can be very adversarial at times and can be trying when the communities you work and live in are affected by major issues that engender strong opinions and positions. Although it can be hard to find a balance when the work you are involved in is so closely linked to your role in the community, providing a balanced perspective and facilitating meaningful dialogue can be hugely rewarding.

When I started in the recreation field, I was very much an idealist (and somewhat naive) about the resource management world I was entering. Over time, that idealism was tempered with a pragmatic outlook that reflected the complex world and complex issues that I worked on. At that point in my career, I experienced fewer opportunities to achieve balance and more pressure to find solutions, even if those solutions didn't resonate with my personal outlook. Today, after more years of experience and insight, I try to model a pragmatic idealism that reflects my early passion and idealistic outlook and an understanding of what is important to the cause I am working on. I try to negotiate outcomes that will result in the greater good.

MY ADVICE TO YOU

When I talk with students who aspire to leadership roles in the recreation field, I like to emphasize the importance of early work experiences and encourage them to enjoy the path they are about to embark on. Although I believe that having focus and goals is important, I also believe that there is a lot of value in having a broad exposure to a multitude of career opportunities. Find the aspects of the recreation field that you truly enjoy and are passionate about. This period of exploration and discovery is valuable on a personal level, but more important, this is a time to be exposed to many of the experiences and leadership styles that you will model in the future. Being conscious of the types of leaders you meet and considering the pros and cons of their management styles will help determine the kind of leader you become over the course of your career.

Perhaps the most significant observation I have made about the recreation and leisure field—and in particular, the resource management arena in which I work—is how fundamental the natural world is in shaping our identities, our sense of place, and the way we interpret and interact with the landscapes around us. My work has provided a unique opportunity to travel and live and learn from people across a wide swath of demographics and geographies, particularly in terms of how they relate to the natural world around them. People's "stories of landscape" are always changing and evolving and are full of regional differences. As I have matured and moved through the various aspects of my professional life, I have appreciated how people and their complex story lines have added depth and character to my life. Their influence on me has been as powerful as my experiences, such as the first wildfire I fought or wilderness I worked in.

▶ Recreation areas and facilities are architecturally, administratively, and programmatically inclusive, and universal design is used in all aspects of operation and management.

▶ Inclusive recreation creates a sense of community belonging.

Inclusion focuses on welcoming people of all kinds and variations into our neighborhoods, work and play spaces, and communities. What are the salient variations in the human condition that leaders must understand to facilitate inclusion effectively?

Variations: A New Way of Thinking

Historically, we have tended to think about people categorically. That is, you are either black or white, gay or straight, a women or a man, and so on. The new way of thinking about human beings is less categorical and more fluid. In the dimensions of humanness that have mattered for equity and social justice throughout history, we now know that people vary on a continuum in many ways. In other words, people do not fit into a yes or no box on any characteristic associated with being human. An older person can be multiracial, identify as

being transgendered, and have the functional ability of a young adult as a result of lifestyle. Categorical labels have become less meaningful and even misleading. Leaders who can conceptualize humanness as a composite of variations on a continuum across dimensions are better able to create an environment in which diversity works. Let's take a closer look at the core dimensions of the human condition. As well, it is important to increase awareness and understanding of the "isms" often associated with the core dimensions. An **ism** is an oppressive and systemic belief system about a group; examples include sexism, racism, and ageism.

Variations in the Human Condition

If diversity is a social mosaic of variations in the human condition, then it is important to understand what the key variations are that make up that mosaic. How do people differ? Researchers in diversity have categorized variations in the human condition as core or secondary.

Core Variations

Core variations are the more permanent and immutable aspects of an individual (Allison &

Schnieder, 2008; Loden & Rosener, 1990). The primary dimensions are important in forming a person's values, self-image, identity, opportunities, and perceptions of others (Loden, 2012). Some core variations have been used historically to treat people differently, giving them different opportunities, levels of power, and privileges. The core dimensions include (in alphabetical order) ability, age, class, ethnicity, gender, race, sexual orientation, and spiritual beliefs (although some scholars identify this last difference as a secondary dimension) (Allison & Schneider, 2008). These primary dimensions, if ignored, devalued, or misunderstood by others, can lead to culture clash (Loden, 2012). We will look briefly at each of these core dimensions of humanness. Although they are presented categorically for ease of learning, it is important to remember that there is wide variation within and across the categories.

Ability   Ability is how one is able to function in the world. All people function in many ways to accomplish daily activities, including recreation. Functioning includes the physical domain (e.g., being able to walk, lift, move, balance, and grasp), the intellectual domain (e.g., being able to think, learn, remember, pay attention, solve problems, read, write, and follow directions), the sensory domain (being able to see, hear, smell, feel, and integrate sensations), communication (expressive, receptive, verbal, nonverbal), and social and emotional functioning (e.g., being able to experience enjoyment, cope with stress, feel good about oneself, interact with others, form friendships, and understand social norms). People vary in their functioning across all of these domains. These variations could be due to a variety of disabilities, obesity, illnesses, injuries, poverty, aging, and more. What matters is not the cause of the variation, but how it affects function and how the level of function affects the person's interaction with the environment. Ability is *not* an inherent attribute of the person but results from interactions with the physical and social environment. It results, in part, from choices society makes about our environment (Institute of Medicine, 2007).

Ableism is a form of discrimination against people with disabilities or other functional differences. When people are judged solely by their disability, when they are viewed as inferior or abnormal, or when differential treatment is justified based on disability, ableism is at play and occurs at the individual and institutional level (Koppelman & Goodhart, 2008). An emerging group experiencing ableism is those who are obese; they experience not only negative attitudes, but denial of membership in groups, loss of jobs, and other forms of discrimination.

Age   In its simplest conception, age is the length of time that one has existed. However, age can be defined biologically, psychologically, or socially (Freysinger, 2008). Biological age has to do with growth and development across the life span and is often thought of chronologically in years. But age is also a social construction and a result of the lived life. It encompasses people's meanings and experiences as well as the kinds of physical and social environments in which they live.

Ageism is discrimination based on chronological age, in which age alone is used to determine a person's roles and capabilities (e.g., "crazy old geezer," "old lady driver"). It is a process of systematic stereotyping based on age with no regard for the capabilities of the whole person (International Longevity Center, 2006).

Class or Socioeconomic Status   Class is a complex dimension of the human condition. Many may wonder why class is included here as a primary dimension and not a secondary dimension. After all, it seems quite changeable over a lifetime. However, research has shown that class, or socioeconomic status (SES), is a relatively stable construction. Social class comprises income, wealth, occupation, and education level (Dawson, 2008; Scott & Leonhardt, 2005). Social class has an aspect of not only shared economic status, but also shared social and cultural practices in relation to positions of power. People who are born into poverty and remain at that level of income over their lifetimes will not have the same opportunities for well-paying jobs or higher education as those with higher SES. Given that the poverty level continues to rise and the distribution of wealth continues to be highly inequitable, many people will continue to experience being poor and likely experience classism.

Classism is the systematic oppression of subordinated groups (people without endowed or acquired economic power, social influence, and privilege) who work for wages for the dominant group (those who have access to control of the necessary resources by which other people

Recreation professionals must ensure that the physical and social environment affords participation for people of varying abilities.

Photo courtesy of Mark E. Fabend.

make their living). Classism is held in place by a system of beliefs that ranks people according to economic status, family lineage, job, and level of education. Classism perpetuates the myth that dominant group members are smarter and more articulate than working class, subordinated group members. In this way, dominant group members (upper-middle-class and wealthy people) define for everyone else what is "normal" or "acceptable" in the class hierarchy.

Ethnicity   **Ethnicity** is the shared cultural practices, perspectives, and distinctions that set one group of people apart from another. That is, ethnicity is a shared cultural heritage that is learned. Typically, that cultural heritage includes language, religion, holiday celebrations or rituals, and family life (Floyd & Nicholas, 2008). Ethnicity is not the same as race, but like race, it can be the basis for experiencing prejudice and discrimination.

Ethnocentrism is the belief that one's own culture is superior to other cultures or ethnicities. It can lead to false assumptions about other groups, unhealthy and distorted comparisons and judgments, and inaccurate communication.

Gender   **Gender** is the culturally specific set of characteristics that identifies the social behavior of women and men and the relationships between them. Gender refers not simply to women or men, but to the relationship between them and the way it is socially constructed (Federation of Canadian Municipalities, 2004). It is defined as more than the biological differences between men and women; it includes the ways those differences, whether real or perceived, have been valued, used, and relied on to classify women and men and to assign roles and expectations to them. Words that refer to gender include *man, woman, transgender, masculine,* and *feminine.* Gender differs from sex, which refers to a person based on anatomy (external genitalia, chromosomes, and internal reproductive system). Sex terms are *male, female,* and *transsexual.* Sex is biological, although social views and experiences of sex are cultural. **Gender identity** is one's internal personal sense of being a man or a woman or a boy or a girl. A person whose birth-assigned sex and internal sense of gender identity do not match is the definition of a transgendered person (Gender Equity Resource Center, 2012).

Gender discrimination, or sexism, is prejudice, stereotyping, and discrimination directed against people on the basis of their sex or gender and is based on the belief that one sex is superior to the other. It often involves the application of stereotypes of masculinity in relation to men, or of femininity in relation to women. Sexism may be evident in organizational and institutional structures, policies, procedures, and programs, as well as in the attitudes and behaviors of individuals (Egale, 2012). Gender discrimination is also sometimes referred to as male or female chauvinism.

Race Race is defined as groups of people who have similarities in biological traits deemed by society to be socially significant, meaning that people treat other people differently because of them (Howard, 1999). Race is inherited and often construed as a difference that is biological. Yet the concept of race continues to be controversial. The categories developed to describe variations in race are confusing, especially when they include Hispanic or Latino (Wallman, Evinger, & Schechter, 2000). For example, the U.S. Census Bureau (2010) defines "Hispanic or Latino" as a person of Cuban, Mexican, Puerto Rican, South or Central American, or other Spanish culture or origin *regardless of race*. In fact, the biological basis for race is even

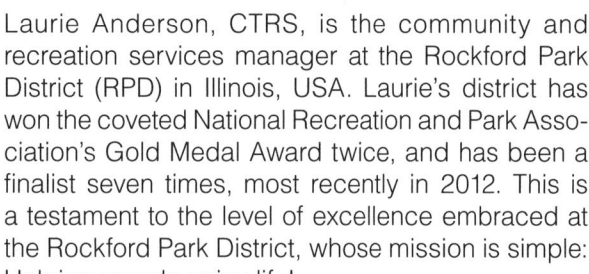

Best Practices From the Field

Laurie Anderson, CTRS, is the community and recreation services manager at the Rockford Park District (RPD) in Illinois, USA. Laurie's district has won the coveted National Recreation and Park Association's Gold Medal Award twice, and has been a finalist seven times, most recently in 2012. This is a testament to the level of excellence embraced at the Rockford Park District, whose mission is simple: Helping people enjoy life!

Laurie brings that mission to life through the programs and services she helps her staff facilitate throughout the year. Inclusion strategies, from the program level to the community level, are evident in all the work of the district. Beginning at the program level, supports and accommodations are readily available for all participants who need them. This statement appears on all communications from the RPD:

> "We welcome the opportunity to assist guests with disabilities to enjoy ALL our facilities, programs, and services. For assistance and information on accessibility, contact RPD Customer Service at 815-987-8800 (TTY, 888-871-6171)."

Pick up a program brochure, and you will see people of all races, ethnicities, abilities, genders, and ages participating in RPD activities. Throughout the program, you will find best practices in communication, from the use of pictures and symbols to the use of plain language to languages other than English. Laurie spearheaded an initiative to have all department managers, including planners and designers, attend "Inclusion U" and has led other diversity and inclusion trainings on a routine basis. Rockford Park District is a model for inclusion. Visit the website and watch the Gold Medal 12-minute video at www.rockfordparkdistrict.org.

Jessica Steinberg, a colleague of Laurie, is the director at the Magic Waters Water Park, a large public water park in the Rockford Park District. Jessica has made inclusion central to the water park's services and facilities. "We have discovered new ways to look at our water park and found small changes to be more inclusive. Don't just think about physical disabilities and people who are in wheelchairs. . . . How about Grandma who needs the assistance of a cane to come watch her grandchild splash down the waterslide? How about the teenage boy who is deaf and can't hear the whistles of the lifeguard? How about the family that has a child with autism who just can't wait in line? Or the uncle who is paralyzed from his military duties but wants to swim with his little nephew? How about the mom who comes to the water park with three children, a stroller, a cooler, and three bags? The dedicated season pass holder who just had surgery but still wants to get some sun and dangle her feet in the water?" Understanding the broad range of needs of Magic Waters Water Park guests has helped Jessica make it more inclusive. Here are some things Magic Waters has done over the past several years: changed its philosophy of inclusion, provided more advanced disability and diversity awareness staff training, reevaluated and changed some park rules and policies, provided adaptive equipment and speed passes for people with disabilities, provided season pass caregiver options, and added family changing rooms. Visit the website at www.magicwaterswaterpark.com.

in question (Venter et al., 2001). In the massive human genome mapping project, Venter and colleagues found that "Many diverse sources of data have shown that any two individuals are more than 99.9% identical in (genetic) sequence, which means that all the glorious differences among individuals in our species that can be attributed to genes falls in a mere 0.1% of the sequence" (p. 1348). Despite this, race continues to be a variation in the human condition that creates vastly different levels of privilege, opportunity, and power.

Racism is the systematic practice of denying people access to rights, representation, or resources based on racial differences. Racism involves more than the personal actions of individuals. It is a thorough system of discrimination that involves social institutions and affects virtually every aspect of society (United Nations, 2010). **White privilege** is the idea that people who are of European descent should have access to privilege and power just because of their race, rather than because of anything they have or haven't done; other groups are denied that privilege (McIntosh, 1988). It is taken for granted that the cultural beliefs, values, and practices of white people are the most common and influential. White privilege pervades much of North American society, and often, people who are white lack awareness of the dominant position of power and influence they hold. Examples of white privilege abound, from the color of children's dolls to the faces we see on popular television programs.

Sexual Orientation   **Sexual orientation**
is who we are emotionally or physically attracted to (or both). Sexual orientation is the direction of one's enduring attraction. *Heterosexual,* or *straight,* is the term used for an enduring attraction to members of a sex other than one's own. *Gay* is used to define an enduring attraction to members of the same sex (used for either men or women), and *lesbian* is the preferred term for women who have an enduring attraction to other women (Gay & Lesbian Alliance Against Defamation, 2010).

Heterosexism is the belief that heterosexuality is the only natural sexuality and that it is inherently healthier than, or superior to, other types of sexuality. Heterosexism is not just an attitude held by individuals; it is systemic as well. Heterosexual privilege means that power and dominance belong to those who are not gay or lesbian. For example, people who are heterosexual do not have to "come out" as straight.

Spiritual or Religious Beliefs   Spiritual
beliefs, and in particular religion, are considered a primary dimension of being human, not because they cannot change over time, but because they have been used to exclude or discriminate against others. In understanding religious or spiritual diversity, it is important to look *within* as well as *among* faith traditions. Just as there are various ways to be Christian, so there are various ways to be Hindu, Muslim, Buddhist, Jewish, or Sikh. When people become aware of the diversity within and between religions, they find stereotypes about religious "others," such as a fear of people who are Muslim (called **Islamophobia**), difficult to maintain.

Secondary Variations

Secondary variations in the human condition include such things as education, family status, geographic location, political beliefs, language, and work style. These differences affect and interact with the core dimensions of diversity, but are changeable over time (Allison & Schneider, 2008). People have some level of choice about and control over secondary dimensions.

Intersectionality

Intersectionality is a theory that seeks to examine the ways various socially and culturally constructed categories interact on multiple levels to manifest themselves as inequality in society. Most people do not identify primarily with one dimension of diversity, but with multiple identities. For example, a woman who is black and uses a wheelchair will have a different experience in society than a white woman or a woman without a disability or even a black man. Intersectionality, as a way of thinking about people, helps leaders avoid the trap of viewing social problems as separate challenges facing specific groups defined in mutually exclusive ways. Instead, as leaders with intersectional awareness work to increase the inclusion of all community members, they need to ask

> *how their approaches address and engage constituent members who are in fact constituents of other social groups as well. How do debates across constituencies sound different when it is recognized that each community contains members of the other? What is the broadest articulation of a problem that would*

embrace more than the interests of the most advantaged? (Crenshaw, 2009, p. 6)

Intersectionality theory helps us see differences as natural variations along multiple continuums. None of us has only one dimension.

Core Variations as a Historical Basis for Differential Treatment

The preceding section gave a brief and superficial glimpse into the multitude of ways humans vary across primary and secondary dimensions, not to categorize or *name* people, but to provide some common meaning and language with which to talk about differences. Open communication and honest dialogue are critical, because these core variations have historically been used to stereotype at best and discriminate at worse. Power, privilege, and dominance have historically been held by certain groups in society: whites, men, people without disabilities, middle-aged adults, heterosexuals, and the upper class, to name a few. Members of these groups are granted privilege just by being members of the group, and for no other reason. And members of other groups have not only been denied privilege, but have experienced negative treatment. Prejudice and discrimination continue in today's world, both at the individual and institutional level.

Stereotypes are generalizations that we make about the characteristics of all members of a group, based on an image, often wrong, about what people in that group are like. **Prejudice** is the act of prejudging, or making a judgment, usually negative, about a person based on that person's group membership without real knowledge of the person and often based on stereotype. **Discrimination** is using power to act on prejudice—treating someone differently (and often negatively) because of their membership in a group. Prejudice and discrimination produce negative outcomes for groups experiencing them. For example, women as a group continue to make 76 percent of the salary men make for doing the same jobs. African Americans continue to experience higher rates of dropping out of high school and prison sentences. People with disabilities continue to be unemployed at a significantly higher rate than those without disabilities. These are systemic outcomes of ongoing prejudice and discrimination at all levels in society.

Overcoming prejudice and discrimination requires bold and sensitive leadership. Leaders in the 21st century must have a sensitivity about and awareness of the social inequities that exist and a repertoire of skills and knowledge to begin to make positive change.

Inclusive Leadership

Diversity is the mosaic of people who bring a variety of backgrounds, styles, perspectives, values, and beliefs as assets to the groups and organizations with which they interact (Howard, 1999). Diversity, which results from inclusion and differentiation, is something 21st-century leaders in the leisure services profession must embrace. But how can leaders move their organizations to higher levels of diversity? If a leader fosters inclusiveness at every level, from the program level to the community level, then diversity can be one natural outcome. Inclusion is a continuous process that invites, welcomes, and celebrates all community members' participation. When leaders foster inclusiveness, they enhance diversity.

Twenty-first-century leaders, then, must have skills and competencies that build diversity at the micro level (groups and programs), at the meso level (agency), and at the macro level (the community and beyond). Overarching all levels of leadership, and a powerful tool in its own right, is language. To be inclusive, leaders must use language well.

Language: A Powerful Tool at All Levels

Language bridges all levels of leadership, from informal conversations with coworkers to formal communications issued by an agency. Language is not only a means of communication, but also an agent for shaping the way people perceive and experience the world (Wilkins, 2012). It welcomes and invites, or it hurts and excludes. Language is powerful. Because of this, and because it is something we can learn, use, and practice, language is a powerful change agent. Leaders must be prepared to learn the language of diversity, and because society is always evolving, relearn that language on a regular basis. This section offers guidelines on how to use language that is respectful and inclusive.

We can assume that most people want to use the most respectful terms. Since we have inherited a system that routinely perpetuates prejudicial attitudes and beliefs about groups,

we often hear well-intentioned people uncon-
sciously reinforcing those beliefs through their
use of words. (Castania, 2003, p. 1)

What words do you use to describe variations in the human condition? What words are inclusive and respectful? Which perpetuate stereotypes and negative views? In choosing words to describe other people, it is important to be accurate, sensitive, and positive.

Accurately describing a person or group avoids stereotypes and assumptions and values identity. For example, instead of calling someone a Native American, American Indian, or First Nation member, call her by the more accurate descriptor of tribal affiliation, whether it be Sioux or Ojibway or Kootenai. Tribal affiliation is a much more accurate descriptor that reflects the heterogeneity among tribal groups. This is just one example that illustrates how accurate language is respectful and honest.

Choosing words that are sensitive shows genuine regard for others. For example, calling a grown woman a girl shows disrespect for her as a mature adult, especially given that people rarely call men boys. The way we phrase things can perpetuate stereotypes as well, and show a lack of sensitivity. In the sentence *John still runs, despite his age,* we are sending the message that older people are usually feeble and inactive. Sensitivity in word choice is respectful of individuals and groups.

Framing language in a positive way also conveys genuine respect. Negativity is often associated with many groups who have experienced historical prejudice and discrimination. Phrases such as *confined to a wheelchair* and *crazy lunatic* are examples of negative word choices. *Handicapped* is a word that has long been used to describe people with disabilities, even though the root meaning is very negative—beggar, loser, or disadvantaged. Yet we see the word *handicapped* everywhere in relation to amenities and services to assist people with disabilities. Reframing language to be positive conveys respect and helps erase stereotypes. *Handicapped parking* becomes *accessible parking. Confined to a wheelchair* becomes *uses a wheelchair.* And *crazy lunatic* becomes *a person with a psychosocial disability.* In choosing words, keeping the person first is the best guideline, and then, if needed at all, the label comes second (Snow, 2009). Table 5.1 provides examples of person-first language and other examples of accurate, sensitive, and positive word choices in relation to diversity.

Because the language of diversity is ever evolving, here are some basic guidelines for choosing language that is most respectful and inclusive:

▶ Ask and listen—don't assume.
▶ Honor self-identification.
▶ Be specific.
▶ De-categorize (disaggregate large categories).
▶ Avoid labels.
▶ Consider the person first.

Language is powerful and affects the culture of an agency and community. Leaders can make a difference in setting the standard for accurate, sensitive, and positive language that includes all people. They can also facilitate inclusion across all levels of their organizations, from the micro to the meso and macro levels (see figure 5.1). A discussion of all of the strategies available to leaders to put inclusion into practice is beyond the scope of this chapter. An introduction to a few of the actions leaders can take is provided next to pique your interest in learning more.

Inclusive Leadership at the Micro Level

What can leaders do to promote program and activity inclusion? At its most basic level, inclusion happens one person at a time. And, at the micro level of the program, group, or activity, inclusion is most easily promoted by the leader. The following suggestions for programs and activities are easily implemented. They do not require much in the way of resources, but primarily a willingness to work toward, and a positive attitude toward, inclusion and diversity.

Staff

All staff members, from permanent to seasonal, need to have an understanding of diversity, what inclusion is, and how it can be facilitated. In hiring staff, leaders must be mindful of diversity and choose staff members who are comfortable with people with differences and are positive about inclusion. Once staff are hired, leaders must provide routine staff training on diversity awareness and inclusion strategies.

Registration and Assessment

All participants in a community must have the means to register for programs and services. Promotional

Table 5.1   Inclusive Language Guidelines

General guideline	Instead of this . . .	Say this.
Use person-first language. Put the person before the disability or difference, describe what the person has, not what the person is, and use the label only if necessary.	Autistic child	Child with autism
	Disabled person	Person with a disability
	Mentally retarded	Person with an intellectual disability
	She is bipolar	She has bipolar disorder
Use positive, sensitive language. Examine your words to ensure that you are not communicating or perpetuating negative images or stereotypes.	Handicapped parking	Accessible parking
	Confined to a wheelchair	Uses a wheelchair
	Afflicted with Alzheimer's	Has Alzheimer's
	Normal people	People without disabilities
	Birth defect	Congenital disability
	Girl (when talking about a grown woman)	Woman
Use nonsexist language. Sexist language permeates our culture and is used unwittingly. Male pronouns are often used to refer to both sexes, and sexist words are used to refer to people in various professions. Purposefully shift language to be gender neutral and inclusive.	"If a leader works hard, he will succeed."	"If a leader works hard, he or she will succeed."
	"Who lost his ticket?"	"Who lost a ticket? or, Who lost their ticket?"
	Firemen, mailmen, cavemen, chairmen	Firefighters, mail carriers, cave dwellers, chairpersons
	Waitress, stewardess (and other gender-stereotyped service roles)	Food server, flight attendant
Avoid qualifiers that reinforce stereotypes. A qualifier is added information that suggests that what is being said is an exception to what is expected.	"A group of intelligent black students helped with the diversity training."	"A group of black students helped with the diversity training."
	"Our board of directors includes a lady professor, a business executive, a woman doctor, a lawyer, and a female engineer."	"Our board of directors includes a professor, a business executive, a doctor, a lawyer, and an engineer."
Avoid language that excludes. Often, we are unaware of the exclusionary nature of language we grew up using.	"You guys" to a mixed-gender group	"You all" or just "You"
	"Dear Mothers, Please bake cookies for the upcoming party."	"Dear Families, Please bake cookies for the upcoming party."
Identify people by characteristics only when relevant. Often, the identifier is not even necessary.	"Mark, our gay recreation director"	"Mark, our recreation director" (You would not say, Mark, our heterosexual recreation director)
Be aware of language that perpetuates dominance. Some words reinforce what is considered normal, mainstream, or standard.	Nonwhite people	People of color
	Normal people	People without disabilities
Do not use hurtful and negative words or phrases.	Lower class	Poor, working class, middle class
	Illegal alien	Undocumented person or worker

Based on Anderson and Kress 2003; Anti-Defamation League 2007; Castania 2003; Klein 1993; Snow 2009.

materials (e.g., advertisements, flyers, brochures, websites) need a statement that says something to this effect: *We welcome all people. If you need certain accommodations in order to participate, please let us know how we can help you be involved.* For programs that require preregistration, the registration form should include a place where people can identify any needs they may have to participate in the program; this request for information begins the individualized process needed to facilitate inclusion.

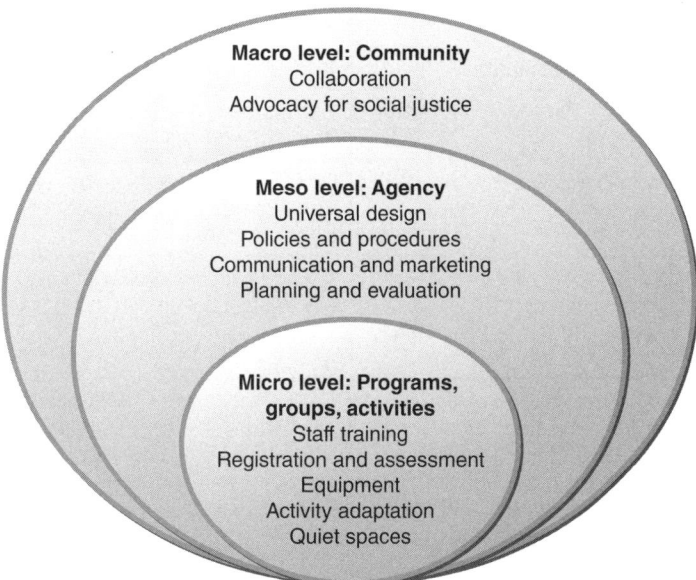

Figure 5.1 Inclusion strategies for leaders at the micro, meso, and macro levels.

In essence, the leader's job is to bridge the gap between the requirements of the activity and the skills and abilities of the participant. This gap, if there is one, is bridged with services, supports, accommodations, adaptations, training, and any other means to help with participation. A wealth of strategies, resources, and practices are available for bridging this gap (Anderson & Kress, 2003; Smith, 2009).

Figure 5.2 illustrates a model for bridging the gap that program leaders can use. Table 5.2 provides some examples of bridging the gap for full participation by people of diverse backgrounds. The examples in table 5.2 are simplified to provide a sense of how the model works. In reality, each scenario would be more complex, with more nuance and depth.

Equipment

A variety of adapted equipment is available to help people with functional differences participate fully in programs and activities (e.g., beach wheelchairs, grasping cuffs, assistive listening devices). Age- and gender-appropriate equipment of the right size and weight facilitates inclusion. Equipment that is culturally and gender appropriate should be available as well. For example, having toys in the playroom that reflect more than one culture and do not promote gender stereotypes facilitates inclusiveness.

Activity Adaptation and Partial Participation

Activity adaptations and partial participation allow community members to partake in the parts of the activity that they can do, or in a different way. For example, providing a child with a significant disability with a personal floatation device will allow that child to participate with peers at a water park. Having a portion of the open swim time available only to females (and blocking any windows or viewing areas) will allow Muslim women to swim.

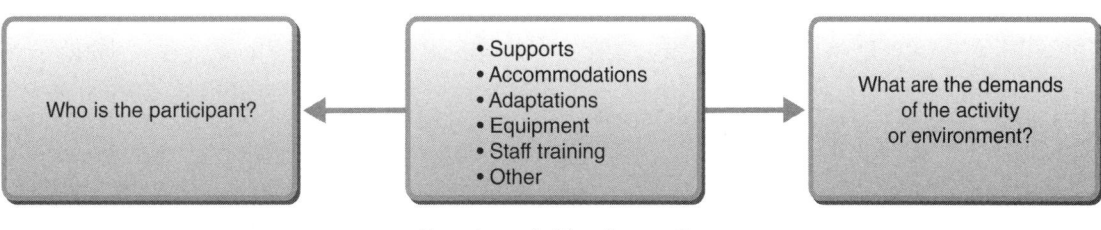

Figure 5.2 Bridging the gap model.

Table 5.2 Bridging the Gap in Action

The person and the activity or environment	Bridge the gap with this strategy
Bob wants to learn to ski. He uses a wheelchair and cannot stand.	Use a monoski (a sitski) with individualized instruction until Bob can monoski independently.
Sarah wants to pursue Zumba to increase her well-being. She is a single mother who works at a very low-paying day job.	Offer Zumba in the evenings, with a concurrent children's program or child care at reduced rates during the Zumba class (or both).
Aamir is a recreation specialist at a local parks and recreation department. His faith requires that he pray five times daily, with two of those times occurring during his workday. His prayers involve certain movements and positions.	Provide a quiet space with solitude and encourage Aamir to schedule his breaks to coincide with his prayer time.
Esther has always enjoyed her water exercise class and has participated for years and years. Her best friends are her water exercise friends. Of late, she has been unable to complete the class because she becomes unbalanced and fatigued. She doesn't want to try a new, less strenuous activity because of the social support she has at her water exercise class.	Ask Esther to see her physician to ensure that her change in functioning is a normal part of aging and nothing more significant. Have Esther complete all of her exercises during class along the wall where she can hang on to the edge of the pool. Install pool stairs with a handrail and provide a chair on the pool deck where Esther can exit and rest when needed during class.
Lyndon wants to join the soccer club, but he noticed that all the other boys in the program are white. He questions whether he can join because he is a person of color.	Actively reach out and invite families and children of color to the soccer club; encourage friends to join together. Revise marketing materials to reflect the diversity of the community.
The parks and recreation department has held an Easter egg hunt every spring for as long as staff can remember. A new staff member questions whether the traditional event is inclusive of the community.	Assess the demographic trends in the community. Create more inclusive celebrations such as a spring fling instead of an Easter egg hunt, or add additional celebrations that reflect the community's diversity.

Quiet Area

A designated quiet area near recreation program areas is a best practice. Recreation environments are often noisy and distracting, and someone who has difficulty integrating stimuli or handling stress may need a quiet place in which to regroup or relax for a short period. A participant may need a quiet space for religious purposes or for feeding an infant. The quiet space doesn't need to be special; it can be an unused room or even a yurt set up outside the mainstream of activity. Leaders must make sure participants know about the availability and location of the quiet space and that it is comfortable and inviting.

These are just a few of the many strategies and approaches leaders can use at the individual program level to encourage and promote the participation of diverse people.

Inclusive Leadership at the Meso Level

It is often said that inclusion happens one person at a time; this happens both from the top down and from the bottom up. At the meso, or agency, level, administrative practices that focus on inclusion can change the culture of agencies. A lack of these practices can unintentionally turn community members away as well. The strategies outlined in this section are readily implemented at inclusive facilities.

Facility and Amenity Design

Who can approach, enter, and use the facilities and amenities at an agency or organization? If the answer is "All people!" then universal design principles are incorporated into the facilities, amenities, programs, and services. **Universal design** is a concept that promotes creating a recreation environment for *all* people that reflects an inclusive culture. Environments, services, and products are usable by as many people as possible regardless of age, ability, culture, or circumstance. Although universal design is often associated with disability, it is a design approach that helps everyone. The principles of universal design are equitable use; flexibility in use; simple and intuitive use; perceptible information; tolerance for error and safe; low physical effort; and size and space for approach and use by all (Center for Universal Design, 2010). Universal design means that a person who is transgendered will find an appropriate restroom to use, as will the person using a wheelchair and the parent with three toddlers in tow. It means there is a barrier-free, well-lit, well-marked route of travel from the parking area or bus stop to the entrance to the changing area and from there to the activity area. Universal design allows all people to approach, enter, and use a facility or program area.

Policies and Procedures

Clear and well-communicated policies and procedures are critical for facilitating inclusion. Policies and procedures for the emergency evacuation of people with disabilities and other functional differences are critical for safety. An agency policy about personal care attendants (those who accompany a person who is older or has a disability and is there only to help, not participate) is needed; many agencies allow personal care attendants to attend programs and activities free of charge, because they are solely there to assist. An agency must develop a clear and inclusive policy on what falls under family rates, family memberships, and the like. Today's families are much more diverse, and policies must reflect this diversity. Policies on how the agency will accommodate service dogs and other animals, mobility devices, burqas or head coverings in certain recreation areas, and spaces for prayer must be in place and shared with the public. All staff, from custodial staff to ticket staff to the executive director, must know the policies to ensure that they are fairly and equitably implemented.

Marketing and Communication

Who is invited to a park? Who are conveyed as appropriate participants for a basketball leagues? Leaders must take a critical look at their organizations' marketing materials to be sure they include images of all kinds of people. Marketing materials and other agency communications should reflect the diversity of the community. The materials should let people know what is available to help them participate. The agency website should include an easily located page that provides detailed information about physical access, safety guidelines, child care, adaptive equipment, quiet spaces, sliding fee scales and scholarships, policies that facilitate participation, an invitation to call ahead for an individual consultation, and other information to help people enjoy what the agency has to offer.

Communication needs can be met in a wide variety of ways, from providing alternative forms of communication to assistive listening devices to apps on a smartphone that facilitate interactions. Alternative forms of communication may include interpreters (sign language and other languages), computer devices, iPads, and online translating programs. The key is to let the public know what forms of communication are available and how they can be accessed or arranged, and to be open to exploring new ways to communicate.

Planning and Evaluation

When undertaking any new construction or renovations, leaders must include a wide variety of people in the planning, to ensure inclusivity from the initial phases of the project. People who experience a disability on a daily basis, for example, or who have young children, or who must take care to not expose their bodies in public will have great insights that can help with the design of projects that truly meet their needs. When planning programs or events, leaders must take into consideration the location of the event, scheduling, transportation, cost, and other cultural considerations. They must be alert to unintentionally excluding segments of the community for any of these reasons.

As well, leaders must continually evaluate strategies for creating inclusive agencies. Satisfaction on the part of current users is important, but so is determining who is still not coming. Who does not yet feel invited? These are important areas to monitor so changes can be made that ensure equity and inclusion.

Inclusive Leadership at the Macro Level

Leaders have a certain level of control at the micro and meso level of their agencies. As they move to the macro level—that is, the community and beyond—partnerships and collaboration become critical to foster inclusion. Advocacy is often needed to make social change beyond the agency level.

Collaborative Partnerships

A best practice in inclusion and diversity is to develop collaborative partnerships across community entities. Partnerships should reflect the diversity of the community and include civic groups, special interest groups, ethnic groups, political groups, and other entities that can add perspective, knowledge, resources, mutual goals, and human resources to the efforts of the recreation agency. Many of us grew up or live in relatively homogeneous communities and may be uncomfortable, albeit subconsciously, interacting with people who are different from us. Leaders must go beyond superficial relationships by consciously developing multicultural coalitions, even starting in informal settings. Such an effort fosters authentic, trusting, and honest relationships. Collaboration is a skill leaders must develop to be effective in a diverse society.

Advocacy and Social Justice

At times, leaders in the 21st century will find themselves in the position of being advocates for social justice and equity. When resources for the public good are scarce, those who most often suffer are people who are marginalized and lack a collective voice. Leaders in the field should be prepared to help give voice to the needs of all community members so that all people can play wherever they choose. Social justice means genuine fairness for all people in the aspects of our lives that matter, based on respect and dignity. Social justice is not so much about creating *equality* as it is about creating *equity*. Equality means that everyone gets shoes; equity means that everyone gets shoes that fit. Leaders who work in communities in which resource distribution is highly imbalanced will need to take an advocacy role often.

Advocacy is speaking, writing, or acting on behalf of the sincerely perceived interests of a disadvantaged person or a group without conflict of interest. Advocacy requires three things: a passionate desire to see positive change, a sound understanding of the issue or idea for which one is advocating, and a willingness to "go public" to effect change (Anderson & Heyne, 2012). Advocacy can occur at the grassroots level, such as joining with other community members to advocate for a particular change through avenues such as organized communication, media events, protests, and rallies; or by attending and testifying at public meetings, providing public input on proposals, or writing letters to the editor. Advocacy can also be more formal, such as working with organizations to change laws, rules, and policies. The steps in advocacy include being clear about the need, having sound information, and having a well-reasoned plan to effect change. Advocacy is a skill that takes

diligence to develop and must be used carefully to preserve collaborative partnerships while still effecting needed change for participants.

The Inclusion Lens

Leaders need to facilitate inclusion across multiple levels of service. But how do they start to make environments, programs, services, and communities more inclusive? One analytical tool to help begin and sustain the inclusion process is the inclusion lens (Health Canada, 2002). A lens is a filter or a way of looking at things that encourages us to consider certain ideas in our workplaces. A lens tool is an assessment tool that provides a way of asking questions about what we do in everyday practice. The inclusion lens tool encourages the application of diversity and inclusion concepts to all that we do for the people we serve. The inclusion lens tool is a set of questions to help administrators, staff, and volunteers consider the concepts of diversity and inclusion in the development, revision, implementation, and evaluation of programs, policies, practices, and environments. An inclusion lens looks at variations in the human condition and asks: Who has privilege? Who has power? Who is marginalized? Who is excluded? Why? An inclusion lens views differences as natural variations in the human conditions and challenges inequity and exclusion.

Figure 5.3 depicts seven lenses: universal design, language, marketing and communication, awareness and diversity training, administrative practices, engaging a diverse audience, and supports and accommodations. Each of these lenses, when used continually, will help leaders identify areas in which change can be made to ensure that all community members are welcomed and included.

Professional Development for Inclusive Leaders

Leaders in the 21st century, then, must be able to facilitate inclusion and sustain diversity that works. One key area of professional development is advocacy, discussed previously. An equally important area for professional development is cultural competence.

Cultural Competence Defined

Culture is defined as the integrated patterns of human behavior that includes thoughts, communication, actions, customs, beliefs, values, and

Inclusion Is a Process; Diversity Is an Outcome

The Inclusion Lens

What is inclusion?
Inclusion is a process of ensuring that everyone is welcome and involved.

What is a lens?
A lens is a filter or a way of looking at things. It encourages us to consider certain ideas in our work.

What is a lens tool?
A lens tool is an assessment tool. It provides a way of asking questions about what we do in everyday practice. The inclusion lens tool seeks to encourage the application of diversity and inclusion concepts to all we do for the people we serve.

What is the purpose of the lens tool?
The inclusion lens tool is a set of questions to help administrators, staff, and volunteers consider the concepts of diversity and inclusion in the development, revision, implementation, and evaluation of programs, policies, practices, and environments.

The lens tool serves to promote inclusion and achieve diversity.

Inclusion Lens Questions

To ensure the inclusion of *all* people in programs, policies, practices, and environments, ask yourself the following questions:

Universal design
- Do we use universal design?
- Can *all* people approach, enter, and use the facilities, programs, and services?

Language
- Do we use inclusive language?
- Is our language accurate, sensitive, and positive?

Marketing and communication
- Do our marketing and communication reflect the diversity of our community?
- Is our communication accessible? Inclusive? Available in many formats?
- Is everyone invited?

Awareness and diversity training
- What is our awareness of variations in the human condition?
- What is our attitude toward diversity?
- Do we train our staff on diversity and inclusion?

Administrative practices
- Do we have policies and procedures in place that promote inclusion?
- Do staff members understand and use the policies and procedures?
- Do our policies or practices unintentionally discriminate or exclude?

Engaging a diverse audience
- Are our facilities and programs readily available to everyone?
- Do we have an inclusive registration process?
- Do we have a process to learn what a person needs to successfully participate?

Supports and accommodations
- Do we provide supports (human resources) for successful participation by all people?
- Do we provide accommodations for successful participation by all people?

Figure 5.3 The inclusion lens.

Adapted from IWK Health Centre, Halifax, Nova Scotia, 2012. IWK Health Centre. Diversity and Inclusion Lens Too (2010). Derived from http://www.iwk.nshealth.ca/index.cfm?objectid=D9031E41-AD9F-52EC-1A999738F4CC8828.

institutions of social groups (Howard, 1999). We each have our own cultural patterns, and it takes focused effort to not only gain an awareness of what those are, but also to learn about cultures other than our own. **Cultural competence** is defined as a set of congruent behaviors, attitudes, and policies that come together in a system or agency or among professionals and enables people to work effectively in a cross-cultural context (Cross et al., 1989). It is a process by which individuals and systems respond respectfully and effectively to people of all cultures, languages, classes, races, ethnic backgrounds, degrees of ability, religions, genders, sexual orientations, and other diversity factors in a way that recognizes, affirms, and values the worth of individuals, families, and communities and protects and preserves the dignity of each (Oregon Office of Equity and Inclusion, 2012).

Being competent in cross-cultural functioning means learning new patterns of behavior and applying them in the appropriate settings (King, Sims, & Osher, 2007). Competence is indicated by the following practices:

▶ Acceptance and respect of differences

▶ Continual expansion of knowledge about inclusion and diversity

▶ Continued self-assessment

▶ Attention to the dynamics of differences

▶ Adoption of sensitive and relevant service delivery models to better meet needs

As with any learning process, developing cultural competence takes time, commitment, and an awareness of one's developmental level on the continuum of cultural competence.

Continuum of Cultural Competence

Cultural competence can be conceptualized as a developmental process along a continuum. Cross (1988) developed a model to help professionals and agencies assess their levels of cultural competence, and to give direction to efforts to gain more competence. The continuum includes five stages and is described in table 5.3. The continuum of cultural competence has been used by leaders, agencies, and systems to develop strategies for improvement and, ultimately, diversity.

Strategies for Improving Cultural Competence

For leaders, perhaps the most important starting point in developing cultural competence is to continually assess themselves and develop higher levels of self-awareness. Exploring their cultural roots; critiquing their own levels of privilege; examining their beliefs, values, and attitudes—all lead to greater self-awareness and increased cultural competence. Actively seeking opportunities to learn about, spend time with, and develop relationships with those different from themselves, closely examining differences, and having honest, open dialogues about differences will all raise leaders' cultural competence levels. Lastly, especially for leaders who are white, coming to terms with their cultural legacy and understanding that they are not their history and did not create the unfair system of privilege and damage will energize them to begin to change that system. Gary Howard (1993), a respected educator in multiculturalism, stated:

> The way for us to overcome the denial, hostility, fear, and guilt of the past and present is to become active participants in the creation of a better future. As whites, once we become aware of the heavy weight of our oppressive past, our role is not to fall into a kind of morose confessionalism about the sins of our ancestors. The healing response for ourselves, as well as for those who have been the victims of oppression, is involvement, action, contribution, and responsibility. The healing path requires all of us to join our efforts, resources, energy, and commitment. No one group can do it alone. Together we are coresponsible for the creation of a new America. (p. 6)

The New Norm

If we embrace diversity and develop solid skills in facilitating inclusion, we will help change the face of our communities and, in turn, our society. We will see a new norm develop. When we shift our gaze to the whole person in the environment and accept increased variation in the human condition, we widen the boundaries of what we consider to be part of mainstream culture. We move from "mainstreaming" to true inclusion (Snow, 2012). This broader and more inclusive view, in turn,

Table 5.3 Cultural Competence Continuum

Stage 1	Stage 2	Stage 3	Stage 4	Stage 5
Cultural destructiveness	Cultural incapacity	Cultural blindness	Cultural precompetence	Cultural competence
This is the most negative stage of the continuum, in which attitudes, behaviors, policies, and practices are destructive or harmful to people and their cultures.	In this stage, the individual or agency does not mean to be destructive to others and their cultures, but does not have the capacity or awareness to meet different cultural needs.	At the midpoint of the continuum, the individual or agency provides services with the expressed intent of being unbiased. They function as if the culture makes no difference and all the people are the same. This is sometimes called color blindness in relation to race.	Individuals and organizations move toward the positive end of the continuum by acknowledging cultural differences and making documented efforts to take them into consideration.	The most positive end of the continuum is indicated by acceptance and respect of differences, continual expansion of cultural knowledge, continued cultural self-assessment, attention to the dynamics of differences, and the adoption of culturally relevant service delivery models to better meet needs.
People in this stage • view culture as a problem; • believe that if a culture or population can be suppressed or destroyed, people will be better off; • believe that people should be more like the "mainstream"; and • assume that one culture is superior and should eradicate "lesser" cultures.	People in this stage • lack cultural awareness and skills; • may have been brought up in a homogeneous society, been taught to behave in certain ways, and never questioned what they were taught; • believe in the racial superiority of a dominant group and assume a paternalistic posture toward others; and • maintain stereotypes.	People in this stage • see others in terms of their own culture and claim that all people are alike; • believe that culture makes no difference ("we are all the same"); and • believe that all people should be treated in the same way regardless of difference.	People in this stage • recognize cultural differences and start to educate themselves and others concerning these differences; • realize their shortcomings in interacting within a diverse environment; and • may become complacent in their efforts.	People in this stage • accept, appreciate, and accommodate differences and begin actively to educate less informed people about differences; • value diversity and accept and respect differences; • accept the influence of their own culture in relation to other cultures; • understand and manage the dynamics of difference when cultures intersect; • examine components of cross-cultural interactions (e.g., communication); and • seek knowledge about diverse cultures, develop skills to interact, and become allies with others in multicultural settings.

Based Mak 2002; Williams 2001.

empowers people. Dr. Patrica Deegan, who has a psychiatric disability and is a respected advocate in the mental health field, stated: "We don't want to be mainstreamed. We say let the mainstream become a wide stream that has room for all of us and leaves no one stranded" (Deegan, 2006, p. 28). The new norm will widen the stream. As leaders, we will be creating the change needed so that no one is left stranded.

I Am Norm: A Model for Attitude Change

The new norm is an attitude change and will be more difficult for those who grew up and live in more homogeneous cultures. Young people today are growing up in an entirely different world. Leaders can look to them for inspiration and as models for positive attitudes about diversity and inclusion. I Am Norm is a wonderful example and training tool (www.IamNorm.org). This project grew out of a youth summit on inclusion and captures the spirit of the mainstream as a very wide stream. Through video, music, and other media, young people send an energetic message that no one is Norm, yet we are all Norm.

A Special Note About Bullying

Because bullying is an urgent issue in the 21st century, it deserves a special note. Most children, and even some adults, who are bullied have some visible difference. As we work toward developing a new norm, perhaps this will change. In the meantime, many excellent resources and approaches have been developed for leaders to put into practice today. One important strategy is to develop and actively market an agency and its services as a "safe zone" by developing, training staff on, widely publicizing, and then enforcing a zero tolerance policy on bullying. If every leader in leisure services embraced the practices of a safe zone and zero tolerance policy, we will have made a significant contribution to a socially just and kind world.

Best Practices in Inclusive Leadership

Diversity is both an ideal and a reality. Inclusion can help to make the reality of diversity closer to the ideal. If we are all invited, welcomed, given fair opportunities, supported, encouraged, and celebrated for who we are, then as an agency, a

community, and society, we can savor the benefits of diversity.

The cost of exclusion is too high: loneliness, pain, loss of opportunity to develop one's full capabilities, missed opportunities to nurture flourishing communities, fear, marginalization, prejudice, discrimination, and the list goes on. As leaders, we need to reframe our question from, How much will it cost to make this inclusive? to, What is so unique about this situation that it could possibly justify exclusion? As leaders, we must embrace the notion that people vary across key dimensions on a continuum, and strive to create and sustain a culture in which all those variations have a respected and valued place. People should not have to fit into a mold to fit into a community. As leaders, we must abandon any outdated perceptions of normalcy and learn to embrace and appreciate diversity.

One best practice helping to make this dream a reality is the work of the Inclusive Recreation Resource Center. Table 5.4 provides an overview of the Center and its powerful training called Inclusion U that is helping to change the face of recreation services so that all people can play wherever they choose. The Inclusive Recreation Resource Center is a university-based center housed at State University of New York at Cortland whose mission is to promote and sustain the participation by people of all abilities in inclusive recreation activities and resources. The Center provides many services, including inclusivity assessments, training, an online database for inclusive recreation, technical assistance, a recreation referral service, partnerships, and research and evaluation. Inclusion U trains an army of volunteers to increase inclusion in recreation. The Inclusion U curriculum shown in table 5.4 is an excellent model for any disability awareness training, but goes beyond awareness to powerful action strategies.

Summary

Diversity is the collective mix of humans who interact positively in a social sphere (e.g., communities, neighborhoods, recreation programs, workplaces), all of whom vary across salient dimensions such as race, ethnicity, age, gender, ability, sexual orientation, class, and spiritual beliefs. A new way to think about diversity is that all people vary, not categorically, but across a range of different dimensions of being human. Diversity can be thought of as variations in the human condition and the intersectionality of those variations. It honors and

Table 5.4 Inclusion U and the Inclusivity Assessment Tool

Module 1: Introduction	The Inclusive Recreation Resource Center (mission, vision, activities) Goals and objectives of Inclusion U Process to complete the course and become a Certified Inclusivity Assessor (CIA)
Module 2: What is inclusion and why is it important?	Definitions and core principles Physical accessibility—built and natural environments Social accessibility—programs, services and events, administration
Module 3: What do I need to know about disability?	Person-first language The social model of disability Functional abilities—physical, sensory, intellectual, emotional, social
Module 4: Assessing inclusivity	How to use the Inclusivity Assessment Tool Steps to approach a site, facility, or program (partnering, collegiality, market potential)
Module 5: What is physical inclusion?	Accessibility—approach, enter, use Universal design The Access Board and other resources The built and natural environments and inclusivity How to measure physical inclusion
Module 6: Social inclusion: administrative practices	Mission, vision, and values Planning and involvement of people with disabilities Administrative and ground-level support for inclusion Staff hiring, training, and evaluation Inclusion point of contact Marketing and promotion, including web page design Communication in alternative formats Policies and procedures (policy on personal assistants, use of service animals, etc.)
Module 7: Social inclusion: program practices	Registration and needs assessment Supports Additional staff or volunteers Peer training or orientation Positive behavioral supports Accommodations Adapted equipment Activity adaptations (e.g., skills, rules, space, goal structure, team formation) Task analysis Partial participation Implementation and monitoring and evaluating supports and accommodations
Module 8: Putting it into action	Completing an assessment at a recreation agency Reporting results to the Inclusive Recreation Resource Center for the online database
Module 9: Networking, partnerships, and collaboration	Benefits of partnerships and collaboration How to identify potential partnerships that are win–win How to form productive partnerships; skills needed for collaboration and partnering Resources available to partnerships Final exam to become a Certified Inclusivity Assessor (CIA)

Reprinted, by permission, from L. Anderson, 2011, *IAT manual* (Cortland, NY: SUNY Cortland), 5-6.

embraces the differences we have, but recognizes that those same differences have provided different levels of privilege, dominance, access, and power. Diversity, then, must also embrace the active pursuit of social justice and equity. Diversity, when it works, has many benefits to society, communities, and individuals.

If communities and agencies have an inclusive philosophy and use best practices in inclusion, then diversity has an opportunity to flourish. In other words, inclusion is a process that can lead to the outcome of diversity. Thus, 21st-century leaders must know how to foster inclusion at all levels (micro, meso, and macro) to help achieve the promise of diversity. Leaders must develop not only competencies in facilitating inclusion, but also cultural competence. Leaders can help society develop a new norm in which the mainstream is a wide stream and there is room for everyone to play wherever they choose.

Questions for Reflection and Discussion

1. What are the benefits of diversity to you, your chosen profession, and your community?

2. To foster diversity, how can you facilitate inclusive services as a future leader? How about inclusive environments?

3. What level of cultural competence are you at as a leader? How can you deepen your cultural competence? How can you improve the cultural competence of your community?

4. How can you use the inclusion lens to understand the systemic values, practices, and attitudes of your community? Who is included and invited? Who isn't included, and why?

Key Terms and Definitions

ableism—A form of discrimination against people with disabilities or other functional differences.

advocacy—Speaking, writing, or acting on behalf of the perceived interests of a disadvantaged person or a group without conflict of interest.

ageism—A form of discrimination based on chronological age, in which age alone is used to determine people's roles and capabilities.

classism—The systematic oppression of subordinated groups (people without endowed or acquired economic power, social influence, and privilege) who work for wages for the dominant group (those who have access to control of the necessary resources by which other people make their living).

cultural competence—A set of congruent behaviors, attitudes, and policies that come together in a system or agency or among professionals and enables people to work effectively in a cross-cultural context.

culture—Integrated patterns of human behavior that include thoughts, communication, actions, customs, beliefs, values, and institutions of social groups.

discrimination—Using power to act on prejudice; treating someone differently (and often negatively) because of that person's membership in a group.

diversity—The collective mix of humans who interact positively and equitably in a social sphere, all of whom vary on a continuum across salient dimensions such as race, ethnicity, age, gender, ability, sexual orientation, class, and spiritual beliefs. Diversity honors and embraces differences, but recognizes that those same differences have provided levels of privilege, dominance, access, and power that demands the active pursuit of social justice and equity.

ethnicity—Shared cultural practices, perspectives, and distinctions that set one group of people apart from another.

ethnocentrism—The belief that one's own culture is superior to other cultures or ethnicities.

gender—The culturally specific set of characteristics that identifies the social behavior of women and men and the relationships between them.

gender discrimination, or **sexism**—Prejudice, stereotyping, and discrimination directed against people on the basis of their sex or gender; it includes the belief that one sex is superior to the other.

gender identity—The internal personal sense of being a man or a woman or a boy or a girl.

heterosexism—The belief that heterosexuality is the only natural sexuality and that it is inherently healthier than, or superior to, other types of sexuality.

inclusion—A process that welcomes people of all kinds and variations into neighborhoods, work and play spaces, and communities, and fosters a sense of belonging.

intersectionality—A theory that seeks to examine the ways socially and culturally constructed categories interact on multiple levels to manifest themselves as inequality in society.

Islamophobia—The irrational fear of people who are Muslim based on prejudice, stereotyping, and discrimination.

ism—An oppressive and systemic belief system about a group (e.g., sexism, racism, ageism).

prejudice—The act of prejudging, or making a judgment (usually negative), about a person based on that person's group membership without real knowledge of the person; it is often based on stereotype.

race—Groups of people who have similarities in biological traits deemed by society to be socially significant, meaning that they are treated differently because of them.

racism—The systematic practice of denying people access to rights, representation, or resources based on racial differences.

sexual orientation—One who is emotionally or physically attracted to (or both); the direction of one's enduring attraction.

social model of disability—A model in which ability level is seen as a variation in the human condition and a function of the environment as much as it is the impairment or disability a person may have.

stereotypes—Generalizations made about the characteristics of all members of a group based on an image, often wrong, about what people in that group are like.

universal design—The concept of creating environments, services, and products that are usable by as many people as possible regardless of age, ability, culture, or circumstance.

white privilege—The idea that people who are of European descent have access to privilege and power just because of their race, rather than because of anything they have or haven't done; other groups are denied that privilege.

Bibliography

Allison, M., & Schneider, I. (2008). *Diversity and the recreation profession: Organizational perspectives.* State College, PA: Venture.

Anderson, L. (2012). Inclusivity: It's not just about pool lifts. *World Water Park Magazine, 11* (5), 42-44.

Anderson, L., & Heyne, L. (2012). *Therapeutic recreation practice: A strengths approach.* State College, PA: Venture.

Anderson, L., & Kress, C. (2003). *Inclusion: Strategies for including people with disabilities in parks and recreation opportunities.* State College, PA: Venture.

Anderson, L., Penney McGee, L., & Wilkins, V. (2011). *The Inclusivity Assessment Tool and user manual.* Cortland, NY: The Inclusive Recreation Resource Center.

Anderson, L., Schlein, S., McAvoy, L., Lais, G., & Seligman, D. (1997). Creating positive change through an integrated outdoor adventure program. *Therapeutic Recreation Journal, 31* (4), 214-229.

Anti-Defamation League. (2007). *Guidelines for achieving bias-free communication.* Washington, DC: Anti-Defamation League.

Bell, J., & Hartmann, D. (2007). Diversity in everyday discourse: The cultural ambiguities and consequences of "Happy Talk." *American Sociological Review, 72,* 895-914.

Castania, K. (2003). *The evolving language of diversity.* Ithaca, NY: Cornell University.

Center for Universal Design. (2010). About UD. Retrieved from www.design.ncsu.edu/cud/about_ud/about_ud.htm

City of Ottawa Equity and Inclusion Lens: http://ottawa.ca/en/city-hall/get-know-your-city/statistics-and-economic-profile/equity-and-inclusion-lens

Coffey, G. (2012, April). *The inclusion paradigm: The key to organizational performance.* Presented at HR & EEO in the Federal Workplace Conference, Washington, D.C.

Crenshaw, K. (2009). *A primer on intersectionality.* New York: Columbia Law School.

Cross, T. (1988). Cultural competence continuum. *Focal Point* (Fall issue), pp. 1-4.

Cross, T.L., Bazron, B.J., Isaacs, M.R., & Dennis, K.W. (1989). *Towards a culturally competent system of care: A monograph on effective services for minority children who are severely emotionally disturbed.* Washington, DC: Georgetown University Center for Child Health and Mental Health Policy, CASSP Technical Assistance Center.

Dattilo, J. (2002). *Inclusive leisure services: Responding to the rights of people with disabilities.* State College, PA: Venture.

Dawson, D. (2008). Social class and leisure provision. In M. Allison & I. Schneider (Eds.), *Diversity and the recreation profession: Organizational perspectives.* State College, PA: Venture.

Deegan, P. (2006). Foreword. In C. Rapp & R. Goscha, *The strengths model: Case management with people with psychiatric disabilities* (2nd ed.). New York: Oxford University Press.

Disability Is Natural: www.disabilityisnatural.com

Diversity Research Lab at the University of Illinois: www.diversitylab.uiuc.edu

Egale. (2012). Diversity = possibility. Retrieved from http://gsanetwork.ca/sites/default/files/resources/Terms___Concepts/MyGSA_ON_Resource_Kit-08_TermsandConcepts_6.pdf

Federation of Canadian Municipalities. (2004). *Increasing women's participation in municipal decision-making: Resource kit.* Ottawa, ON: Federation of Canadian Municipalities.

Florida, R. (2012). *The rise of the creative class revisited: 10th anniversary edition.* New York: Basic Books.

Floyd, M., & Nicholas, L. (2008). Trends and research on race, ethnicity, and leisure: Implications for management. In M. Allison & I. Schneider (Eds.), *Diversity and the recreation profession: Organizational perspectives.* State College, PA: Venture.

Freysinger, V. (2008). Acting our age: The relationship between leisure and age. In M. Allison & I. Schneider (Eds.), *Diversity and the recreation profession: Organizational perspectives.* State College, PA: Venture.

Gender Equity Resource Center. (2012). Definitions. Berkeley, CA: Gender Equity Resource Center. Retrieved from http://geneq.berkeley.edu/lgbt_resources_definiton_of_terms.

Gay & Lesbian Alliance Against Defamation. (2010). *Media reference guide: Words and images matter.* New York: Author.

Harper, D. (2012). *Online etymology dictionary.* Retrieved from www.etymonline.com/ index.php?term=diversity.

Health Canada (2002). *An inclusion lens: Workbook for looking at social and economic exclusion and inclusion.* Halifax, NS: Population and Public Health Branch, Health Canada.

Heyne, L., Schleien, S.J., & McAvoy, L. (1993). *Making friends: Using recreation activities to promote friendship between children with and without disabilities.* Minneapolis: Institute on Community Integration, University of Minnesota.

Howard, G. (1993). *Whites in multicultural education: Rethinking our role.* Gary Howard Equity Institutes. Retreived from www.ghequityinstitute.com/writings/writings.html.

Howard, G. (1999). *We can't teach what we don't know: White teachers, multiracial schools.* New York: Columbia University Teachers College Press.

I am Norm: www.iamnorm.org

Inclusive Recreation Resource Center: www.inclusiverec.org

Institute of Medicine. (2007). *The future of disability in America.* Washington, DC: The National Academies Press.

International Longevity Center. (2006). *Ageism in America.* New York: International Longevity Center—USA.

It Gets Better: www.itgetsbetter.org

IWK Health Center. (2012). *Diversity and the inclusion lens tool.* Retrieved from http://iwk.nshealth.ca/sites/default/files/Lens_Tool_Bookmark%20(1).pdf

Keil, M., Amershi, B., Holmes, S., Jablonski, H., Erika Lüthi, E., Matoba, K., Plett, A., & von Unruh, K. (2007). *Training manual for diversity management.* Brussels, Belguim: European Commission. Retrieved from http://ec.europa.eu/social.

King, M., Sims., A., & Osher, D. (2007). *How is cultural competence integrated into education?* Retrieved from Center for Effective Collaboration & Practice, http://cecp.air.org/cultural/Q_integrated.htm#def.

Klein, J. (1993). *Avoiding sexist language.* Retrieved from www.hamilton.edu/writing/writing-resources/avoiding-sexist-language.

Koppelman, K., & Goodhart, R.L. (2008). Understanding human differences: Multicultural education for a diverse America. Boston: Pearson.

Loden, M. (2012). *Primary and secondary dimensions of diversity.* Retrieved from www.loden.com/Site/Dimensions.html.

Loden, M., & Rosener, J. (1990). *Workforce America: Managing employee diversity as a vital resource.* New York: McGraw-Hill.

Mak, J. (2002). *What is cultural competence.* Diversity and Human Rights Commission. Retrieved from http://peer.hdwg.org/sites/default/files/T%20%20Cross%20Model%20Information_0.pdf.

McIntosh, P. (1988). *White privilege: Unpacking the invisible knapsack.* Wellesley, MA: Wellesley College Center for Research on Women.

Merriam-Webster Dictionary. (2012). Definition of diversity. Retrieved from www.merriam-webster.com/dictionary/diversity.

Mirrors of Privilege, Making Whiteness Visible: http://world-trust.org/mirrors-of-privilege-making-whiteness-visible

National Center for Cultural Competence: http://nccc.georgetown.edu

Oregon Office of Equity and Inclusion. (2012). Diversity. Retrieved from http://cms.oregon.egov.com.

Phillips, K., Liljenquist, K., & Neale, N. (2009). Is the pain worth the gain? The advantages and liabilities of agreeing with socially distinct newcomers. *Personality and Social Psychology Bulletin 35*, 336-350.

Rioux, M, & Carbert, A. (2003). Human rights and disability: The international context. *Journal of Developmental Disabilities, 10* (2), 1-14.

Schleien, S.J., Ray, M.T., & Green, F.P. (1997). *Community recreation and people with disabilities: Strategies for inclusion* (2nd ed.). Baltimore: Paul H. Brookes.

Scott, L., & Leonhardt, D. (2005, May 15). Shadowly lines that still divide. *The New York Times.*

Smith, D. (2009). *Diversity's promise for higher education.* Baltimore: John Hopkins University Press.

Snow, K. (2009). *A few words about people first language.* Disability is Natural. Retrieved from www.disabilityis-natural.com.

Snow, K. (2012). *Mainstreaming, integration, inclusion: Is there a difference.* Disability is Natural. Retrieved from www.disabilityisnatural.com.

Statistics Canada. (2010). Demographic change. Retrieved from www.statcan.gc.ca/pub/82-229-x/2009001/demo/int1-eng.htm.

Stop Bullying: www.stopbullying.gov

Tapia, A. (2010). Canada's open arms immigration policy: A stark contrast with US and Western Europe. The Inclusion Paradox. Retrieved from http://inclusionparadox.com/open-arms-immigration-policy-canada-poised-to-benefit-from-increasingly-diverse-and-foreign-born-population.

Thomas, R.R. (1996). *Redefining diversity.* New York: American Management Association.

United Nations. (2008). *Convention on the rights of persons with disabilities and optional protocols.* New York: United Nations.

United Nations. (2010). *Discrimination curriculum.* Retrieved from http://cyberschoolbus.un.org/discrim/race.asp#B.

Unzueta, M.M., Knowles, E.D., & Ho, G.C. (2012). Diversity is what you want it to be: How social dominance motives affect construals of diversity. *Psychological Science, 23*, 303-309.

U.S. Census Bureau. (2010). *Overview of race and Hispanic origin: 2010.* Washington, DC: U.S. Census Bureau.

Venter, J.C., Adams, M.D., Myers, E.W., Li, P.W., Mural, R.J., et al. (2001). The sequence of the human genome. *Science, 291*, 1304-1351.

Wallman, B., Evinger, S., & Schechter, S. (2000). Measuring our nation's diversity: Developing a common language for data on race/ethnicity. *American Journal of Public Health, 90* (11): 1704-1708.

Whitney, L. (2012). 2011 ends with almost 6 billion mobile phone subscriptions. *CNET.* Retrieved from http://news.cnet.com/8301-1023_3-57352095-93/2011-ends-with-almost-6-billion-mobile-phone-subscriptions.

Wilkins, V. (2012). Communicating humanness: Attitudes and language. *Social Advocacy and Systems Change Journal, 3* (1), 38-43.

Williams, B. (2001). Accomplishing cross cultural competence in youth development programs. *Journal of Extension, 39* (6), 1-7.

World Health Organization. (2003). *International Classification of Functioning, Disability, and Health Version 2.1a.* Retrieved from www.who.int/classifications/icf/site/checklist/icf-checklist.pdf.

Chapter **6**

Leadership Styles and Ethics

Mary Breunig

" *Action indeed is the sole medium of expression for ethics.* "

—Jane Addams

Jenna was working her second summer at Camp Happy Trails. She was enthusiastic about her new job as the head of the counselor-in-training (CIT) program. This position was one of some notoriety given that Jenna would be working with older, presumably more mature kids as both a counselor and a member of the camp administration, and she would be training these 17-year-old CIT members to be future counselors at Camp Happy Trails. Jenna had earned this position as a result of her previous years' successes at Happy Trails, where she demonstrated exceptional leadership capacities and sound decision making in her role as camp counselor and water ski instructor.

As was the tradition at the start of the camp season, all of the counselors, including the CIT members, arrived at camp for leadership training one week in advance of the arrival of the campers. Throughout this week, counselors were introduced to the camp mission and vision, engaged in team-building activities, learned about leadership theories and decision-making models, and prepared the camp for the campers' arrival (e.g., cleared brush and put in the docks). At the end of that week of work and fun, there was a big celebration party involving a large meal and music. After the camp directors had retired for the night, the counselors brought out beer and wine and continued with the celebration. Jenna wanted to have a beer herself but believed this would be poor role modeling for her underage CIT members. One of them approached her partway into the night asking if she could have a beer, stating that one of the other CIT members was already drinking. Jenna was surprised by the question but even more surprised by the news that one of the 17-year-old girls was drinking beer.

Jenna had to make a quick decision about what to do and how to respond to this turn of events. She wondered what would be in the best interest of the girls. Was there a hard-and-fast camp policy about this? What was her role as the girls' supervisor? She had to consider how to best approach this situation to encourage the girls to be both honest with her and trust her. She had to think about the group, the need for ongoing positive dynamics in deciding what to do, and how to communicate with not only the girls but also the counselors and staff as a whole. She had to think about what she had (or had not) already communicated about expectations. Were there possible legal implications to this decision? Jenna began to think back to her past experiences in considering her next steps. She also thought back to her outdoor recreation courses and the decision-making models and methods she could employ to help inform this decision.

Jenna removed herself from the group for a short period of time as she contemplated how to proceed and integrate her past experiential and theoretical knowledge to this case.

Learning Outcomes

At the conclusion of this chapter, students will be able to:

▶ Describe select leadership theories and styles.
▶ Discuss ethical theories and the distinction between an ethic of justice and an ethic of care.
▶ Explain decision-making frameworks and methods.
▶ Outline a model for ethical decision making.

Jenna's quandary raises some interesting considerations regarding leadership and decision making. This chapter presents some foundational knowledge about leadership theories, styles, ethics, and decision making that will help burgeoning recreation and leisure services leaders determine what to do when faced with challenging leadership situations such as the one in the opening scenario.

Leadership Theories

Attempting to define leadership is a relatively recent academic activity, although the phenomenon of leadership has been ever present throughout the history of human relationships (Stogdill, 1974). Early definitions of leadership and leadership theories were based on current meanings and interests, many of which have been applied to our present situations (Martin et al., 2006).

In 1939 a group of researchers led by psychologist Kurt Lewin set out to identify styles of leadership. They concluded that most leadership styles, at least at that time, could be categorized as authoritarian, democratic, or laissez-faire. Authoritarian leaders, also known as autocratic leaders, provide clear expectations of what needs to be done, when it should be done, and how it should be done. This leadership style also has a clear division between the leader and the followers. Authoritarian leaders make decisions independently with little or no input from the rest of the group, and decision making is thus often less creative under authoritarian leadership (Lewin, Lippit, & White, 1939).

Lewin's study found that participative leadership, also known as democratic leadership, is generally the most effective leadership style. Democratic leaders offer guidance to group members, but they also participate in the group and allow input from other group members.

Participative leaders encourage group members to be involved in decisions, but they retain the final say over the decision-making process. A laissez-faire, or delegative, leader provides little or no guidance to group members; decision making is in the hands of the group members.

Lewin's theory of leadership remains relevant today, although a contemporary application of this theory should involve close attention to context, including the leadership site, individuals, the leadership goal, the group composition, and leader epistemology (more will be said about this later in this chapter). For example, authoritarian leadership is best applied when there is little time for group decision making or when the leader is the most knowledgeable member of the group. The delegative, or laissez-faire, style can be effective when group members have a lot of expertise.

The next generation of leadership theories, often referred to as "early leadership theories" included trait, behavioral, and situational perspectives on leadership. **Trait theories** focus on the capacities, talents, and physical characteristics of the leader. An early trait theory focusing on people who occupied significant positions that affected society in important ways was referred to as the great man theory. Numerous trait studies tried to identify the qualities or traits that defined leadership and included such factors as age, height, weight, physique, health, appearance, fluency of speech, intelligence, scholarship, judgment and decision, dominance, self-confidence, mood, optimism, social and economic status, social skills, popularity and prestige, cooperation, and task-related characteristics (Stogdill, 1974). Charismatic (sometimes referred to as heroic) leadership is rooted in trait theory and involves energizing people and envisioning solutions specifically during times of crisis or change. More contemporarily, Sashkin (1989) concluded that to understand leadership, one must go beyond a consideration of personal characteristics and examine behaviors and situations. Starting in the mid-twentieth century, behaviorists focused on observable phenomena. Gardner (1990) argued that most leadership behaviors are learned and are not characteristics with which people are born. Researchers at Ohio State University and the University of Michigan conducted studies to identify the behavioral characteristics of leaders that appeared to be related to measures of performance. The study results identified two dimensions of leadership: consideration (exhibited by people-oriented behavioral leaders) and initiating structure (exhibited by task-oriented leaders).

Situational theories entered the leadership theory literature in the 1960s, further expanding on the elements of task and relationship. These theories assert that each situation requires that the leader adjust her style and behavior to best fit the circumstances, including the task and the social–emotional needs of the group. In 1967 Fiedler proposed the **contingency leadership theory**, which states that any leader has a primary style that is either more task oriented or more relationship oriented and that determining the task or relationship orientation of a circumstance or group will determine the best leader fit.

Aparna Rajagopal-Durbin is a field instructor and the diversity and inclusion manager at the National Outdoor Leadership School (NOLS), an experiential wilderness education program that uses the outdoors as a classroom to teach leadership, outdoor skills, and environmental ethics.

An industry conceived and historically dominated by the privileged, wilderness education in the United States is seeing more racial, ethnic, and socioeconomic diversity in its participants as demographics shift. At NOLS, more Americans of color are attending courses than ever before. Along with this diversity come varying values, beliefs, communication styles, expectations, abilities, needs, and perceptions.

In more traditional classroom settings, less conflict arises from this diversity because students spend a limited amount of time with their peers and teachers and return to their homes or dorms at the end of the day. But on a NOLS course, diverse groups spend extended periods of time together—24 hours a day, seven days a week, for weeks at a stretch. They physically exert themselves over long days, sleep next to each other, cook and eat meals together, and work together on teams to make decisions that have real and immediate consequences. Students who are already outside their comfort zones on day one because they are "different" eventually find themselves pushed to the "red zone"—in which their only instinct is fight or flight. Whereas the real learning on NOLS courses happens when students are outside their physical comfort zones, no learning happens when students are pushed so far outside their social comfort zone by their peers' behavior that all they can think about is leaving.

As more of these "inclusion incidents" occurred, NOLS' largely white, economically and socially privileged faculty were feeling less and less equipped to provide positive experiences for students so unlike themselves. The result was that many nontraditional students from diverse backgrounds were feeling like outsiders, which resulted in bad behavior, lack of motivation, and ultimately, separation from NOLS courses because they did not believe that their instructors could meet their needs.

Realizing that the cultural competency of NOLS faculty was not keeping pace with the growing diversity of its students, NOLS hired diversity consultants in 2005 to develop staff training. This training was geared toward a traditional office setting, not extended wilderness expeditions. "It turns out that

Photo courtesy of Janeen Hutchins.

you just can't fit the square peg of corporate diversity training into the round hole of experiential outdoor education," says Aparna. "So it was no surprise that NOLS staff left these trainings feeling like they had just jumped through yet another administrative hoop. Diversity training—Check."

Fast forward to today. With the benefit of input from of NOLS' experienced faculty, Aparna has developed an engaging cultural competency workshop for outdoor educators to help them learn how to be more inclusive in the field and how to teach students to be inclusive of each other. "Our mantra is, Diversity is what we are, inclusion is what we do, and cultural competency is why we need to do it," says Aparna.

NOLS defines cultural competency as the ability to interact effectively across various dimensions of diversity; in other words, the ability to "flex" with each other's differences. Cultural competency requires three things: (1) self-awareness, or an understanding of your own culture, assumptions, values, styles, biases, attitudes, and privilege; (2) "other" awareness, or an understanding of others' cultures, assumptions, values, styles, biases, attitudes, and privilege (or lack thereof) without judging them; and (3) an understanding of your impact on others and the ability to adopt a situationally appropriate style for greater inclusion and effectiveness, whether in communication, decision making, or any other aspect of outdoor education.

Participants in the NOLS cultural competency seminar typically spend two days standing up, running around, dancing, talking, playing, and doing a little bit of sitting and listening to a cadre of facilitators

continued

Best Practices From the Field *(continued)*

who discuss the language of diversity and inclusion, how to foster inclusion in the outdoors, and how to respond to inclusion-related conflict in the field. Many participants have transformative experiences at these seminars as they come to terms with their own privilege and power and how it can affect students, often unintentionally. Participants leave with a list of activities they can facilitate with students and hopefully a deeper understanding of what it takes to be truly inclusive in the outdoor education industry.

"This is not to say that NOLS has done it right," acknowledges Aparna. "NOLS isn't just an experiential education institution, but an experiential learning institution, which means we are constantly learning from our mistakes. And in the world of cultural competency, we will always have more work to do."

Notwithstanding the fact that NOLS continues to discover areas in which it can improve in the realm of cultural competency and inclusion, its cultural competency seminars are a great example of a best practice of leadership in recreation and leisure services for the 21st century.

Hersey and Blanchard's (1982) research on situational leadership is based on the premise that most leader activities can be classified into either task or relationship dimensions. About one decade after Fiedler, Hersey and Blanchard forwarded a **situational leadership theory**, in which they stated that leaders and leader styles are more flexible than Fiedler suggested. They maintained that leaders should change their behavior as followers' maturity increases. Hersey and Blanchard identified four levels of leader maturity (M1 through M4):

▶ M1 (low)—Leaders generally lack the specific skills required for the job at hand and are unable and unwilling to do or to take responsibility for this job or task.

▶ M2—Leaders are still unable to take on responsibility for the task being done; however, they are willing to work at the task.

▶ M3—Leaders are experienced and able to do the task but lack the confidence to take on responsibility.

▶ M4 (high)—Leaders are experienced at the task and comfortable with their own ability to do it well. They are able and willing to not only do the task, but also take responsibility for the task.

Maturity levels are also task specific. A person might be generally skilled, confident, and motivated in his overall work, but might have a maturity level of M2 when asked to perform a task requiring skills he doesn't possess. For example, Jenna's capacities as a camp water ski instructor and her commitment to that work do not necessarily translate into having the administrative capacities or previous experiences to exercise sound judgment related to the conundrum in the opening scenario.

Hersey, Blanchard, and Johnson (1996) further developed the situational theory by identifying and categorizing group readiness and its impact on leadership. Readiness level is defined in terms of three components: the group's ability, motivation, and prior experience. The four levels of group readiness are as follows:

▶ R1 (low)—Members are unable and unwilling to do a task or feel insecure about it.

▶ R2 (moderate)—Members are unable to do the task, but willing to try and confident about trying.

▶ R3 (moderate)—Members are able to do the task, but unwilling to try or insecure about trying.

▶ R4 (high)—Members are able and willing to do the task and feel confident about it.

The behavior of the leader is thus determined by both the readiness level of the group and the group's orientation to the dimensions of task and relationship. Figure 6.1 illustrates this. The key assumption of the situational model of leadership is that leaders are both able and willing to adapt their leadership approach to the group's situation.

In terms of the opening scenario, Jenna's decision about how to proceed with her leadership challenge will thus be influenced by the fact that it was only the first week of her interaction with the new CIT group, and group readiness and capacity were thus low.

When researchers and theorists focus on a broader, more philosophical conception of leadership based on **values**, morals, culture, inspiration, motivation, needs, wants, influence, and power, for

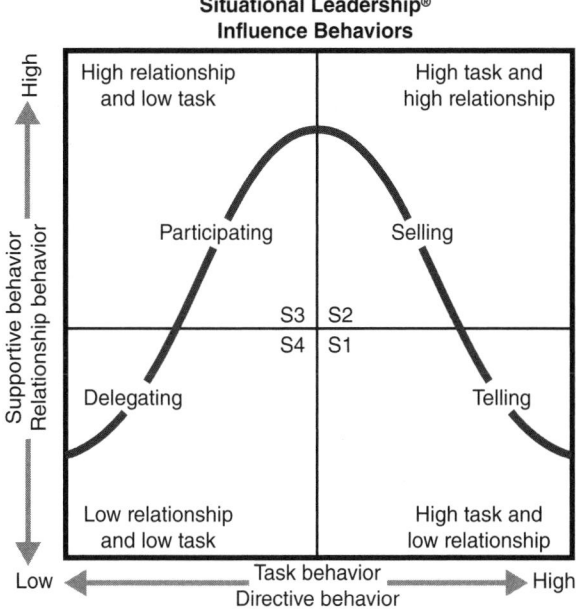

Figure 6.1 Situational leadership model.

example, a shift to values-based leadership theories occurred. In the late 1980s and early 1990s, values-based theories began to appear in the leadership literature (Bass, 1990). Values-based leadership theorists believed that something unique about leadership transcended the situation and remained constant despite the contingencies. The primary leadership role is integrating the values of all followers into programs and actions that facilitate the development of both the leader and the follower (Bass, 1990).

One contemporary form of values-based leadership can be found in Greenleaf's (1977) servant leadership theory. In *Servant Leadership*, Greenleaf describes how service, first and foremost, qualifies one for leadership and that leading as an act of service is the distinctive nature of true leaders. He focused his discussion of leadership on an explicitly moral dimension, defining servant leadership as the natural feeling that one first wants to serve and focusing on the care taken by the servant to make sure other people's highest-priority needs are being met. Burns (1978) referred to the transformational potential of this form of leadership, one that must incorporate a central core of moral values. Leaders address the needs, wants, and values of their followers (and their own) and, therefore, serve as an independent force in changing the makeup of followers' values.

Much of the leadership practice of recreation and leisure professionals is servant based. In this field, the focus is on an ethic of care. A recreational specialist at a local Boys and Girls Club, for example, plays an active role in working with youth who may come from a socioeconomic background different from that of the leaders or facilitators. Much of the time spent with youth involves understanding what brings them to the center and determining how best to care for and serve them in a safe physical and psychological space. Delivering "canned" programs rarely works when trying to be contextually responsive and serve others' interests and needs. Recreation professionals try to create context-specific programs based on group needs to serve a variety of program participants. A Boys and Girls Club program with male youth at risk may include some programming for active or group sport participation but may start with some group games so participants can first get to know each other, to set a positive, less competitive tone.

Another contemporary view of leadership is **wisdom-led leadership,** which promotes a new way of understanding the world and the development of an awareness of how to synthesize and integrate what Branson (2009) referred to as a "seemingly chaotic world." According to Branson, in our rationally dominated world, our consciousness has been trained to objectify, externalize, and specialize leadership and decision making by striving to limit any subjective influence. "This is a kind of dichotomized consciousness, a consciousness associated with either/or, good/bad, right/wrong, true/false type perspectives, which cannot lead to synthesis and integration" (Branson, 2009, p. 26). Branson calls for a more actively and holistically involved approach to leadership that involves the subjectivity of the leader and encourages the development of a more global perspective. "This is about enabling the leader to see the world not as divided, separated, and dichotomous but as harmonious, united, and interdependent" (Branson, 2009, p. 27) and about seeing the world through "vision logic" (Foucault) or "centaur consciousness" (Heidegger), in which the body and mind, the objective and the subjective, are reunited to create a more integrated self but also, ultimately, to create a better world (Branson, 2009).

The Boys and Girls Club program facilitator would encourage participants to expand their ways of knowing and viewing the world beyond their own communities and beyond previous stereotypes held about other youth involved in the program. The leader or facilitator would discourage fierce competition, for example, by nurturing collaboration and full group participation. Likely, a group game or sport activity would include the randomized assignment of group members rather than the outdated and potentially dichotomizing strategy of picking team leaders based on popularity and then having those leaders choose their teams based on traditional notions of strong and good players.

Coaching-based leadership is another contemporary approach to leadership. Generally, coaching is about establishing a helping relationship between the coach and the person or group with whom the coach is engaged. The coach is a facilitator whose aim is to help the coachee to learn, as a kind of self-directed learning (Moen & Federici, 2012). This leadership approach is influenced by the field of humanistic psychology, which emphasizes the importance of listening to the subjective beliefs of the client (Kahn, 1996). Attention to the coachee's world is therefore essential in coaching. The importance of asking the right questions coupled with the ability to listen deeply to what the coachee is saying are two important principles that define the coaching process (Kvalsund, 2005). Powerful questioning and active listening help coachees increase their ability and take responsibility for their own growth and development. The true nature of a coaching relationship is therefore based on mutuality: both parties are equal in the relationship and promote each other's independence while working and learning together (Moen & Federici, 2012).

Coaching can be used with leisure professionals who are developing their leadership practice. For example, senior leaders are often paired with new leaders who shadow them. Take, for example, an adventure course that involves low ropes course elements. The senior leader may frame the initial activities, coaching program participants about their involvement and creating a supportive environment for the participants as the new leader observes. The new leader may then facilitate a subsequent activity with the senior leader observing and taking mental or written notes about aspects of the facilitation that went well and those that require improvement. A coaching session between the senior and new leader may follow the day's activities with the participants. In this way, both participant coaching and leader or facilitator coaching (i.e., mentorship) occur concurrently.

Values and Ethics

Contemporary leadership theories strongly emphasize the importance of values, leader and participant subjectivities, and **ethics** in leadership. This section focuses on ethical decision making and introduces ethical theories, which can help you clarify your own worldview and its influence on your practice.

There are many ways to introduce and frame a discussion of ethics and ethical decision making. This section draws on Starratt's (2010) emphasis on three ethical perspectives, an ethic of justice, an ethic of care, and an ethic of critique. We first explore the concepts of values and ethics and related terminology.

Developing an understanding of values and ethics in the recreation and leisure services field is essential to professional practice given that values and ethics inevitably influence leadership practice. This section will help you better understand your personal values and ethics and how these affect the way you lead, the style or leadership approach you employ, and some of the potential shortcomings and pitfalls that may result.

To better understand values and their influence, leaders need to first understand the lens through which they "know" and "see" the world (Martin et al., 2006). This process is akin to the old adage that you must "Know thyself" before you can authentically engage with or lead others.

Epistemology is the branch of philosophy that studies the nature, sources, and validity of knowledge. Roughly translated, epistemology means "ways of knowing." It seeks to answer such questions as What is true? and How do we know? Epistemology is therefore rooted in an understanding of the sources of truth alongside an understanding of the particular lens through which one views the world and interprets these sources.

Draw a layered circular lens like that shown in figure 6.2. Now consider your upbringing and some of the factors that may have contributed to your view of the world (i.e., your epistemological lens). Include such factors as your home environment, family composition, education, religious belief, sexuality, gender, peer group, and socioeconomic class. Write socially identifying factors from your early years, such as your family composition, in the smallest circle (e.g., two siblings and married, heterosexual parents). Continue to work your way out, writing more present-day life context factors in the more outer rings of the circle. In other words, you are working, or writing, your

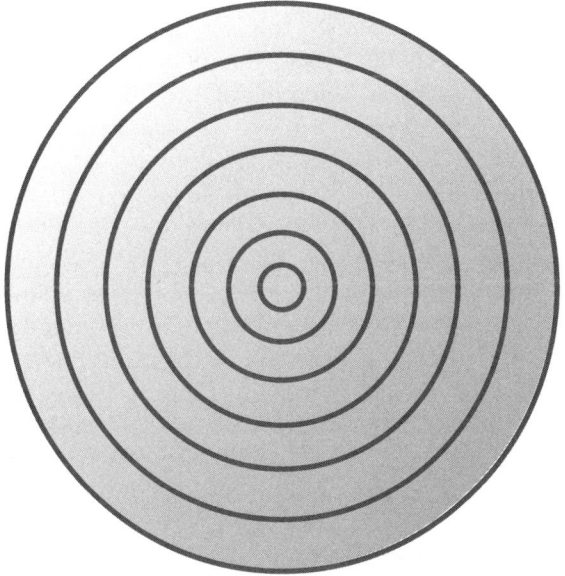

Figure 6.2   Draw a layered circular lens and write down factors that have influenced you from your earliest days (inner rings) to now (outer rings).
Reprinted, by permission, from B. Martin et al., 2006, *Outdoor leadership: Theory and practice* (Champaign, IL: Human Kinetics), 91.

way historically from the most inner circle to the outer rim (roughly speaking, of course, because some events may co-occur).

Identifying your epistemology not only highlights your predominant leadership style tendencies but also your biases, which is a primary consideration in any discussion of ethics.

Let's consider an example of how epistemology influences leadership style and decision making. Write a one-minute response to the leadership challenge presented in the opening scenario, including some consideration of epistemology (i.e., name the biases and partiality that you likely bring to any response you might have to this challenge). Incorporate some mention of how both epistemology and leadership style might influence your response.

Pair with a partner and share your lens. Can you see the role of epistemology in the decision-making process? This exercise provides an example of the role of personal values in decision making. But is a personal values-based decision always an ethical one? Not necessarily. How then might you go about making a decision based on ethics?

The next sections introduce three primary views of leadership: an ethic of justice, an ethic of care, and an ethic of critique.

Ethic of Justice

An **ethic of justice** focuses on societal rules, those reinforced by bureaucratic organizational systems, as the basis for decision making. **Kohlberg's model of moral development** and moral reasoning (see figure 6.3) provides the foundation for this ethic. This model identifies six developmental stages in forming moral reasoning (Kohlberg, 1981). That development moves from the preconventional level, where we see simple negative and positive reinforcement of specific behaviors ("My teacher told me to stay in my seat"; "She says I am a good boy when I stay seated"); to the conventional level, where begins a sense of mutuality ("When I share my toys with my younger brother, my mom hugs me and says I am a good girl") that eventually becomes a large, generalized sense of what is socially approved ("Good girls would never do that"; "That's what bad boys do"); to the postconventional level, where first there is a sense of general rules ("It's wrong to lie") that society lives by and finally a sense that some rules are more important to observe than others (e.g., lying to save someone's life) (Starratt, 2010).

Preconventional level	**Stage 1.** The focus is on punishment and obedience. **Stage 2.** The focus is on satisfying needs, mainly one's own.
Conventional level	**Stage 3.** The focus is on conformity and gaining approval. **Stage 4.** The focus is on authority and fixed rules.
Postconventional level	**Stage 5.** The focus is on the social contract and public interest. **Stage 6.** The focus is on moral principles.

Figure 6.3 Kohlberg's six stages of moral development.
Reprinted, by permission, from B. Martin et al., 2006, *Outdoor leadership: Theory and practice* (Champaign, IL: Human Kinetics), 95.

An ethic of justice operates on the principles of fairness and reciprocity, giving credence to the concept of the *summmum bonum* ("highest good"), which gives ethics a mathematical and logical appearance and moves the discussion beyond the sphere of actual human activity. It has been argued that Kohlberg's model of moral development overemphasizes a hierarchy of moral reasoning (Noddings, 1984).

Ethic of Care

Gilligan (1982) and Noddings (1984), among others, have challenged Kohlberg's research as applying more to males than to females, whose moral reasoning tends to involve a greater concern for relationships and the responsibilities relationships impose. That more relational approach to ethical decision making is often referred to as an ethic of care. An **ethic of care** takes a relationship-oriented approach to moral development. It considers not only relationships but also the effect of decisions over a period of time (Mitten, 1996). Mitten maintained that although this is a feeling mode, it is not necessarily an emotional one. "At the heart of this ethic is the maintenance of the caring relationship" (p. 166). The universal aspect of this ethic is the caring attitude—being able to be cared for and being able to care about others.

Gilligan (1982) argued that men and women differ in moral reasoning; women focus on care and responsibility, whereas men are preoccupied with rights and justice. Neither method of reasoning is superior to the other, but Gilligan suggested that both need to be considered.

In thinking through the key distinguishing factors of these two ethical perspectives, consider the character Jean Valjean in Victor Hugo's novel *Les Misérables*. Valjean was imprisoned for stealing bread for his starving sister and her family and then imprisoned 14 more times for numerous escape attempts.

Studies have shown that adolescent boys and girls address the ethical dilemma presented in Valjean's story in different ways. Gilligan, in her book *In a Different Voice* (1982), highlighted this disparity. She suggested that a boy would locate truth in logic. He would most likely rationally derive a solution to this dilemma in a similar manner to how he would solve a mathematical problem. The preadolescent boy would reason that laws have mistakes and you can't have laws written for every possible scenario, condoning Valjean's imprisonment and claiming that the act of stealing and attempting to escape are simply "wrong." The boy would likely reason at the conventional stage of Kohlberg's scale, relying on social norms and laws as the measure of what is right.

In contrast, Gilligan suggested that a preadolescent girl's response to this dilemma would convey a very different impression of her moral development. When asked whether Valjean should have taken the bread, her reply would mostly likely convey uncertainty. A girl might not consider moral norms or the law but rather the effect that the theft would have on the relationship between Valjean and his family and society. A preadolescent girl may reason that if Valjean steals the bread, he may prevent his sister and her family from being hungry for the day, but he may also end up in jail, and then the family would be in an even more dire situation. She would approach this ethical dilemma not as a mathematical problem to be solved but as a dilemma involving relationships that extend over a period of time. The preadolescent girl's solution might lack moral logic and structure, and Kohlberg's stages of moral development thus might not even apply to her, thus highlighting a limitation of this theory. In fact, if Kohlberg's stages were applied to the girl's view of the issue in this instance, her moral judgments might appear to be a full stage lower in maturity than those of the boy.

These two children see two very different moral problems. Kohlberg's (1981) theory of moral development provides a ready response to the boy's logic but seems to be unable to address the girl's approach to solving this dilemma. Her response appears to lie outside the moral domain. Both of these preadolescents are intelligent and perceptive about life. The disparity lies in the way they think about conflict and choice and in their different modes of moral understanding. Gilligan's discussion suggested some serious limitations to Kohlberg's theory of moral development.

For a leisure professional, Kohlberg's theory of moral development may also present certain limitations, but it may be useful as an initial framework. For example, some leadership decisions may need to be based on the law and social norms. For example, as a summer camp counselor, you may be required to insist that all participants on a canoe outing wear close-toed shoes because the program procedures manual identifies this as a fixed policy. This represents a principle ethic that is nonnegotiable regardless of participant preference. Other decisions may provide participants and you with more agency, moving beyond the self-interest preconventional and law-based conventional stages into the postconventional stage of moral development.

The National Outdoor Leadership School (NOLS) starts its trips with the development of a positive learning environment (PLE) social contract that everyone can agree to uphold. This involves the leader and participants co-negotiating aspects of program participation (e.g., consensual decision making) that they jointly wish to include in their environment and those aspects (e.g., put-downs) they wish to keep out. That said, there may be instances that negate the social contract and lie outside of Kohlberg's theory (e.g., a life-threatening situation that requires a hasty and definitive leader or expert decision).

Ethic of Critique

An ethic of critique requires confronting entrenched assumptions about the presumed legitimacy of the status quo, and may require taking a stance against people who support, even by their own passivity, that status quo (Starratt, 2010). An ethic of critique involves the proactive analysis of a situation and requires leaders to look at their own epistemological leanings in exploring how to approach a situation. Starratt cautions that leaders should not be allowed the luxury of simply identifying ethically questionable practices of injustice, lack of care, or institutional, systemic disadvantaging, but rather, that they should be required to work out practical, short-term, intermediate, and long-term strategies to change those practices into ethically positive practices. The point is not simply to develop ethical critics, but to develop ethical leaders who will actively counteract and transform environments into places that promote just, caring, and critical practice.

For the recreation and leisure professional, an ethic of critique may mean actively questioning aspects of a specific program procedure. Are program policies and procedures fitting for all participants? How does program policy support dominant norms that privilege certain people over others? How might the **hidden curriculum** contained in program manuals and standards marginalize certain people and groups? The hidden curriculum consists of the transmission of norms, values, and beliefs conveyed in a specific context. For example, until recently the Boy Scouts had a zero tolerance policy about homosexuality and did not welcome gay youth. What did the zero tolerance policy communicate to young people about who were included and who were excluded, and what did it communicate about "right" and "wrong"? An ethic of critique provides a proactive foundation from which to question and hopefully reshape certain policies and practices, both overt and hidden, within the recreation and leisure studies profession.

Leisure Leaders

Mo Kappes

MY PREPARATION

- BA in psychology—College of William and Mary, Williamsburg, VA
- MEd in curriculum and instruction with a focus in experiential education—Ferris State University, Big Rapids, MI
- American Canoe Association (ACA) Level 3 tandem and solo canoe; wilderness first aid (WFA); expired wilderness first responder (WFR)

MY CAREER

I am the adviser and experiential educational specialist for a student-run organization at the University of Wisconsin at Madison called Adventure Learning Programs (ALPS). The mission of the organization is to challenge people through adventure-based learning to discover themselves and understand those around them. We provide team-building and high and low ropes course experiences to the campus and surrounding community. There are up to 40 student facilitators in the organization, and we serve over 7,000 students every year.

My primary duties include advising ALPS student coordinators in their leadership of the organization; acting as a liaison between the students and faculty and staff; supporting the students in the continued development and growth of the organization; training student staff; maintaining challenge course industry safety standards; and developing an experiential education curriculum for the organization as well as the campus at large. I am a mentor, a resource, an educator, and a support system to my students as they develop as facilitators, educators, leaders, and thoughtful citizens.

I was introduced to the field of adventure education when I led my first weeklong canoe trip at Camp Manito-wish YMCA in Northern Wisconsin. I loved being "on trail," traveling through the north woods of Wisconsin via canoe—the lifestyle, the serenity, the challenge, the beauty, and most important, the personal growth of myself and my campers. It was amazing what we could accomplish working together to complete the daily tasks

Photo courtesy of Monica Kappes.

of life on the trail, and the growth that occurred when we were challenged by the trail experience—whether it be carrying a canoe, cooking in the rain, or dealing with an annoying tent mate. When the trip was over, my only thought was, How do I do this for the rest of my life? I spent the next 12 years in the field developing my skills as a wilderness trip leader, environmental educator, and facilitator at various organizations throughout the country from wilderness therapy programs to team-building and ropes course programs.

It was 10 years into my journey as a field practitioner that I realized that I wanted to do more than just work with clients. I wanted to educate others to be outdoor leaders and facilitators. So I returned to school and got my master's degree in education. This degree combined with my practical field experience is what got me the job I have today—teaching college students to be facilitators and leaders.

I love my job! I have the opportunity to work with motivated, committed, and eager students who want to learn about adventure education, develop as leaders, grow as individuals, and change the world around them. The only thing missing in the ALPS quiver of offerings is a wilderness trip component, but there is always room to grow!

I am a big proponent of the collaborative leadership model in which everyone works to accomplish tasks and the unique talents of all are valued and used to help the whole. There is no one leader; rather, each person is doing his or her part to get the job done. This philosophy meshes well with my position as adviser as well as with the structure of ALPS. As a student organization, ALPS is run *for* students *by* students. It is truly my job to advise and support the students in where they want to take the organization versus where *I* want it to go. I spend a lot of time collaborating with the student coordinators, the leadership council (composed of coordinators and committee chairs), and the student facilitators to get things done. Everything we do is based on this model—from planning and implementing workshops to developing and expanding our programs. I meet regularly with members of the leadership council as they develop trainings, new forms, marketing strategies, the budget, and so on. It is a wonderful process to be a part of—everyone is growing, including myself, as a leader and as a supportive member of ALPS and the other communities we are part of.

MY ADVICE TO YOU

Get in there and do it! Find a job or internship at an organization or business that is doing the work you are interested in, and work there. Gain real-life experience—you will learn quickly what you love and what you don't, you will make connections in the field, and you will begin to learn about your own philosophy.

Make connections with practitioners in the field and use them as resources. Everyone I have ever met in the field has been more than excited to help others who are interested in exploring it.

Follow your heart—do what you are passionate about.

Take advantage of opportunities. You have one life to live—go out and live it!

I believe that this field is a great place for people to learn more about themselves and those around them. And, with these insights, they can work toward a more compassionate, equitable world.

Decision Making

Within an ethic of justice, decision making is based on a hierarchical structure of moral reasoning. It focuses on the establishment of principles that can be logically applied to any situation. According to this ethic, using principles keeps ethical decision making rational and objective. For example, in relation to the opening scenario, if Jenna were basing her decision on a pure ethic of justice, she would likely turn to the written camp policies and procedures manual to make a decision, likely leading to her telling the CIT that underage drinking by camp staff is against policy. But how then would Jenna approach the CIT who was already drinking, and would Jenna's decision lead to the CIT continuing to drink but doing so privately, which might place her (and the camp) at even greater risk? What other sources of ethics and perspectives and people could Jenna rely on to make the best decision, not just for this singular event, but for the full summer that lies ahead?

The ability to make well-informed decisions from established frameworks is essential to the achievement of program outcomes for both recreation and leisure programs (Martin et al., 2006). Authors have highlighted the distinction between judgment and decision making. Petzoldt and Ringholz (1984) asserted that **judgment** is an informed opinion based on past experience, which suggests that judgment cannot be taught but can be developed. **Decision making**, on the other hand, is the process of choosing the best option from a collection of possible options and can be taught, leading to theory development and decision-making frameworks. This section presents some of those frameworks.

Classical decision-making frameworks, also referred to as maximum utility theories, rational theories, or normative models of decision making offer a starting point for approaching decisions, with a focus on gathering and processing information about expected probabilities and outcomes (Shooter & Furman, 2011). Given that decisions involving outdoor leadership and outdoor leisure pursuits are often constrained by time pressures and incomplete information (e.g., about weather, individual and group needs, and changes in the physical environment), classical decision-making models face considerable challenges in the outdoors (Shooter & Furman, 2011). Thus, alternatives to classical decision-making models have been explored in recent years.

One of these is the dual-process model. Dual-process models are a means to express that two features of human cognitive process exist; one involving a conscious, rational, controlled, deliberative process, and another involving unconscious, automated, intuitive processes (Shooter & Furman, 2011). This shift has brought various issues to the fore, including the role of heuristic biases and traps, intuition, naturalistic decision making, and decision-making methods that are situation dependent.

Heuristics refers to experience-based techniques for problem-solving. Decision makers develop rules of thumb based on past successes and are often attracted to familiar situations and contexts in which these can be applied. Expanding on experience-based decision making, Klein (1998) suggested that expert decision makers use an intuitive process that involves recognition-primed decision making within naturalistic environments that result in fast, accurate, and effective decisions. In other words, expert decision makers use their past experiences and intuition to recognize and inform a given decision, one that is informed by their past experiences and successes. Boyes and O'Hare (2003) introduced and emphasized the importance of context awareness in recognizing key situational factors when making decisions and projecting the decision outcomes. This context awareness, coupled with experience-based decision making, contributes to a leader's capacity to determine what decision-making method may best "fit" any given endeavor or situation.

Situational Methods of Decision Making

The main methods for making decisions are these:

- The *leader decides* without consulting group members.
- A *pros and cons* list gets developed to determine the decision.
- A *consensus* decision may occur if the leader would like the group to come to full agreement about a particular decision.
- A group may strive to achieve *unity*, whereby most group members agree on a course of action but some wish to note their dissent without impeding the group majority.
- A *voting* decision may occur if the leader wants to get input quickly from the group and is not seeking unanimity.

- *Arbitration* may occur if the leader lacks expertise in a certain area or if the group is at a standstill and needs an outside source to be involved in the decision-making process.
- *Flippism* involves leaving a decision to *chance* if the decision is a simple one (e.g., flipping a coin to decide whether to have quick-cook oatmeal or pancakes in the morning).
- If a group is unable to come to consensus or unity, a *compromise* decision may be the best method. In this instance, opposing members work together to formulate a decision that redirects the decision to one that everyone can agree on.
- On some occasions, the decision may be left to an *expert*. The group leader may lack the expertise to make the decision, and an expert in the group may be better informed and able to decide.

It is important to note that the decision-making method employed depends on the situation. It is equally important to note that these categories are more discrete theoretically than they may appear in practice. For example, a leader under a time constraint makes a decision, communicates that decision to the group, and expects the group members to follow that decision. Under a different set of conditions, the leader may ask for group input. Group members may act in a consultative role, whereby the ultimate decision is still made by the leader but that decision is made with the input of the group. Leadership theories, models, and practice thus merge with decision-making frameworks and methods.

Consider the following scenario:

You are one of several facilitators leading group activities with a class of eighth-grade students to help the group form as part of a team-building day at the recreation center where you work. During the opening tag game activity, you observe three girls moving off to the sidelines and audibly giggling and pointing to certain students, mocking them while the group runs around the field. You look toward the other facilitators, and you all shrug your shoulders, gesturing, What should we do? The teacher of the class is meeting in the main office with the program director and is unable to provide context or direction. During the next activity, the group of girls on the sidelines has grown to 12.

Think-pair-share how you would manage this situation? Ask students to first think about how they would manage the situation if they were in the leadership role, writing down some preliminary thoughts. Then have students pair with another member of class to exchange their ideas. Then pair with a group of four and try to determine a response to the leadership challenge based on your collective insights. Be prepared to "share out" your response with the larger class. What leadership style might you employ, and how might you go about deciding how to proceed?

Your ability to respond to scenarios and questions and your overall capacity to make sound (and quick, given the context in which we work) decisions will mature and develop alongside your overall leadership ability. It is important to be attentive to the outcomes of your previous decisions and to try to recognize any patterns that may be developing as a result of your past successes and failures. It is equally important, however, not to become paralyzed by some of the negative outcomes of your past decisions. This form of experience-based judgment will develop as your leadership practice develops.

Two Decision-Making Models

This section presents two decision-making models, an analytic one that is based on some of the early leadership theories and classical decision-making theories, and one for making ethical decisions (figure 6.4). Studying leadership and thinking about ethical matters will help you with decision making and make you a better leader. A theoretical understanding of ethics and ethical models is insufficient. You must put ethical decision making into practice.

Early leadership theories and those rooted in a more linear approach to decision making might consider an analytic model and its stepwise process useful in providing a framework with which to analyze a situation. General questions in an analytic model might include the following: (1) What is the problem? (2) Why is it a problem? (3) When is it a problem? (4) Where is it a problem? and (5) How is it a problem? Consider the opening scenario using this model. Identify the preceding five questions in light of the scenario and propose a solution.

The more contemporary models of leadership, as well as some of the aforementioned limitations of rooting decisions in logic alone, have led to more sophisticated and nuanced models of decisions, including a consideration of the role of values and ethics in decision making. Figure 6.4 is one example of an ethical decision-making model. This model has a great degree of sophistication and analysis of the problem at hand, but that does not necessarily mean that it requires more time; rather, it demands a complete consideration of the

State problem	• Do I have a conflict of interest? • Does this make me uncomfortable?
Check facts	• Some problems disappear on closer examination of the situation. • Other problems change radically.
State specifications	• What are the limits (e.g., laws, policies, or regulations)? • What are the objectives?
List options	• List a minimum of five options. Be imaginative!
Test options	• Submit each option to a series of tests: harm, publicity, defensibility, reversibility, virtue, professional, colleague, organizational.
Make tentative choice	• Based on results of previous steps, did you solve the problem?

Make final choice	• After reviewing steps 1-6, ask:
	    What would make it less likely you will have to make this decision again?
	    What precautions can you take and what supports do you need?
	    What changes can you make to the organization or society?

Figure 6.4 Sample ethical decision-making model.
Adapted, by permission, from M. Davis, 1997, "Developing and using cases to teach practical ethics," *Teaching Philosophy* 20(4): 353-385.

situation, including a consideration of values and ethics. Consider the opening scenario in light of this model and propose a solution. Is your solution the same using the analytic model as when you used the ethical one? What differences, if any, were there? What kinds of scenarios might require the ethics-based model?

Summary

According to Deborah Britzman (2003), "Practice makes practice." Effective leadership comes with practice and more practice. An understanding of your epistemology and leadership tendencies alongside a knowledge and awareness of leadership styles will help you develop your leadership competency. Understanding recreation and leisure services leadership in context is important. How you become a leader and how you lead are important considerations. Understanding your own natural inclination and leadership style will help you begin to develop a leadership ability that is balanced and situation dependent. Your ability as a leader is further enhanced by adopting a flexible approach to leadership that allows you to apply a variety of styles to fit the situations at hand.

Values and ethics define a person. Participants and coleaders look for high standards, clear ethics, and the exercise of appropriate values in leadership. An understanding of some of the ethical principles and theories will help you develop these high standards and make ethical decisions. It is good to know that there are policies and procedures in place to help you with this process. It is equally important to know that these represent only part of the equation. You will need to examine your own values and beliefs and superimpose those on the principle ethicsc that are already in place.

You are involved not only in developing your own individual leadership practice but also in establishing recreation and leisure services as a profession. Your individual efforts and attention to ethical matters will contribute to developing the recreation and leisure profession.

Questions for Reflection and Discussion

1. What characteristics and traits contribute to successful leadership?
2. What is situational leadership theory, and in what leadership context might it be useful?
3. List two contemporary leadership styles and identify a leadership setting in which each might be applied.
4. What is the role of values in leadership?
5. Can a leader be unbiased? What are some strategies for managing leader biases?
6. Under what circumstances as a leader might you apply an ethic of care to a leadership challenge you are facing?
7. What is your personal leadership motto?

Key Terms and Definitions

coaching-based leadership—A contemporary approach to leadership. The leader serves as coach and mentor rather than in a directive manner.

contingency leadership theory—A theory that states that leaders are motivated from either a task orientation or a relationship orientation.

decision making—The process of choosing the best option from a collection of possible options.

epistemology—The branch of philosophy that studies the nature, sources, and validity of knowledge. Roughly translated, epistemology means "ways of knowing."

ethic of care—An ethic based on relationships.

ethic of justice—An ethic that operates on the principles of fairness and reciprocity, giving credence to the summum bonum, which gives ethics a mathematical and logical appearance and moves the discussion beyond the sphere of actual human activity.

ethics—The study of both moral values and conduct.

hidden curriculum—The transmission of norms, values, and beliefs in a specific context that are not explicitly communicated and are thus hidden.

judgment—An informed opinion based on past experience. It cannot be taught but can be developed.

Kohlberg's model of moral development— A measure of moral development that identifies six developmental stages in forming moral reasoning (see figure 6.3).

principle ethics—Ethics guided by a proactively determined set of rules, often determined by a governing professional organization or by the current professional standards of behavior.

situational leadership theory—A theory that takes into account the leader, the followers, and the situation.

trait theories—Theories that assume that certain physical and psychological characteristics predispose some people to leadership.

values—Beliefs (as opposed to facts) that affect how one thinks, judges, feels, and acts.

wisdom-led leadership—A leadership theory and practice that emphasizes the importance of "wisdom" to guide the actions of leaders.

Bibliography

Action Wheel Leadership. Leadership Theories: www.action-wheel.com/leadership-theories.html

Bass, B.M. (1990). From transactional to transformational leadership: Learning to share the vision. *Organizational Dynamics,* (Winter): 19-31.

Boyes, M.A., & O'Hare, D. (2003). Between safety and risk: A model for outdoor adventure decision-making. *Journal of Adventure Education and Outdoor Learning, 3* (1), 63-75.

Branson, C.M. (2009). Leadership for an age of wisdom. *Studies in Educational Leadership 9*, 17-33.

Britzman, D. (2003). *Practice makes practice: A critical study of learning to teach* (2nd ed.). Albany: State University of New York Press.

Burns, J.M. (1978). *Leadership.* New York: Harper & Row.

Center for Ethical Deliberation (University of Northern Colorado, Institute of Professional Ethics): James M. DuBois, Facilitating Case Discussions https://docs.google.com/viewer?a=v&pid=sites&srcid=bmFycmF0aXZlYmlvZXRoaoaW NzLmNvbXxlbWhyfGd4OjdjYWU0MTA1MWNlYmMxMjU; James M. DuBois, A Framework for Analyzing Ethics Cases https://docs.google.com/viewer?a=v&pid=sites&srcid=bmFycmF0aXZlYmlvZXRoaoaWNzLmNvbXxlbWhyfG d4OjRmNjQ5YmIwZmM5YTM2Y2M

Fiedler, F.E. (1967). *A theory of leadership effectiveness.* New York: McGraw-Hill.

Gardner, J.W. (1990). *On leadership.* New York: The Free Press.

Gert, B. *Common morality: Deciding what to do* (Oxford University Press, 2004, pp. 20, 151, 152); flow chart prepared by Reinhold Schlieper: http://faculty.erau.edu/schliepr/ethics/flowchart.html

Gilligan, C. (1982). *In a different voice: Psychological theory and women's development.* Cambridge, MA: Harvard University Press.

Greenleaf, R. (1977). *Servant leadership.* Mahwah, NJ: Paulist Press

Hersey, P., & Blanchard, K. (1982). Management of organizational behavior: Utilizing human resources (4th ed.). Englewood Cliffs, NJ: Prentice Hall.

Hersey, P., Blanchard, K.H., & Johnson, D.E. (1996). *Management of organizational behavior: Utilizing human resources* (7th ed.). Upper Saddle River, NJ: Prentice Hall.

Kahn, E. (1996). The intersubjective perspective and the client centred approach: Are they one at their core? *Psychotherapy, 33*, 30-38.

Klein, G. (1998). *Source of power: How people make decisions.* Cambridge, MA: MIT.

Kohlberg, L. (1981). *The philosophy of moral development.* San Francisco: Harper & Row.

Kvalsund, R. (2005). *Coaching, metode: prosess: relasjon.* Norway: Synergy.

Lewin, K., Lippit, R., & White, R.K. (1939). Patterns of aggressive behavior in experimentally created social climates. *Journal of Social Psychology, 10*, 271-301.

Martin, B., Cashel, C., Wagstaff, M., & Breunig, M. (2006). *Outdoor leadership: Theory and practice.* Champaign, IL: Human Kinetics.

Mind Tools. Decision-Making Techniques: www.mindtools.com/pages/main/newMN_TED.htm

Mitten, D. (1996). The value of feminist ethics in experiential education teaching and leadership. In K. Warren (Ed.), *Women's voices in experiential education* (pp. 159-171). Boulder, CO: Association for Experiential Education.

Moen, F., & Federici, R.A. (2012). The effect of coaching based leadership. *Journal of Education and Learning, 1* (2), 1-14.

Noddings, N. (1984). *Caring: A feminine approach to ethics & moral education.* Berkeley, CA: University of California Press.

Petzoldt, P., & Ringholz, R.C. (1984). *The new wilderness handbook.* New York: Norton.

Sample Recreation and Leisure Program Standard: http://www.tcu.gov.on.ca/pepg/audiences/colleges/progstan/humserv/reclei.html

Sashkin, M. (1989). *Visionary leadership. The perspective from education.* New York: The Westview Press.

Shooter, W., & Furman, N. (2011). Contextualizing recent judgment and decision-making concepts for outdoor leadership research. *Journal of Outdoor Recreation, Education, and Leadership, 3* (3), 189-203.

Starratt, R.J. (2010). Developing ethical leadership. In B. Davies & M. Brundrett (Eds.), Developing successful leadership. *Studies in Educational Leadership, 11,* 27-37.

Stogdill, R. (1974). *Handbook of leadership.* New York: The Free Press.

Young, P. Mediations. Basic Principles of Ethical Decision Making: http://publicsphere.typepad.com/mediations/2006/05/post.html

Part II

Leading as a Professional in Leisure Services

Working with others, whether they are program participants, coworkers, volunteers, or community members, is a staple of being a recreation and leisure services professional. The way a recreation and leisure services leader goes about working with these groups varies based on the goals and objectives of the groups, the purpose for their existence, and the demographics of group members. Leaders need to be prepared to recognize the differences among these groups and choose the appropriate leadership strategies and facilitation techniques to address any number of situations that may arise. In light of this, recreation and leisure services leaders also need to be aware of how to do this while being mindful of risk and risk management. The chapters in part II provide insight into what it takes to help groups achieve their fullest potential in a rapidly changing modern world.

In chapter 7, Tim O'Connell and Michael Van Bussel trace the process by which groups develop, explore the various roles that individuals take in groups, and present implications for practice for recreation and leisure services leaders. Although a large part of the chapter focuses on the group as a whole, the authors also look at the experience of individual members in the group context. Factors such as environmental conditions (which play a role in most recreation and leisure settings), noise, and physical setting are also discussed so leaders are aware of their impacts on groups and individuals. Finally, O'Connell and Van Bussel provide a troubleshooting guide to common group problems and suggest some easy solutions to these issues.

We hear again from Michael Van Bussel in chapter 8 about direct leadership—that is, the face-to-face interaction, ground-level motivation, and problem solving in which recreation and leisure services leaders are involved on a daily basis. The chapter begins with a discussion of what motivates people to participate in recreation and leisure activities and programs and how that translates to preferences for leadership behavior. It also explores how situational characteristics and the traits of group members influence what is theoretically expected from leaders (e.g., preferred leader behavior) versus what they really do in practice (e.g., actual leader behavior). Chelladurai's (1990) *Multidimensional Model of*

Leadership is used as a framework to explore these topics and applications to 21st-century leadership practice.

In chapter 9, Marilynn Glasser discusses supervision and working specifically with staff and volunteers. Because recreation and leisure services leaders have busy jobs, they need to know how to delegate responsibilities to others and to manage their completion of those tasks. Glasser provides an outline of what supervision entails, explains why it is important, and gives insights into the typical duties supervisors encounter in their jobs. This chapter ends with an exploration of why people volunteer, the unique nature of working with volunteers, and the processes and techniques for creating a positive and successful volunteer culture.

As Greg Robinson notes at the beginning of chapter 10, 21st-century recreation and leisure services leaders are increasingly seen as members of a team instead of separate from it. This chapter covers the important subjects of the history of team development and training, the differences between team and individual leadership, program delivery, and team development. Topics such as team learning, chaos, team organization, conflict, and trust are discussed, and suggestions for recreation and leisure services leadership are provided. The chapter ends with an explanation of factors that influence the successful or unsuccessful development of teams. Robinson includes some poignant tips for beginning leaders about why letting go is important as well as troubleshooting tips for addressing some common difficulties in working with teams in recreation and leisure settings.

The final chapter in this section (chapter 11) addresses risk and risk management. In an increasingly litigious society, recreation and leisure services leaders must be aware of their duties and responsibilities to minimize exposure to risk, not only for those with whom they work, but also for the agency or organization that employs them. In this chapter, Robert Kauffman provides an overview of basic legal terms of which recreation and leisure services leaders should be aware and suggests several risk management strategies to use in professional practice. Several scenarios and real-life events are used to highlight specific topics and outline methods to reduce or prevent accidents.

Chapter 7

Understanding Group Dynamics

Tim O'Connell and Michael Van Bussel

" To associate with other like-minded people in small, purposeful groups is for the great majority of men and women a source of profound psychological satisfaction. "

—Aldous Huxley, *Beyond the Mexique Bay* (1934)

Abby and Jack, both intercollegiate soccer players, were hired to run an elite soccer camp for players 15 to 18 years of age. The camp ran for two weeks and had 22 participants, both male and female. The activities were located outside at the outskirts of a large soccer complex, far from any buildings or shelter. Abby and Jack organized drills, games, and scrimmages for the participants and tracked their progress. As the camp progressed, the two instructors allowed the campers to make certain decisions regarding the daily agenda, such as selecting their favorite drills and activities. The opportunity to have input on the agenda had gone over well with the participants.

The weather for the first week had been excellent, not too hot, not too cold, and not a cloud in the sky—great soccer weather. On the Monday of the second week the instructors had a terrific session planned for the players. As they began their second session in the afternoon, the sun was out in full force and the temperatures increased significantly prompting a heat warning from the local weather advisory. Abby and Jack knew they should probably cancel the afternoon session and find shelter in the distant clubhouse. They called the group in and suggested they pack up and make their way back to the clubhouse. The meeting, however, turned into a heated argument. Some believed that the heat would pass and did not want to pack up the equipment. Another group stated that they would like to work on their tans. Others wanted to move to the clubhouse immediately because they were uncomfortable from the heat. As the conversation continued, it was clear that no consensus was going to be reached. What should Abby and Jack do as the leaders of this group? Should they allow the group to make this decision?

Learning Outcomes

At the conclusion of this chapter, students will be able to:

▶ Define the term *group.*

▶ Discuss the ways groups form.

▶ Understand how groups behave as collectives.

▶ Appreciate the roles individuals may take in groups and how individuals behave in a group context.

▶ Identify common problems groups encounter and consider solutions.

▶ Apply various leadership styles and theories to groups.

Groups are one of the basic building blocks of society. Although a myriad of individual transactions occur in leisure services provision every day, working with groups is the bread and butter of what most recreation leaders do. Groups are a powerful force—they influence how people behave and communicate and even shape attitudes and beliefs. Many people participate in recreation and leisure activities with others to have fun and to attain other psychological, physical, emotional, and spiritual benefits. Although some people prefer to engage in recreation and leisure activities by themselves, taking part in group activities often provides an enhanced experience. The goals and objectives of the group, individual members' goals, the conditions in which the group is operating, how people are getting along, and the work that needs to be done all shape how a leader goes about leading a group. The purpose of this chapter is to assist recreation and leisure services professionals in preparing to work with groups and to help group members achieve a basic understanding of group dynamics and what makes groups tick.

Groups Defined

What exactly is a group? It does not seem that difficult to pinpoint exactly what a group is and does. However, considering all the groups to which people might belong (e.g., family, baseball team, work department, political party), defining the essence of a group can be difficult. For the recreation and leisure professional, understanding some of the key features of a group will help determine the best way to approach working with that group as well as specific leadership strategies to implement at certain stages of the group's existence. Depending on the context, the definition of group may change, particularly for people who are members of that group. A cricket team is together for very different reasons than is a family attending a concert in a park over a summer holiday weekend. We refer to a **group** as two or more people who are socially connected to one another. In terms of recreation and leisure professionals, this will most often be through participation in a specific activity with others or through working with people to accomplish a specific goal or task (e.g., putting

Best Practices From the Field

Tony DiCicco was the head coach for the U.S. Women's National Soccer Team from 1994 to 1999. During his tenure, the team won an Olympic gold medal in 1996 and a FIFA World Cup title against China in 1999. His success as a coach derived from a balance of a knowledge of the game and an understanding of the athletes for whom he was responsible. As a former goalkeeper who played for his country, he was able to bring this experience to the table. But Tony also had to understand female athletes and the factors that motivated them individually and as a group. Regarding the differences in coaching men and women, Coach DiCicco believes that even though there are similarities, the motivating factors for men and women are different:

> The women on the national team wanted to be challenged like all elite athletes, but they did not want a coach screaming in their faces or singling anyone out for criticism or behaving in a manner that might jeopardize their relationship with each other or with the coaching staff. (Longman, 2001, p. 172)

Tony DiCicco focused on this relational approach to coaching by providing a sound foundation centered on the team and grounded in positive and constructive communication. As recreational leaders or coaches, we may think that our approach should be the same for all groups that we're charged to lead. Coach DiCicco was receptive of the group's needs and accommodating in his approach. His democratic style that involved active listening, player engagement, and empowerment was a change from the traditional autocratic approach to coaching that had been prevalent earlier in his playing career. The ability to build, focus on, and maintain solid relationships with the many players that comprised the team speaks to the best practice of positive communication. This positive philosophy is reflected in the National Team's performance as it compiled a 103-8-8 record. Ultimately, this record speaks for itself, but it also reflects the importance of constituent awareness and positive communication in leadership.

together a new therapeutic intervention program at a rehabilitation center).

History of Groups

Groups have had a significant role in helping individuals meet their basic needs such as food, shelter, clothing, protection, and companionship since the beginning of human history. As individual humans' abilities changed, so did groups' capacities for more sophisticated interactions. Survival techniques (e.g., acquiring food) became more focused on group efforts, and the resulting surplus of food and materials led to trading with other groups. Slowly, larger societies and cultures developed as a result of these shared group experiences. This led to the development of group recreation and leisure activities that individuals began enjoying with others. Today, this is evident around the world through the popularity of sports leagues, the Olympics, packaged group vacations, and other group recreation and leisure events.

The family is the first group to which most people belong. Most people (in North America, at least) spend most of their time living, working, playing, and recreating with others. Although the family provides stability, other groups become more important than family at various points in a person's life. For example, peer groups are more important, particularly for recreation and leisure activities, as children grow older and enter adolescence. This continues into adulthood as people begin to move away from the family group. As they continue to age, the family may again become the central group in their lives, although in the form of their own families created by marriage and children of their own. People's recreation and leisure are certainly shaped by the groups that are most influential at various stages of their lives.

Group Development

How do groups develop? Do all groups develop in the same way? Initially, these may seem like simple questions. However, the complexity and variability of groups, and the characteristics associated with them, may make the answers much more difficult to conceptualize. **Group development** examines the how and why of change within groups over a period of time. Elements measured during the group development process include roles within the group, the interaction of the group members, levels of cohesion, group structures, and member

orientation. Forsyth (1999) placed these theories into three categories: sequential stage or linear models, recurring phase or cyclical models, and equilibrium models. This section provides examples of models from each of these categories.

Sequential Stage Models

Sequential stage models, or linear models, contextualize group development as a progression through multiple stages. Once certain characteristics of the stage have been reached, progression to the next phase occurs. Tuckman's (1965) theory of the stages of group development is probably the best known and most widely used of the sequential stage models. Initially, the theory had four stages: forming, storming, norming, and performing (Tuckman, 1965). In 1977, the model was revised to include a fifth stage, adjourning (Tuckman & Jensen, 1977).

Forming

Forming, the initial stage of Tuckman's (1965) stages of group development, includes a preliminary orientation of the group members. During this stage members become familiar with fellow members and try to establish what their role is in relation to the others in the group. The behavior of group members is characterized by caginess as they get to know the personalities and attributes of others. People attempt to find out whether they belong in the group and may also participate in social comparison, weighing themselves against others. For example, at the initial meeting of a sport team, players may need to spend a certain amount of time getting familiar with their teammates and coaches. In recreation and leisure environments leaders must be cognizant of this stage and develop strategies to help group members familiarize themselves with others in the group prior to the initiation of the activity (e.g., a backcountry trip).

Storming

The second stage of Tuckman's (1965) model, storming, includes elements of tension concerning leadership in the group, the formation of norms that regulate members' behavior, the designation of roles, and even personality clashes between members. Opposition by group members is perpetuated to establish control or highlight certain visions of the group construct. Tension continues until the group identifies and selects a viable leader. During this process interpersonal conflict,

© Tim O'Connell

In recreation and leisure environments, the leader may need to be more directive in the forming stage as group members begin to get to know one another.

jealousy, emotional resistance, and genuine lack of trust may be present. As the group works through issues such as the creation of group roles, norms, and leadership levels, conflict may decrease. Recreation managers need to accept that storming is an important part of the group development process. However, although this stage can help the group learn how to deal with issues, the conflict should not be allowed to undermine positive group interaction or detract from the real purpose or goals the group has established.

Norming

The third stage, norming, is highlighted by group members uniting in a productive and goal-oriented manner. At this stage group norms are established, lines of communication are created, and modes of decision making are formed. A general commitment by all members of the group to the overall functioning and success of the group is present. Increased satisfaction among group members may proliferate as the group works together toward common goals. Overall, in the norming stage, members understand their roles, the other members of the group, and the task at hand.

Performing

The fourth stage, performing, is characterized by the successful integration of human resources to complete the task. The group members come together, focus their energy on the particulars of what needs to be accomplished, and begin to achieve success. The interpersonal relationships of members of the group have harmonized and matured to the point that the group becomes efficient at accomplishing the task. Recreation leaders must recognize that this stage may not arrive quickly. Often, performing is reached after a long period of storming and norming, and it is achieved only by a limited number of groups (Forsyth, 2006). Groups in which structural issues have been rectified, goals have been established, and roles have been clearly designated may reach this stage (Forsyth, 2006). Intergroup support also helps the group complete the task. Group members work together, provide mutual support, and encourage each other throughout the process. Recreation leaders should promote a positive environment in which the achievements of group members are recognized.

Adjourning

The final stage, adjourning, added by Tuckman and Jensen in 1977, occurs once the group has completed its task and disbanded. At this point the members of the group may join other groups. Depending on the circumstance of the disbanding of the group, conflict may or may not be present. If the group was not successful, finger pointing and accusations may occur. Recreation leaders should facilitate the transition from the group to individual endeavors. Providing feedback during end-of-season meetings, promoting opportunities for recognition and reflection, and facilitating opportunities for members to become involved in other activities are ways leaders can smooth the transition.

Recurring Phase Models

In **recurring phase models**, a group experiences a variety of stages multiple times throughout its existence. Stages may be encountered multiple times, and the order in which groups experience these phases is not predetermined. In addition, groups may not experience certain stages at all.

One recurring phase model of group formation and development includes six stages. The initial stage, which includes feelings of distance and a lack of connection to the group, is known as *discontent* (Worchel, 1994). These feelings are accentuated when joining a new work group (e.g., an individual climber meeting a preestablished group of climbers for the first time). This new member may feel marginalized when not included in conversations with established members. Progressing from this first stage requires a *precipitating event,* which can be minor (e.g., a disagreement between group members) or major (e.g., a protest against the status quo) (Worchel, 1994). Ultimately, the precipitating event highlights a general displeasure with the current situation and possibly produces a venue to create commonality among group members (Worchel, 1994).

Once members identify with the group or have a connection with the other members, they progress to the stage of *group identification*. At this stage the need for compliance within the group is accentuated as members seek to establish and maintain cohesiveness (Worchel, 1994). The *group productivity* stage is highlighted by higher levels of task orientation as members work toward a common goal established by the group. As mem-

bers of the group become more comfortable with this process, there is time for self-reflection and analysis (Worchel, 1994). The *individualization* phase is characterized by a yearning for recognition of one's personal accomplishments once the group has achieved success. The final stage, *decay,* is characterized by a lack of focus to complete the tasks assigned. Personal needs becomes the focus and group activities decrease. At any point in the model the cycle may be broken, and if the group does not disband, a progression through some or all of the stages may happen again (Worchel, 1994).

Equilibrium Models

The final perspective, **equilibrium models**, emphasizes the maintenance of balance throughout the organization. Task and social elements of the group must maintain this balance to be successful (Bales, 1965). This perspective does not support the premise that groups progress through stages. The concept of robust equilibrium models supports the notion that groups have an early period of change followed by a time of stability (Carron, Hausenblas, & Eys, 2005). This theory is quite applicable to recreation and leisure groups. Once a group is established, often only minimal changes to the channels of communication or the overall structure of the group are needed to maintain its productivity. Another equilibrium perspective, the punctuated equilibrium model, highlights the quick reactions taken by groups when imbalances occur (O'Connell & Cuthbertson, 2009). Task and social imbalances can occur without warning and may be addressed by reassigning roles or reallocating resources (O'Connell & Cuthbertson, 2009).

These perspectives of group development are important for leisure leaders to understand. How do you know which theory is most applicable? Or, once you have selected a theory, how do you know which stage of development your group is in? These are difficult questions to answer. At the same time, this is the beauty of group dynamics. Experience in a variety of circumstances will help you grow in your ability to facilitate and make decisions as a leisure services leader.

Norms

What are norms, and how do they influence leisure groups? Does an understanding of group norms influence leaders? **Norms** are parameters that guide the behavior in a group. Behavior falling

Photo courtesy of Myles Clinton.

Understanding group dynamics can help leaders choose appropriate facilitation and leadership styles, regardless of the group makeup or situation.

outside these parameters is deemed unwanted by the organization, group, or team. Those not abiding by these norms are evaluated negatively and may suffer consequences. For example, if you are late to work on a regular basis, you may be reprimanded or even lose your job.

Norm Development

Referring back to Tuckman's (1965) stages of group development, norms tend to be created during the storming stage and are ultimately agreed upon and solidified during the norming stage. Carron, Hausenblas, and Eys (2005) stated that interaction is a prerequisite to the emergence of norms; member interactions facilitate the creation of the parameters of behavior for the group. Along with these interactions must come reinforcement: "The behaviours that the vast majority of team members find acceptable are reinforced; unacceptable behaviours are discouraged. Consequently, each individual comes to understand the standards (norms) deemed appropriate" (Carron et al., 2005, p. 175).

Leisure leaders may be able to facilitate the development of norms by stating, modeling, or importing (O'Connell & Cuthbertson, 2009). Stating involves telling the group which behaviors are suitable and which are not. Modeling consists of demonstrating the prescribed behavior (e.g., not arriving late after telling the team about consequences for coming late to practice). Remember, as a leader "your words and actions must be consistent. Group members will be confused and lose respect for you as a leader if you don't walk your talk" (O'Connell & Cuthbertson, 2009, p. 27). Finally, importing involves employing norms that are used in other situations. An example of importing is the highlighting of active listening techniques for students participating in a skills seminar. A combination of techniques may be beneficial in establishing norms for leisure groups (O'Connell & Cuthbertson, 2009).

Norm Adherence

Leisure leaders must also pay attention to how group members adhere to the established norms, keeping in mind that conforming to norms can be either a positive or a negative thing. From a positive perspective, conformity to norms allows individuals to focus on the social and task orientations of the group and eliminates worry about the appropriateness of behavior. On the other hand, conforming to restrictive norms may deter new membership to the group or limit creative thinking. Ultimately, "conformity is not just behaving as other people behave; it is being influence by how they behave" (Carron, Hausenblas, & Eys, 2005, p. 178). O'Connell and Cuthbertson (2009) highlighted numerous factors that influence conformity to group norms:

▶ Explicitness or implicitness of the norm

▶ Punishments for breaking rules or not abiding by the norm

▶ Feelings of shared responsibility and obligation to follow agreed-upon norms

▶ Development of group identity

▶ Individual qualities of group members

▶ Percentage of others in the group who conform to the norm

▶ Wish to continue membership in a group

▶ Status level within the group (p. 27)

Understanding these factors may help leaders cultivate appropriate norms and make positive choices in leisure groups.

Roles

Roles may be defined as "a set of behaviours that are expected from the occupants of specific positions within the group" (Eys et al., 2006, p. 164). People may be assigned to their roles or may find their niches within the group. Roles may be task focused or social in nature. Task roles include seeking information, giving opinions, and evaluating the group itself. Social roles include mediator, facilitator, or observer. These are but a few of the many roles people can play within a group.

Mabry and Barnes (1980) highlighted two general categories of roles: formal and informal. Formal roles are established by the group and are promoted as positions of importance. Often, these roles have titles such as team leader, captain, and coach. Informal roles grow out of experiences within the group. These roles are created as deemed necessary by the group. Examples of informal roles are team comedian and entertainment coordinator. Promoting role diversity is an important task of leisure leaders, as they should encourage their group members to fulfill a range of roles. If competition for a role occurs or roles are left empty, conflict and group ineffectiveness may result.

Role ambiguity is a lack of clarity regarding one's role within the group (Eys et al., 2006). This may be caused by an absence of information such as the goals of the group, the resources available, or how to perform certain roles. **Role conflict** is an incongruity between the requirements of two roles (Kahn et al., 1964). Leisure organizations can limit the potential for role ambiguity and role conflict by instituting mentorship programs and consistent evaluation procedures.

Group Size

Does the size of a group matter? The number of participants can have a significant impact on elements of leadership, productivity, and performance. The question of whether group size should be limited is addressed in this section.

Group size certainly affects leisure leaders (Carron, Hausenblas, & Eys, 2005). As group size increases, the stress placed on leaders increases as they strive to meet the needs of more constituents. Also, as numbers increase, leaders have fewer opportunities to connect with their constituents personally. The straining of lines of communication can have negative consequences such as a lack of member motivation, delays in decision making, and a disconnect between the goals of the organization and individual roles. In turn, as group size increases, more leaders may be necessary. Lastly, the potential for leaders to adopt coercive and authoritarian styles of leadership increases with the size of the group (Hare, 1981). A democratic leadership style can be difficult with large numbers of people and may force leaders to opt for handing down decisions from the top.

What is the optimal group size? There are varying opinions about this. Hare (1981) completed a meta-analysis of group size research over 75 years and concluded the following:

The optimum size for a small discussion group may be five members, since members are generally less satisfied with smaller or larger groups. In smaller groups members may be forced to be too prominent, and in larger groups they may not have enough opportunity to speak. In the group of five, strict deadlocks can be avoided and members can shift roles swiftly. (p. 697)

However, many activities require more than five members. In sport a hockey lineup requires six

© Tim O'Connell

As the size of the group increases, the demands on the leaders increase.

starters, and soccer and American football both require eleven players. Ultimately, the group must have enough members with the requisite skills to complete the task (Forsyth, 2006).

Cohesion

What causes groups to stick together? Is cohesion unique for leisure groups? What factors of cohesion should leisure leaders promote to maximize productivity within groups? Carron, Brawley, and Widmeyer (1998) provided the quintessential definition of **cohesion**: "Cohesion is a dynamic process which is reflected in the tendency for a group to stick together and remain united in the pursuit of its instrumental objectives and/or for the satisfaction of member affective needs" (p. 213). This definition highlights several very important aspects. The notion of cohesion being a dynamic process addresses the fluidity and ever-changing nature of groups. As group members and groups themselves share a variety of experiences, perspectives may change and ultimately shift the focus of the group's goals and objectives. Next, groups stick together for a variety of reasons. A team may remain cohesive in search of a repeat championship, whereas a group of scuba divers may remain together because they enjoy the social interactions. Finally, cohesion has multiple components. In its simplest form, cohesion contains both social and task-related components. As Carron, Hausenblas, and Eys (2005) explained,

"cohesion reflects the social and task-related bonds among members of the group" (p. 227).

The behavior of the leader may have an impact on the cohesiveness of the group. One way to promote a cohesive environment is to establish group goals and provide a means to accomplish these goals. Also, a democratic style of leadership, social support, and positive feedback are associated with higher levels of task cohesion (Westre & Weiss, 1991). A democratic leadership style may empower group members to make decisions and in turn create more of a connection to the group. Should a similar decision-making approach be promoted for all groups? As Carron, Hausenblas, and Eys (2005) explained, "in groups that are low in cohesiveness, task-oriented behaviors produce better performance, greater role clarity, and higher individual satisfaction. In groups that are high in cohesiveness, person-oriented behaviors are better" (p. 251). Ideally, recreation leaders must understand the multidimensional nature of groups because different factors may influence different levels of cohesion within the group and ultimately affect performance (Carron, Hausenblas, & Eys, 2005).

Socialization

People who join groups are not absorbed into them as faceless and mindless members of the crowd. They are engaged and interested in the group at varying levels over time. A person's journey through group membership is called **socialization**. Many leaders make the mistake of maintaining a greater focus on the group experience and lose sight of the attention required to foster positive individual experiences. Leaders are most successful in leading groups when they remember that groups are made up of individuals!

When people consider joining a group, one of the things they think about is how much membership will cost in terms of time, effort, and lost opportunities. For example, someone who chooses to participate in a tennis league that conflicts with another recreational activity gives up the chance to participate in that activity. People also consider what they are going to gain from joining a group (Moreland & Levine, 1982). It is important to remember that while a person is sizing up the group, the group is evaluating the person. If the group has a positive view of the member, it will try to keep that person involved with the group. If the evaluation is negative, the group may directly or indirectly encourage the person to leave the group. Moreland and Levine's (1982) model of group socialization is similar to the models of group formation discussed earlier in this chapter. Following are the five stages of group socialization:

1. Investigation
2. Socialization
3. Maintenance
4. Resocialization
5. Remembrance

This model is illustrated in figure 7.1.

Investigation

During the investigation stage, a person identifies possible groups to join. This involves evaluating the costs and benefits of a number of groups. The person also figures out which group will best help him reach his goals and objectives and fulfill his needs. In a similar manner, groups try to attract new members and are determining the costs and benefits of having a particular person join the group. Once someone accepts an invitation to join a group (entry), the second stage of the socialization process begins (socialization). The investigation stage is similar to the forming stage of group development.

Leaders can help in the investigation stage by recruiting new members and giving them a realistic picture of both the costs and benefits of group

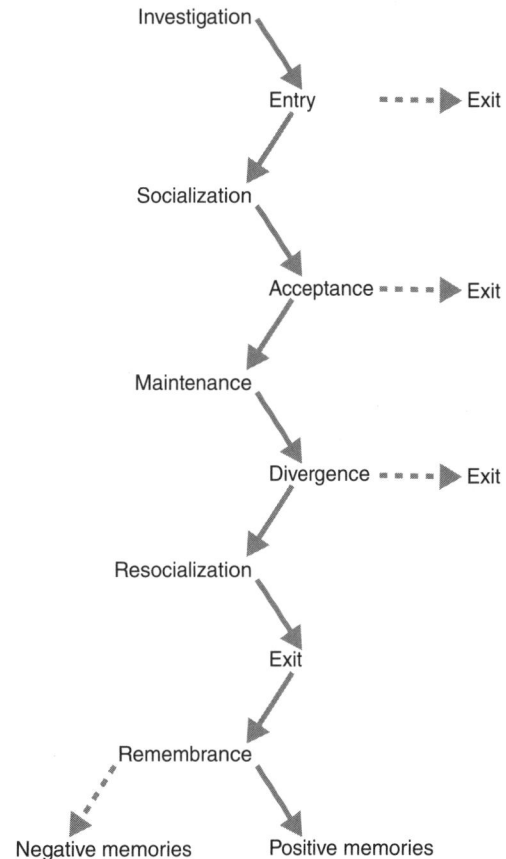

Figure 7.1 Stages of socialization.

Reprinted, by permission, from T. O'Connell and B. Cuthbertson, 2009, *Group dynamics in recreation and leisure: Creating conscious groups through an experiential approach* (Champaign, IL: Human Kinetics), 32.

membership. In our experience, many groups advise potential members only of the benefits of membership. Groups tend to gloss over the costs, or negative aspects, of membership until later in the socialization process. However, all potential members should have adequate information for making their decisions about whether the group is for them. This will save the leader, the group, and the potential member lots of time and effort. Promotional materials and group representatives should provide appropriate information at presentations and recruitment drives; this will help avoid problems later on.

Socialization

The socialization stage involves the collective comprehending of how the new person will fit into the group. This may involve old members' shifting roles and an overall redefining of group processes.

From the group perspective, this is called accommodation. Meanwhile, the new member must assimilate, or learn the group's operating procedures, norms, standards, and methods of communication. Through this process, the new member is accepted into the group and gains access to the full benefits of group membership.

The socialization process can be compromised in a number of ways. First, as in the storming and norming phases of group development, if either the new member or existing members do something to cause the other to perceive them in a negative way, the new member may exit the group or be forced out. Consider a group of therapeutic recreation specialists who have been working together for a number of years. A new specialist who has worked at a different facility for three years is hired and challenges the ways the existing group has been doing things. The new specialist might be seen as an outcast by the others for suggesting that they do things differently. On the other hand, the new specialist might believe that the others are purposefully snubbing her and that she will never be accepted into the group.

Recreation or leisure services leaders must focus on the relationship function of the group. They should consider using team-building activities, assigning mentors to new group members, and facilitating group discussions about the transition process for both new members and the group as a whole. Informally, this may take on characteristics of an initiation, during which new members are taught how the group operates. Leaders need to be aware of the positive and negative aspects of such a process and do what they can to prevent hazing or any other negative behaviors. On a formal level, many recreation and leisure groups host training days during which processes are specifically addressed. Usually, policies and procedures are available in staff manuals to help with this process as well.

Leaders working with groups of participants in recreation and leisure activities can help groups set the standards for how they work. For example, in the challenge course industry, many leaders use the full value contract (discussed at length in chapter 4) or optimum participation models to encourage groups to develop their own operating procedures. Leaders must ensure that the procedures they use are inclusive and fair and that they will help both individual members and the group as a whole succeed.

Maintenance

The maintenance stage of socialization is identified by continued accommodation and assimilation on the part of all group members. Generally, during this stage everything is working well, and the group is able to accomplish both its task and relationship functions. The maintenance stage is similar to the performing stage of group development. However, during this stage, both the group and individuals are constantly evaluating the costs, benefits, and value of their involvement.

Leaders need to carefully monitor what is happening with the group as a whole and with individual group members during the maintenance phase. Regular check-ins and group debriefing sessions can help. When things are going well, new leaders (and many seasoned leaders as well) will take this time to relax and focus on other aspects of their work. However, this is not the time to let their guard down. Small issues that are not attended to can simmer and have disastrous consequences if they are not identified and dealt with immediately. When this occurs, people will become less committed to the group, and the group may begin to question those people's value to them. This point is called divergence and marks the transition to the resocialization phase.

Resocialization

Resocialization is similar to the socialization stage in many ways. Assimilation or accommodation happens once again in both the individual and the group. There are two outcomes of resocialization. First, the individual and group may be in agreement about the current and future picture for the group. In a process called convergence, the individual recommits to the group and the group recommits to the individual. Second, the individual and group may decide to part ways. This is referred to as divergence. Through this process, a person leaves the group. This is similar to the adjourning stage of group development. The group must then determine how it will fill the hole left by the departing member.

Leaders need to consider a few things during the resocialization phase. First, they may question whether convergence makes the most sense for the group. This is not to say that they should determine by themselves whether a member should remain in the group; rather, they can objectively consider whether it is in the best interests of both the individual and group for the person to remain a member. Sometimes people stay in a group out of obligation or a fear of letting the group down, thereby putting the group's needs ahead of their own. Although this is certainly admirable, leaders must be cognizant of how this might affect everyone down the road, and implement appropriate strategies to point out the pros and cons of someone remaining in the group. This process can be tricky to navigate, but if handled diplomatically, it will most likely result in positive outcomes.

The resocialization stage is the time to celebrate individual members' contributions to the group—leaders can throw a party, bring members together in other ways, or give outgoing members a card and gift to let them know their efforts were appreciated. Recognizing others seems to be becoming a lost art—saying thanks can help ease the transition out of a group for both the individual and the group as a whole.

During the resocialization stage, as the group converges, leaders can take the opportunity to determine whether it is time to shake up the group. Do roles need to be reassigned? Are the group norms still acceptable to the group and its individual members? Are the goals of the group still appropriate and meaningful? Now is the time to take advantage of the renewed energy that often comes with convergence and put it to good use! This may require that members go through assimilation and accommodation again, but the outcomes will be worth it.

Remembrance

The last stage of socialization, remembrance, occurs when people debrief their experiences in the group, both as individuals and as members of the collective. Many people who were viewed positively by group members live on through a group's history and tradition. This is common in recreation and leisure services settings through the naming of gymnasiums, function rooms, and buildings after influential group members. If a group member is not viewed positively, that person may be talked about in negative tones or erased from the collective memory. People tend to remember their group experiences in much the same way. If it was positive, they often integrate parts of their experience into how they go about working with future groups. People who have a good experience with a group often recommend that group to others, tell stories about the group, and fondly remember it for a long time. If the experience was negative, people have the opposite reaction—they purposefully avoid doing certain things in a group setting, tell others to stay away from that group, or try to erase the experience from memory.

Celebrating a group's accomplishments is important.

Recreation and leisure services leaders can help group members with the remembrance process. They may decide to create a website where group members can stay in touch after a member leaves, schedule times for past members to visit the group (reunions), or create awards named after influential people to be sure they stay in the collective memory. Leaders can also learn from people who leave a group on less than positive terms—for example, by conducting an exit interview or sending a follow-up email to determine what went wrong or why the person felt the way he did. This will give the person the opportunity to vent some of his feelings (and maybe feel better about the group experience) while giving the leader food for thought on how to avoid similar situations in the future.

Recreation and leisure service leaders cannot always ensure that everyone has a positive experience with a group. However, an understanding of the socialization process will help them become aware of what group members experience as a group forms and members join and leave. This will help them figure out whether individual and group needs are complementary, address situations as they arise, and assist people in having a positive group experience. Because many groups centered on recreation and leisure are in transition for most of their existence, these are important concepts to understand.

Environmental Factors

People are exposed to various environmental factors that affect their experiences in groups. Think about how many times in a day people transition from one environment to another—they leave their homes in the morning, go outside, go to work, get some exercise, and go home again. Each of these experiences, as well as the time between them, is potentially affected by environmental factors such as weather, noise, temperature, perceptions of personal space, and even seating arrangements. The social conditions of each of these environments also affects people's ability to work or play. Understanding how environmental and social factors might influence group functioning is important because the environmental context is often a large part of a group's experience, particularly when the group is engaged in recreation, leisure, and experiential education activities.

Part of our existence on earth is our ability to adapt to whatever atmosphere is present. Wearing a rain coat or putting on sunscreen, shivering in the cold or complaining that the air conditioner is broken, listening to the wind blowing through the trees or plugging our ears as a police car goes by with its siren wailing, sinking into a leather lounge chair with a martini or feeling uncomfortable because the wallpaper doesn't match the curtains—these are all examples of how we navigate changes in both natural environments and those constructed by humans.

Whether natural or built, environmental factors also shape individual and group behaviors, as well as peoples' expectations about what happens or what can happen in a particular place at a particular time.

Think about what happens when students walk into a large lecture hall at a university. Most people assume that the students who sit up front are the "serious" students, whereas those who choose the back row are less serious about their studies. Once a student has chosen a seat, he will most likely sit in the same place for the remainder of the course, and may become acquainted with students who sit nearby. Most people also assume that the person standing behind the podium is the instructor, and that the primary purpose of entering the lecture hall is to take notes, listen to the instructor talk, or take an exam. The lights are dimmed or turned off to watch a DVD, the air conditioning comes on when the weather is warm, and the heat comes on when the weather is cold. Seating is usually heavy-duty, institutional, and uncomfortable, causing students to fidget to allow blood to flow to various extremities.

When people are comfortable in their environments, they can devote energy to the task at hand (e.g., listening to a speaker or playing basketball). When people are uncomfortable in their environments, they tend to experience some type of stress or feel agitated in an emotional, cognitive, physical, or behavioral manner. Although it is not always possible, manipulating the recreation, leisure, or experiential education environment so that people are comfortable helps groups perform to the best of their ability.

Temperature

Research has shown that most people are comfortable when the temperature ranges from 60 to 80 degrees Fahrenheit (16 to 27 °C). When the temperature gets above or below this range, people start to pay more attention to regulating their body temperature than to what is going on around them. This may lead to irritability, frustration, lack of focus, or withdrawal from group processes. Recreation and leisure services leaders may be challenged on two fronts: being comfortable with the temperature and dealing with participants who may be more focused on cooling off or warming up.

Although recreation and leisure services leaders cannot always control the temperatures, especially if they are outdoors, they can take measures to ensure that participants have the time to respond to temperature changes and make themselves comfortable. For example, regular breaks for water and rest, conducting programs in the shade, or scheduling events during cooler portions of the day (i.e., morning or evening) are fine strategies in hot temperatures. Sometimes simply acknowledging that it is hot is enough to focus participants on the program or task at hand for enough time to get something done or make a decision. In terms of cold temperatures, leaders should provide breaks for physical activities such as brisk walks or provide warm beverages. Depending on the context and situation, recreation and leisure services leaders may choose to keep some extra warm clothes or blankets on hand if a workspace is traditionally cool or if participants such as the elderly are more apt to get cold. Of course, the easiest strategy is to con-trol the temperature through heating and cooling systems. However, because this is often not possible, recreation leaders should be aware of how people react to temperature extremes. Responding to temperature challenges and making people comfortable will help get things done and provide conditions for a good experience for all.

Weather

In addition to temperature, recreation leaders need to be aware of the influence of weather on group dynamics. Weather conditions may stop a group from having an important meeting, or may force a group to spend unexpected time together. Strong winds may blow materials away, create too much noise, or generate hazardous conditions. Effects of the sun and hot temperatures may affect peoples' abilities to work in group settings. Lack of access to water or other liquids will cause dehydration, which often leads to irritability, may strain relationships, and will certainly affect a group's ability to make decisions.

Many people become preoccupied with weather conditions or anticipated weather conditions, which may affect the group as a whole. In places that receive heavy snow, people may worry about whether they will make it home in the evening, or whether their children will be stuck at school; such concerns reduce the focus on group dynamics

© Tim O'Connell

There are many ways weather can interfere with a group's function.

and the tasks at hand. Many recreation and leisure organizations, agencies, and schools close early in preparation for severe weather. As group members leave, the ability of the group to complete its work is compromised. Leaders should be sensitive to these feelings and be prepared to respond accordingly.

Groups that operate in environments affected by weather on a regular basis usually have plans in place to deal with adverse weather events. Teleconferences, Internet chat meetings, and e-mail enable groups to deal with difficult weather situations. Leaders should consult (or develop) agency risk management plans that outline specific procedures for dealing with weather emergencies. Many agencies have sessions to practice responding to severe weather conditions. During a weather emergency, leaders should strive to promote good communication among group members, stress cooperation and watching out for one another, and work for the common good of the group. One positive outcome of going through perceived or real weather emergencies is an increased sense of group identity and cohesion, and an enhanced ability to work together as a group. Savvy leaders take advantage of these situations (e.g., being stuck in a blizzard) to focus on interpersonal relationships or the task function of the group. Doing so often takes peoples' minds off worrying about the weather and refocuses them on getting things done.

Environmental Conditions

Some recreation and leisure services leaders work with groups and participants in places where other environmental conditions may affect group dynamics. For example, in the spring season in certain areas of North America, blackflies come out in full force. When groups are not prepared to contend physically and psychologically with these biting insects, group dynamics can suffer. We have observed some groups so absorbed in escaping these insects that group members barely speak to one another. The best strategy to deal with difficult insect situations is to know about and be prepared to deal with local conditions. This may include having appropriate clothing, insect repellent, or shelters (such as bug tents) in which groups can conduct their business or go about their activities. Leaders should also educate participants about dealing with insects because it is often the psychological aspect of swarming insects (and not their bites) that affects most people.

Another environmental condition to contend with is altitude. Many people respond to high altitudes with shortness of breath, headache, and upset stomach. Severe cases can lead to an abnormal buildup of fluid in the brain or lungs and require immediate medical attention. Obviously, these things will affect group dynamics. Leaders working with groups at high altitudes must be aware of how group members are feeling and respond accordingly. Leaders who are used to being at higher elevations should be aware that some of their participants may have just arrived from much lower elevations and adjust their expectations for the group accordingly. For example, some tour companies in the Rocky Mountain regions of both the United States and Canada offer guided mountain hikes to tourists visiting from other parts of the world. Although the tour leaders are acclimatized to the elevation from living there, they must remember that participants come from other places (usually lower in elevation). These leaders set a slower pace, allow more time for rest, provide plenty of fluids, and ease into group work to give people time to adjust to the new environment.

Noise

Noise is another environmental factor that influences how groups function. Most people are uncomfortable with noise that is over 80 decibels. Groups may be able to function in the presence of loud noises for short periods of time by simply ignoring them. In the long term, however, people begin to expend unnecessary energy coping with the environment and less energy on the task at hand. Long-term effects such as headaches and interpersonal conflict may occur as a result of repeated exposure to continuous loud noise. From a practical standpoint, loud noise impedes communication, which further curtails the productivity of the group. The best way to address the problem is to stop the noise or move the group to another location. If neither is possible, the group may have to disband for a period of time until the noise is gone or can be addressed.

Setting

The physical setting may have a great effect on a group. Imagine walking into a room that is messy, has flickering lights, and is smelly and very hot.

Leisure Leaders

Jalynn Bosley (Director), Christie Pettingill (Associate Director), and Sam Dear (Associate Director)

OUR PREPARATION

Jalynn Bosley

BPHE—Queen's University, Kingston, ON

BEd—University of Maine at Presque Isle

Wilderness first responder (WFR)

Christie Pettingill

BPHE, BA, BEd—Queen's University, Kingston, ON

Wilderness first responder (WFR), National Lifesaving Society (NLS)

Sam Dear

MA in leisure studies—Brock University, St. Catharines, ON

Postgraduate certificate in international project management—Humber College, Toronto, ON

HBOR of outdoor recreation, parks and tourism and BA in geography—Lakehead University, Thunder Bay, ON

Wilderness first responder (WFR); National Lifesaving Society (NLS); swiftwater rescue technician (SRT); graduate teaching assistant of the year, Brock University, 2010; member of the Association of Experiential Education

OUR CAREERS

ALIVE Outdoors is a service provider in that it does not own or maintain a "home" program delivery site or have a full-time instructor team. ALIVE currently partners with numerous camps to host programs at their properties and use their facilities, equipment, and select instructors. Our office is in Toronto, Ontario.

ALIVE Outdoors was founded in 2000 and has evolved from a canoe-tripping company into an experiential education company whose main goal is to offer meaningful and empowering experiences to people of all ages. ALIVE Outdoors' main clientele are school groups; however, as we continue to grow, so does the range of people we connect and work with.

Photo courtesy of Jalynn Bosley, ALIVE Outdoors Inc.

The backbone and essence of each ALIVE Outdoors experience is right in our name: **A**dventure, **L**eadership, **I**ndividuality, **V**alues, and **E**mpowerment. Our mission is to use experiential education to empower people to recognize and embrace their inner potential. Our customized programs inspire confidence to embrace challenge in a caring and supportive atmosphere. In a society that encourages competition, we help people learn the importance of cooperation.

Learning through experience allows students to become more aware of who they are and gives them the chance to align their behavior and choices with their values. We emphasize the idea that leadership begins from within and that personal leadership is defined by all the small actions we do—especially when no one is watching.

Students in our programs develop key qualities such as responsibility, communication skills, healthy decision making, community living, independence, and cooperation. Self-empowerment and decision-making skills emerge from this type of hands-on learning. ALIVE Outdoors programs stimulate the development of interpersonal skills, as well as encourage people to be physically active and supportive of one another. In our world of television, computers, cell phones, and other unhealthy distractions, these skills are extremely important to nurture. Although vital to life, they

continued

are not always fostered in the classroom or the corporate environment.

Our personal leadership programs help participants flourish and recognize their strengths and talents. Our programs lead people to build enriching and respectful relationships with themselves, with others, and with nature.

Jalynn Bosley (Owner/Director)

What do I do? Everything! Literally, I do everything from accounting to insurance to scheduling to marketing, and from leading writing workshops to delivering programs, addressing risk management, and mapping canoe routes. When you start a business from scratch, you must be a jack-of-all-trades.

I have always worked at camps, guiding canoe trips; for a few years I was the leadership director at a few camps. I was a classroom teacher for kindergarten to grade 8 physical education for a few years before deciding that my passion was to teach young people life skills through outdoor education. I started ALIVE Outdoors in 2000 as a canoe-tripping company with an emphasis on personal leadership, and it has evolved into a year-round experiential outdoor education company.

I like knowing that what we do makes a difference. I love being my own boss and not being caught up in the bureaucracy of a bigger organization. I love being able to dream up ideas and write programs and put them into action. I love being outside when I can get away from the office side of things. I love the community of people in this field. Some of the most passionate and sincere people on the planet work in the outdoor education industry, and I am so grateful to cross paths with so many of them. I dislike the massive amount of paperwork to attend to, e-mails to answer, and risks to manage (e.g., dietary needs and allergies). Needing to tend to, and keep track of so many details can be very tedious at times.

As the owner of ALIVE Outdoors, it's my job to unite and support our team. My philosophy is quite simple—express my appreciation to everyone involved, and show my deep-rooted gratitude. Because we do not own a program delivery site, we have to work hard at making people feel part of something special. I am committed to aligning my words and actions to ensure that all instructors and our director team understand that without

them sharing their gifts and talents, ALIVE would not be ALIVE!

Christie Pettingill (Associate Director)

My job at ALIVE Outdoors is varied as well. I coordinate with many of our schools and partner outdoor education centers to ensure that we are creating and providing meaningful and quality programs. I am largely responsible for hiring 80 contract instructors and keeping up with our instructor communications. I help create and update schedules and ensure that all of our information packages are up-to-date and in line with industry standards. As the tripping specialist, I also plan canoe and hiking routes. I facilitate many of our programs and occasionally get to instruct as well.

I first went to summer camp at the age of nine. That quickly turned into my favorite thing to do all year as I cherished the friends and confidence that camp brought to my life. When I became old enough to instruct at camp, it was my dream come true; I quickly realized that I love educating and inspiring youth. I spent many years in various leadership roles at camps, I have guided for a few canoe-tripping companies, I have taught English overseas, I have spent some time in the classroom substitute teaching, and I have taught at numerous outdoor education centers. I met Jalynn while working at one of these outdoor education centers; she sensed my passion and brought me on to the ALIVE full-time team, where I have been since April 2011.

I love inspiring people through the outdoors. It's so rewarding to see and hear how our programs are truly making a difference. I don't like all of the paperwork; it really seems never-ending at times.

I want to give 110 percent to everything I do and to do it with integrity. I'm very aware of the need to treat other people with kindness and always try to get a few laughs out of coworkers, clients, and students. I want our programs to be the absolute best they can be, so when I am bogged down by paperwork, I think of the goal. When leading a program, I work long hours to ensure that our instructors, clients, and students have all of their needs met and are having a positive, meaningful, and fun experience. I am known to throw in a few jokes at appropriate times to keep the mood light and uplifting.

Sam Dear (Associate Director)

I break down my job into two parts: when I'm in the office and when I'm not. In the office, my responsibilities are multifaceted and include keeping in close communication with partner outdoor centers and schools, improving and creating new programs and workshops, marketing initiatives, writing proposals, and addressing students' dietary and medical issues. When I am out of the office (approximately 90 days per year), my responsibilities include facilitating programs for schools, delivering workshops, mentoring staff in working toward professional goals, and troubleshooting.

After my first canoe trip in grade 8, I knew I was bound for a career in the outdoor industry. I started my career working as a camp counselor in various positions, which further solidified my love for canoe tripping and the outdoor classroom. To gain a greater understanding of the field, I studied recreation and leisure at Lakehead University in Thunder Bay, Ontario. Throughout my time at Lakehead and following my graduation, I worked for a variety of organizations in various roles: guide, instructor, educator, and manager.

Following international volunteer and travel experiences, I took a break from the field and returned to school to study international development. As a result of this experience, I became interested in the idea of using outdoor experiential education and play as tools for international collaboration. In an attempt to bridge outdoor education and international travel, I found myself at Brock University co-creating a program that brought outdoor recreation students to Cuba while completing a master's thesis on the ethics of international volunteering.

Wanting to get back into the outdoor classroom, I applied to work on ALIVE Outdoor's fall instructor team. As an instructor, I was incredibly impressed with ALIVE's programs and knew it was a place where all of my skills and interests would be fueled. It was not a hard decision to apply for the associate director's position, which was posted five months after my instructor contract had ended.

When accepting a job, I ask myself two questions: (1) Will the position provide me with opportunities to grow on a personal and professional level, and (2) will I be surrounded by people who inspire me? As an associate director with ALIVE, I can say with certainty that the answer to these two questions is yes. Further, working with ALIVE provides me with the opportunity to live with integrity and purpose every day. This I value beyond measure. I am also grateful that the position provides a supportive space in which new ideas are welcomed and fueled. Finally, although at times ALIVE's instructor team is large, the full-time team is small. This makes the decision-making process quick and efficient. We rarely deal with bureaucracy.

My personal leadership philosophy is rooted in my belief that the ultimate aim of outdoor education programs is to help people realize their strengths and, further, to help them understand how those strengths can contribute to their becoming active, engaged, and inspired citizens of both their local and global communities. On a day-to-day basis, having a clear sense of why I do what I do helps me stay integral and congruent in all aspects of my work.

OUR ADVICE TO YOU

Jalynn

People may tell you that finding a job in this field of work is very challenging. It's not. You have to think outside the box. You have to be willing to sit with uncertainty between contracts, and you have to work hard at finding meaningful work. It's out there, but you have to be persistent, make long-term connections, and be 100 percent reliable and committed. You will go to work every day feeling as though you are living your passion—and that is the greatest feeling. More than anything, we look for people who have authentic energy and who can inspire young people. Show your heart to people. Know that this work truly matters and leaves a lasting impression on those you share your passion with.

I believe that some of life's greatest lessons can happen over the course of a few days and that some of our most profound lessons come from the simplest moments. Experiential and outdoor education programs are more important than ever before. We find ourselves in a time of materialism in which people spend more time in front of screens than ever before. One of the things we want young people to recognize is that the true

continued

Leisure Leaders *(continued)*

valuables in this world are relationships and caring for our environment. There is no better place to nurture key life skills than in the outdoors with inspiring and passionate role models leading the way.

Christie

Show your passion. I interview well over 100 candidates a year, and the thing that always shines through is the passion to be in this field. Be excited, learn as much as you can, and immerse yourself in as many new situations as possible.

Sam

It is important to recognize that certifications and theory-based knowledge provide only a small starting point to your career. The combination of what you learn in a formal setting, your own unique ambition, and your formal and informal experiences in the field makes you a well-rounded leader and very employable. During your undergraduate years, get outside as much as possible with your friends. Make mistakes and learn from them.

Take your role as a leader in this field seriously. You are ultimately a teacher who has the ability to create powerful experiences for people of all ages.

The outdoor classroom is the most powerful environment in which to realize your strengths and to understand how those strengths can help you become an active, engaged, and inspired citizen of both your local and global communities.

For most people, such a setting is not attractive and will cause them to focus on their surroundings and not the group or work to be done. Now imagine a sunny room that has nice couches, smells good, and is thoughtfully laid out. This setting will most likely attract people to use it.

The atmosphere of a particular setting affects how people and groups using that space feel. Ultimately, this affects groups' ability to function. For the most part, people judge their settings in terms of their perceptions of how hectic or calm they are, as well as how enjoyable they are. Although personal tastes and cultural preferences play a role in these perceptions, people prefer settings that are clean and lit appropriately for the activity.

Another component of the setting that influences how effectively a group operates is how enjoyable it is for group members. A setting that is overstimulating may be distracting to some people, whereas an environment that is perceived as understimulating may create feelings of boredom or disconnection. Stimulating settings may overload people's ability to process and evaluate the stimuli. Providing a setting that is suitable for the task at hand and meets the needs of group members will help ensure group success. Although recreation and leisure services leaders might not be able to work with groups in a perfect setting for every situation, they should try to provide a pleasant environment. This will help participants feel comfortable with their surroundings and focus on what the group is doing.

Environmental factors are sure to play a role in group dynamics. Recreation and leisure services leaders must be aware of how these factors and settings affect groups and individual group members and respond accordingly. If no action is taken, people will be more focused on making themselves comfortable or thinking about what is irritating them than on the group or the task at hand. Often, leaders try to tough it out and expect group members to do the same. Although this may work once in a while, we do not recommend making this a standard practice. We do recommend responding to or addressing environmental concerns as conditions warrant.

Leadership Theory and Working With Groups

We often hear students comment that what they read in textbooks is just common sense. However, when it comes to applying leadership theory to working with groups, there are intricacies that are not so apparent to many people, especially new leaders when they are in the midst of a group dynamics crisis. For example, some new leaders (particularly those in the field of recreation and leisure services) become focused on developing interpersonal relationships in a group that is just forming, allowing people to find their own way in the group. In other words, they adopt a hands-off, or laissez-faire, approach. However, most groups, particularly when they are forming, require more direction from the leader in terms of both the task and relationships. This section examines the joint application of leadership theory and group dynamics theory to working with people.

Trait Theories of Leadership and Group Dynamics

As discussed in chapter 6, trait theories of leadership assume that leaders are born with certain characteristics, or traits, that make them effective. Some traits do relate to leadership, such as an achievement orientation, adaptability, a sense of responsibility, self-confidence, and a high energy level (Wilson, 2005). Other traits that have been found to predict leadership include aggressiveness, alertness, emotional control, independence, integrity, and creativity (Forsyth, 2006). In terms of applying these to group dynamics situations, emerging leaders should be aware of the traits required for particular situations. For example, when a group is struggling with low energy levels, the leader should respond with increased energy.

Another way to think about applying trait theories of leadership to group dynamics is to think about the stage of development the group is in and decide which traits are most appropriate to exhibit at that time. For example, if a group is in the storming phase, the leader may choose to exhibit self-confidence to assure the group that even though things are tough at the moment, the leader is in control and will help the group get through the difficulty. What happens when a leader doesn't possess a certain trait or is uncomfortable acting a certain way? Regardless of the context, recreation and leisure services leaders can always turn to this basic guideline: clearly defining the role of the leader and what is expected from group members will promote cohesiveness, satisfaction, and group productivity (Johnson & Johnson, 2003). Of course, leaders also need to consider the stage and condition of the group. However, if they follow

these basic guidelines and take advantage of their strong traits, things will improve.

For leaders who do not have certain traits or are uncomfortable in certain situations, there are other ways to gain the skills necessary for addressing group dynamics emergencies. First, there are plenty of opportunities to develop leadership traits through practice. We suggest reading and responding to scenarios, talking with other leaders to see what they would do in a specific situation, and taking advantage of every opportunity to develop leadership traits. A second way is through formal leadership training. Many universities and colleges offer continuing education courses in leadership that help new leaders identify and develop the traits they need to improve. Finally, there are many professional development opportunities to practice leadership skills and build traits through organizations such as the National Recreation and Park Association, American Camp Association, and Association for Experiential Education.

Situational Theories of Leadership and Group Dynamics

Most people understand how situational theories of leadership (such as Hersey and Blanchard's 1982 model) fit with group dynamics theory, and in particular Tuckman's (1965) stages of group development. Recreation and leisure services leaders who can pinpoint their group's stage of development can choose the appropriate style of leadership by combining these theoretical areas.

As shown in figure 7.2, a leader should consider using a telling style of leadership with a group that is forming. This is because the group has yet to establish norms, and individual members have not yet assumed the roles needed for optimal functioning. In essence, the leader must do this on behalf of the group until it is ready to attend to the task and relationship functions to come. For a group that is storming, a selling style of leadership is best. This style is best because the group

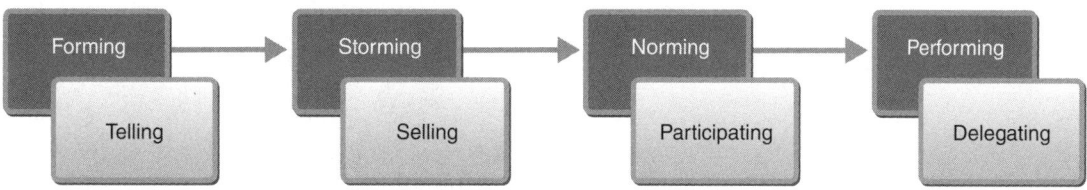

Figure 7.2 Leadership styles and stages of group development.

still requires direction and support, particularly when determining operating procedures and filling roles. The selling style is sometimes also called coaching, which is perhaps a better way to think about leading a group in the storming stage. For groups in the norming stage, a participating style of leadership is appropriate because the group is focused on the relationship function as people take on roles and finalize decisions about how the group will work. When working with groups in the norming stage, leaders can help them reach consensus. A delegating style of leadership is best for groups in the performing stage. Because the group is working well together on the task at hand as well as getting along, the leader can turn over control of decision making to the group.

Perhaps a simpler way to consider the intersection of group dynamics theory and leadership theory is to consider Tannenbaum and Schmitt's (1973) idea that the control of the leader should decrease as a group is able to handle more freedom in terms of decision making and positive relationships. This is not to say that the leader is completely removed from interactions with the group, but that she should be aware of how proficient the group is and allow it the freedom to operate on its own if it is capable of doing so. The leader can always step in and exert influence or control if needed. Figure 7.3 shows Tannenbaum and Schmitt's continuum.

Most people are comfortable with one or two styles of leadership. Recreation and leisure services professionals should be aware of their preferred styles as well as those they need to develop further. Strong leaders are able to quickly identify the needs of the group (i.e., stage of development) and respond with an appropriate style of leadership. Correctly identifying the stage of development and

leading with a particular style does take practice, particularly if the leader is new or if the style required for the situation is not one with which the leader is comfortable. Although leadership style and stage of group development are one area in which leadership theory and group dynamics theory overlap, there are others, including groupthink, polarization, and social loafing. These are discussed in the next section.

Common Issues With Groups

Working in a group is usually a good way to get things done, especially in recreation and leisure settings. Bringing together diverse people with their own opinions and ways of doing things can create a rich environment for success. However, traps and pitfalls can occur; leaders can avoid them by understanding some of the warning signs and responding accordingly. Common pitfalls include groupthink, polarization, and social loafing.

Groupthink

The concept of groupthink was introduced by Irving Janus (1972), a social psychologist who was interested in how some groups make such disastrous decisions. **Groupthink** is the tendency for group members to seek agreement with one another. The desire for agreement is so strong that any potential concerns about a decision from individuals in the group are pushed aside in favor of absolute consensus (Janus, 1972). Because of this desire, group members support and express confidence in a decision that may be problematic. Janus (1972) indicated the following warning signs that a group is headed toward groupthink:

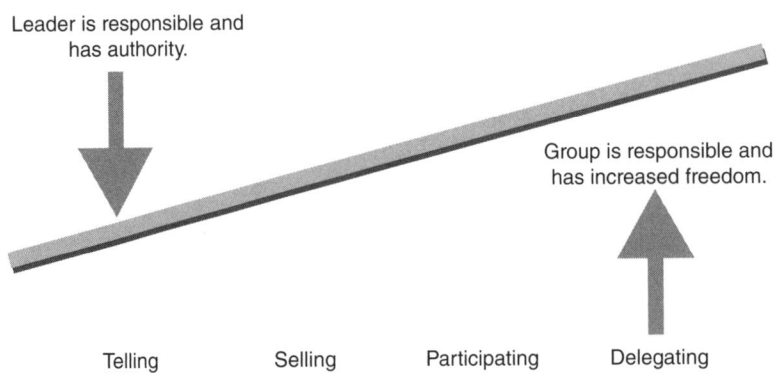

Figure 7.3 Tannenbaum and Schmitt's continuum.

▶ Pressure on those who disagree with the majority or favored opinion

▶ **Mindguards**, or group members who block information and opinions that oppose the decision

▶ Stereotyping of those who are outside the group who disagree or provide alternative solutions

▶ Self-censorship to keep individual concerns quiet

▶ Appearances of invulnerability, or the wrong idea that the group is making positive progress with a discussion or decision

▶ Incorrect justification that the discussion or decision is right, even though a careful examination would reveal many issues in the process

▶ False impressions of morality in which the group believes its decision is a good one despite potential ethical issues and consequences

▶ Appearances of total support, or the belief that everyone in the group is in agreement with the decision, when in fact, not everyone agrees with the decision (Janus, 1972)

These signs of groupthink might not be easy to notice right away, and may not even be recognized until after an incorrect decision has been made. However, some conditions contribute to a group's chance of falling into groupthink. These include separation from outside sources of information; leadership styles that repress people who disagree with where the group is headed; a lack of different experiences, ranges of experience, and backgrounds of group members; strong cohesiveness and bonds among group members; a lack of decision-making skills; and having to make fast decisions. Recreation and leisure services leaders should consider whether a group is predisposed to experience groupthink or if the conditions are right for groupthink to occur. If a leader believes that a group is headed toward groupthink, it is best to call a time-out and carefully consider the proposed course of action. This may be difficult if group members are working well together and the group has experienced success with decisions in the past.

Polarization

Working in a group certainly has many advantages, but there are disadvantages as well. Being in the presence of others can sometimes overwhelm individuals. This is part of a process called social facilitation in which people perform reasonably well on simple tasks and less well on complex tasks in the presence of others. Through this process, groups regularly adopt either more risky or more cautious positions than those initially held by any of the individuals. This was originally called risky-shift, but is now called **group polarization**. Researchers have found that groups make cautious decisions (cautious shift) as well as more risky decisions than the average of individual group members' decisions. Figure 7.4 shows the continuum of group polarization.

The starting positions of individuals and the group as a whole provide key information as to whether the eventual decision is either cautious or risky. Individuals and groups tend to assume more severe positions as discussion and the decision-making process unfold. If at the start a position is cautious, it will become even more cautious as the process continues. If it is risky at the start, it will get more risky. Recreation or leisure services leaders can help groups make good decisions by paying attention to the conditions, opinions, and positions at the start of decision-making process. By reminding the group of its initial attitude toward the issue or decision, a leader can encourage the group to reconsider, especially if the leader recognizes that it is polarizing in a cautious or risky way.

What makes group polarization happen? The way people are influenced by and influence the group contributes to the chance that polarization will occur. The thing that attracts people to groups, how norms are created, the feelings of connectedness that develops, and communication structures all factor into group polarization. The following conditions may result in group polarization:

• *Information sharing.* People often confirm what the rest of the group already knows. However, people who have information not known to

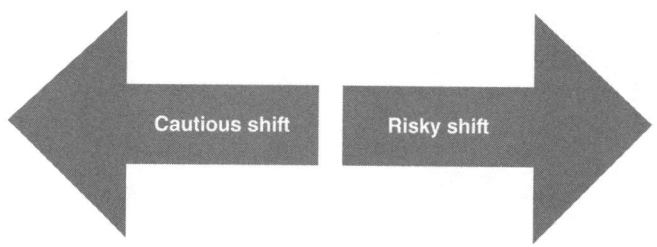

Figure 7.4 Group polarization.

the rest of the group might not share it because they want to gain an edge or have control over the process. Furthermore, if this information is distinctive or "out there," they may choose not to share it because they don't want to be embarrassed or sanctioned by the group. Fresh information may also influence group members if it is sensible, convincing, and well thought out. Finally, people may change the information they have to fit within the values held by a group.

• *Loyalty.* People may go along with polarized decisions because they want to stay in a group or be on good terms with other group members.

• *Norms.* The norms a group sets for itself around decision making may set the stage for polarized decisions, particularly if the group has had similar experiences in which things worked out favorably. People may believe that they need to support the cautious or risky stance to be looked at in a positive light. These people tend to become strong supporters of the proposed decision and disregard the polarized nature of the decision.

• *Convincing points of view.* People tend to support decisions the more they hear persuasive arguments. The more the ideas are discussed, the more people believe that the decision is sound. This is especially true if the decision is shared with others outside the group. People are not apt to easily switch positions once a decision has been made public—they believe they have to stick to their guns.

Group polarization can result in either positive or negative decisions. Recreation and leisure services leaders should be aware of the factors that contribute to group polarization so they can help groups benefit from the positive aspects of group decision making.

Social Loafing

Some group members see the group as a way to reduce their input to the decision-making process. People who tend to hide in a group and not contribute to their full capability are called **social loafers**. They turn the old adage of "Two heads are better than one" to their benefit. In essence,

When group members pull their own weight, this can help minimize the effects of group polarization.

© Human Kinetics

these people purposefully lose themselves in the crowd and do not work hard as a result. This may occur as a result of low group cohesion, individual inputs that are not recognized or evaluated, a group that is too big, the perception that others are not working, or a decision that is not considered meaningful or interesting.

On a similar note is the phenomenon of **free riding**. This is social loafing to an extreme, in which a member does not contribute to the group process in any way. The person gets the most from the group for the least amount of energy. People who have previously experienced this with other group members may be inclined to follow suit to avoid feeling taken advantage of. These people do not want to be easy targets or get stuck doing everything for the group. If individual contributions are supported and the rest of the group members are pulling their own weight, these feelings can be circumvented.

Summary

In the recreation and leisure services field, leaders will most likely spend much of their time working with groups of people. Understanding how groups work and some of the theory of group dynamics will help leaders help groups go about their business. Leaders need to attend to how groups develop as well as how individual members enter and leave groups, particularly groups that have a long history and are well established. Environmental factors, which are often overlooked, can have strong influences on group dynamics, especially in recreation and leisure groups. Leaders should not only be aware of how the environment is influencing their groups, but also be aware of some of the internal processes that happen in groups (e.g., the development of norms and roles) and be prepared to step in with an appropriate leadership style and strategies to address any hiccups along the way. Likewise, recreation and leisure services leaders should be aware of some of the common difficulties groups encounter such as groupthink, polarization, and social loafing. Appropriate leadership techniques can help groups avoid these pitfalls and make life easier for everyone involved.

Questions for Reflection and Discussion

1. What is a group? Why is it important for recreation and leisure services professionals to understand groups and group dynamics?

2. Identify and discuss some of the ways that groups form. How can a leader use this information to help groups better reach their goals and objectives?

3. What are group norms? Why are they significant for group members and leaders to understand?

4. Why are roles important in groups? List some positive and negative roles you might encounter as a leader in recreation and leisure services settings. What can you do to promote positive roles and confront negative roles within a group?

5. Environmental factors such as weather and temperature can affect a group's performance. Name some strategies for both indoor and outdoor recreation and leisure settings that you can use to enhance conditions for a group's success.

6. In terms of working with groups in recreation and leisure settings in the 21st century, what do you think are some of the biggest challenges you will face?

Key Terms and Definitions

cohesion—The tendency for groups to stick together when working toward reaching goals.

equilibrium models—Models of group development that focus on the stability of the task and social elements of a group.

free riding—When an individual claims membership in a group but does not contribute in any meaningful way to the group process.

group—Two or more people who are socially connected to one another.

group development—The growth and change within a group over time.

group polarization—The tendency of groups to take a more cautious or more risky course of action than individual group members would.

groupthink—The tendency for group members to seek agreement with each other.

mindguard—A group member who blocks information sharing and opinions that oppose his or her beliefs.

norms—Rules or parameters that guide the behavior in a group.

recurring phase models—Models of group development that suggest that groups may experience a stage of growth or change several times.

role ambiguity—A lack of clarity around a specific role in a group.

role conflict—The incompatibility of the behaviors required to fulfill two or more roles.

roles—Behaviors that are expected from a person who holds a specific position in a group.

sequential stage models—Models of group development that suggest that groups move through a series of stages in a step-by-step manner.

socialization—The process by which a person is integrated into and out of a group.

social loafer—A group member who contributes very little to the group and assumes that others will do more to complete the task.

Bibliography

Bales, R.F. (1965). The equilibrium problem in small groups. In A.P. Hare, E.F. Borgatta, and R.F. Bales (Eds.). *Small groups: Studies in social interaction.* (pp. 450-456). New York: Knopf.

Carron, A.V., Brawley, L.R., & Widmeyer, W.N. (1998). The measurement of cohesiveness in sport groups. In J.L. Duda (Ed.), *Advancements in sport and exercise psychology measurement* (pp. 213-226). Morgantown, WV: Fitness Information Technology.

Carron, A.V., Hausenblas, H.A., & Eys, M.A. (2005). *Group dynamics in sport* (3rd ed.). Morgantown, WV: Fitness Information Technology.

Eys, M.A., Burke, S.M., Carron, A.V., & Dennis, P.W. (2006). The sport team as an effective group. In J.M. Williams (Ed.), *Applied sport psychology: Personal growth to peak performance* (pp. 157-173). Boston: McGraw-Hill.

Forsyth, D. (1999). *Group dynamics* (3rd ed.). Belmont, CA: Wadsworth.

Forsyth, D. (2006). *Group dynamics* (4th ed.). Belmont, CA: Wadsworth.

Hare, A.P. (1981). Group size. *American Behavioural Scientist, 24,* 695-708.

Hersey, P., & Blanchard, K. (1982). *Management of organizational behavior: Utilizing human resources* (4th ed.). Englewood Cliffs, NJ: Prentice Hall.

Janus, I.L. (1972). *Victims of groupthink.* Boston: Houghton Mifflin.

Johnson, D.W., & Johnson, F.P. (2003). *Joining together: Group theory and group skills* (8th ed.). Boston: Pearson Education.

Kahn, R.L., Wolfe, D.M., Quinn, R.P., Snoek, J.D., & Rosenthal, R.A. (1964). *Occupational stress: Studies in role conflict and ambiguity.* New York: Wiley.

Longman, J. (2001). *Girls of summer: The U.S. women's soccer team and how it changed the world.* New York: HarperCollins.

Mabry, E.A., & Barnes R.E. (1980). *The dynamics of small group communication.* Englewood Cliffs, NJ: Prentice Hall. Moreland, R., & Levine, J. (1982). Socialization in small groups: Temporal changes in individual-group relations. *Advances in Experimental Social Psychology, 15,* 137-192.

O'Connell, T.S., & Cuthbertson, B. (2009). *Group dynamics in recreation and leisure: Creating conscious groups through an experiential approach.* Champaign, IL: Human Kinetics.

Tannenbaum, A.S., & Schmitt, W.H. (1973). How to choose a leadership pattern. *Harvard Business Review, 51* (3), 162-180.

Tuckman, B.W. (1965). Developmental sequences in small groups. *Psychological Bulletin, 63,* 384-399.

Tuckman, B.W., & Jensen, M.A.C. (1977). Stages of small group development revisited. *Group and Organizational Studies, 2,* 419-427.Westre, K.R., & Weiss, M.R. (1991). The relationship between perceived coaching behaviours and group cohesion in high school football teams. *Sport Psychologist, 5,* 41-54.Wilson, G.L. (2005). *Groups in context: Leadership and participation in small groups* (7th ed.). New York: McGraw-Hill.

Worchel, S. (1994). You can go home again: Returning group research to the group context with an eye on developmental issues. *Small Group Research, 25,* 205-223.

Worchel, S., Coutant-Sassic, D. & Grossman, M. (1992). A developmental approach to group dynamics: A model and illustrative approach. In S. Worchel, W. Wood, & J.A. Simpson (Eds.). *Group process and productivity.* Newbury Park, CA: Sage.

Chapter 8

Direct Leadership in Recreation, Leisure, Hospitality, and Tourism

Michael Van Bussel

" *Leadership rests not only upon ability, not only upon capacity—having the capacity to lead is not enough. The leader must be willing to use it. His [or her] leadership is then based on truth and character. There must be truth in the purpose and will power in the character.* "

—Vince Lombardi

G ary, the recently elected president of a recreational hockey organization, was mandated to lead the executive board and the organization for a three-year period. He is a front-line leader and is not afraid to get his hands dirty working alongside the members of the executive board.

Every year the hockey organization holds a tournament that is a major fund-raiser and vital to the operations of the club. Gary appointed two board members, Sharon and Bill, to lead the organization of the tournament. Both were new to the board and to the job of organizing the tournament. Bill was a friend of several members of the board, and Sharon was new to the community. Gary, Bill, and Sharon sat down and divided the tasks: Sharon was charged with organizing the banquet, running the concessions, and creating the program for the tournament, whereas Bill was responsible for booking the arena and banquet venues and organizing the volunteers.

As the weeks passed, Gary began to hear rumblings that work was not completed. Sharon complained that no venues had been booked and that she needed volunteers for the banquet but none were yet available. When Gary approached Bill, he was dismissive, saying that work had been extremely busy and he had not had the time to complete his tasks. Gary reminded Bill that the success of the club depended on this tournament. Gary asked Bill if he needed more assistance. Bill said no and that he would get right on it. Gary left the meeting with some lingering questions: *What do I do if these tasks are not completed? Should I have taken on some of these tasks myself? Should I replace Bill? If I do replace Bill, how will this affect the other members of the board?*

As a direct leader, what should Gary do? What could he have done to avoid the situation in the first place?

Learning Outcomes

At the conclusion of this chapter, students will be able to:

▶ Discuss direct leadership in recreation and leisure.

▶ Appreciate the dimensions of leader behavior.

▶ Explain the multidimensional model of leadership.

▶ Understand the gender dynamics that exist in the leader–constituent relationship.

▶ Use goal and objective setting in recreation and leisure contexts.

Grassroots recreation and leisure organizations generally possess a simple organizational structure, often a flat configuration with little to no middle management and minimal formalization (Slack & Parent, 2006). The most significant characteristic of this structure is the impact of the leader on the decision making and coordination of the organization. Leaders on the front line who work directly with individuals or groups in leisure settings have the proximity and ability to influence the experience and satisfaction of the workforce and recreational participants alike (Slack & Parent, 2006).

Direct leadership involves an immediate or face-to-face relationship between a leader and subordinate which affects approaches to motivation and problem solving. In this direct environment, group members are in contact with the leader all the time. Direct leadership allows for an immediate assessment of the productivity or problems of the group and provides an opportunity for quick problem solving. Thus, direct leaders have more opportunity to influence and develop the people in their charge than organizational or strategic leaders do, who have little or no contact with constituents.

Consider the owner of a river rafting company. This person acquires the resources, sets the policy, trains the guides to work on the river, and is also the front-line contact with client groups. The owner is able to quickly solve problems and deal with issues that involve both the river guides and paying customers. Or consider a dive shop owner who takes a group out on a dive charter on a nearby wreck. The owner is involved with collecting fees and registrations, filling air tanks, piloting the boat, providing a briefing for the dive, and ensuring that both participants and crew comply with safety protocols. As a hands-on leader, the dive shop owner can swiftly react to emergent situations or changing weather conditions.

Direct leaders such as the owners of the river rafting company and the dive shop have real-time access to the situation and to the information necessary for making decisions. In other organizations, owners may be somewhat removed from the operations, may not have access to the appropriate information, and thus may not be able to make decisions that best address the situation at hand.

Recreation and leisure endeavors provide unique venues in which to examine human interaction, communication, and leadership. Depending on the style of leadership, the environment, and the demands of the situation, recreation leaders maintain a level of responsibility for the people under their charge and are a driving force behind the decision making of the group. This chapter addresses participant motivation, preferred leader behavior, models of leadership, gender issues in front-line leadership, and new ways to consider leading a group.

Motivation

What motivates people to become involved in recreational, leisure, and sporting activities? Several theories explain leisure choices. Whether viewed from the perspective of Neulinger's (1981) paradigm or Csikszentmihalyi's (1990) theory of flow, a variety of factors influence involvement in leisure. In sport, motivators for participation seem to be equally varied. Research on motivation in sport reveals different reasons for participating for males and females. Males, for instance, tend to focus on **extrinsic motivation**, which can come in the form of awards for successful achievement in comparison to their fellow athletes (Gill, 1992). Females, in contrast, focus on **intrinsic motivation** (e.g., the common good of the group as a whole) (Jaffee & Manzer, 1992).

The importance of understanding the needs of participants and creating an environment that meets their needs cannot be overstated. Direct leaders must be able to anticipate and adapt to the needs of the groups for which they are responsible. A failure to do so could negatively influence participants' enjoyment, leading to demoralization and the potential for risks to health and safety.

Equally important are the reasons people quit chosen activities. Indeed, the rate of disengagement can be directly linked the intrinsic motivation of participants (Sarrazin et al., 2002). Thus, a direct leader's focus should be on promoting intrinsic motivational elements to increase participant satisfaction in recreational or leisure experiences. Moreover, the behavior of leaders, particularly in terms of leadership style, can have a substantial effect on participants' motivation (Vallerand & Losier, 1999). Consider a person who is leading a group on a backcountry camping expedition for the first time. Although appearing confident on the outside, this person actually lacks confidence in their ability to lead the group. To control the situation, this person adopts an autocratic style of leadership and micromanages every aspect of the trip. Everything from the camp setup to the daily agenda (including curfew) is strictly enforced. Lacking any input into the trip and even permission to ask questions, the participants experience a decrease in intrinsic motivation and a lack of enjoyment. Providing opportunities for input, choice, and engagement results in a more empowering experience that may increase intrinsic motivation.

Preferences in Leadership Behavior

What do people want in leaders? Is there a list of characteristics to help us identify quality leaders? In the early 1950s, scholars began to categorize leader behaviors. For example, some Ohio State University studies selected *consideration* and *initiating structure* as the main dimensions of leader behavior (Hurd, Barcelona, & Meldrum, 2008). Creating a foundation of mutual trust and respect is the basis of *consideration*; *initiating structure* ensures that the leader is responsible for defining roles and structures through an assessment of work (Hurd, Barcelona, & Meldrum, 2008). Leadership researchers at the University of Michigan developed two dimensions as well, *employee-oriented leadership* and *production-oriented leadership* (Hurd, Barcelona, & Meldrum, 2008). A production orientation focuses on completing the task, whereas an employee orientation concentrates on getting to know employees and seeking a connection with the workforce (Hurd, Barcelona, & Meldrum, 2008). Both Ohio State and Michigan promoted caring and concern for group members; however, the latter focused on member productivity in completing the task.

The relevance of these studies to a discussion of direct leaders rests in their focus on the individual group member. Gone are the days of motivation by intimidation and fear. Understanding the unique needs of those who make up the organization and empowering them to make decisions provides intrinsic motivation and ensures happier and more productive group members. A failure to do so could result in dissatisfaction, higher turnover, and ultimately more costs to the organization as a whole.

Dimensions of Leader Behavior

In the search for clear descriptions of leadership, Chelladurai and Saleh (1980) came up with five distinct dimensions of leader behavior:

1. Training and instruction
2. Democratic behavior
3. Autocratic behavior
4. Social support
5. Positive feedback (Chelladurai & Saleh, 1980)

Table 8.1 presents examples of leader behaviors and the elements of leadership that relate to the five dimensions.

Training and instruction focuses on the performance level and skill acquisition of the participants. Daily instruction during practice and the coordination of activities would be considered

Table 8.1 Dimensions of Leader Behavior

Leader behaviors	Examples	Elements of leadership
Training and instruction	Improving performance level Teaching techniques, tactics, and skills Coordinating activities	Process and task accomplishment
Democratic behavior	Allowing participants to be involved in the decision-making process Getting group members involved in goal formation	Decision style of the leader
Autocratic behavior	Focus on authority Leader makes the decisions	Decision style of the leader
Social support	Satisfying the interpersonal needs of participants Being concerned about participants and a positive group environment	Concern for the needs of participants Motivational
Positive feedback	Rewarding positive performance Expressing appreciation for contributions and performance	Process and task accomplishment Motivational

Adapted from Chelladurai and Saleh 1980.

training and instruction (Chelladurai & Saleh, 1980). From a recreation and leisure perspective, training and instruction could include teaching correct rock climbing or paddling techniques.

Democratic leadership refers to involving participants in the process of decision making. Allowing members of the group to have input regarding processes or the formation of group goals reflects democratic behavior (Chelladurai & Saleh, 1980). Democratic leadership is not a laissez-faire approach to leadership (e.g., allowing group members to do whatever they want). It does, however, provide opportunities for feedback and discourse between leaders and subordinates. These discussions may lead to collaborative decision making and the creation of a culture in which everyone's input is valued.

When leaders demand compliance and separate themselves from the group, they are using an **autocratic leadership** style (Chelladurai & Saleh, 1980). Direct leaders who issue orders and ultimatums without consulting with the workforce or constituents exhibit autocratic behavior. This type of behavior is often seen in emergent situations when leaders lack time to make a decision (Chelladurai & Saleh, 1980).

Social support refers to the interpersonal relationship between leader and member and the attentiveness of the leader to specific member needs. An example of social support would be listening to participants and helping them with their problems (Chelladurai & Saleh, 1980). Finally, positive feedback consists of complimentary remarks regarding performance and a genuine appreciation of effort and participation (Chelladurai & Saleh, 1980).

Does Chelladurai and Saleh's (1980) dimensions of leader behavior constitute a comprehensive list of conduct for direct leaders? Do direct leaders use all of these dimensions all the time? Direct leaders need to assess group members as well as the situation they are in to determine which dimension of leader behavior to use, or if a combination of behaviors is most appropriate at the time.

Multidimensional Model of Leadership

To address the questions in the preceding section, Chelladuarai (1990) sought to create a model of leadership that encapsulates leader, group member, and situational characteristics. The multidimensional model of leadership, illustrated in figure 8.1, examined leader behavior from three perspectives: required, actual, and preferred (Chelladurai, 1990). The previously mentioned characteristics form antecedents that lead to specific leader behavior. Ultimately, that behavior may indicate the level of performance and satisfaction of participants in the activity (Chelladurai, 1990). For recreation

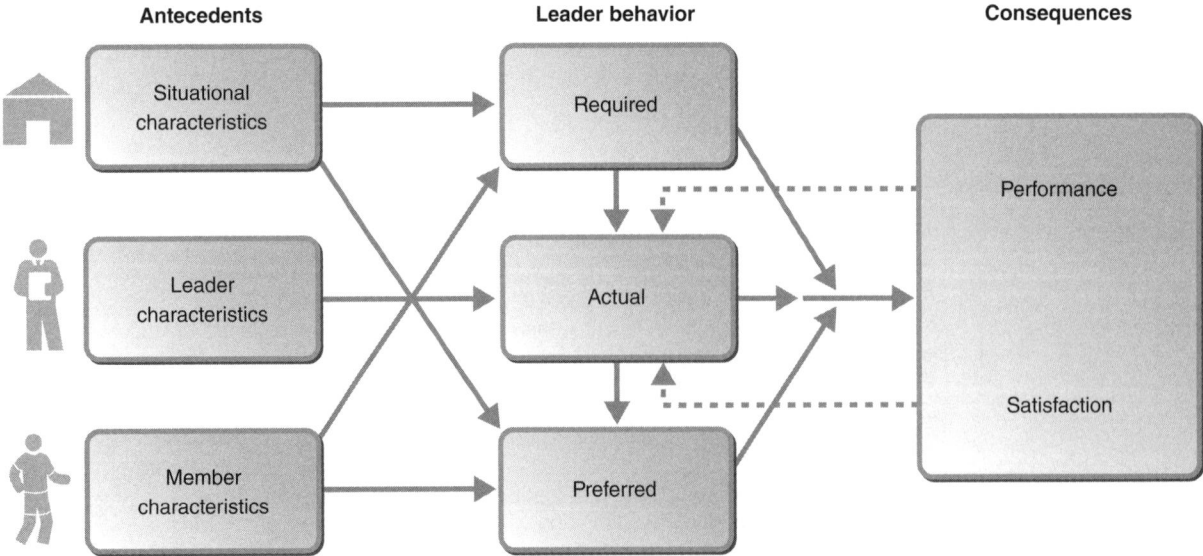

Figure 8.1 The multidimensional model of leadership.
Reprinted from P. Chelladaurai, 2006, *Human resource management in sport and recreation*, 2nd ed. (Champaign, IL: Human Kinetics), 194; By permission of P. Chelladaurai; Adapted from P. Chelladaurai, 1990, "Leadership in sport: A review," *International Journal of Sport Psychology* 21(4): 328-354. By permission of P. Chelladaurai.

leaders, and direct leaders in particular, this model highlights the multifaceted nature of leadership, the unique needs of group members, and most important, distinct situational elements that front-line leaders must face and adapt to on a daily basis.

Required Leader Behavior

Required leader behavior is seen by the organization and the environment as necessary for dealing with the demands and constraints of a situation. A failure to act in the prescribed manner leads to a decrease in the respect or admiration for the leader and ultimately decreases the leader's performance and effectiveness (Chelladurai, 2006). When comparing a recreational swim meet for kids and a competitive swim meet for young adults; the level of officiating for these two events would be very different. Comparing the expectations of participants, parents, and spectators, the need for high-level officials with extensive experience is much higher for the competitive meet than for the recreational swim meet for kids. A failure to provide appropriate officials for the competitive meet would destabilize the competition, frustrate the competitors, and undermine the leadership of the organizing committee. These demands set the bounds of required leader behavior.

Situational Characteristics

The situational characteristics leaders face may be extensive and varied. An analysis of any situation must include the goals of the group, the tasks at hand, the social norms for the group, the size of the working groups, formalized rules that govern group dynamics, and technologies that can be used to complete the tasks (Chelladurai, 2006). Using an example from sport, compatibility between a coach and an athlete is essential to the creation of an environment in which productivity is the norm. During high-stress situations, such as games, athletes who feel more of a connection with their coaches have fewer negative psychological effects and also feel that they can communicate in a much more positive manner (Kenow & Williams, 1999).

To examine situational leadership in a recreation setting, consider novice rock climbers who experience accentuated levels of stress due to the real threat of physical injury. In certain circumstances stress promotes increased effort and performance (Hardy & Hutchinson, 2007). The role of climbing instructors is similar to that of team coaches: they must be aware of the comfort level and level of technical skill of their participants. Positive communication and support during the initial experience with climbing helps participants with their outlook and encourages them to continue in the activity.

Member Characteristics

The nature of the group may also influence the behavior of a leader (Chelladurai, 2006). For example, a high ropes course facilitator may treat a group of 10-year-old students differently than a work group of 30-year-olds. Based on participants' level of maturity and physical ability, the focus could be quite different for these two groups. However, the facilitator should not rush to judgment. In this case, the young group could be supremely talented and focused, and the work group could be quite unfocused and disinterested in the activity. Direct leaders should constantly evaluate the membership of the group to determine their approach.

Just as leisure facilitators need to understand their constituents, so too should participants understand their leaders. Understanding gender differences in communication is beneficial for both leaders and participants. The gender difference in communication has been examined extensively by many theorists, including Deborah Tannen. Her research highlighted a need for people of both genders to understand communication differences and to appreciate the unique nature of gendered communication (Tannen, 1990). The examination of gender and communication has revealed that distinct speech identities are formed in females and males through socialization (Wood, 2007). The use of rough language, highlighted by aggressive posturing, has often been associated with male communication (Fasting & Pfister, 2000). Conversely, females tend to use an approach that focuses on dialogue and relationship building and promotes caring and understanding (Fasting & Pfister, 2000). Direct leaders need to be aware of these subtleties when analyzing group members to draw out the best in their groups.

Preferred Leader Behavior

What do participants want from their leaders? These preferences may be dictated by what is happening in the environment, the timing, the situation, the group, and ultimately the individuals themselves. A survey of students regarding the elements of leadership that appealed to them the most revealed that males preferred autocratic behavior (command style leadership), whereas females preferred democratic leadership (participant involvement in decision making) (Beam, Serwatka, & Wilson, 2004). This information is important to consider when choosing a leadership approach. For example, the coach of a female team may want to involve the players in the formation of team goals. Such a collaboration should yield a set of goals that are shared equally by the team and the coaching staff, and in the end group members will be active participants in the realization of these goals. This empowering activity should also enhance players' intrinsic motivation.

Leaders on the front line must be cognizant of their constituents and in a position to determine the unique needs of the groups they are charged to lead. This may change from year to year and from group to group. Therefore, the ability to adapt and alter one's leadership approach may be critical to maximizing participant satisfaction. Promoting independence in employees is also an excellent example of preferred leader behavior (Chelladurai, 2006). A therapeutic recreation specialist might prefer to create recreation programming for seniors herself rather than involve the general manager of the adult community, who may not have any qualifications in this field, in the oversight and approval of every activity in the program. Therefore, the leadership style of the general manager and other factors should be considered when making the decision.

Situational Characteristics

As mentioned previously, goals, tasks, social norms, group size, formalization, and technology may all influence a person's preference in leadership behavior (Chelladurai, 2006). The type of task and the ability to work independently are driving forces behind the need for leader monitoring and intervention (Chelladurai, 2006). With too much intervention, the element of empowerment may be lost; with too little monitoring, employees may not focus on the tasks as they should. In either case, dissatisfaction or complacency may cause a drop in productivity. Also, when direct leaders must wait for confirmation from superiors of their decisions, their ability to respond quickly to front-line problems may be compromised. Micromanagement by supervisors can lead to tension, disengagement, and ultimately dissatisfaction with direct leaders.

Communication in direct leadership situations differs substantially from the hierarchical and multilayered communication that occurs in larger organizations. The ability to communicate with front-line staff and respond to participant feedback directly allows direct leaders to make quick decisions and implement pragmatic solutions to everyday problems. Also, direct leaders must pay attention not only to their own actions but also to the actions of those around them. Using both verbal and **nonverbal communication** such as body language and expressions, direct leaders collect real-time information to help them make decisions and implement plans swiftly. Written communication such as e-mails and instant messages also increases their contact with subordinates and clients. A leader's ability to decipher small details in communication in shorter amounts of time may be the difference between providing a successful recreation experience and a terrible one. Ultimately, the recreation leader is responsible for creating an environment in which all participants may enjoy, grow, and succeed. Developing a process for environmental scanning, both internally and externally, will allow the direct leader to receive up-to-date information on what is happening in the leisure environment and feel confident in the decisions made with this information.

Member Characteristics

The unique needs of individuals also comes into play when considering preferred leader behavior. People who require a consistent level of affirmation may need more interaction with leaders, whereas those who seek autonomy within their workplace may need less interaction with their leaders (Chelladurai, 2006). Getting to know the people who make up the fabric of the organization is key in keeping one's finger on the pulse of the group and ultimately understanding members' needs. For instance, a democratic leadership style and elements of social support may be more appealing to female than male participants (Zhang, Jensen, & Mann, 1997). In contrast, in some situations the behaviors and preferences of both male and female participants are similar (Sherman, Fuller, & Speed, 2000). All athletes may prefer positive feedback and democratic behavior and may not appreciate autocratic behavior (Sherman, Fuller, & Speed, 2000). One study suggests that both males and females may gravitate to coaches who allow them to experience more freedom and personal investment without the anxiety of retribution (Sherman, Fuller, & Speed, 2000). As Fasting and Pfister

Best Practices From the Field

For over 20 years, leadership researchers Kouzes and Posner have interviewed and examined numerous leaders to learn their secrets to success. These stories of change and extraordinary leadership highlight important practices for leaders. Understanding the exceptional experiences of everyday leaders provided a rich resource from which these researchers developed their five practices of exemplary leadership. These five practices, and subsequent ten commitments, are as relevant today as they were when they started their research in 1983 (Kouzes & Posner, 2007).

Five Best Practices and Ten Commitments of Leadership

Practices	Commitments	Direct leadership examples
1. Model the way.	1. Clarify values by finding your voice and affirming shared ideals. 2. Set the example by aligning actions with shared values.	*Lead by example.* If the leader has emphasized punctuality, then the leader should always be early.
2. Inspire a shared vision.	3. Envision the future by imaging exciting and ennobling possibilities. 4. Enlist others in a common vision by appealing to shared aspirations.	*Promote your ideas.* Inspire others through your enthusiasm for a plan that has considered constituents' needs.
3. Challenge the process.	5. Search for opportunities by seizing the initiative and looking outward for innovative ways to improve. 6. Experiment and take risks by constantly generating small wins and learning from experience.	*Provide opportunities to take risks.* Elements of growth can be realized through risk. However, leaders must understand the capabilities of their constituents to create a safe environment in which they can grow.
4. Enable others to act.	7. Foster collaboration by building trust and facilitating relationships. 8. Strengthen others by increasing self-determination and developing competence.	*Empower your constituents.* Engendering trust by allowing constituents to make decisions promotes feelings of confidence and capability that will exceed all expectations.
5. Encourage the heart.	9. Recognize contributions by showing appreciation for individual excellence. 10. Celebrate values and victories by creating a spirit of community.	*Reward exceptionality.* In volunteer environments, it is essential to create a proper reward structure, recognize exceptional performance, and celebrate the success of individuals and the group.

Adapted, by permission, from J.M. Kouzes and B.Z. Posner, *The leadership challenge*, 4th ed., pgs. 14-26, copyright © 2007 by John Wiley & Sons, Inc. All rights reserved.

(2000) explained, "an awareness of the strong gender order in sport, and its implications for young women and men, is essential for both teaching and coaching and is a prerequisite if a change in the sporting culture is to take place" (p. 106). It is up to recreation leaders to promote change for the betterment of all constituents.

Many member characteristics can influence the direct leader's approach to communication, goal setting, and expectation management. Those in direct supervisory relationships may use member characteristics to maximize the experience for themselves and the people entrusted to them. Leisure leaders should adopt and refine their approach to member characteristics to meet the group's needs. Understanding these characteristics may result in a successful leisure experience for all.

Actual Leader Behavior

The true test of a direct leader is adapting and reacting to what is happening around them. The personality and ability of the leader influences his or her capacity to change and ultimately to choose the correct plan of action (Chelladurai, 2006). Task-oriented leaders tend to focus on performance outcomes and seek to control situations to achieve success (Fiedler, 1967). Relationship-focused leaders, on the other hand, are concerned with group dynamics and seek to promote a positive working environment (Fiedler, 1967). The inclination to choose one style or the other may be driven by experience, prior mentorship, or comfort level. Either approach can be successful, and the level of success may be influenced by situational and member characteristics.

Aspects of communication have also been highlighted as actual leader characteristics. The use of humor increases the bond between superiors and subordinates (Grisaffe, Blom, & Burke, 2003). On the other hand, the use of aggressive comments decreases constituents' level of approval of their leader (Kassing & Infante, 1999). A final aspect of communication to be considered is criticism. Criticism can be used by recreation leaders in a constructive and positive manner. Constructive feedback from the direct leader can motivate group members to improve their performance. Negative criticism has the opposite effect; in certain circumstances it places strain on the relationship and may ultimately affect personal elements such as confidence and self-esteem (Fisher, 1996). Direct leaders who fail to use criticism in the correct way may lose members or cause demoralization or disengagement within the entire group. The ability of the leader is another factor that affects behavior. Knowledge and expertise applied to the task is essential for its completion. For example, backcountry guides should have knowledge of the surroundings, techniques for lodging and food preparation, navigation skills, and emergency first aid practice. Without these skills, the guide may put others in danger along with themselves. Another key element is the ability to conceptualize how all the pieces fit together. Technical knowledge without an ability to use it in conjunction with other knowledge may limit its impact. However, if a leader can synthesize multiple items into a single plan, the effectiveness of the instruction and output of the group will be increased (Chelladurai, 2006). Likewise, group members seek the leader's expertise to maximize their performance and enjoyment. Indeed, putting all the pieces together is an important part of direct leadership.

Performance and Satisfaction

The concluding stage of the multidimensional model of leadership involves performance and satisfaction (Chelladurai, 1990). Creating a situation in which required and preferred leader behaviors closely resemble actual leader behavior bodes well for increased satisfaction and performance. As Chelladurai (2006) stated,

> The degree to which the three states of leader behavior are congruent (i.e., the actual behavior is consistent with both the preferred and required behaviors) influences performance and satisfaction. Thus, any of the states of leader behavior could be a limiting factor. . . . Similarly, if actual leader behavior deviated from the requirements of the organization or member preferences, it would detrimentally affect performance and satisfaction. (p. 198)

In the end, the multidimensional model of leadership describes the antecedent factors in leader behavior (required, preferred, and actual) and the consequences relating to performance and participant satisfaction (Chelladurai, 1990). Direct leaders need to be able to anticipate and forecast group needs. This ability may lead to flexibility and adaptation and maximize productivity and satisfaction. Whether organizing a backcountry expedition or coordinating a recreational sport league, having in-depth knowledge of the participants and subordinates and adapting one's approach to these constituents will result in increased levels of performance and satisfaction. Ultimately, the most important factor to consider is the front-line contact with staff and participants and the feedback this experience provides. Another way to gain an understanding of constituents is to examine similar groups in similar circumstances. Furthermore, looking at the preferred leader behavior found in these examples also provides a base line for the development of a leadership approach.

Tools for Direct Leadership: Setting Goals and Objectives

There are a variety of tools that direct leaders can utilize to motivate their group members. One of these tools is goal setting. Involving your team in the formation of both short-term and long-term

Leisure Leaders

Mark Eys

MY PREPARATION

- BA, BSc, MA, and PhD in kinesiology—Western University, London, ON
- Canada Research Chair (Tier II) in Group Dynamics and Physical Activity
- Early Researcher Award, Ministry of Research and Innovation—Province of Ontario; Canadian Interuniversity Sport (CIS) Coach of the Year—Western University women's soccer
- Ontario University Athletics (OUA) Women's Soccer Coach of the Year

Photo courtesy of Mark Eys.

MY CAREER

I am an associate professor and Canada Research Chair (Tier II) in Group Dynamics and Physical Activity in the Departments of Kinesiology/Physical Education and Psychology at Wilfrid Laurier University. On a day-to-day basis my responsibilities include teaching undergraduate and graduate students, conducting research focused on social/psychological issues within sport and exercise contexts, and helping in the administration of the academic programs of which I am a faculty member. I am also a member of the Healthy Communities Partnership within the Waterloo Region and part of the steering committee for the Waterloo Region Active Living Network, both of which are devoted to promoting active living as part of their mandates.

My career path to an academic position was fairly typical, consisting of the completion of undergraduate, master, and doctoral degrees. The first academic position I held was at Laurentian University within the School of Human Kinetics, specifically, in the Sport Psychology program (2004-2009). In 2009, I accepted my current position at Wilfrid Laurier University.

There is not too much to dislike about my job beyond the small obstacles that can arise at times (which can be overcome). Overall, I have the opportunity to pursue interesting research questions that I develop in conjunction with my graduate students, interact with students of all levels through instructing, and contribute to community initiatives devoted to promoting physical activity in our region.

I have the privilege of acting in a leadership role with students on a daily basis but consider leadership to be a continual improvement process. Overall, I try to employ a full range of leadership behaviors including both transactional and transformational approaches. These concepts are addressed in our research projects and in the sport and exercise psychology field more generally.

MY ADVICE TO YOU

I believe very strongly that the reason I have a career that I am very passionate about is that I have been fortunate to have had the opportunity to interact and collaborate with incredibly stimulating, trustworthy, and intelligent colleagues. Building these relationships, in my opinion, has given me opportunities to lead (and follow), in addition to the mutual provision of social support as I have moved forward in my career.

I view the field of recreation and leisure as incredibly valuable to individual health and quality of life. From a physical activity standpoint, recreation and leisure specialists can help to answer a multitude of challenging questions related to the promotion of an active lifestyle.

goals provides an opportunity for member input and ultimately creates buy-in for all those involved in the process.

Goal Setting

One of the first tasks in group development when leading a team or recreational group is to establish goals. **Goals** are intended aims of an individual or group to meet certain targets. Goals themselves can be short term or long term and involve several objectives. **Objectives** are specific measurable actions that are the building blocks for achieving the goal. The key element of an objective is its measurability. When an objective is completed, group members can move on to complete the next objective. The creation of objectives and their realization are influenced by direct leadership and the interactions of leaders.

Setting goals and objectives can occur in a couple of ways. First, direct leaders may choose to assign goals. This method has the benefit of timeliness and may allow the direct leader to promptly drive the direction of the group. Conversely, the autocratic nature of this approach may have a negative influence on morale and limit the impact of the goals themselves. Involving group members in the process of goal setting can have a positive effect on the individuals and the group. As described by Carron, Hausenblas and Eys (2005), "cooperative or participant-set goals produce double the effect of assigned goals. Possibly the sense of 'ownership' of goals is greater and therefore, [participants] work harder to achieve them" (p. 269). Soliciting input from participants during goal setting also increases their buy-in, making them more willing to work to achieve the goals. Therefore, participant-set goals instill an added responsibility for group members, highlighting the realization of the goals that they have agreed on and their duty to achieve those goals.

Another factor to consider when setting goals is the level of the goals. The direct leader must consider the level of the group and the ability of the participants. This information will dictate the level, complexity, and number of goals to establish. Goals that are established at too low a level may leave the group unmotivated. On the other hand, goals that are established at too high a level may cause frustration due to a lack of success. Establishing goals that provide early experiences of success can provide motivation. More challenging goals should be scheduled for later in the season so that participants have a long-term target on which to focus.

Be SMART

As mentioned previously, the building blocks of goals are objectives—the elements that must be completed to realize the goals. Peter Drucker, in his 1954 work *The Practice of Management*, introduced the SMART approach to formulating objectives:

S—Specific: Objectives must be concise and deal directly with the main issues in order to ensure success.

M—Measurable: Objectives must contain some way to measure their level of completion.

A—Achievable: Objectives must be established at an appropriate level, finding a balance between challenge and quick success.

R—Realistic: Objectives must reflect the unique circumstances of each group; not all objectives may be attainable by all groups.

T—Time bound: Objectives must be able to be completed in a certain time frame.

(Drucker, 1954)

The completion of SMART objectives ensures that the building blocks of goals are soundly constructed allowing a realistic and relatively predictable progression in their completion. Research has proven that the creation of goals and objectives for groups has a positive and lasting impact (Brawley, Carron, & Widmeyer, 1993). As a direct leader brings the group together to form goals and objectives, a sense of connection and togetherness and a true belief in the goals may occur (Brawley, Carron, & Widmeyer, 1993). However, the increased performance and satisfaction of group members is not due only to the establishment and implementation of goals. Rather, the maintenance and achievement of those goals also contribute group members' satisfaction.

Once goals and objectives have been established, they must be revisited and often altered to fit the situational constraints that are ever present in recreation and leisure environments. An example of an outdoor recreation trip highlights the importance of the flexibility of goals and objectives.

A group leader responsible for leading a back-country hiking expedition took the time to set goals and objectives with the group before leaving. The expedition was to take the group over mountainous terrain. The goal established by all group members was to reach the peak of one of the tallest mountains in the area. One of the final objectives was to reach the summit via a fairly challenging pass. The pass has several localized streams that are not usually significant obstacles. The group started out with clear weather and in high spirits. However, on the second day and for several days following, they encountered significant rainfall. The mountain rivers swelled with the sudden and consistent downpour. The deluge of water made their final chosen passage extremely challenging, and the leader was concerned about the safety of the group. The inclement weather had also dampened the spirits of the group.

The leader had to act. He brought the group together and discussed the alternatives: take the pass at extreme risk, take an alternate path that was significantly less challenging and reach the summit, or head back to base camp. After discussing the alternatives, the group decided to take the more heavily traveled alternate path. The rain continued as they set out, but as they got closer to the summit, the weather cleared and the sun began to shine. A sense of accomplishment washed over everyone because they had achieved their goal of reaching the summit safely.

Indeed, the ability to adapt to circumstances is an essential tool for direct leaders working with recreation and leisure groups in the field.

Summary

Working with leisure constituents on the front line, direct leaders are essential members in the operation of recreation organizations. This chapter began with a definition of direct leadership and emphasized the importance of this position as well as the motivations of leisure consumers. It is true that not all constituents want the same things in their leaders. The discussion of preferences in leader behavior provided insights into numerous direct leader experiences.

The discussion of the dimensions of leadership and the multidimensional model of leadership provided a context and focus for an understanding of direct leader behavior. Also discussed was the influence of gender on leader behavior. Furthermore, several suggestions regarding communication in direct leadership were forwarded. Finally, a discussion of setting goals and objectives highlighted the unique influence direct leaders can have on both employees and recreation and leisure participants. Truly, direct leadership is a complex, sometimes daunting, but ultimately rewarding task. At the end of the day, a smile on a participant's face, the thank-you card received from a team, and the accomplishments of a group are how direct leaders know they have been successful.

Questions for Reflection and Discussion

1. What are two characteristics of direct leadership that differentiate it from other forms of leadership?

2. Why is it important for direct leaders to understand the motivations of participants and employees under their care?

3. What is the difference between intrinsic and extrinsic motivation?

4. Chelladurai's (1990) multidimensional model of leadership highlights characteristics of leader behavior that are required, actual, and preferred. Think about a recreation leadership position you have seen or been involved with, and highlight two leader behaviors for each of the three categories. How did the convergence of these three elements affect the performance of the group?

5. You have been placed in a direct leadership role in a local recreation organization. Your first task is to create goals for the group. Using Drucker's (1954) SMART philosophy, create one short-term, one mid-range, and one long-term goal for your organization.

Key Terms and Definitions

autocratic leadership—Leadership that demands compliance and seeks little to no input from the group.

democratic behavior—Leadership that involves participants in the process.

direct leadership—Front-line leadership that involves an immediate or face-to-face relationship between leader and subordinate which affects approaches to motivation and problem solving.

extrinsic motivation—Motivation from an outside source (e.g., based on money or rewards).

goals—Intended aims of an individual or group to meet certain outcomes.

intrinsic motivation—Motivation that is generated internally (e.g., feeling good about the building of relationships).

nonverbal communication—Communication without words or sounds (e.g., facial expressions or body gestures).

objectives—Specific measurable actions that are the building blocks for achieving a goal.

Bibliography

Beam, J.W., Serwatka, T.S., & Wilson, W.J. (2004). Preferred leadership of NCAA Division I and II intercollegiate student-atheltes. *Journal of Sport Behavior, 27* (1), 3-17. Brawley, L.R., Carron, A.V., & Widmeyer, W. (1993). The influence of the group and its cohesiveness on perceptions of group-related variables. *Journal of Sport and Exercise Psychology, 15,* 245-260.

Carron, A.V., Hausenblas, H.A., & Eys, M.A. (2005). *Group dynamics in sport* (3rd ed.). Morgantown, WV: Fitness Information Technology.

Chelladurai, P. (1990). Leadership in sport: A review. *International Journal of Sport Psychology, 21,* (4), 328-354.

Chelladurai, P. (2006). *Human resource management in sport and recreation.* Champaign, IL: Human Kinetics.

Chelladurai, P., & Saleh, S.D. (1980). Dimensions of leader behavior in sports: Development of a leadership scale. *Journal of Sport Psychology, 2,* 34-45.

Csikszentmihalyi, M. (1990). *Flow: The psychology of optimal experience.* New York: Harper & Row.

Drucker, P. (1954). *The practice of management.* New York: Harper & Row.

Fasting, K., & Pfister, G. (2000). Female and male coaches in the eyes of female elite soccer players. *European Physical Education Review, 6* (1), 91-110.

Fiedler, F.E. (1967). *A theory of leadership effectiveness.* New York: McGraw-Hill.

Fisher, C. (1996). The perils of criticism. *Performance Edge, 5* (3), 1-3.

Gill, D.L. (1992). Gender and sport behavior. In T.S. Hom (Ed.), *Advances in sport psychology* (pp. 143-160). Champaign, IL: Human Kinetics.

Grisaffe, C., Blom, L.C., & Burke, K.L. (2003). The effects of head and assistant coaches' uses of humor on collegiate soccer players' evaluation of their coaches. *Journal of Sport Behavior, 26* (2), 103-108.

Hardy, L., & Hutchinson, A. (2007). Effects of performance anxiety on effort and performance in rock climbing: A test of processing efficiency theory. *Anxiety Stress and Coping: An International Journal, 20* (2), 147-161.

Hurd, A.R., Barcelona, R.J., & Meldrum, J.T. (2008). *Leisure services management.* Champaign, IL: Human Kinetics.

Jaffee, L., & Manzer, R. (1992). Girls' perspectives: Physical activity and self-esteem. *Melpomene: A Journal for Women's Health Research, 11* (3), 14-23.

Kassing, J.W., & Infante, D.A. (1999). Aggressive communication in coach-athlete dyads. *Communication Research Reports, 16,* 110-120.

Kenow, L.J., & Williams, J.M. (1999). Coach-athlete compatibility and athlete's perception of coaching behaviors. *Journal of Sport Behavior, 22* (2), 251-259.

Kouzes, J.M., & Posner, B.Z. (2007). *The leadership challenge* (4th ed.). San Francisco: Jossey-Bass.

Luminary Group. (2010). Vince Lombardi. Retrieved from www.vincelombardi.com.

Neulinger, J. (1981). *To leisure: An introduction.* Boston: Allyn & Bacon.

Sarrazin, P., Vallerand, R., Guillett, E., Pelletier, L., & Curry, F. (2002). Motivation and dropout in female handballers: A 21-month prospective study. *European Journal of Social Psychology, 32,* 39-418.

Sherman, C.A., Fuller, R., & Speed, H.D. (2000). Gender comparisons of preferred coaching behaviors in Australian sports. *Journal of Sport Behavior, 23* (4), 389-406.

Slack, T., & Parent, M.M. (2006). *Understanding sport organizations: The application of organization theory* (2nd ed.). Champaign, IL: Human Kinetics.

Tannen, D. (1990). *You just don't understand: Women and men in conversation.* New York: William Morrow.

Vallerand R.J., & Losier G.F. (1999). An integrative analysis of intrinsic and extrinsic motivation in sport. *Journal of Applied Sport Psychology, 11,* 142-169.

Wood, J.T. (2007). *Gendered lives: Communication, gender, and culture* (7th ed.). Belmont, CA: Thompson Wadsworth.

Zhang, J.J., Jensen, B.E., & Mann, B.L. (1997). Modification and revision of the Leadership Scale for Sport. *Journal of Sport Behavior, 20,* 105-122.

Chapter 9

Supervising Staff and Volunteers

Marilynn R. Glasser

" *Supervisors who leave their egos at home and offer* "
staff opportunities to learn, grow, and implement
ideas will have an easier job than their peers
and will be recognized by people throughout the
organization.

—Rich DiGirolamo, speaker and author of
Diary of the Happiest Employee on Earth

F ollowing college, Zoe worked for three years as a recreation leader with a small municipal recreation and parks agency. She has just accepted a new position, a great career step, as a recreation supervisor, and she's thrilled that she was the candidate selected. However, because this municipality is considerably larger than the one she previously worked for, five department employees will be reporting to her—and she's never been a supervisor. So, as happy as Zoe is to begin her new job, it's a bit scary, and she is understandably anxious about doing well and pleasing her superiors.

Fortunately, Zoe is the kind of young professional who wants to learn as much as possible about a new endeavor. She fully realizes that it will take time and experience to become the kind of terrific supervisor she hopes to be. However, she also knows that gathering, learning, and absorbing quality information about supervising will certainly provide a good start.

Because supervision is the essence of Zoe's new position, she will first need to learn what supervision actually means and why it's important. She will need to understand the many roles of a supervisor as well as the variety of responsibilities of a supervisor in the field of parks and recreation. Also, she will need to determine the expectations of her that her superiors and subordinates have. Through this learning process, additional topics will include delegation, motivation, training, communications, discipline, and evaluation. Volunteers represent an important resource in a number of programs and events in Zoe's new agency, so she will also need to learn about the differences between supervising paid staff members and supervising volunteers. Finally, she should learn the characteristics of the best supervisors and the common mistakes supervisors often make so she can avoid them.

Learning Outcomes

At the conclusion of this chapter, students will be able to:

▶ Define supervision, realize the importance of supervision to agency success, and identify the typical expectations of both supervisors and supervisees.

▶ Identify and explain a variety of responsibilities of parks and recreation supervisors, including overseeing supervisees and their work, assigning duties and projects, training, problem solving, decision making, motivating, delegating, evaluating, promoting professional development, enforcing policies, communicating, and disciplining.

▶ Describe the supervisor–supervisee relationship and its importance.

▶ Examine the realm of volunteers in the field and differentiate their roles, characteristics, motivations, and training needs from those of paid parks and recreation employees, especially in relation to supervision.

▶ Identify and evaluate positive and negative qualities of parks and recreation supervisors to determine the common mistakes supervisors should seek to avoid and the attributes and practices they should endeavor to adopt.

The recreation and parks profession is all about people. Practitioners in this field must truly enjoy people and should look forward to the leadership role they will play in providing parks and recreation services, the essence of which is enabling and encouraging the enhancement of quality of life. Thus, supervision must foster and motivate capable, enthusiastic employees who appreciate their positive impact on the lives of those they serve.

This chapter provides an overview of the knowledge and skills you'll need and the challenges you'll face as a recreation supervisor and presents ways to deal with your new responsibilities as you begin to develop your abilities. You'll gain confidence and be on your way to becoming a skilled, respected, and capable recreation supervisor.

Supervision is an integral component of leadership. After all, directly or indirectly, a leader oversees people, much like supervisors do. Exhibiting good supervision qualities is an important characteristic of being a good leader. Plus, a supervisor who demonstrates good leadership skills can inspire the highest level of performance from their subordinates and establish positive, productive relationships with them.

It should not be difficult to identify the connection supervision has with leadership. The related skills and abilities promote quality parks and recreation agencies. Supervisors are trained to monitor, oversee, and indeed, *supervise*, others. Whereas a definition of leadership highlights the ability to influence others, supervision tends to be more about delegating tasks to subordinates and then following their progress and results.

To be effective, supervisors must develop and put into practice skills and abilities that will enhance their leadership roles. Although some believe that supervision entails only overseeing the productivity and development of supervisees, certainly leadership skills are involved and play a great role in the success of a supervisor. This success then translates to the overall success of the organization. Thus, although leadership and supervision have different definitions, the relationship between them is an important one.

Table 9.1 provides a view of the differences between, and nuances of, leaders and supervisors.

Defining Supervision

Just what is the meaning of supervision, and why is it important to supervise staff and volunteers in our parks and recreation agencies? Let's begin by exploring a few of the ways supervision is defined by several organizations.

A firm called Rising Sun Consultants defines supervision as "A developmental process designed

Table 9.1 Differences Between Leaders and Supervisors

Subject	Leader	Supervisor
Focus	Leading people	Managing work
Have	Followers	Subordinates
Truth	Seeks	Establishes
Dynamic	Proactive	Reactive
Concern	What is right	Being right
Direction	New roads	Existing roads
Wants	Achievement	Results
Risk	Takes	Minimizes
Credit	Gives	Takes
Seeks	Vision	Objectives
Approach	Sets direction	Plans details
Power	Personal charisma	Formal authority
Appeals to	Heart	Head
Energy	Passion	Control

Adapted, by permission, from *Changing Minds*. Available: http://changingminds.org/disciplines/leadership/articles/

to support and enhance an individual's acquisition of the motivation, autonomy, self-awareness, and skills necessary to effectively accomplish the task at hand" (Pierce & Roswell, 2006, p. 1).

"Supervision is the process of getting others to become self-directed," states the Association of Professional Mentors, whereas the Free Management Library (managementhelp.org) says, "Typically supervision is the activity carried out by supervisors to oversee the productivity and progress of employees who report directly to the supervisors" (Shukla, 2009, p. 47). A more academic definition comes from the Syracuse University School of Education, quoting Bernard and Goodyear (2004):

Supervision is an intervention that is provided by a senior member of a profession to a junior member or members of that same profession. This relationship is evaluative, extends over time, and has the simultaneous purposes of enhancing the professional functioning of the junior person(s), monitoring the quality of professional services offered to the clients she, he, or they see(s), and serving as a gatekeeper of those who are to enter the particular profession (p. 8).

Lastly, William R. VanDersal (1968), defined supervision as "the art of working with a group of people over whom authority is exercised in such a way as to achieve their greatest combined effectiveness in getting work done" (p. 25).

Thus, reflecting on the preceding, we can define **supervision** as a means of directing, supporting, and monitoring those for whom a supervisor is responsible. Supervisory duties may include training new staff members, developing and assigning projects and tasks, verifying that plans are being carried out properly, providing support, assisting employees as needed, and providing discipline. Essentially, employees have their duties and responsibilities assigned, and supervisors monitor that these are fulfilled correctly. The staff is accountable accordingly, and the supervisor's responsibility is to ensure that the assignments are accomplished accurately and efficiently.

Why Supervision Is Important

A number of relevant points can be made about the importance of supervision and the benefits of quality supervision. Supervision geared toward helping supervisees gain competency enables

them to feel supported and valued, making the organization more effective. A well-supervised staff does a better job, makes the supervisor's job easier, allows the supervisor to be more efficient, and again, improves the effectiveness of the agency. Good supervisors can explain the requirements and responsibilities of supervisees, the methods they are expected to use, and the organizational norms and culture so that expectations are clear from the beginning; this can prevent a variety of problems. Supervision, with constructive feedback, can result in better employees who feel more fully integrated with their team of other employees, which, in turn, also makes for a stronger agency.

Good supervisors demonstrate to their supervisees that someone cares about them and their work. Their supervisees also know that they will have the support they need if they run into problems. Attending to these aspects helps to keep people happy with their jobs and encourages them to stay with the organization. Without good supervision, poor work may go unnoticed for a while, but eventually it will be realized, perhaps by the agency's administration or, perhaps more upsetting, a community member. Quality supervision can assist in recognizing and addressing issues before they can become serious problems. Finally, good supervisors who truly understand their jobs treat all their supervisees with respect and focus on the professional and personal needs and development of those they supervise and inspire enthusiasm about the work and loyalty to the organization's mission. This fosters positive attitudes, a happy, productive workplace, and ultimately, an agency dedicated to enhancing the quality of life for everyone it serves. Such dedication should be the basic mission of all parks and recreation agencies.

Volunteers, often integral members of a parks and recreation agency, also provide assistance with a variety of tasks, and thus, they, too, must be supervised. Their roles, however, are different from those of paid staff. Because they are motivated by different things, they require different forms of monitoring and supervision. A discussion of volunteers and the ways they should be supervised is provided later in this chapter.

What Is Expected of a Supervisor?

Providing effective supervision requires developing a repertoire of skills that may initially seem intimidating. Each supervisory position and group of people a supervisor works with will require different skills or combinations of skills. Although the field of parks and recreation has particular nuances, it is similar to other fields in many ways in terms of staff supervision. Developing supervisory skills is an ongoing process that should continue throughout one's career. The topics and challenges of providing quality supervision are numerous but extremely important for any practitioner to learn, understand, and appreciate.

Supervisors play a number of roles in performing their duties. They must be motivators, leaders, helpers, mentors, directors, coaches, supporters, empowerers, teachers, and often role models. Although that all sounds quite challenging, and it can be, the job of a supervisor can also be very rewarding. All supervisors take on these roles differently; some perform some roles better than others and may realize the need to shift their roles for particular employees or particular projects. Supervisors in the field of parks and recreation need to remember that their work is always about people—and, today, in our modern world, that often means not only people of different ages and backgrounds, but also from a variety of cultures and ethnicities as well as degrees of physical ability. All of these people have their own needs and wants and thus require different forms of motivation, types of assistance, and teaching styles. Finding supervision methods that will be successful for all employees under all circumstances is extremely unlikely. Thus, supervisors need to get to know their employees and determine how to encourage them to do their best, most productive work.

Because supervisors are usually expected to get things done through others, they are often caught in the middle between administrative or management personnel (such as a recreation director or parks superintendent) and the front-line employees (such as program leaders, camp directors, and sport coordinators). The expectations from both ends of an organizational structure can easily place supervisors between a rock and a hard place. Figure 9.1 shows typical duties both management and employees expect of supervisors.

Obviously, a good deal is expected of supervisors. They are indeed truly in the middle, above

---

Managers expect supervisors to do the following:

Demonstrate loyalty to the agency and all staff.

Understand and communicate management's philosophy and goals.

Follow and enforce all policies.

Delegate tasks.

Schedule work in an appropriate, timely manner.

Solve problems as needed.

Monitor and evaluate employees.

Staff various programs, events, facilities, and miscellaneous tasks as needed.

Be ever mindful of the budget.

Develop and maintain good morale.

Keep management regularly informed and updated.

Enforce discipline.

Set and follow priorities.

Employees expect supervisors to do the following:

Provide goals and direction.

Delegate tasks.

Support them.

Exhibit respect for them.

Be consistent.

Exhibit fairness.

Provide feedback.

Motivate them.

Represent their interests.

Provide training.

Defend them when necessary.

Recognize their efforts and successes.

Figure 9.1 Typical duties expected of supervisors.

those they supervise, yet below their own superiors. It's easy to see how important supervisors are in accomplishing the work of the agency; they are critical to ensuring that the goals of the organization (developed and expressed by senior management) are delivered to the organization's clientele (through the direct actions of the front-line staff).

Supervisors' Responsibilities

In addition to explaining what constitutes a supervisor, their importance to an organization, and what is expected of them, it is also critical to acknowledge their numerous and varied responsibilities. These responsibilities clearly indicate that a recreation supervisor must develop an extensive array of abilities and skills to provide the supervision required for a professional parks and recreation agency.

A look at the many responsibilities of recreation and parks supervisors reveals the variety of people they relate to in the workplace. In modern society, these people will be from different cultures, ethnicities, abilities (and disabilities), backgrounds, and of course, ages. These differences can be significant and directly affect the delivery and receptiveness of the supervision provided.

Consider that for the first time in history, four generations are working side by side in the workplace. Each generation has distinct attitudes, behaviors, expectations, habits, and motivations. Because research indicates that people communicate based on their generational cultures, effective supervision of workers of varying ages depends on learning about and understanding their differences. Supervisors can tailor their communications to encourage all supervisees to work as productively as possible. Table 9.2 shows how those born in four different time periods view and

Table 9.2 Workplace Characteristics of Various Generations

	Veterans (1922-1945)	Baby boomers (1946-1964)	Generation X (1965-1980)	Generation Y (1981-2000)
Work ethic and values	• Hard work • Respect authority • Sacrifice • Duty before fun • Adhere to rules	• Workaholics • Work efficiently • Crusading causes • Personal fulfillment • Desire quality • Question authority	• Eliminate the task • Self-reliance • Want structure and direction • Skeptical	• What's next • Multitasking • Tenacity • Entrepreneurial • Tolerant • Goal oriented
Work is...	An obligation	An exciting adventure	• A difficult challenge • A contract	• A means to an end • Fulfillment
Leadership style	• Directive • Command-and-control	• Consensual • Collegial	• Everyone is the same • Challenge others • Ask why	TBD*
Interactive style	Individual	• Team player • Love to have meetings	Entrepreneur	Participative
Communications	• Formal • Memo	In person	• Direct • Immediate	• E-mail • Voice mail
Feedback and rewards	• No news is good news • Satisfaction in a job well done	• Don't appreciate it • Money • Title recognition	• Sorry to interrupt, but how am I doing? • Freedom is the best reward	• Whenever I want it, at the push of a button • Meaningful work
Messages that motivate	Your experience is respected.	• You are valued. • You are needed.	• Do it your way. • Forget the rules.	You will work with other bright, creative people.
Work and family life	Ne'er the twain shall meet	• No balance • Work to live	Balance	Balance

*As this group has not spent much time in the workforce, this characteristic has yet to be determined.

Reprinted, by permission, from G. Hammill, 2005, "Mixing and managing four generations of employees," *FDU Magazine* Vol 12(2). © Fairleigh Dickinson University.

value concerns such as work ethics and attitudes, leadership and communication styles, motivation, and work life versus family life. Being cognizant of these characteristics and learning how to communicate with employees of different generations will maximize supervisory effectiveness and minimize misunderstandings and confrontations.

Creating, Assigning, and Assisting With Projects

Working on projects as a supervisor includes developing, planning, scheduling, and determining time lines and deadlines. It may also involve organizing supervisees for some projects or creating teams for assignments to be performed. In many cases, because of the nature of the work, supervisors should encourage creativity and initiative in employees, especially in relation to areas such as program and event development. In most cases, at any given time, each employee may have a number of assignments and responsibilities, some of which may be ongoing, seasonal, or annual. There will be both short-term and long-term projects, and the related budget planning will be an important part of this responsibility. In addition, some projects will take longer to develop and implement than others. Some will require just one or two employees, and others may need a large team of employees. Ensuring that the most appropriate employees have been assigned to particular projects based on their abilities, knowledge, interests, and experience is another important aspect of this responsibility.

Supervisors may certainly assist supervisees as needed, especially with newer projects. Going beyond the role of overseer and actually working with supervisees, especially to demonstrate duties, can provide valuable supportive lessons as well as establish confidence and foster goodwill. Supervisors should be comfortable with these scenarios and take advantage of these opportunities whenever possible.

Problem Solving and Decision Making

Supervisors must look ahead to anticipate problems, recognize them when they occur, ascertain their causes, and be able to assist employees in developing responses and solutions. In some cases, they may need to learn and implement systematic methods to make good decisions or solve problems. However, whether the decisions to be made or the problems to be addressed are serious or minor, quality skills in these areas are extremely important to develop.

Whereas **problem solving** refers to determining solutions to correct the discrepancy between a desired state and a current reality, **decision making** is choosing from two or more alternatives. Although these terms each have their own characteristics, they are clearly related, because either can precede the other; problem solving can produce a decision, and decision making can solve a problem. These are important facets of supervisory work to address and implement.

Typically, two types of decisions are encountered in supervisory work: programmed and nonprogrammed. Programmed decisions are typically routine decisions that are made based on policies. The policy helps supervisors know what to do and what decision to make. Programmed decisions are less time consuming and less difficult to make than nonprogrammed ones because they are largely prescribed. Nonprogrammed decisions tend to be more challenging because they are typically required for new, unique, and often unexpected circumstances. Most issues requiring a supervisor's attention are complex and don't fit neatly into a prescribed set of rules; more time and thought are needed to consider all angles of the problem. Thus, these types of issues require nonprogrammed decisions. Following is a step-by-step method for developing solutions to problems:

1. *Identify and define the problem.* This can be more challenging than it seems. The problem at hand may actually be a symptom of a larger problem that must be identified. It may also be important to obtain multiple viewpoints.

2. *Define the objectives for the solution.* Determine what the result should achieve. Because others may be affected, their anticipated reactions may require consideration.

3. *Generate possible solutions.* Seek multiple possible solutions, think outside the box, brainstorm, and acknowledge that any solution may be affected by emotional attachments to programs, products, or people. Sometimes, simply the idea of change can impede solution generation.

4. *Evaluate possible solutions.* All the solutions generated in step 3 should be considered and

then screened based on the objectives for the solution (as defined in step 2). It may be necessary or desirable to compare solutions, adapt them, or combine them.

5. *Select and implement the solution.* This is done by determining which solution will be the most beneficial and least detrimental. It is also important to make sure the selected solution is aligned with the agency's general goals and objectives, mission, and strategic organizational plan (and possibly the agency's master plan).

6. *Evaluate and monitor the solution.* This is often a learning opportunity as the consequences of the decision are examined, outcomes are identified and measured, and a determination is made as to whether the best decision was made. If this is not the case, perhaps due to unforeseen or uncontrollable factors, the process may need to be repeated.

It's important to note that it takes time and experience to master problem solving and decision making. Trial and error will invariably be part of the process.

Orientation and Training

Orientation and training help new supervisees get off to a positive start with the organization and enable all supervisees to be current with new techniques, procedures, and technology. A supervisor must be adept at providing guidelines and basic information to ensure that work is done correctly and efficiently.

An orientation enables employees to learn about the agency's culture, values, mission, and vision, as well as its structure, roles, policies, methods, and procedures for conducting business. Personnel policies outlined in an orientation should include topics such as compensation, benefits, safety information, and union relations (if applicable). In addition, employees should be given an overview of the functions and responsibilities of the agency, job duties, standards, rules, and performance expectations. Finally, a comprehensive tour of the offices and facilities should be a feature of the orientation, and attendees should also receive information about the community and the customers or residents the agency serves.

Following are five important purposes of an employee orientation:

1. It establishes a favorable impression of the organization.

2. It provides agency and job information.

3. It enhances interpersonal acceptance by coworkers.

4. It helps accelerate a new employee's socialization and integration.

5. It ensures that new employees can begin to perform well more quickly.

A mentoring program, either formal or informal, may be used for orienting new employees, or as an extension of an orientation. A mentor is a go-to person for the new employee, someone who can provide advice and support as well as a relationship of comfort and trust.

Supervisors need to make sure that supervisees are trained in how to obtain the information, supplies, equipment, and skill sets required for performing their responsibilities. In addition, they may need to teach specific tasks to help employees accomplish the goals and objectives of various projects, programs, and events. Supervisees must be trained in the nuances of the agency's ways of doing things—including basic issues such as where to find keys, office equipment, and suppliers and how to contact people and find local school information. Ideally, training will enable supervisees to develop expertise in their work, which they can

Mentors provide advice and support in an environment of trust.

Photo courtesy of Andrew Porto.

use in future assignments. However, supervisors will continually have training responsibilities, especially with new projects or procedures.

Another type of training that has become somewhat commonplace in many agencies and is often offered to all employees of a municipality includes topics such as time management, stress management, conflict resolution, customer service, and sexual harassment prevention. Although not specific to parks and recreation, it's easy to see how these types of courses can improve any employee's job performance.

Evaluation

Supervisors must ensure that job descriptions accurately represent an employee's qualifications and responsibilities. They must also set performance standards and appropriate, realistic job goals. Whether called an evaluation, performance appraisal or annual review, these must be conducted to assess employees' performance and develop improvement plans as needed. Performance appraisals may take any one of a number of forms depending on the agency's preference.

Although it is often said that the purpose of evaluations is to determine whether employees should be promoted, trained, given a raise, or fired, they are really supposed to help them develop and improve their skills and abilities. The objectives of an employee evaluation should be as follows:

▶ Help existing employees focus on their abilities, skills, and interests

▶ Improve employee job performance

▶ Provide formal periodic feedback to let employees know how they're doing

However, conducting employee evaluations can be very challenging for most supervisors. Actually, many supervisors do not like the task of evaluating employees. Unless a supervisor has had the experience of truly assisting an employee develop and improve in a job via an evaluation, she may question the time and effort put into conducting evaluations, given the discomfort it causes. Although all levels of parks and recreation agencies—employees, administrators, supervisors, and leaders—should appreciate the advantages of employee appraisals related to performance, development, and the better use of human resource power, few truly understand them. Evaluating an employee's performance requires training and

experience that few supervisors have, which is why it is an important supervisory skill to develop. Supervisors should explore the various formats, forms, and techniques used to evaluate employees and discuss the possibilities with agency administrators to develop and implement quality, equitable employee evaluation tools and procedures for the benefit of all agency employees as well as the organization itself.

The evaluative discussion should not only provide the supervisor with an opportunity to review the employee's work, but also enable the employee to provide feedback about the training, supervision, and support received from the supervisor. This maximizes the benefits of the evaluation for both people.

Encouraging Professional Development

Experienced parks and recreation professionals should assist in the development of their less-experienced employees. A priority for the agency, as well as a responsibility of supervisors, development can be considered an important extension of employee training. As an employee develops more skills and gains valuable knowledge and experience, the agency benefits along with the employee. For example, encouraging employees to attend and participate at professional conferences and workshops provides both formal and informal learning and networking opportunities and can result in new ideas, solutions to problems, and new resources for supplies and equipment. In addition, membership in professional parks and recreation associations should be encouraged and supported—ideally at local and regional, state or provincial, and national levels. Active participation in these associations creates true professionals who value and appreciate the opportunities to develop their skills, knowledge, and expertise, which benefit their agencies and communities as well as their careers. Finally, attaining and maintaining professional certification should also be encouraged.

Supervisors should also encourage their employees to keep current with the larger field of parks and recreation by reading professional journals, contacting colleagues to maintain networking relationships, and even seeking advanced college degrees. In addition, depending on employees' specific responsibilities, supervisors may suggest courses to obtain certifications offered by organizations

Pride in Parks (PIP) is a "performance-based management program" of the Westchester County Department of Parks, Recreation and Conservation in New York State, USA. It involves a comprehensive, outcomes-based performance measurement system that monitors the conditions encountered by the public when using the county's parks, and compares those conditions to standards developed by the department. Westchester County is responsible for the maintenance and operation of 18,000 acres of parkland. The Pride in Parks mission states: "Creating life-enriching experiences at safe, clean, affordable parks through responsible leadership and preserving our natural resources."

The parks receive unannounced inspections to compare conditions against a list of criteria for the variety of types of areas and facilities in each park. General categories include restrooms, picnic areas, playgrounds, roadways and parking lots, grounds, camping areas, and swimming pools and beaches. Each general category has subcategories more specifically identifying items such as signage, litter and cleanliness, surfaces, lawns, and floral areas. Some aspects, such as restrooms, are weighted more than others to emphasize their importance.

Following the inspections, a meeting is held with the PIP team members and the staff members from the park being reviewed. A PowerPoint slideshow is presented featuring photos of the conditions present during the inspection. Additional materials presented at the meeting include the inspection rating, a summary report, and comments from park visitors.

The meeting discussion centers on the overall well-being of the facility from the perspective of park users. The inspection results indicate what has been accomplished in relation to expectations and the circumstances that existed at the time of the inspection. Successes and areas needing improvement are clearly noted.

So how does this system relate to this chapter on supervision?

Park staff members were initially, and perhaps understandably, resistant to the PIP program. They were particularly upset about the surprise inspections by the PIP supervisor. Previously, they would know when supervisors would be coming so they could prepare their parks. They were able to make an extra effort as the day approached to make sure their parks were in excellent condition. The PIP program essentially put them on notice that their parks needed to be in tip-top condition every day!

Over time, the PIP program simply became a fact of life for the park staff. The inspections resulted in a number of positive changes in park staff. It increased their motivation, for example. Once the program became more accepted, park employees were more willing to follow through. Increased teamwork became evident. Even some friendly competition evolved among the park crews. As harsh as the program may have seemed at first, the results from this somewhat unusual supervisory experience have been positive for all:

- As the park employees became more accountable, they also developed more pride in their work.

- The department administration is extremely proud of the marked, ongoing improvement in the condition of the county's parks.

- Perhaps most important, the residents of Westchester County are truly fortunate to be able to enjoy the tremendous improvements created by the PIP system. Indeed, for them, "creating life-enriching experiences at safe, clean, affordable parks" has become an ongoing reality.

The PIP program has resulted in the Westchester County parks' being maintained in outstanding condition, virtually at all times, through a unique type of supervision that has encouraged excellence. Moreover, the majority of county park staff members have embraced the program.

The Westchester County PRC administration is quick to point out that the PIP program isn't perfect. The system itself is periodically evaluated and evolves to meet new demands and circumstances encountered in the parks and related facilities. Thus, supervision—the essence of the program—is applied to the program itself, which must recognize needed changes and be ready to evolve as well. This chapter presents many aspects of supervision. The PIP program is just one example of a modern approach and perspective that fosters professional, exceptional quality in the field of recreation and leisure.

such as the American Red Cross or state or provincial agencies. Certifications make employees more valuable to the agency and provide additional credentials for their personal professional development.

Supporting Personnel and Organizational Policies

Supervisors are responsible for ensuring that employees follow organizations' policies and procedures. They must be knowledgeable about this information and explain it as needed to employees when necessary. Policies include both human resource policies such as sick leave, personal leave, and vacations, and public policies such as dealing with the media and confidentiality issues.

Although problematic issues may come up infrequently, supervisors should know how to respond, or be prepared to contact the human resources office or peruse the personnel manual as needed. They must exhibit loyalty to the organization by communicating the importance of adhering to the established policies. Supervisors must be advocates for their agencies and convey that positive attitude to their supervisees.

Observing, Monitoring, and Providing Feedback

Once an employee has been given assignments, the supervisor's primary responsibilities involve observing, monitoring, and providing feedback. The supervisor must keep track of all employees, their assignments, and their progress in meeting expectations. The following points will help supervisors with these tasks:

- Be sure supervisees fully understand and accept responsibility for assignments and know what must be done.
- Explain to supervisees how their assignments fit into the big picture of the agency—how they contribute to the agency's overall business and services.
- Ensure that supervisees have all they need to accomplish their assignments (e.g., information, supplies, equipment, staff, and funds) and that they know what to do if additional needs arise.
- Keep the lines of communication with supervisees open.

- Create an environment in which supervisees feel comfortable approaching their supervisors, even with problems.
- Listen actively by focusing on supervisees when they are speaking and concentrating on the information they are conveying.
- Provide feedback by describing employees' work, not judging it; appraise how well employees are meeting assignment goals or objectives, as well as how they are reflecting organizational standards.
- Praise employees for good or improved performance.
- Be aware of tasks being worked on and whether supervisees are encountering difficulties.
- Avoid micromanaging, but provide direction and assistance as needed. **Micromanaging** refers to excessive control over people and projects, a preoccupation with the work to be done, and anxiety over how the work is being done. This can have a variety of negative results such as employees feeling that they are not trusted and consequently losing motivation.
- Encourage employees to be creative, try new ideas and methods, and accept new responsibilities. This can benefit not only supervisees, but also supervisors, the administration, the agency itself, and those the agency serves.

Delegation

Delegation can be defined as assigning subordinates tasks for which a superior has the ultimate responsibility. Delegation can help employees develop new skills, gain confidence, and develop a sense of ownership of tasks and projects. Delegation is directly related to the overall success of an organization. It is an extremely important concept but somewhat complicated and one of the least understood business management principles; thus, it is not an easy skill to develop.

Supervisors' attitudes toward delegation are important. They must be willing to delegate and let go of power, and they must trust supervisees, even if they are worried about minor mistakes. Effective delegation involves selecting the right people for particular tasks based on their skills, capabilities, and interests. Supervisors must clearly specify their preferred results; they should provide information

Supervisors must ensure that supervisees have all they need to accomplish their assignments.

about what, why, when, who, and where, and often, leave the how to supervisees. Supervisees can then complete assignments the way they choose as long as the results are what supervisors have specified. Summarizing the delegated task or assignment to their supervisors before beginning can help avoid misunderstandings.

As always, supervisors should maintain open lines of communication, seeking feedback from employees on the project's progress, as well as providing ongoing feedback. If they are not satisfied with the progress being made, supervisors should continue to work with the employee to achieve the desired results rather than take back the job. Ideally, for the growth of employees and related benefits, employees should perceive projects as *their* responsibility. Finally, the supervisor should address insufficient performance and problems and reward success.

Delegation can be very specific or very general. The more specific it is, the less flexibility and creativity the supervisee will have, whereas the more general it is, the more opportunity the supervisee will have to take initiative and be creative. Understandably, supervisors are more likely to delegate in a general manner to employees with more experience, education, and training.

Successful delegation takes thought, careful planning, knowledge of supervisees' areas of competence, good personal communication skills, and a willingness to take risks. Because this is a challenging skill to develop, supervisors should be aware of some of the obstacles they may face, such as the following:

▶ Believing that only *they* can do the assignment correctly, or that they can do the assignment better and faster than anyone else

▶ Being concerned about the quality of the work delegated because they have the ultimate responsibility for the tasks

▶ Not wanting to take the time to teach an employee how to perform the task

▶ Believing that the employee isn't competent to do the work or doesn't have the necessary training

▶ Feeling guilty for passing on tasks to employees who they believe are already overworked

▶ Fearing that an employee might outshine them

▶ Being unwilling to delegate tasks that they enjoy doing

▶ Demanding perfection

▶ Not wanting to take risks and being generally uncomfortable with delegating

To delegate successfully, supervisors should do the following:

▶ Recognize that delegation is not a technique for eliminating responsibility, but rather for dividing it up

▶ Know their supervisees' capabilities

▶ Know not only what is to be done, but also why, when, with what resources, and under what priorities

▶ Correct problems and errors with tact

▶ Show genuine, sincere interest in supervisees' work

▶ Reward supervisees for good work (more authority and responsibility can be particularly meaningful)

▶ Be cautious about taking back delegated assignments or authority. This action should be considered only when a serious problem occurs, such as a significant breach in safety procedures or a major policy violation; simple mistakes are not generally sufficient reasons to retract delegated responsibility.

Motivation

Motivation is defined as the drive to work toward certain goals and to expend considerable energy in reaching them. There are many resources on the subject of how to motivate others, including a number of well-known theories, but motivation must actually be initiated within the person.

Some of the common, accepted, conventional ways of stimulating motivation are through raises, promotions, and activities such as contests. Often, however, these methods are out of the reach of supervisors in civil service types of positions common to municipalities. They also may have limited effectiveness for certain employees and may even backfire, resulting in problems rather than increased motivation. For example, employees motivated by material rewards may flourish with a material rewards system, whereas those motivated by achievement will not. Contests may motivate employees who have a high need for recognition and thrive on competition, but a postcontest letdown period following intense productivity to reach contest goals can cause productivity levels to decrease dramatically.

Given that the recreation and leisure services profession is all about people, it's important to mention that employees and volunteers in the field have unique personalities, with their own needs, desires, goals, and expectations. They decide how much effort they will exert, and they are responsible for their own behavior, although external factors in the work environment will influence their behavior as well. Supervisors must be aware of these differences and take them into consideration when developing motivation strategies.

Quality supervision is perhaps the most important element in motivating supervisees. A good supervisor helps supervisees feel responsible and strong, recognizes and praises good performance and productivity, is willing to listen to both suggestions and complaints, provides opportunities for involvement in decision making, and fosters cooperation. One often overlooked motivator that should also be mentioned, especially in the parks and recreation field, is fun. Fun can reduce stress and often makes people want to work, encouraging them to perform better.

Figure 9.2 shows motivation dos and don'ts for supervisors.

Motivation, like delegation, is difficult to master. It's important to remember that motivation not only increases productivity but also improves supervisees' well-being, satisfaction, and morale, which makes for more valuable workers.

Communication and Meetings

Agencies need to have strong, ongoing internal communication. Again, with our profession's emphasis on people, this is an extremely important aspect of parks and recreation. With just a few exceptions, such as sensitive personnel issues, all employees should feel up-to-date on the latest activities and concerns of the agency. The following basic communication guidelines can help any agency or department:

• *Have all employees provide weekly status reports to supervisors.* These can be somewhat general or very specific, but they should include both what has been accomplished to date and what is expected to be done in the next week. They should include items such as problems or setbacks encountered or the need for additional resources. These reports help ensure that the employee and supervisor have a mutual understanding of the work in progress and can stave off issues before

Do	Don't
Communicate standards and be consistent.	Belittle or embarrass a supervisee.
Be aware of personal biases and prejudices.	Criticize a supervisee in front of others.
Give praise where appropriate.	Fail to give undivided attention, or seem preoccupied when conversing with a supervisee.
Inform supervisees of changes that may affect them.	
Care about supervisees.	Vacillate when making a decision.
Be tactful with supervisees.	Play favorites.
Be willing to learn from supervisees.	Be insensitive.
Encourage independence and confidence.	Fail to help supervisees grow.
Encourage ingenuity and freedom of expression.	

Figure 9.2 Dos and don'ts for supervisors regarding motivating employees.

they become more serious problems. Although some may see this as a tedious exercise, these reports are helpful for current and future planning and enable busy supervisees to stand back and reflect on their work.

• *Hold monthly meetings with all supervisees.* This provides an opportunity for all to catch up and review current activities and recent successes. These meetings can foster teamwork and agency pride and create an opportunity for employees to assist one another with particular challenges. Staff can also discuss and share their work with each other and request input if needed.

• *Meet individually with supervisees monthly.* All of the supervisee's work activities can be reviewed, feedback can be provided, and questions from both the supervisor and supervisee can be addressed.

Meeting management is an often overlooked set of skills that supervisors should develop. The following list can help supervisors hold quality meetings:

Selecting Participants

▶ Choose participants based on what the meeting is expected to accomplish.

▶ Contact meeting participants to inform them of the meeting's purpose and why their attendance is important. This contact should also include the location, date, and time of the meeting as well as a list of the expected attendees and whom to contact with questions.

▶ Provide a copy of the meeting's proposed agenda, in advance, to all participants.

▶ Designate someone to record important actions, assignments, and dates discussed and determined at the meeting. This person should ensure that this information is distributed to all participants shortly after the meeting.

Developing Agendas

▶ Develop the agenda along with participants. Let everyone know the overall outcome expected and the meeting activities to achieve that outcome.

▶ Design the agenda to encourage participants' involvement early in the meeting (e.g., something for them to do right away so they arrive on time).

▶ For each major agenda topic, indicate the needed action, the expected result, and a time estimate for addressing it.

▶ Post the agenda and encourage participants to refer to it as needed.

Opening and Conducting the Meeting

▶ Always start the meeting on time, welcome attendees, and thank them for their time in advance. This respects those who arrive on time and reminds late-comers that scheduling is serious.

▶ Review the agenda at the beginning of the meeting, and make sure all participants understand the major topics to be discussed.

▸ Clarify the supervisor's role in the meeting, and make sure attendees are familiar with the ground rules (e.g., being on time, speaking one at a time, turning off cell phones or putting them on vibrate, being respectful and courteous to all participants).

▸ Once the meeting has begun, keep up the momentum.

▸ Keep track of the time to avoid having the meeting run longer than planned (a common problem). If the meeting runs over, request input from participants about a satisfactory resolution.

▸ Given that complaints about meetings typically occur *after* meetings are conducted, request feedback during the meeting to keep the process on track, and encourage participants to indicate how they think the meeting is going.

Evaluating and Closing the Meeting

▸ Leave a few minutes at the end of the meetings for all participants to participate in evaluating the meeting.

▸ Also at the end of a meeting, review all actions and assignments. In addition, set a date and time for the next, or follow-up, meeting, and ask participants whether they can attend.

▸ Inform participants that they will receive a follow-up report about the meeting or meeting minutes, preferably within a few days; a week at the most.

▸ Make sure the meeting ends on time and, ideally, on a positive note.

Discipline

Discipline is handled somewhat differently from one agency to another, but it is an important facet of supervisory duties, albeit often an uncomfortable one. Even the best of agencies have staff members or volunteers who aren't working up to their potential or meeting the supervisor's expectations or who may be causing interpersonal or other problems. In these situations, the supervisor must intervene, keeping in mind that sensitivity to everyone's needs—the employee in question, the other staff and volunteers affected, and the agency itself—should be a prime consideration.

Supervisors should work to develop meeting management skills.

Most agencies' disciplinary policies reflect some version of the following four-step format:

1. *Verbal warning.* The supervisor confronts the employee, identifies the problem, and explains acceptable behavior and consequences if there are further incidents. (Although this first step is verbal, not written, the supervisor should make notes.)

2. *Written warning.* If the problem recurs, the supervisor documents the incident. The employee is asked to sign the warning; whether the employee signs it or not, the warning is placed in the employee's personnel file. The employee should be given the opportunity to respond in writing.

3. *Intervention.* Intervention usually involves developing an employee improvement plan, ideally with input from the employee. The plan identifies the problem and the effects of the problem, reviews the expected performance standards, and indicates possible solutions. The plan is then formally prepared and presented to the employee.

4. *Termination.* This serious, difficult step requires a great deal of documentation by supervisors and perhaps others. Most agencies have a number of policies and procedures regarding this step that may go beyond a supervisor's realm of responsibility. In addition, termination policies related to civil service or union concerns may have to be addressed.

Initially, when first encountering a disciplinary problem, the supervisor may need to cool off first or monitor her own reactions to the problem. She should avoid speaking in the heat of the moment, which often results in harsh words that tend to be more personal than objective. Privacy should be sought; the employee or volunteer should not be confronted in public, in front of others, or in a degrading manner. It's important that the supervisor be as supportive as possible—it may be an opportunity to learn why an employee or volunteer is not working as well as expected or why he has been disruptive or problematic. The supervisor must act objectively by focusing on the employee's behavior and the problem at hand, rather than on the person or his personality. Although such situations can be challenging, if the supervisor can determine the root of the problem, she may be able to find a way to transform the worker into an asset to the agency.

If the problem is poor job performance, the supervisor should clearly state the deficiency. Specific, not general, examples should be provided because they tend to be more difficult for the employee to refute. The supervisor should give the employee the opportunity to discuss her perspective and sincerely listen to the employee. There may be information or reasons for the behavior that the supervisor is not aware of and should hear. The supervisor should then identify the requirements for correcting the problem and solicit the employee's input on the corrective measures. The supervisor should be sure the employee is informed of the consequences if there are further problems and then monitor the employee's progress.

If the problem is a policy violation, the supervisor should first give the employee a chance to explain his actions. The supervisor should listen carefully because circumstances can sometimes justify a violation, which would require a different response. The supervisor should follow through with his responsibility and not apologize for the need to adhere to the policy. As indicated, his job involves enforcing rules. The employee must be informed, without equivocation, about what will happen if the behavior occurs again. If there is another occurrence, the defined consequences should be carried out immediately in a professional, impartial manner.

Discipline is a challenging aspect of a supervisory job that must be faced with know-how and confidence. Because serious problems often involve administration or management, new supervisors should make every effort to learn from their superiors as they gain the experience needed for handling these types of problem.

Supervisor–Supervisee Relationship

The relationship between supervisor and supervisee is often described as a partnership. The two work together to determine the best ways for the supervisee to learn and practice skills, solve problems, and continue to improve and grow as a parks and recreation professional. The relationship is a critical aspect of the workplace and promotes productivity and cohesiveness. This partnership concept should be the basis for all supervision.

Although some of the following may have already been mentioned, there are key points about the supervisor–supervisee relationship that can't be emphasized enough. To strengthen their relationships with supervisees, supervisors should do the following:

▶ Always show supervisees respect, trust, and confidence.

▶ Be available to supervisees and make it easy for them to talk with you by keeping an open mind.

▶ Discuss expectations with supervisees—both your expectations of them and their expectations of you.

▶ Make regular rounds to see supervisees in action. Let them know you are interested in them and what they are doing and feeling.

▶ Support supervisees, stand up for them, look out for their interests, appreciate them, and try to reduce pressures on them whenever possible. These behaviors will go far in endearing them to you.

Having examined the many responsibilities of a recreation supervisor in relation to subordinate staff, the next section discusses the important area of supervising volunteers. Although supervising volunteers is similar to supervising paid staff, the

differences are significant and must be recognized and addressed. Supervisors must acknowledge the importance of volunteerism in the field of recreation and parks and understand the skills needed for supervising volunteers.

Supervising Volunteers

Volunteers play an enormously important role in most parks and recreation agencies. They are an essential, valuable, and appreciated resource. Simply defined, **volunteers** are people who perform services without remuneration. They serve in numerous capacities, and many agencies, departments, and organizations would not be able to function without them. They extend agency leadership resources by serving in many programs and at many events, sites, and facilities. This section provides an overview of the many aspects of volunteerism found in the recreation and leisure field.

Characteristics

Volunteers who work in parks and recreation agencies may be of almost any age, from teenagers helping with sports, day camps, or special

Volunteers play an enormously important role in most parks and recreation agencies.

© Human Kinetics

events through senior citizens giving back to their communities. Both males and females serve as agency volunteers, and married people volunteer more than those in other marital status groups. People of all education, income, and occupational backgrounds volunteer, although those with higher incomes, higher education levels, and higher-level occupations predominate. Also, individuals and families with children are more likely to volunteer than those without children. Although research on the race and ethnicity of volunteers is minimal, the numbers in the United States appear to be proportional to national demographics.

Volunteers' Roles

Volunteers' roles in agencies can be generally divided into the following categories:

- ▶ *Direct service.* These types of volunteer positions relate to recreation programs, senior citizen services, sport programming, and activities in centers and other facilities.
- ▶ *Clerical or administrative work.* These tasks involve functions such as filing, telecommunications, program or facility registration, mailings, and serving as receptionists.
- ▶ *Public relations.* Volunteer efforts in this category include writing publicity or news releases, editing brochures, or speaking publicly on behalf of the agency.
- ▶ *Fund-raising.* This important area, fundamental to many parks and recreation agencies, involves planning or organizing fund-raising efforts, making phone calls, helping with mailings, or taking part in door-to-door fund-raising campaigns.
- ▶ *Policy making and advising.* Volunteers serve on boards, commissions, advisory committees, and councils. People volunteering in this capacity can be a particularly important component of the agency and often represent the interests of various community neighborhoods and groups.

Motivation

Why do people volunteer? Following are some of the many reasons so many people are happily motivated to donate their time to parks and recreation agencies:

- ▶ *Self-satisfaction.* It feels good to volunteer. People like to feel needed and to keep busy by helping their communities.
- ▶ *Altruism.* People often believe that helping others is the right thing to do, or something they *should* do. This motivation may relate to religious beliefs, family values, upbringing, or family tradition.
- ▶ *Companionship and meeting others.* This reason may motivate someone who is new in a community or perhaps recently lost a spouse.
- ▶ *Learning about a field.* Many people volunteer to receive training opportunities.
- ▶ *Helping to maintain an organization.* A volunteer may feel a sense of pride in helping an organization succeed.
- ▶ *Developing professional contacts.* Volunteering often presents excellent opportunities for professional networking.
- ▶ *Getting ahead in a particular field or occupation.* Volunteer work is valued by many, and some corporations even seek volunteer opportunities for their employees. In addition, many know that volunteer activities often look good on a resume.
- ▶ *Obtaining training or experience.* Volunteer work may be a route to a paying position, especially if new skills are learned in the process.
- ▶ *Providing entry to a particular organization.* A person with a desire to become involved in a greater capacity within an organization may do so by volunteering in order to get their foot in the door.
- ▶ *Social panache.* Some volunteers enjoy the prestige of being associated with a particular agency; volunteering could relate to obtaining a desired status.

Benefits

The benefits for volunteers can translate into motivation. Although they don't receive monetary compensation, they do reap valuable, meaningful benefits (as does the parks and recreation agency or department itself). The benefits of volunteering, to the volunteer, include the following:

- ▶ The satisfaction of helping to provide programs that wouldn't exist without substantial support from unpaid workers

Leisure Leaders

Erin Riedel

MY PREPARATION

- MS in recreation education—Lehman College, New York, NY
- BS in liberal studies (three minors: management, psychology, and wellness)—Southern Connecticut State University, New Haven, CT
- National Recreation and Park Association, member
- New York State Recreation and Park Society
  - Region 1 representative: 2012/2013
  - Young Professional Award: 2011/2012
  - Fundraising conference co-chair: 2011/2012
- Westchester Recreation and Parks Society
  - Auditions chair: 2013
  - Auditions co-chair: 2011, 2012

MY CAREER

I currently work for the Town of Yorktown Recreation and Parks Department in Yorktown Heights, New York. We serve about 36,000 residents. The department consists of 3 recreation professionals, 2.5 office staff, 12 parks laborers, and roughly 275 part-time/seasonal staff (camp, swimming pool, seasonal labor, and special events).

As recreation supervisor, I'm responsible for planning, promoting, developing, training, coordinating, and supervising some of the major segments of the department's programs and services for the community. I supervise all toddler and youth programs as well as some adult and senior programs and leagues. I supervise our seven-day camp programs and most specialty camp programs. I also have general promotional responsibilities including updating the website, sending e-blasts, communicating with local media, and coordinating flyers. I serve as liaison between the recreation and parks department and the Yorktown Community and Cultural Center.

Photo courtesy of Wilma Riedel.

I started in recreation as a child participant and later as an employed teen, lifeguarding. When I was about to graduate with my bachelor's degree, I thought, What am I *really* going to do with the rest of my life? I called my summer supervisor and asked her how she got into the field of recreation. She put me in touch with the recreation education program at Lehman College in the Bronx, and I decided I would get my master's degree in recreation. While attending Lehman, I started to work part-time for the City of Rye, New York, in the recreation department as well as in several other local recreation departments. After six months, a full-time senior recreation leader position opened; I applied and was lucky enough to get the job. I then worked for the City of Rye Recreation Department from April 2008 through April 2012, when I came to my current position in Yorktown.

My favorite part of the job is seeing participants enjoying themselves in programs and special events. I love to interact with the customers. If I could sit at the registration desk all day, I would, or if the summer camp could be all year round, I would be a happy camper (no pun intended).

My least favorite part of the job is dealing with politics.

I strongly believe that we lead by example. I follow the same rules my camp counselors have to follow. If I don't believe in something, how will my staff? I believe in helping with a job if it needs to get done and staying an extra 15 minutes if need be. No job is too large or too small. I believe in delegating but staying connected, saying *please* and *thank you*, and being understanding.

MY ADVICE TO YOU

Be passionate. Love what you do. If you don't believe in it, how will your customers or your boss?

Network! I got to where I am today because of the colleagues I pushed to associate with.

Try to get part-time work experience in many venues in recreation to become a more rounded candidate or employee (e.g., camps, pools, leagues, special events).

Ask questions.

I feel honored to work in the field of recreation. I get to provide quality, fun leisure programs for thousands of people throughout the year. We recreation professionals work in this field because we love it. We work when others play, and we are honored to do so. We love to provide, care, and give back to the communities we serve. Our field and the players in it are constantly changing, keeping us on our toes and making our jobs nowhere near boring!

- ▶ The opportunity to offer special skills, expertise, or leadership talents that staff members are unable to provide
- ▶ The opportunity to provide a new emotional ingredient such as a fresh outlook, enthusiasm, and interest
- ▶ The satisfaction of serving as a special link between the community and the agency by helping regular staff understand the needs and wishes of the constituency and by helping interpret agency goals to that same constituency
- ▶ Enjoying a recreation activity

Recruitment and Placement

The best volunteers are those who are actively recruited to meet specific agency needs. Examples of recruitment techniques include general publicity addressed to the community via local media; written appeals to community clubs and associations; volunteer recruitment fairs; and information listed in agency bulletins, newsletters, brochures, or websites.

Unfortunately, in today's world, some caution is needed when recruiting volunteers for recreation agencies. Those interested in volunteering may be required to provide as much information as an applicant for a paid position, and in many communities, that includes background checks conducted by local law enforcement agencies. Liability concerns are also extremely important for any agency or government in modern society. In addition, for some volunteer positions, such as coaches and umpires who work with young people, many agencies require that volunteers take specific training courses or obtain certifications via regional or national associations. Thus, recruiting volunteers can be challenging as agencies increasingly require a good deal of personal information from volunteers as well as hours of training prior to being accepted as a volunteer. Hopefully, volunteers will realize the importance of these requirements in today's unpredictable and litigious society.

Volunteers should be assigned to roles that appropriately and adequately match their skills, abilities, interests, and needs. They want meaningful responsibility and to be taken seriously and appreciated.

Some people have only a vague idea of the volunteer opportunities available, whereas others come with particular assignments in mind; those folks often expect the agency to be happy to have them. Sometimes, however, agencies have enough volunteers performing certain services or simply have greater volunteer needs in other areas but don't want to lose potential volunteers. This demonstrates the challenge of placing volunteers. An honest discussion with people interested in volunteering can help supervisors create good matches with the agency's needs. Supervisors can do this by (1) determining a potential volunteer's interests and desires, (2) presenting the agency's available volunteer options and needs, and (3) explaining exactly the tasks to be performed to encourage the person to give a particular volunteer job a try, even if it is not what the person envisioned doing. The supervisor must be willing to alter the volunteer assignment, if need be, or risk the volunteer seeking satisfying volunteer work elsewhere. Volunteer placement often requires understanding and sensitivity on the part of supervisors to make matches that work well for all—the volunteer, the supervisor, the agency, and the people served.

Orientation and Training

The purpose of orienting and training volunteers is to ensure the highest possible degree of satisfaction with their contributions to the agency. Like paid employees, volunteers should receive an initial, planned orientation followed by training,

© Hill Street Studios/E/ Blend Images RM/age fotostock

It's important to try to find a match of volunteers and tasks that works well for all.

as needed, to prepare them to perform their responsibilities. During an orientation volunteers should receive an assortment of agency materials to familiarize them with the agency's programs and services, a tour of the agency's offices and facilities, and an opportunity to meet with staff and other volunteers. Training begins with a review of the volunteer's job description, an explanation of the tasks, including how they are to be accomplished, introductions to the people the volunteer will be working with, and a review of the volunteer's anticipated schedule.

Supervision

Generally, supervising volunteers is really quite similar to supervising employees, but there are some important differences. One is that paid staff members usually require more structured and stringent supervision than volunteers do. Supervising employees varies depending on position level; those at higher levels require less supervision, and those at lower levels require more. These differing amounts of supervision and monitoring do not typically apply to volunteers. The additional struc-

ture required for employees relates to the higher expectations the agency has for them.

Supervising volunteers tends to be a somewhat sensitive task and, for some supervisors, can be challenging, especially when problems arise and there is the risk of hurt feelings. Because volunteers don't necessarily know the inner workings of the agency, they may require ongoing guidance from a supervisor to perform well. Ideally, this additional guidance may taper off as they gain knowledge and experience in performing their particular tasks.

Frequently, volunteers are not adequately supervised. Most of the reasons quality supervision is important for paid employees apply to volunteers as well. Volunteers, after all, deserve the same consideration to be conscientiously observed and assisted by supervisors to maximize the quality of their work and garner appreciation for their time and efforts. A parks and recreation supervisor should recognize the importance of this and provide that support and encouragement all supervisees seek and thrive on—both paid and unpaid.

Evaluation

Evaluating volunteers is another responsibility of agency supervisors, just as with employees. Volunteers deserve to be evaluated honestly, though again, because they are not paid for their work, evaluating them can be challenging. However, the feedback provided is important and meaningful. Volunteers are there to help and support the agency, and they will surely want to know whether they are performing their duties properly and meeting the agency's expectations.

Many agencies don't evaluate their volunteers. They may believe that because volunteers are freely giving their time, putting them through an evaluation would be unfair or even unappreciative. However, among other motivations, volunteers expect that they are providing service to well-run, dedicated, competent agencies. Conducting evaluations on volunteers as well as paid staff can be viewed as an indication that the organization is indeed a professional one.

Some agencies conduct informal or casual evaluations of their volunteers; however, we recommend using the same evaluation process that is used for paid employees. In most cases, the same evaluation forms and procedures can be used for both. However, some organizations may prefer to use evaluation forms or other resources specifically designed for volunteers.

Before joining the agency, volunteers should be informed that they will be evaluated periodically. This avoids any surprises. In addition, the evaluation should involve a two-way discussion, just as with paid employees, in which volunteers have the opportunity to evaluate the training, supervision, and support received in addition to being evaluated on the quality of their work.

Recognition and Retention

Agency volunteers must be recognized for their work, and their efforts must be explicitly appreciated. Recognition of volunteers is extremely important and often not done enough. Following are some of the many ways to recognize volunteers:

- Present certificates, gifts such as T-shirts or pins, and public praise at events.
- Write about them in articles in publications.
- Send letters of appreciation.

- Present special awards such as plaques.
- Thank them regularly.
- Request advice and follow through when received.
- Host formal thank-you presentations such as luncheons in their honor.

Recognition of agency volunteers is not solely to reward them for their time and energy; it also improves the agency's volunteer program and retains the excellent leadership resource volunteers represent. The best volunteers should be encouraged to stay and grow with the agency.

Problems and Challenges

Although supervising volunteers is mostly similar to supervising paid staff, following are some problems unique to supervising volunteers:

- *Dependability.* This is perhaps the most common problem with volunteers. Because they receive no monetary compensation, they may feel only a minimal obligation to arrive on time or to work regularly.
- *Liability.* The agency must establish legal responsibility for working volunteers.
- *Getting to job sites (transportation).* Transportation is often a problem in suburban and rural geographic areas or with teenage volunteers. Solutions include arranging car pools, agency vehicle programs, and parent transportation.
- *Assembling groups of volunteers.* Because volunteers often work on different days and times based on their availability and agency volunteer needs, arranging meetings and trainings can be difficult, if not impossible.
- *Developing or maintaining camaraderie among volunteers.* Volunteers' different schedules minimize their opportunities to share, bond, or compare notes with fellow workers, which can hinder their developing a sense of belonging.

Certainly supervisors need to address these problems as best they can and find ways to reduce the impact of these problems. They must not lose sight of the importance of what volunteers contribute to the overall success of the agency.

How to Be a Top-Notch Parks and Recreation Supervisor

As you take on the important responsibilities of overseeing others, remember times when you might have said or thought, "If *I* were the supervisor, I would . . ." Recalling those times can help you adopt positive behaviors and avoid mistakes in your own practice. Remembering again that the recreation field is all about people, it's important to note that the opportunities for both positive and negative interactions related to various supervisory duties are extensive. This is especially true in the early stages of gaining practical experience. Table 9.3 provides concrete advice on some dos and don'ts as you develop your knowledge and skill as a supervisor. Strive to respect your supervisees, encourage them to excel, and be mindful of your organization's mission. This will help you become an invaluable asset to the people you supervise and to the organization you serve.

This chapter explored many of the important aspects of supervision in the recreation and parks field. Clearly, supervisors must exhibit many qualities of both leadership and supervision regardless of their employment positions, titles, or responsibilities. Learning and developing the capabilities of a good supervisor can also make you a good leader, especially as you look toward future management and executive parks and recreation opportunities.

Table 9.3 Dos and Don'ts for Becoming a Top-Notch Supervisor

Do	Don't
Treat others as you would like to be treated That means, first and foremost, treating your supervisees with respect. You will always have an easier time keeping things running smoothly by respecting workers. That also means treating all supervisees fairly and equitably. In addition, you should model courtesy and civility in the workplace to create a respectful, caring, and professional atmosphere.	**Create perceptions of favoritism** Some supervisees are more likable than others. Yet, again, remember the field's people focus. You must separate supervisees' work contributions from your likes and dislikes of personalities. Treating all supervisees equally, with respect, is an important aspect of a supervisor's position.
Look and act like a leader Supervisees are more likely to respond to a supervisor who looks the part. This refers to dressing appropriately, being well groomed, and carrying yourself with a modest amount of confidence and authority. Supervisees will look up to you as role model in the agency—and as a professional.	**Be too emotional** Keeping your cool is key here. If you allow emotions to show, particularly anger, you may find yourself being considered temperamental or easily rattled, or worse, you may lose credibility. Being defensive or crabby when dealing with challenges to authority can be very upsetting, especially to newer supervisors, but modeling calm behavior and avoiding emotional displays can build confidence and exhibit authority.
Be trustworthy Along with respect for their superiors, supervisees need to be able to trust them and expect that they will be honest and ethical at all times. These characteristics also make supervisees feel safe and comfortable with speaking to their supervisors about problems and concerns.	**Vent or listen to venting** Avoid the all-too-common workplace habit of complaining. Venting to another supervisor may be acceptable, but even the appearance of acknowledging other employees' venting can be problematic. Venting is similar to gossiping and should simply be avoided, certainly by supervisors. Thus, don't vent to nonsupervisors, don't talk about others when they are not present, and don't even listen casually to employee venting.

Do	Don't
Get to know and care about your supervisees Remember that your staff is made up of multifaceted human beings with needs, interests, and lives that are important to them. When supervisees feel that their supervisors care about them as individuals, it can make a huge, positive impact on how they perform their jobs. Be friendly and interested, but don't attempt to be a friend *and* a boss.	**Rely solely on your experience with other supervisors** It's perfectly natural to emulate previous supervisors. Especially in the recreation field, many supervisors begin employment as teenagers (e.g., camp counselors or lifeguards), and they may have a number of supervisors before becoming supervisors themselves. It can be very tempting to act, or *re*act, as your former supervisors may have done in certain situations. However, it's better to communicate with a trusted resource (another supervisor, a superior, or a mentor at your agency) about your concerns. You should also develop your own style of supervising and handling challenges. Because your education should be ongoing, you can also read up on supervising and managing to learn how to hone your supervisory skills.
Practice mindfulness Mindfulness refers to paying attention to each interaction, each decision, and each communication you make. This means focusing on each of these simple actions when they occur. Consciously think about the way these actions will be perceived by others and the impact they might have.	**Be bossy** The most effective supervisors listen to their supervisees. With supervisees' input, you have the opportunity to make better decisions and obtain helpful feedback. A positive, open attitude toward your supervisees will foster respect, a positive attitude, and most important, a good relationship with them.
Listen really well The more you truly listen to what your supervisees say, the more they will feel that they are valued and respected and the more they will care about what you have to say and be engaged.	**Be unclear about your expectations** If expectations, especially for particular assignments or tasks, are not clear to employees or volunteers, you really can't expect them to meet them. Direct, clear, one-on-one communication with your supervisees can clarify expectations and thus ensure understanding—for both parties. By the same token, be sure you're clear about what the administration or management expects of *you*.
Realize that problems will occur You need to accept that problems are a normal occurrence in any agency. Approach them with an attitude of finding solutions rather than placing blame.	**Be unnecessarily harsh** "Using a hammer when a nudge will do" is another way to describe this pitfall. Small mistakes by supervisees are not uncommon and, at least to some extent, should be expected from time to time. Focus on handling these less significant issues with understanding and tact, while recognizing more serious problems that deserve a more serious consequence and reaction.
Provide appreciation, praise, and recognition Don't take supervisees for granted. Praise should be offered to both encourage and reward them. Be sure not to just praise supervisees for exceptional work; take the time to show those who regularly perform their work adequately that you appreciate their efforts. Good performance that goes unrecognized may diminish. However, don't praise too often. If you are always complimenting work, it ceases to have much meaning.	**Lie your way out of situations** When you make a mistake, simply admit it and take the consequences. This is about ethical behavior that *all* workers should exhibit. If you don't know the answer to something, admit it, but indicate that you'll try to find the answer. Both supervisees and the administration look to you for honesty. Your level of honesty will directly affect how trustworthy and credible you are perceived to be. A trusted reputation takes time and effort to build and will almost certainly be compromised, likely for a long time, by a single untruth.

continued

Table 9.3 *(continued)*

Do	Don't
Remember that supervisors are people too Show your supervisees that you too are human. Let them get to know you, share with them, laugh and have a sense of humor. The more genuine and authentic you are, the more your supervisees will care about what you think of their work and the more they will care about doing a great job for you.	**Take credit for a supervisee's success** Learn to take pleasure in your supervisees' accomplishments. Take pride in their work, which often makes you look good. Realize, too, that often their accomplishments are making a statement about your supervisory abilities. However, taking the joy of employee success away from those who worked hard to earn it breeds resentment and can seriously, and negatively, affect their future work.
Provide feedback and motivation Endeavor to let supervisees know that you really do notice the work they do. You've hopefully set fair and achievable goals for them and set them up for success instead of failure. Now provide motivation to encourage peak performance.	**Blame the administration for problems** A difficult, but necessary aspect of your job is defending management decisions, whether or not you had input and regardless of how you feel about the decisions. The administration expects support and loyalty, and thus you must refrain from any behaviors or actions that may sabotage administrative decisions.
Provide a positive employment climate This relates to fostering a healthy sense of self-esteem. When employees feel good about themselves and their work, they are far more likely to be cooperative and display a willingness to go the extra mile for you when needed. That can be a much appreciated attitude. In addition, an optimistic supervisor helps set a tone of positivity throughout the workplace.	**Sell out your supervisees** All employees and volunteers want their supervisors to represent them in a positive light to administration, to fight for them when necessary. They count on that. Even if you can't always obtain everything requested, you must be willing to work to get the resources, information, supplies, and rewards your supervisees want and need.
Confront supervisee problems quickly and decisively Never ignore nonperformance or problem performance. Identify and discuss the problem and review and clarify the assignment needs and expectations; this is not about blame, shame, or threats. Let the employee know that you require their compliance. Supervisors who aren't willing to deal with poor performance or behavior damage overall workplace morale and respect. Other supervisees notice and wait for their supervisor's appropriate response.	**Be afraid to say no** You may be asked to do more with less, especially in these tough economic times. Resources are often limited or scarce, including money, people, and time. There is only so much you can do, and attempting to do more may affect the quality of your other responsibilities. Altering your priorities may cause more harm than good. Don't be afraid to request help when additional, unanticipated responsibilities are assigned to you. Because working extra hours is often an expected requirement of supervisors, especially in relation to activities and events conducted on weekends or in the evening, you may be tempted to work excessive hours simply to avoid saying no to your superiors. You then run the risk of exhaustion or burnout and thus lose effectiveness anyway.
Spread goodwill When you act in a thoughtful, considerate manner, you inspire others to do the same. Supervisees' morale will be high and they will feel encouraged to do their best. That will have a positive impact on the entire agency.	**Give up your personal life** Despite the essence of our profession being about quality of life, recreation, parks, and leisure professionals often sacrifice their personal lives for their work. Many parks and recreation professionals are passionate about their work. However, when your work becomes the priority and it takes a toll on your health and personal relationships, the quality of your work as well as your personal life may suffer. You may become chronically tired with little time or energy for your family or yourself. Then, at work, you will become ineffective. Thus, find a balance, set limits, take vacations, have hobbies, and enjoy your life. Enjoy your work, and make sure your life reflects the values of your profession.

Summary

An understanding of supervision regardless of the settings in which it is conducted is important, as is an awareness of its value and the expectations of both supervisors and supervisees. Supervisory responsibilities in the parks and recreation profession include creating, assigning, and assisting with projects; problem solving and decision making; evaluating; delegating; communicating and holding meetings; dealing with discipline; and maintaining the supervisor–supervisee relationship. Although many aspects of supervising agency volunteers are similar to those of supervising paid employees, supervisors must be familiar with the differences so they can deal appropriately with people in both categories.

Parks and recreation professionals can be truly outstanding, valuable, and capable supervisors by avoiding common mistakes. Clearly, becoming a quality parks and recreation supervisor takes time, training, and experience.

Questions for Reflection and Discussion

1. What are some of the main reasons quality supervision is important in parks and recreation agencies? What might be the result of minimal or poor supervision?

2. What are some of the critical supervisory skills parks and recreation supervisors should develop to handle their numerous responsibilities? Which might be considered the most difficult to learn and perform? Why?

3. What are some of the characteristics that foster good supervisor–supervisee relationships? Which might be the most challenging to develop and exhibit? Why?

4. What are some of the reasons people volunteer their time and effort with parks and recreation agencies? Why should they be supervised?

5. What are some of the common mistakes supervisors make? How do these contrast with the characteristics of competent, effective supervisors?

6. Look back to the scenario presented at the beginning of this chapter. What steps might a new parks and recreation supervisor take when beginning a new job? Suggest steps that can be taken initially, and others that may take some time and experience to develop.

Key Terms and Definitions

decision making—Choosing from two or more alternatives.

delegation—Assigning subordinates tasks for which a superior has the ultimate responsibility.

micromanaging—Excessive control over people and projects, a preoccupation with the work to be done, and anxiety over how the work is being done.

motivation—The drive to work toward certain goals and to expend considerable energy in reaching them.

problem solving—Determining solutions to correct the discrepancy between a desired state and a current reality.

supervision—A means of directing, supporting, and monitoring those for whom a supervisor is responsible.

volunteers—People who perform services without remuneration.

Bibliography

Anderson, D.M., & Hurd, A.R. (2011). *The park and recreation professional's handbook.* Champaign, IL: Human Kinetics.

Bannon, J.J. (1999). *911 management: A comprehensive guide for leisure service managers.* Urbana, IL: Sagamore.

Barcelona, R.J., Hurd, A.R., & Meldrum, J.T. (2008). *Leisure services management.* Champaign, IL: Human Kinetics.

Bernard, J.M., & Goodyear, R.K. (2004). *Fundamentals of clinical supervision.* Boston: Pearson Education.

Brinckerhoff, P.C. (2010). Evaluating volunteers. *Mission-Based Management Newsletter,* www.missionbased.com/newsletters/july10.htm.

Campbell, C. (2011). *Leadership and its impact on supervision being an effective supervisor: Learned behavior or innate characteristic.* Unpublished manuscript, Southern Illinois University at Carbondale.

Coyne, K. (n.d.). Skills of a successful supervisor, http://ehow.com/list_5950149_skills-successful-supervisor.html.

David, I. (2011). How to be a good supervisor, http://ehow.com/how_4443631_good-supervisor.html.

Grossman, A.H. (1980). *Personnel management in recreation and leisure services.* South Plainfield, NJ: Groupwork Today.

Haag, R. (2008). Six steps to becoming a good supervisor. *The glasshammer,* http://theglasshammer.com/news/2008/07/23/six-steps-to-becoming-a-good-supervisor.

Hammill, G. (n.d.). Mixing and managing four generations of employees, www.fdu.edu/newspubs/magazine/05ws/generations.htm.

Heathfield, S. (n.d.). 7 ways to foster employee motivation—today, http://humanresources.about.com/od/motivationrewardretention/a/employee_motivation.htm.

Jamison, L.M., Murphy, J.F., Niepoth, E.W., & Williams, J.G. (1991). *Leisure systems: Critical concepts and applications.* Urbana, IL: Sagamore.

Kendrick, S. (2009). Evaluating volunteers. Volunteer Hub, www.volunteerhub.com/blog/evaluating-volunteers.

Lee, D. (2007). Want to be a "super supervisor"? Here are 11 things you can do. HumanNature@Work, www.humannatureatwork.com/Employee-Retention-Articles-Want-to-Be-a-Super-Supervisor.htm.

Lutzin, S.G. (1980). *Managing municipal leisure services.* Washington, DC: International City Management Association.

Mask, D. (n.d.). Everyday rules for every supervisor. Isnare.com, www.isnare.com/?aid=171093&ca=Business+Management.

McNamara, C. (n.d.). Free basic guide to leadership and supervision. Free Management Library, http://managementhelp.org/management/guidebook.htm.

McNamara, C. (n.d.). Guidelines to conducting effective meetings. Free Management Library, http://managementhelp.org/misc/meeting-management.htm.

McNamara, C. (n.d.). Roles and responsibilities of a supervisor. Free Management Library, http://managementhelp.org/supervision/roles.htm.

Nagy, J., & Wadud, E. (n.d.). Providing supervision for staff and volunteers, http://ctb.ku.edu/en/table-of-contents/leadership/effective-manager/staff-supervision/main

The nine pitfalls of new managers (n.d.), http://piecesofme.typepad.com/NewSupervisorPitfalls.pdf.

Opperman, M. (1999). Characteristics that make a good supervisor, http://theuniversityfaculty.cornell.edu/forums/pdfs/SupervisorQualities991217.pdf.

Pandey, K. (2010). Supervisor duties. Buzzle, www.buzzle.com/articles/supervisor-duties.html.

Pierce, R.A., & Roswell, J.S. (2006). The 10 keys to effective supervision. Retrieved from http://www.risingsunconsultants.com/resources/whitepapers2.html

Russell, R.V. (1986). *Leadership in recreation.* St. Louis, MO: Times Mirror/Mosby College Publishing.

Schwartz, A. (n.d.). Supervisor-employee relations: Tips for managers, http://ezinearticles.com/?Supervisor-Employee-Relations:-Tips-for-Managers&id=53912.

Shukla, R. (2009). *Talent management: Process of developing and integrating skilled workers.* New Delhi: Global India Publications.

Supervisor essentials—Supervisory tips & training. (n.d.). Supervisor Essentials, www.supervisoressentials.com/articles_sub7.html.

Supervisor's basic responsibilities. (n.d.). http://pbsbo.ucsc.edu/personnel_payroll/staff/basi_resp.html

The top 3 reasons why staff supervision is a manager's most important task. (2010). The Capable Manager, https://thecapablemanager.wordpress.com/2010/01/26/top-3-reasons-why-staff-supervision-is-a-managers-most-important-task.

Van Dersal, W.R. (1968). *The successful supervisor in government and business.* New York: Harper & Row.

Wolf, T. (1999). *Managing a nonprofit organization in the twenty-first century.* New York: Simon & Schuster.

Chapter 10

Team Development and Team Leadership

Greg Robinson

> " *The results across our numerous data points to one conclusion: Leadership is changing and approaches focusing on flexibility, collaboration, crossing boundaries and collective leadership are expected to become a high priority.* "
>
> —André Martin, *The Changing Nature of Leadership* (2007)

Ben is a leader of an established and successful program. He has a staff with a variety of tenure and experience. Although historically the program has been among the premier programs of its kind in the country, for the past several months Ben has noticed that enrollment has decreased. Those activities that were popular in the past are no longer filling up. At first, he thought it was just a temporary dip, but the trend is downward and has been for some time. This is not just a slow time; there is something fundamentally wrong with the program.

Ben's solution is to revise the type and structure of the program. In doing so, he will be changing the business model of the program dramatically. Activities that were once the flagship will be a smaller part of the program. And shorter, more accessible programs will become more prominent. The challenge is that Ben has a long-tenured, well-respected staff director with ties to the organization and community. In making this change, Ben will be reducing the very programs this director has made his career focus. The director is resistant, to say the least. There has been no room for discussion or compromise, and his efforts have kept any change from occurring. All the while, enrollment continues to decline. Some members of Ben's team, including his first assistant and some newer members, are on board with the change. Other long-tenured members are not necessarily against change, but they have deep relationships with Ben's resistant director and do not want to see him hurt or embarrassed.

What should Ben do?

Learning Outcomes

At the conclusion of this chapter, students will be able to:

▶ Explain what makes a team healthy and productive.

▶ Discuss how to design an effective team.

▶ Describe the role of a leader in forming and maintaining healthy teams.

We live in an age in which leadership and teams are not simply connected, but merging into each other. As a result of client requirements, work complexity, or limited resources, organizations are pressed to push responsibility and decision making lower in their chains of command. At the same time, leaders need to rely on others for broader perspectives and to develop solutions that are both sustainable and good for the organization at large. Leaders are no longer leading from the forefront, but rather, operating as an integral part of the teams they service. This is the demand of the 21st century.

This chapter explains not only how to form good teams, but also how to participate and lead alongside others. Various subjects are explored. The first is understanding team development. People cannot fully appreciate where they are and where they need to go unless they also know something about where they have been. This section provides some foundational concepts that will inform the later discussion. Among these concepts are stages of team development, a systems perspective of teams, and the paradoxical concept of individual factors for team success. Building strong teams depends as much on the maturity and competence of individual members as it does on team development.

The chapter then explores the differences between team and individual leadership. To lead a team successfully, leaders must know themselves well and clearly understand the issues at hand. Leading teams is primarily about clarifying a shared direction and creating the conditions for team members to do their own self-awareness and self-leadership work. Team leaders establish the atmosphere, expectations, and processes and continue to help the team make choices that lead to team improvement. This facilitative leadership approach can be challenging to leaders who prefer to demonstrate their personal competence through action, but it is necessary to ensure team success.

Next, the chapter explores team formation or team formation guidelines, as well as teaching teams how to be successful. Understanding the role of a team leader and being clear on the kind of leadership that will help the team is only the first step. What must leaders do to actually form their teams? How do they teach team members to take responsibility for themselves and equip their teams to be successful in a world that is constantly changing? Today's teams must use a different kind of teamwork than that used by teams of the past. Customer and client expectations, the mobility of the workforce, and rapid and constant change have resulted in the need for a new kind of teamwork. This section considers what a team development process might look like, as well as the type of infrastructure needed for sustainable teamwork and collaboration.

Importantly, this chapter also looks at examples of successful and unsuccessful team development. Looking at real-world examples of how teams are formed provides insights into how the ideas discussed earlier in the chapter appear when enacted.

Understanding Team Development

The foundation of good team leadership is an understanding of how teams develop. This section introduces the evolving understanding of teams over the last 45 years. The earliest work of researchers focused on understanding how teams moved through predictable stages as they worked out power and task issues. In more recent years, systems theory has enlightened researchers, who have focused more on teams as learning entities. Consequently, this section will explore the implications of systems theory on team dynamics. We will look at how systems theory explains how teamwork has changed over the years as well as the critical factors for individuals who want to be good team members.

Stages of Team Development

Every leader in a modern organization is concerned with teams. Gaining some understanding of how teams work and developing a model to guide assessment and intervention are crucial for success. The most widely known and accepted model of team development is from the work of Tuckman and Jensen (1977). From a survey of team research in 1965 and then again in 1977, Tuckman outlined a five-stage model for how teams progress through their life cycles. Table 10.1 summarizes the atmosphere, group tasks, and leader tasks in each of the five stages.

In Tuckman's model, teams start in a polite and anxious state as members try to understand their place, purpose, and role within the team. This first stage is called forming. At this stage, the team needs a hands-on leader to provide direction,

Table 10.1 Group Development Stages

Stage	Atmosphere	Group tasks	Leader tasks

Forming	• Pleasant
	• Some anxiety and tentativeness
	• Ignoring or being unaware of individual differences
	• Avoiding conflict
		• Joining the group (from me to we)
		• Finding a place in the group
		  • What is my role?
		  • How does this group work?
		  • What is expected of me?
		• Establishing trust
		• Learning names
		• Exploring commonalities
			• Being directive, providing structure
			• Helping the group deal with anxiety
			• Helping members define a safe group
			• Modeling looking out for everyone by listening, drawing out silent members, and enforcing rules of safe communication

Storming	• Internal strife (conflict that is going nowhere) • Trying to establish norms by destroying differences • Attacking the leader	• Trying to define who is going to control the group • Determining how safe the group is	• Acknowledging the chaos and helping members know it is okay • Helping members understand why they may feel anxious again • Teaching new skills that may be needed • Continuing to promote equal participation of members • Modeling calmness and confidence in the group
Norming	• Accepting individual differences • Some relaxation and togetherness • Beginning to experiment with new ideas and becoming ready to take more risks	• Relinquishing preconceived expectations and solutions • Giving up the need to be in control • Trusting the group • Communicating openly and honestly	• Beginning to be less directive and letting the group take responsibility for itself • Encouraging the group • Continuing to empower silent members
Performing	• Appreciating differences • Feeling safe • Renewed confidence • Shared leadership	• Good communication • Dealing with conflict in a healthy manner • Working on individual goals • Preparing to generalize learning • Self-disclosure	• Being less directive • Evaluating the group to see if it has returned to an earlier stage • Playing devil's advocate • Encouraging the group to work together • Monitoring safety issues
Adjourning	• Some sense of sadness or anger • Some distancing as members prepare to leave	• Reflecting on the experience as a whole • Planning for the future • Saying goodbye	• Becoming more directive again, providing structure • Normalizing feelings

create structure for team interaction, and promote relationship building. After some time, teams typically experience what Tuckman called storming. This stage is marked by intragroup conflict as differences become known, power roles are determined, and the group tests the roles and relationships forming within the team. This struggle is typically part of the trust-building process as team members push relationships to determine each team member's commitment to the group. This is a crucial stage because unresolved conflict can cause the team to fail or retreat to the polite forming stage, thereby limiting its ability to excel. The leader can again provide immediate support by being present and providing guidance and structure to help the team articulate the conflict sources and begin to acknowledge team norms that will facilitate progress.

This leads the team into Tuckman's third stage; norming. In the norming stage, group cohesion begins to form as members reach agreement on their task, their roles, and the relationship dynamics of the team. Members begin to comply with an accepted standard for the sake of the team's work. Individual members begin to let go of preconceived ideas about the team and enter into solidarity with their teammates. The leader's role is less directive and more supportive at this point as the team begins to take more responsibility for its own functioning.

With relationship expectations defined, the team can now move full force into its work. Tuckman called this fourth stage of development performing. Teams that reach this stage are fully engaged in their task. This is the most productive period. The leader is no longer at the forefront because the team can handle its work with minimal support and guidance.

The fifth stage is called adjourning. As the team's work comes to an end, there is often a regression to behavior that can resemble the politeness of the forming stage or the conflict of the storming stage. As members begin to release relationships and start to pull away from the team, ambivalent and even powerful emotions may surface. Some members may be sad that a good experience is ending. Some may become angry over missed opportunities or perceived failure, either of the team or of themselves personally. The leader's role once again shifts to a more directive stance as the team begins to end. The leader can help team members articulate their feelings by providing structure and processes to help them reflect, assess, and confirm the lessons learned from the experience.

Teams as Systems

From Tuckman's perspective, teams were understood in terms of their relationship to their task and the orientation of power in the team. This perspective, consistent with early leadership research, focused on task and relationship dimensions (Priest & Gass, 1997). Framing the issues through these lenses worked well for traditional teams focused on completing tasks. However, as the world began to move toward the knowledge era, a new understanding was required.

In his seminal book *The Fifth Discipline*, Peter Senge (1990) proposed that we look at teams as learning systems. A **system** is an entity made up of interdependent parts that form a complex or unified whole. From a systems perspective, we cannot really understand the part or individual unless we understand the context of the relationships of the whole system. This perspective moves the focus toward the quality of interactions as a key to understanding teams. Seeing teams as systems provides insight into how the relationships among the team members influence not only the atmosphere of the team, but also the assumptions the team holds and how the team thinks as a whole.

Team learning has to do with the ability of a group to gain access to the assumptions, both individual and collective, that guide the team's values, beliefs, and actions. Through dialogue, the team enters into a relationship of trust in which members try to suspend their personal judgments while also freely sharing their assumptions. When a critical mass of members possesses the self-awareness and courage to hold such conversations, team members will be able to see things together that they could never have seen as individuals. In this sense, the whole becomes more than the sum of the parts. As Senge (1990) stated, "When teams are truly learning, not only are they producing extraordinary results but the individual members are growing more rapidly than could have occurred otherwise" (p. 10).

Senge's (1990) work coincided with that of Edwin Friedman (1999), who extended Bowen family systems theory to organizations. In the Bowenian framework, groups, like families, are understood as emotional systems. As in other forms of system theory, there is a focus on relationships and the mutual influence team members have on each other. Whereas Senge explored the cognitive aspect of team functioning and improvement, Friedman sought to understand the emotional aspect of a team. The key to understanding a team is to recognize the ways anxiety influences its development and success. All living entities have **emotional process**, which is the ability to take in information from the environment and respond to it.

Figure 10.1 describes the emotional process cycle and the typical pitfalls people encounter. The emotional process is a survival process in which people scan the environment for potential threats. Discovery of a threat triggers an anxiety response. This strong emotion stimulates action to return to a state of security. As a result of cognitive processing, human beings can further complicate the process. Most of us are raised in a culture that builds on the

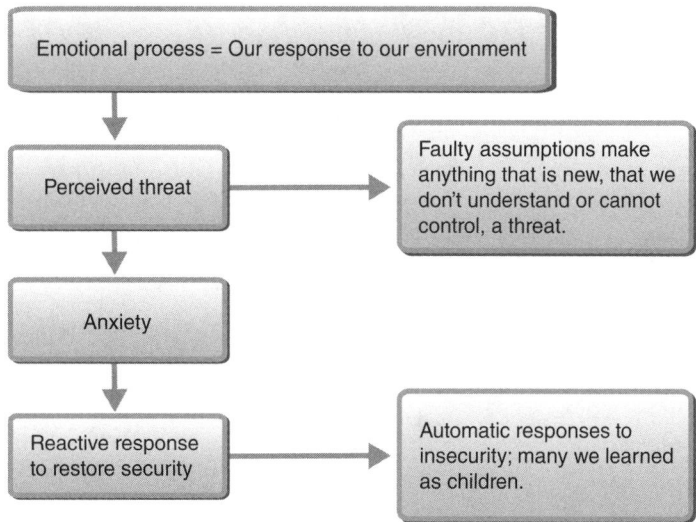

Figure 10.1 Emotional process cycle.

faulty assumption that anything that is new, outside of our control, or unfamiliar is a potential threat with the potential for failure, embarrassment, or ridicule. Thus, we see many things as threats that are really opportunities for growth. We then set in motion automatic responses to combat anxiety. Most of these automatic responses are strategies we learned as children and typically represent our least creative and least effective responses.

When put together, Senge (1990) and Friedman (1999) paint a clear picture as to why so many teams are ineffective. The team's effectiveness is limited by faulty assumptions that both individual members and the team as a whole may hold. To bring these assumptions to the surface and challenge them, team members must be willing to encounter the unknown, make known individual differences, and explore new perspectives on issues that once were thought to be certain. This creates a great deal of anxiety, which sets in motion a series of protective strategies that can limit the ability of the team to learn. The team is then stuck, emotionally unable to move forward and trapped in the fear of discomfort.

Teamwork in the 21st Century

To fully appreciate the value of the systems perspective of teams, we need to consider the very nature of teamwork. Although teams have been around for a long time, the way they work and their purpose has changed. Those changes have

brought new demands that leaders need to consider. Table 10.2 contrasts traditional teamwork with more modern perspectives.

Historically, team members worked in close contact with one another. The purpose of a team was to accomplish a task defined by leaders. Team members worked in close contact because their primary purpose was to make, build, or move something—all work done with tangible raw material. In that setting, feedback was immediate. When mistakes were made or decisions changed, the team knew it because there were immediate and concrete consequences. The team's actions were highly coordinated, requiring a focus on efficiency to carry out the task as quickly as possible; stability was crucial. Teams worked together for long periods of time developing an awareness of and comfort with each other's abilities. Differences were minimized because the efficiency of the work was primary. Teams in this environment were typically formed from a single part of an organization with a singular voice of authority. The demands and expectations were clear because they came from one leader. The team members had clear policies and procedures that held their focus as they found their purpose in the task.

Teams of this generation have a different fundamental purpose from teams of the past, although some still work in more traditional environments. Most teams today work in the context of the information age. They are tasked with work that is service oriented or knowledge dependent. Many teams today are dispersed. The members work

Table 10.2 The Changing Nature of Teamwork

Traditional perspective	New generation teams
Close contact	Dispersed
Immediate feedback	Delayed feedback
Actions highly coordinated	Actions independent but coherent
Interdependence is observable and tangible	Interdependence is less obvious (i.e., at the knowledge level)
Stability is crucial	Agility, flexibility is crucial
Teams formed from one part of the organization with a single voice of authority	Teams formed from many parts of the organization with multiple voices of authority
Teams held together by codes, procedures, and rules	Team cohesion and agility maintained by shared vision and values
Team identity organized around a task	Team identity organized around purpose

in a variety of locations; they may be in different offices or cities or even countries and communicate via technology. Because of the distance, feedback can be delayed. The consequences of an action or decision may not be apparent for weeks or months after it was made. Identifying what needs to be remedied can be difficult because the source of the consequences can be difficult to pinpoint. The interdependence of the team is less obvious because it is more about knowledge than tangible raw materials.

Rather than working the same way at the same time, members of today's teams work independently on their parts and integrate their products at a later time. The work is more complex, requiring multiple specialties and areas of expertise. Thus, teams are often formed from many parts of an organization with multiple voices of authority giving direction. Agendas are frequently in conflict as team members walk the tight line of supporting their teams but also representing their divisions and leaders. Typically, teams of this generation are not given clearly defined tasks; rather, they are given problems or desired results and must determine the issue at hand and develop their own strategies for achieving the desired results. Teams are held together by a shared vision rather than a clear set of rules. In the end, flexibility and the ability to maximize the various perspectives, knowledge areas, and levels of expertise is what makes the team successful.

Team Learning Dynamics

Today's fast-moving and demanding environment requires teams that can learn and respond quickly.

By learning, we mean accessing the **collective intelligence** of the team and putting that together into broad-based systemic solutions that work for everyone and not just one part of an organization or constituency. A critical balance is necessary. Leaders must recognize that the dynamics being discussed occur simultaneously at both the individual and team level (learning wheel model). Focusing on one level to the exclusion of the other will result in an incomplete picture of what is in motion. Additionally, every team member should be equipped to assess and intervene or make adjustments for the team, as well as to his or her own personal involvement. Figure 10.2 illustrates the learning cycle of individuals and teams to demonstrate how each can adjust to be more effective.

Learning

Beginning with the end in mind, **learning** enables teams to prosper in the contemporary environment. Learning in this context, which goes beyond mere information assimilation, includes at least three markers (Robinson & Rose, 2007). The first is a growing awareness and willingness to challenge **assumptions** and mental models. Individuals, teams, and systems at all levels have logic processes that guide not only what they do but also what they pay attention to, what they deem valuable. Thus, for change to occur, these assumptions must be brought to the surface and challenged. It is not so much that all assumptions are wrong, but rather that they, and their associated judgments, should be kept in the realm of awareness so that they can be changed as necessary. This willingness to suspend judgment and consider other ways

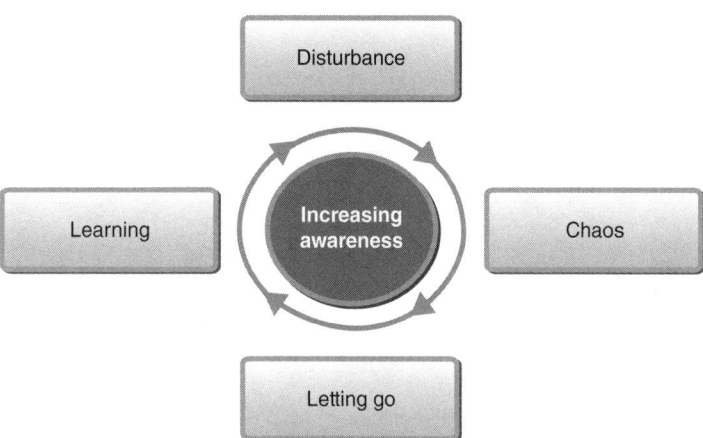

Figure 10.2 Learning wheel model.
From Robinson and Rose 2004.

of thinking is a key indicator that true dialogue is possible among team members (Bohm, 1996; Isaacs, 1999). With this awareness, true learning is within the grasp of the team, which can find new and innovative ways of responding to threats and challenges rather than remaining stuck in ineffective and restrictive practices.

The second learning marker is growing the ability to be purposeful and less **reactive**. This ability is particularly apparent in how the team responds to differences. This second marker, unlike the first, involves an emotional rather than an intellectual shift. Too often, choices made in a team environment are not purposeful, but rather, reactions to emotional discomfort; conflict is avoided because doing so is more comfortable than confrontation. Hard questions are not asked because the possibility of introducing uncertainty is too risky. Different ideas are not considered because of the fear of change or being wrong. Although how we think determines what we see and value, unless we grow our ability to tolerate discomfort and separate what we think from what we feel, we will be unable to change. The only way to grow this emotional maturity is through awareness and challenge, by putting ourselves in positions of discomfort and being purposeful rather than choosing safety (Friedman, 1999). Leaders who can tolerate struggle and refrain from rescuing their teams at the first sign of discomfort encourage this **emotional maturity**. Those who quickly rescue a team make that team more dependent on leadership and less capable of independent action.

The third marker of learning is what results from being competent at the first two. When people have enough openness and awareness to challenge their thinking and tolerate differences, the result is a broader perspective. Having a broader perspective increases the ability to see more durable and effective responses. Seeing more of the world, or the situation or the problem, increases the likelihood of creating sustainable responses and solutions. Moreover, it diminishes the probability of encountering unexpected consequences, which can happen when a solution solves one problem but creates others in the broader system. Obtaining a broader perspective requires sharing and respecting others' ideas because openness to alternative ways of thinking expands team intelligence.

Disturbance

Learning begins with **disturbance**, an external force that creates the demand for change (Robinson & Rose, 2004). A new supervisor, a change in an organization's vision, new regulations, or a changing population can all be forms of disturbance. Disturbance can also be internally driven, such as a desire to improve or the need to be creative. Disturbance does not necessarily result in learning. It is possible to ignore, neglect, or discredit the source as a way to avoid disturbance. This is typically the first place teams begin to struggle in the learning process. The uncertainty of change promotes an avoidance of disturbance and, thus, missed opportunities for growth and improvement.

Let's go back to the opening scenario. After realizing that his programs are atrophying and that long-time constituents are losing interest, what should Ben do? His first step is to acknowledge the disturbance and listen to what is being communicated. Simply trying to work harder is an avoidance strategy that will perpetuate the struggle. If people are not responding to Ben's programs as they once were, the question he needs to ask is, Why not? Engaging in that conversation, particularly with clients and customers, is critical. The alternative is to spend his time trying to convince people to do what he wants them to do, which is always an uphill battle.

Leisure Leaders

Rob Ribbe

MY PREPARATION

- BS in exercise science and MA in educational ministries—Wheaton College, Wheaton, IL
- PhD in education—Biola University, La Mirada, CA
- Member ACA, CCCA, AEE

MY CAREER

I am the director of HoneyRock, Wheaton College's outdoor center for leadership development located in the Northwoods of Wisconsin. We specialize in leadership development of college and graduate students through applied learning as leaders in a camp environment. HoneyRock's mission is to build Christ's church and improve society worldwide by developing whole and effective people through transformational outdoor experiences. We serve 3,000 young people and college students per year and have 24 permanent staff with up to 150 college students and 15 graduate students engaging in our experiential leadership programs each year.

As director of HoneyRock, I am the senior administrator of the college on site, which is 370 miles from Wheaton's main campus in Illinois. I am also an assistant professor in Wheaton's Christian Formation and Ministry department, teaching four to six courses per year.

Three years after I finished college I was hired full time as a program leader at HoneyRock after completing a graduate internship. From there I have grown up through the program over the past 23 years, moving to program director, associate director, and then director. Overall, I love the job. There are many challenges supervising a site and staff so far away from the main campus. I

Photo courtesy of Rob Ribbe.

enjoy the variety of working at a Christian camp that is also a college campus; I enjoy the best of both and the synergistic relationship. The camp provides a fantastic human development and leadership laboratory for developing college and graduate students. I spend the majority of every day engaging people and working to empower them to grow and develop through the tasks of running the organization.

MY ADVICE TO YOU

I suggest that you get experience in a variety of organizations. Develop a strong work ethic, a high sense of integrity, and emotional and relational maturity. If you are in this business for the fun of being outdoors, check your motives. As you move into leadership, you leave the everyday world of outdoor fun. The challenges inherent in the outdoor environment provide a fantastic place for people to learn, grow, and develop. The outdoors is a means to this end, not an end in itself.

Chaos

Once we are disturbed, either by choice or force, a period of uncertainty and **chaos** always follows. When significant change is occurring, it is common to struggle between letting go of what has been known and grasping a new understanding. This can be a time filled with anxiety, stress, and discomfort as each person and the team look for the way forward. This is the primary stage in which panic sets in and the learning process is abandoned. Many passive and active strategies are available to reclaim some sense of security and comfort. Passive strategies include withdrawing, entering into quick agreement, sustaining the status quo, and looking to a hero or leader to rescue and repair the situation. Active strategies include taking control, blaming, organizing behind rules and procedures, and medicating and using other distracting mechanisms.

Leaders must be aware of a number of important things when chaos occurs. First, just because there is chaos does not mean that the leader is doing something wrong. We often believe that chaos is bad and a sign of leader weakness or ineffectiveness; in reality, it is a necessary part of learning. Mental models and assumptions do not change unless questioned. The very act of questioning creates a state of uncertainty or chaos until new assumptions or models reorient thinking.

Second, chaos is a time when leaders need to be present but not rescue. Too many well-meaning leaders step in and rescue struggling people or teams only to make them more dependent and less capable. Struggle is a consequence of chaos and, as such, is a necessary part of learning. Struggle, even failure, can be a key experience in growing and maturing a team. On the other hand, being too distant can be as problematic as being too close. When individuals or teams experience the disorientation of chaos, the presence of the leader can lend them confidence to stay with something that feels very uncomfortable. If a leader is too distant, members may begin to feel abandoned and lose heart, opting for expedient rather than necessary options.

Consider an experiential learning exercise in which team members wear blindfolds. Although they are capable of working out the solution, if the facilitator (leader) is too quiet or team members do not sense their presence, they will call out to see if the facilitator is still present. In such instances, the inability to see for themselves creates a level of stress that can be calmed if they know the facilitator is close and involved. This applies to the workplace. Anytime the level of uncertainty increases, the team will seek greater exposure to the leader.

One leader's response to his team's need for reassurance was to set up monthly lunch meetings during times of change. The leader specifically asked the team to bring concerns, rumors, and questions that might be circulating in the organization about potential changes. This helped team members clarify what was true and reassured them that the leader was keeping tabs on things so they could focus on their work.

Finally, clarity is of utmost importance during a time of chaos. The role of the leader is to provide some structure that helps the team slow down and understand the source of the chaos and identify what is needed to move forward. The natural response may be to react, but the necessary action is to wait, listen, and consider. Teams need the calming influence of a mature leader to slow down enough to arrive at an understanding.

Letting Go

The bridge between chaos and learning is the counterintuitive action of **letting go**. This does not mean an unconditional surrender to the wishes of others or even to circumstances. The idea behind letting go is to loosen the grip on certain things to create openness. Peck (1987) referred to this as emptiness; the important point is for team members to "empty themselves of barriers to communication" (p. 95). Teams must let go of their egos, their preconceived ideas, the need to always be right, the desire for comfort, and the illusion of control. This opens the minds and hearts of those participating to hear what has not been heard before and to see what has not been seen before. In a sense, letting go creates a different kind of listening. "When we listen in the normal way, for what is right and what is wrong, then we won't be able to hear what is possible; what might be but is not yet" (Kahane, 2004, p. 77).

Letting go is difficult, and often it is the leader who can set this course by going first. Letting go is always, on the outside, an act of vulnerability. It can take the form of asking for help, asking a question that one does not know the answer to, or disclosing one's own experience or current feelings. In this lonely first step, the leader can set the stage for a level of collaboration and learning that the group could not achieve on its own.

Consider a leader participating in a workshop designed to promote a collaborative culture across departments of the organization. At one point, a small group was working on a case study to practice a process called co-discovery. As the group was trying to determine the best course of action, one of the leaders spoke up and said, "I don't think I know enough yet . . . ." Her comment revealed some vulnerability that provided space for another team member, who was an expert on the subject, to provide his expertise without the appearance of trying to take over the team. The leader's openness created an environment conducive to questions and concerns as well as a sharing of knowledge free from confrontation.

Coming Full Circle

As a team lets go of the barriers to communication, learning begins. Yet, as the team challenges its assumptions and grows less fearful and more purposeful, the potential for a new disturbance increases. Learning promotes more learning. This endless cycle, though at times slow in the beginning, speeds up with practice. Once a team develops the courage to participate, less energy is spent trying to avoid the changes the team is facing and more is spent doing the valuable work of learning together.

Team Formation

Leaders must be able to assess team dynamics and make interventions that will develop the team to the level of functioning necessary for success. This job, however, can be much easier when leaders build teams well in the beginning. With this in mind, let us look into a number of key factors to consider as a team is being put together. The research related to team effectiveness and specific factors is very complex and, at times contradictory, if not inconclusive. Consequently, this section provides a number of perspectives team leaders should consider when designing a team and some ideas that could moderate the effects of team characteristics and organizational circumstances.

Size and Diversity

Two issues at the forefront of the issue of group composition are size and diversity. The first is often a practical issue that can greatly affect the nature of team communication. How many people can talk or think together? The second issue, diversity, determines the quality of that thinking and talking. Too much diversity and there may be no alignment, no common vision. Too little diversity and there is really no value in having a team. If everyone thinks the same, the team will become locked in a perspective that could be wrong or incomplete. In fact, some research (Nieva, Fleishman, & Reick, 1985) suggests that either too few or too many people may reduce team effectiveness. With too few people the leader risks a lack of diversity, not only of perspectives and values but also of the requisite knowledge, skill, and time to complete the job. With too many people the leader risks being unable to deal with the nuances of an idea and being left with oversimplified bullet points that may quickly devolve into sides and debates. A team that is too big can also influence how much effort or ownership individuals take in the work of the team (Bell, 2007).

Personality Factors

Team member personalities have a strong influence on team performance (Driskell, Hogan, & Salas, 1987; Hackman, 1987). In her meta-analysis of team performance factors, Bell (2007) suggested that leaders should seek team members who are conscientious, agreeable, and open to experience. The conscientious person is "hard working, achievement oriented and persevering" (p. 597). The agreeable person, one who is considerate, trusting, and friendly, will likely value good interpersonal interaction and, thus, minimize intrateam competition. The person who is open to experience is broadminded, original, imaginative, and daring (McCrae & Costa, 1987), proving to be adaptable and flexible in the ever-changing team environment.

This research may suggest that a certain level of maturity and personal identity is important to being a good team member. With maturity comes the courage and emotional awareness (Robinson & Rose, 2004, 2007) necessary to be open-minded, inclusive, and flexible. A strong personality can be an asset to a team but only if the strength of that personality is tempered by self-awareness and self-regulation. Without these, the strength could simply become a barrier to agreement and establishing a common vision for the team.

Best Practices From the Field

Many team leaders busy themselves trying to figure out what they need to do to be effective leaders. What processes do they need to create? What policies or rules do they need to institute? How can they get and maintain power? However, this approach only leads to anxious, dependent, and ultimately immature teams that cannot act on their own. The greatest gift a team leader has to offer is a nonanxious presence. That free gift of self alongside others frees the team to exceed expectations.

This sense of presence was a critical component of what made Phil Jackson so successful as a leader. Here is how Michael Jordan described Jackson's presence:

With Doug [Collins, former coach] you could always feel the tension, while Phil was poised at all times. Doug was more emotional. He wasn't afraid to show you exactly how he was feeling. As a player you connect with the

atmosphere the coach creates. With Phil it was like we were in harmony with each other in the heat of battle. We were comfortable not only with each other but also with the situation no matter how difficult the moment. We were able to find peace amid the noise, and that allowed us to figure out our options, divine solutions and be clear-headed enough to execute them. That's what Phil Jackson brought to the Chicago Bulls and that's what we all connected with. (Jordan, 1998, p. 53)

What many leaders do not recognize is that most groups do not need a leader to tell them what to do. This creates dependency and works against the maturing of the group to handle the difficulties of life. A leader's greatest gift is presence, which creates the emotional space to calm rampant anxiety and allow group members to think clearly. The solutions will undoubtedly follow (Robinson & Rose, 2006 p. 73).

Team Formation Guidelines

The bigger the team is, the greater the complexity of communication will be. Consequently, making sure there are some commonalities of language, tools, reporting, and structures can mitigate potential complications (Cusumano, 1997). Also, implementing a **meeting strategy** with regular times for integrating work and evaluating the culture, organizational practices, and individual assumptions and efforts for their alignment with the direction of the organization is key. The greater the complexity of communication, the more important it is for the team to reconnect on a regular basis. Common models and a common language to describe the desired results and barriers to overcome will facilitate understanding amid a vast array of ideas.

The bigger the team is, the higher the likelihood that ownership will be diffused and accountability diminished. As the saying goes, If we all own it, no one owns it. In large teams, individuals often assume that someone else is taking responsibility for particular items. With size also comes the difficulty of tracing back decisions and actions that lead to certain outcomes; accountability is difficult to determine, and attitudes of blame can be preva-

lent. Therefore, leaders need to make sure that the ownership of specific outcomes is clear. The goal for the leader is to make sure that what the team is trying to do is clear, as are assignments; however, how work is accomplished is left to the creativity of the team. If the leader tries to control the means or process, the level of complexity will increase even more.

The smaller the team is, the greater the risk of a lack of diversity. The team members may think too much alike, and their skills may not be complementary. The key for a small team is to choose people who have multiple areas of expertise and who complement each other. Also, a team can seek other perspectives through interviews, focus groups, and interactions with experts who hold different positions. Small teams have more pressure to guard against groupthink and unchallenged assumptions. Designing a process that requires the team to pause periodically and ask questions about its assumptions can mitigate this.

Finally, a leader who wants a strong team should choose mature and motivated individuals. Attitude is always a difficult aspect to change. Choosing mature team members who are open to working with a team will result in a more effective team process than choosing members based strictly on knowledge or position and trying to change their attitudes after they are on the team. Changing a person's values, maturity level, or identity is often a long and difficult path that distracts the team from its work. If, however, attitudinal change is necessary, the leader should be open and straightforward about it rather than use peer pressure to make individuals compliant. Informed choice and increased self-awareness, as opposed to coercive tactics, will serve this type of change.

Organizational Context Factors

Beyond the personality characteristics and size of the group lie the contextual factors of the organization that need to be considered for team success. These factors include structure, task design, rewards, leadership, and culture.

Structure refers to the way authority and roles are organized. The traditional hierarchy is the most typical design in which authority is layered through the organization with increasing power, information, resources, and control as one moves toward the top of the organization. San Martin-Rodriguez and colleagues (2005) indicated that a move away from these typical structures toward more horizontal structures, in which authority and decision power are distributed across the organization more equally, is more supportive of collaborative interactions. Hierarchical relationships introduce power differences that can impede the ability to collaborate.

Leaders have two options for dealing with power differences. First, they can change the structure; however, this can be difficult when the entire organization is unwilling to adopt a flatter structure. The second is to create a culture of trust in which members have the maturity and courage to speak their minds and leaders are not afraid to empower those they lead. Culture can overcome structure with the right attention.

Task design refers to the organization of work or tasks for which the team is responsible. Kozlowski and Ilgen (2006) indicated that work that provides for self-management and interdependent goals and processes produces strong teams. Hansen (2009) also emphasized interdependence as a requisite for collaboration. Campion, Medsker, and Higgs (1993) as well as Campion, Papper, and Medsker (1996) also indicated that task variety and task significance contribute to a more empowered team. The bottom line is that strong teams really own their work, determine how the work is done,

and believe that their work is significant.

A third contextual factor is rewards. The right reward systems can be difficult to identify because those that focus strictly on team output can result in a lack of focus on individual accountability. On the other hand, reward systems that focus on individual contributions can lead to a lack of concern for team efforts. The key is to find a system that focuses on both collective and individual contributions (Kozlowski & Ilgen, 2006). This idea is described a bit later in the discussion about action learning.

Leadership is another key aspect of the contextual agenda. Without clear and effective leadership, the team may flounder. Leaders contribute to team success by helping to set the vision, providing time and opportunities to collaborate, and connecting efforts to the bigger picture (Kozlowski & Ilgen, 2006; San Martin-Rodriguez et al., 2005; Thomas, 2000). Leaders, as the keepers of the story, can provide energy and direction that enable the team to focus on its work. Distant leaders who provide little contact, presence, or process create anxiety in the team (Friedman, 1999).

All of these components of organizational context are both in service of and contribute to the culture of the team. Schein (1996) described **culture** as a set of shared assumptions passed on because they are deemed sound enough to deal with the issues of "internal integration and external adaptation" (p. 17). Team leaders often focus on engineering the components of the context but forget to implement them in a way that supports a culture that enables collaboration. Cultures that value participation, self-management, flexibility, freedom of expression, and choice and are characterized by integrity and high levels of trust produce better teamwork than cultures that value autonomy, compliance, and limited initiative. A trust-based culture promotes self-motivation, self-management and empowerment, which have been correlated with more effective teams (Kozlowski & Ilgen, 2006).

Internal Processes

Contextual factors, as discussed, provide stability for the team. They are generally defined once and have a long duration in the life of the team. Yet, what often causes the downfall of teams is their inability to manage the dynamic and ever-changing forces at work inside the team—the processes of conflict, trust, and decision making.

Conflict and Trust

Teams are often formed to capitalize on the diversity of skill, knowledge, and abilities of team members. This diversity, however, introduces conflict, a key process that must be managed. Tuckman and Jensen (1977) recognized conflict as a key component in the life cycle of a team in the stage he called storming, which is part of the transition as a group moves from being a new team to being a formed team. It would also appear that working through conflict is a way for teams to assess their trust level. Lencioni (2002) suggested that an important connection exists between trust and conflict. Without a foundation of trust, conflict is feared and avoided. "Teams that lack trust are incapable of engaging in unfiltered and passionate debate of ideas. Instead, they resort to veiled discussions and guarded comments" (Lencioni, 2002, p. 188). Consequently, there is no full and honest conversation, resulting in a lack of true commitment to the solution or the decision of the team. Without commitment, there is no accountability, which leads to poor results.

Not all conflict is the same, nor is the understanding of the role of conflict conclusive (De Dreu & Weingart, 2003; Kozlowski & Ilgen, 2006). Traditionally, research has differentiated between interpersonal conflict (e.g., personal styles, tastes, preferences, and values) and task conflict (e.g., differences in resource allocation, policies, procedures, and the interpretation of facts) (De Dreu & Weingart, 2003). Jehn (1994, 1995, 1997) suggested that task conflict has a positive effect on team effectiveness, but relational conflict has a negative effect. The positive effect is related to the idea that conflict makes teams focus more and consider the issues more deeply than they would without conflict (Simons & Peterson, 2000). Low levels of conflict may help sharpen the interaction among team members, but too much conflict takes away from their ability to think, process information, and make good decisions. It also seems that trust moderates the impact of conflict. It may be that trust reduces interpersonal conflict and provides a safer environment in which to discuss ideas.

Team leaders need to remember that conflict is always possible during team interactions. Effective teams acknowledge the existence of conflict and have processes in place to deal with it. The following could be included in a conflict process.

True trust is not known until it has been tested by difference of opinion.

Steven Prorak | Dreamstime.com

▸ A regular meeting or forum in which disagreements are discussed

▸ Agreed-on team norms that lay out expectations to deal with conflict quickly, directly, and personally

▸ Team member training in active listening and conflict resolution strategies

It is also important for the leader to actively participate early on to demonstrate the value of conflict management and coach team members in conflict resolution processes until they have learned to manage conflict themselves. Having an objective third party can limit the escalation of emotion. Leaders must continue to help team members develop personal maturity, which creates a level of emotional awareness and courage and, thus, increases their ability to work through differences without being polarized in conflict (Robinson & Rose, 2004).

Decision Making

Decision making, a process that readily reveals team dynamics, is difficult for most teams to accomplish well. Among the many forces at work that make decision making difficult are a lack of information, a lack of a clear process, competing agendas, time pressures, political pressures, a lack of self-awareness, and the need to maintain goodwill. To help teams make good decisions, leaders need to consider process, criteria, and a culture of learning. Process refers to the way the decision is to be made. With a clear sequence of steps, a variety of ideas can surface; but for this diversity of ideas to be most effective, teams will need a set of criteria by which the team will prioritize and ultimately choose a final decision. For this process to work there needs to be a culture of learning—a shared expectation that multiple perspectives are good, that difference of opinion is helpful, and that asking hard questions is necessary for the best decisions to surface.

Many decision-making meetings start with an undefined process. Often, meetings start with the team jumping into conversation, which typically has a poorly defined outcome, no steps or order to the conversation to provide discipline, and a limited awareness of how the team is talking to each other. This unstructured process makes it too easy for the team to wander from the real decision that needs focused on. Garvin and Roberto (2001) framed the options of decision-making meetings as inquiry or advocacy. **Inquiry** sees the process as open and seeks to generate a diversity of opinions, whereas **advocacy** sees decision making as a contest. Too often, teams default to the advocacy process, which leads to decisions being based on the opinions of the first, loudest, or longest-speaking person. For inquiry to flourish, teams should ensure that all problems are clearly understood and that **decision criteria** are in place to evaluate options.

Individual Factors for Team Success

A team is only as strong as the quality of the people that comprise it; team leaders need to keep this paradox in mind. A team of mature people with the ability to think critically will be a very capable team. Consequently, the key individual factors to focus on are maturity and critical thinking.

Maturity

Maturity is "the willingness to take responsibility for one's emotional being and destiny" (Friedman, 1999, p. 7). It is being aware enough to understand and manage emotions and anxiety. It is remaining purposeful and intentional even in the face of tension or stress. It is standing alone, thinking for yourself, and having the strength to be vulnerable. Maturity is the ability to experience emotional discomfort without panic. Team leaders need to consider maturity because it affects how people respond to anxiety or fear.

As previously mentioned, emotional process influences how we think, what we see and pay attention to, and how we respond to things we do not understand or cannot control. Hansen (2009) identified fear as a core factor in barriers to collaboration in organizations. The fear of revealing problems and the fear of losing power limit people's ability to collaborate. So what is the answer? How do people get beyond fear?

Maturity is a matter of both **self-awareness** and **self-regulation**. Self-awareness alerts us to the fact that we are experiencing a strong emotion. Something important to us is at work, and we need to address it to keep from being controlled by fear. Self-regulation is the ability to stay calm in the midst of stress and anxiety and choose our actions rather than just being reactive to the emotion in the moment. The key is to be able to separate what we feel from how we think. Just because we feel threatened does not mean there is actually a threat. This must be thought through and considered from multiple perspectives. The very act of being able to step back from an emotion and consider its source and purpose is an act of maturity.

In addition to being aware of their internal emotional processes, team members must be able to act purposefully and courageously in the face of anxiety—theirs or the team's. Ambrose Redmoon was quoted as saying, "Courage is not the absence of fear but rather the judgment that something else is more important than fear" (Miner & Priest, 2000, p. 14). Maturity requires us to remain calm in the face of discomfort, to stay put and consider what else is at stake. It calls on us to do what is right and necessary in spite of how we feel.

Friedman (1999) suggested that systems that are stuck in or dominated by immaturity and anxiety share three traits. The first he called the treadmill effect, the belief that if more effort is put into accumulating data or better technique, things will change. It manifests as a focus on changing others rather than looking to oneself. Second, he talked about the focus on finding answers rather than reframing questions. In systems that are stuck, the need for safety limits the questions asked so that members continue to work hard at finding answers to the old questions. Reframing the question and asking things that seem outside the dominant paradigm result in contact with new possibilities, which can move a stuck system forward. Finally, Friedman proposed that stuck systems are dominated by polarized thinking. There is a focus on either/or, black/white, all or nothing thinking that seeks simple answers. "Intense polarizations also are always symptomatic of underlying emotional processes rather than the subject matter of the polarizing issue" (p. 45). Differences that could make for a greater collective understanding and capability push members into choosing sides and becoming reactive to each other.

Maturity is not something that can increase simply with more thinking, more information, or better technique. It increases when people are put into situations in which they have to be uncomfortable, not when they seek an easy way out. It increases when leaders do not rescue teams and help them avoid the consequences of their decisions or the discomfort of doing things that are difficult, new, or untested. Maturity is critical to the ability to learn and change in a sustainable way.

Critical Thinking

If maturity is a process of emotional growth and change, **critical thinking** is the companion intellectual development opportunity. Although different in function, thinking is not separate from feeling; they are mutually supporting mechanisms. Because thinking promotes certain ways of interpreting situations, how we feel influences what we think and how deliberate we can be in the thinking process. In fact, Argyris (1990) asserted that feelings of embarrassment or threat can generate organizational defenses that prevent learning for individuals, teams, or the organization as a whole.

The purpose of critical thinking is to move beyond simple behavioral adjustments, which is often called single-loop learning (Argyris, 1997). Critical thinking is the empowering process behind double-loop learning. "Double-loop learning corrects mismatches by first changing the underlying governing values and then the actions" (Argyris, 1997, p. 10). Teamwork involves ongoing adjustments as members attempt to coordinate actions, integrate diverse talents and skills, and use divergent perspectives. The underlying opportunity is for the team to allow its differences to emerge, bringing the members' individual and collective assumptions to the surface. As the team learns to challenge its assumptions, it refines what Argyris referred to as governing values and Senge (1990) referred to as mental models, both for the individuals and the team. When individuals cannot or will not think at that deeper level, however, learning cannot happen because the differences are dismissed or become the energy for ongoing conflict.

Team and Individual Leadership

The discussion of teams to this point is consistent with the paradoxical idea that teams are built at both the individual and group levels. This section summarizes the role of the leader at both levels. First, the leader has a responsibility for self-leadership. This provides the maturity to then create a healthy team system which promotes mature self-leadership among the team members. Mature team members are capable of organizing around a shared direction and working together to accomplish this goal. Yet, to do this kind of work, the leader must focus on both growing the individuals and forming the team at the same time.

Individual Leadership

"All leadership begins with self-leadership, and self-leadership begins with knowing oneself" (Lowney, 2003, p. 98). The greatest gift leaders bring to their teams is themselves (Lowney, 2003; Robinson & Rose, 2007). So, although many leadership theories focus outward on how leaders interact with followers, it seems that the more prudent strategy would be to first look inward. Thus, the first task of individual leadership is self-awareness. Lowney echoed the sentiments of Friedman (1999) when he said, "A leader's most compelling leadership tool is who he or she is: a person who understands what he or she values and wants, who is anchored by certain principles, and who faces the world with a consistent outlook" (p. 19). This is similar to the notion of **self-differentiation**, which can be conceptualized as leaders who do the following:

- ▶ Think for themselves and set goals and vision based on their own beliefs
- ▶ Regulate and manage themselves in the face of the resistance and anxiety of others
- ▶ Maintain relationships in which boundaries are respected and do not try to do for others what they should do for themselves (Friedman, 1999)

Once again, the differentiation process requires leaders to not only discern what they believe, but also improve their capacity to manage the emotional processes in the system. There is both an intellectual and emotional development agenda. Leaders with a clearly defined sense of self are better able to manage their relationships with others than are those who lack self-awareness.

A final area of consideration in the area of self-leadership is personal competence. Leaders can be clear about who they are and get along with others, but without a level of competence to do the job, the trust will just not be there. The ability to follow through on one's promises builds trust based on competence.

Team Leadership

The difference between individual and team leadership is not simply that team leaders focus on the team. The team leader serves a facilitative function within the team system. The job is not to do for others, control others, or even motivate others as much as it is to establish the conditions that allow others to lead themselves in collaborative interactions. The systems leader looks beyond the task and even the people to consider whether the

The greatest gift leaders bring to the team is themselves.

© Yanlev | Dreamstime.com

conditions exist to promote personal responsibility, collective learning, and collaboration. To establish the right conditions, the leader should focus on how teams are formed and how individuals are trained, and on developing an infrastructure that facilitates collaboration.

Team Delivery Programs

Facilitative leaders need to understand that how teams are formed and how people are trained is as important as the content they are taught. To develop effective teams, leaders need to provide experiential learning, promote learning sustainability, and address team infrastructure.

Experiential Learning

To become collaborative, teams need experiential learning, a term that may conjure up images of outdoor pursuits, ropes courses, or wilderness excursions. Although these activities are experiential, the term is not that limited in scope. **Experiential learning** involves learning in context, taking action, and reflecting on that action. In this context, meetings, projects, and performance reviews can all be experiential. In fact, all of the work of a team is experiential. What is often missing in these things is a critical, purposeful guided reflection on the experience. This is the skill set that traditional experiential learning mediums bring to the table. It is not about adrenaline or bonding or even problem solving. For teams, the most important aspects of experiential learning are reflecting on their experiences, understanding what is happening among them and why, and identifying new experiments that will help the team system become healthier and more productive (Bodner, 1997).

Why is experiential learning so important? The reason is that most of the things that strengthen a team—trust, self-efficacy, conflict management, maturity, and collective learning—are best learned, if not only learned, by doing rather than talking. Too many teams talk about their goals and key points of change only to live contrary to them. Committing to talking straight or being authentic without any emotion or personal risk is noble but often naive. Real change occurs in the moment choices are made and actions are taken. No amount of planning, brainstorming, or competency mapping can prepare a person for making the right choice in the heat of the moment. Only living through the event and continuing to work

on being aware of such moments and considering one's options in the heat of emotion can help the person become more effective. Experiential learning is about providing a venue in which to take action in the pressure of the moment and then offering the opportunity to take the time to understand that action.

Experiential methods also close the gap between the subject and the application of that subject. "In school contexts, it is common to impart book smarts without providing experiential linkages that inform knowing. Students can acquire only words or symbols; they must then find contextual connections to provide meaning for such 'empty concepts'" (Cowan, 1995, p. 18). In the training realm, this is called **transfer of learning**. Learning that happens in an artificial setting must be taken into the real world of work and applied. It is often during this transfer that learning is lost. Experiential methodologies allow for learning in context with a guide, coach, or facilitator present to help with the transfer of learning.

Learning in context aids in other important areas. It reduces learning segmentation. In moments of action people think only of performance and not of learning or improvement. Traditional learning environments, however, generally involve no thought of performance. Learning in context allows teams to close the gap by learning and performing at the same time, so the two complement each other. Learning in context also often involves the unexpected, which introduces the need to consider alternatives. "The relevance to a learning context is that too often we attend only to the well-worn paths and fail to recognize the value of variation" (Cowan, 2005, p. 18). Part of the reason we choose the well-worn paths is that, in the short term, variation is inefficient; however, in the long term, variance is necessary for growth. It acts as a disturbance that initiates new learning. Experiential learning introduces variance and the need to seek alternatives. That is why no two experiences are ever the same.

Sustainability

In addition to experiential learning, teams need **sustainability**. Sustainability is about actually learning what you're attempting to learn, and about being attentive to the teaching process. Sustainability involves not only solving the dilemma of the day but also preparing to solve the issues of tomorrow.

Leaders can develop sustainability in their teams be providing shorter, more frequent sessions that teach teams to facilitate their own process. What does **self-facilitating** demand? Teams need to be able to assess their performance, diagnose issues needing attention, and create strategies for correcting their course. This would suggest, at a basic level, that teams must value reflecting on their performance and have an established process for doing so. The ultimate goal of sustainability is not only learning the needed skill or knowledge, but also establishing the infrastructure that promotes ongoing collaboration and team learning.

Team Infrastructure

For teams to perform well over time, they need elements or work practices that make it easy to connect with each other and collaborate. These elements create an infrastructure for the team. Following are the elements of team infrastructure:

> ▶ Mind-set
> ▶ Opportunity
> ▶ Process
> ▶ Catalyst (Robinson & Rose, 2004, 2007)

This model is illustrated in figure 10.3.

The first element of building a teaminfrastructure is developing a mind-set of valuing teamwork and collaboration. Such a mind-set requires some competency in **collective learning**, listening, inquiring, and advocating for one's own position. It includes the facilitation skills of assessment, diagnosis, and intervention. In short, the goal of almost all team events is to bring team members to a point at which they want to work together and believe they have the capacity to do so.

Even if a team has the requisite mind-set for teamwork, it will not be able to sustain it without opportunities to connect. Teamwork and collaboration are like any other skills. Without ongoing practice, team members will lose their ability to learn and work together quickly. The labor of trying to get back to an efficient and effective team process often prevents teams from trying. A lack of opportunities to practice working together results in team members slipping back into their solo mind-sets and focusing only on their individual tasks. Most teams already have opportunities of collaboration built into their work processes, so this is not necessarily about adding new things; rather, it is about repurposing already existent opportunities such as staff, project, and performance review meetings and planning sessions. Any time a team can get together to solve problems or make decisions, it has an opportunity to work on the competencies necessary for keeping the collaboration sharp.

Teams can have the right mind-set and even opportunities to collaborate, but without effective team processes, meetings and team gatherings can quickly go stale. Teamwork requires more than just being in the same place and hoping something important happens. The process must be about learning and getting better at thinking and working together (Robinson, 2005).

Finally, a team can possess the right mind-set and have opportunities to collaborate and a clear process for learning, but without a catalyst, the team effort will eventually deteriorate. The role of the catalyst is to bring new energy and focus to the team's work. It helps a team evaluate where it is, where it wants to be, and in some cases, what is possible. A catalyst can come in many forms. Reviewing a team vision often results in new energy from a renewed connection to the team's purpose. Feedback and metrics can also refocus a team and are essential for regulating the team's efforts, as well as measuring performance and competence (Kozlowski & Ilgen, 2006; Thomas, 2000). Benchmarking (comparing a team to another team in a similar industry or role) can stretch team members' imagination about what is possible and motivate them to try to maximize their potential.

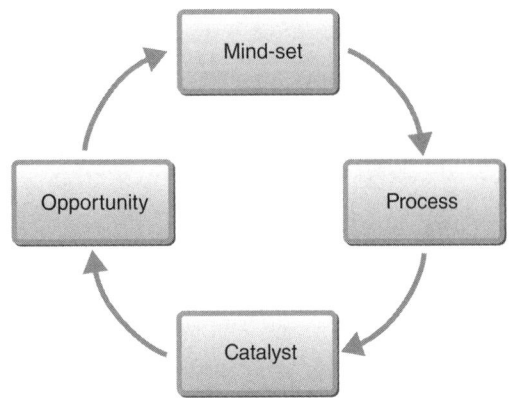

Figure 10.3 Infrastructure model.
From Robinson and Rose 2007.

In the end, the organization must support collaboration and teamwork. That support must be more than occasional statements that teamwork is important. The support is reflected in the work and actions of the leader. A critical leadership action is protecting the new team from superiors, peers, and customers as it learns and grows, because these people might not have such a discerning eye when it comes to evaluating a team's progress.

Successful and Unsuccessful Team Development

To this point, the discussion of team leadership has been largely conceptual. To move concepts to action, however, it is necessary to discuss their application to real-world experiences. This section begins with a case study that reflects team learning dynamics and the creation of a collaborative infrastructure to support ongoing teamwork. Additionally, common elements that lead to unsuccessful team development are considered.

Successful Team Development

Our case involves the safety and loss control leadership of a Fortune 500 company (Robinson, 2003). The change process began with an external *disturbance* in the form of an audit of the safety and loss control function. This function was responsible for safety practices in the large company and monitoring and managing losses from accidents, equipment failures, and environmental incidents. The audit revealed that the function was so fragmented that the company could not even determine the exact level of loss or the quality of safety protocols across the organization. Thirteen departments throughout the company dealt with safety and loss control, and all of them reported to different managers. Many leaders of the function did not even know one another. There was no common approach, no common information, and no agreement across the company as to how safety should be approached. The edict given to the corporate director of safety, and monitored by an internal audit department, was to create a common management system that would work for all parts of the company, including convenience stores, refineries, and telecommunications operations.

Team leadership often means being willing to step out first.

© Human Kinetics.

A good bit of *chaos* resulted from the audit. The corporate director had no idea where to start. His first courageous act was not to use a typical top-down directive strategy, but to promote a learning approach that would involve changing the minds of the other leaders and developing a culture and infrastructure for cross-company collaboration. The goal was to implement a management system based on guiding principles. This would promote not only commonality in language and goals, but diversity in application based on the various business units and geographical locations. Chaos also arose in the first session of the team's change process, which involved many people with different ideas and commitments to their own individual success. In the first meeting, it took the team six hours to define one principle. The team demonstrated many of the common distractions typically present in situations of chaos. Some members tried to take control, whereas others withdrew and tried to wait it out. In the end, the team was so focused on irrelevant minutia that it was drowning in details.

The breakthrough for the team came at the end of the first day. One team member risked an honest observation. He called his fellow team members on what they were doing and promoted the idea that they could do better if members would only *let go* of existing agendas and extend some trust. The next day, the team entered with a new mind-set and focus. Team members completed the definition of nine more principles and ended early. The willingness to let go of things that hindered them enabled a new, shared vision to emerge. They were on their way to establishing real and sustained change.

Over the course of two years, this group implemented an infrastructure for collaboration. Although tentative in the beginning, the infrastructure eventually resulted in a culture shift that brought true cross-functional collaboration to this group. The guiding principles and an understanding of collaboration formed the *mind-set* that would define this group's work. Knowing that the mind-set could not be maintained without practice, the team committed to meeting once a quarter in a central location for one and half days. These meetings were the primary *opportunities* for the team to practice and embed its new mind-set. The *process* used was a modified action learning process. At each meeting, the team would choose one principle to discuss. Team members would say how they understood the principle and how it was being applied in their areas. Ideas would be shared and innovations discussed.

The team members decided that they needed to quantify their efforts and thereby justify the expense in money and time to their respective managers. They also needed to track their progress to see whether they were actually learning and collaborating. The *catalyst* that would perform these two functions took the form of a learning scorecard, which showed the following:

▸ Who took an idea away from the last meeting

▸ Where the idea came from so credit could be shared

▸ What was done with the idea (e.g., whether it was being studied or had been implemented)

▸ The outcomes of applying the idea

In the first 18 months of using the scorecard, team members documented $100,000 in savings from their efforts. Over time, this team became a model to the organization. After nearly 10 years of practice, with multiple changes in personnel, the company's board of directors recognized the process as an exemplary way to manage shared functions across the company (Robinson, 2003; Robinson & Rose, 2007).

Unsuccessful Team Development

Many teams try to improve, and most fail. Change efforts in organizations succeed at only about a 30 percent rate (Bashein, Marcus, & Riley, 1994). There are many reasons for this; this section outlines several of them.

Because a team is a system, every part, or member, has some responsibility in how the team is performing. Yet one of the most frequent mistakes made in team development is to assume that only the team needs to change and not the leader. Consider a team that is having difficulty or is underperforming. The leader has spent some time trying to diagnose the team independently. She presents to the team facilitator the list of issues that she believes underlie the team's struggles. As is typical for human beings, however, the leader believes that she sees the team's issues clearly and fails to consider, or diminishes the importance of, her impact on the team's performance. Thus, as the team development process starts, the efforts are focused exclusively on the team.

The fact is that a leader is never wholly divorced from what is happening with the team. If the team hopes to achieve any sustainable improvement, everyone must change at some level. However, an unmotivated leader cannot be changed with a team process. Some believe that if a leader's behavior is brought forth in a public team event, peer pressure will take over and motivate a personal change. More often than not, however, the leader either denies the behavior or uses the leadership position for personal protection or to quash the team process altogether. A team process for motivated leaders who are aware and ready to work on their part of the equation can be a beautiful thing. Such leaders can generate a level of openness and authenticity that no other team member can create. But unaware and unmotivated leaders undermine the team development process, if only by being distant or removed from the change effort.

A second error in team development is a common response to team anxiety. When things are not going well, teams often look for the quick fix of focusing blame for the situation on a certain person or subgroup within the team (Friedman, 1999). The problem with this practice is twofold. First, the team becomes fixated on only one part of the issue and one person's or group's role in that part of the issue. As team members solidify their beliefs, they continue to see things that confirm their beliefs and dismiss things that contradict their beliefs. Consequently, the team fails to ask additional questions, and the issue, which is certainly the result of multiple forces at work, is oversimplified. The second problem with the scapegoat strategy is that it focuses team members' efforts on trying to change others and away from personal responsibility. This builds a position of false power. Trying to change another may lead to short-term success, but it usually exacerbates the team issues. The team will likely go through a series of changes such as a person changing roles or leaving the team altogether only to have the same or a similar issue come up again with a different person as the focus. Teams create sustainable change only when all members take responsibility for their part in the team process.

Team members often make the same mistake with their personal problems as they do with work-related problems. They too quickly jump to conclusions and immediately try to solve a problem that they do not fully understand. To illustrate, consider how teams often try to improve their meetings with surface changes rather than addressing the issues. Team members may be struggling to stay focused, to reach decisions, and to listen actively to one another. To improve the process, they implement a series of strategies to discipline the conversation. They limit who can talk by having a leader do all the talking, or they institute a timekeeper to limit how much time people have to speak. Over time, the team discovers how cumbersome the weight of rules can be, and that the rules have not solved the issues. The team has failed to understand the underlying causes of the problems, which are its own lack of discipline and collaboration.

Finally, too often leaders take a short-term view of a long-term issue. Leaders can generate a good amount of focus and enthusiasm to tackle current issues. They invest themselves in a process and make the right adjustments to help the team improve. But too often, as soon as the pain of the current situation begins to subside, the leader delegates to others the responsibility for sustaining the changes and moves on to other issues perceived as more pressing. John Kotter (1996) referred to this as "declaring victory too soon" (p. 12). Without long-term attention, the changes will not be anchored in the culture and will die a slow death as atrophy takes place. Leading successful teams is not an event, but an ongoing process in which the leader must be personally invested for the long haul.

Summary

Working with teams is part of every leader's job description. The key to success is to have a model that helps you make sense of what is happening in the team and provides guidance in how to intervene when the team needs help. Team leaders need to focus on a dual development path, realizing that not only are teams only as good as the maturity of the people who make them up, but also that team members mature only when they are part of a healthy, authentic community. Equipping team members to be emotionally mature and self-aware is foundational to the effectiveness of the team. The team leader, who must also be mature and self-aware, not only provides direction and guidance, but also, through a calm presence and purposeful intent, creates a context for learning and adaptation as the team responds to the changing world around it. Trust, maturity, learning, listening, and questioning are all traits that must be developed experientially; information alone is not enough to produce effective teamwork.

Questions for Reflection and Discussion

1. What influences are there on contemporary teams?

2. What are the key success factors and barriers of teams?

3. What do teams need to sustain their success?

4. What should be the leader's role and focus in building or improving a team?

5. What strategies would you use to develop a new team?

6. What role does learning play in a team's success?

7. Answer the following questions based on the information in the scenario at the beginning of the chapter:

   • What would you do to understand the scope of the decay of the program?

• How would you begin to define a new vision for the future?

• How would you deal with the resistant team member?

• How would you handle the fallout from other team members who support the tenured member?

• How can you help the team broaden its perspective and challenge the long-held assumptions?

• How would you begin to rebuild the culture once the resistant members were no longer a part of the team?

• What would you do to prevent this situation from recurring as programs run their course and need to be revised or reinvented?

Key Terms and Definitions

advocacy—The process of articulating and promoting one's own perspective.

assumptions—The taken-for-granted ideas that guide our understanding of who we are and how the world works.

chaos—A period of uncertainty as a person learns and changes.

collective intelligence—The combined experience, knowledge, and insight of a group.

collective learning—Using the perspectives of others to raise one's awareness of one's assumptions and the appropriateness of them. It also includes the ability to manage the individual and collective emotional process to reduce reactivity to the differences of others.

critical thinking—The process of bringing assumptions and values to the surface to determine whether they are valid.

culture—A set of shared beliefs, customs, and assumptions of a particular society or group.

decision criteria—A set of values, ideas, or results that allow members to evaluate the validity of a given decision.

disturbance—An external force that creates the demand for change.

emotional maturity—The ability to take responsibility for one's emotional process and actions.

emotional process—Taking in information from the environment and responding to it.

experiential learning—Learning that involves learning in context, taking action, and reflecting on that action.

inquiry—The process of using questions and active listening to understand the perspective of another person.

learning—The intentional act of clarifying one's assumptions and managing the impact of anxiety on one's actions.

letting go—Creating a level of openness to consider a different perspective or way of understanding.

maturity—The ability to take responsibility for one's decisions and actions regardless of how others respond to you.

meeting strategy—A plan that lays out the purpose, frequency, and duration of a team's meetings.

reactive—Having an anxiety-driven, automatic response.

self-awareness—The ability to be aware of one's values and assumptions as well as the impact emotion has on one's responses.

self-differentiation—The ability to determine one's own beliefs, manage one's reaction to the anxiety of others, and maintain healthy interpersonal boundaries with others.

self-facilitating—The ability of a group to self-assess and self-correct to improve the group's effectiveness.

self-regulation—The ability to manage one's responses in the presence of strong emotion.

structure—The way authority and roles are organized in an organization.

sustainability—As applied to team development, the ability to create lasting change or increase the capacity of the team to change in the future.

system—A complex or unified whole made up of interdependent parts.

task design—The organization of work or tasks for which the team is responsible.

transfer of learning—The process of taking lessons learned in one context and applying them to another context.

Bibliography

Argyris, C. (1990). *Overcoming organizational defenses.* Needham, MA: Allyn & Bacon.

Argyris, C. (1997). Learning and teaching: A theory of action perspective. *Journal of Management Education, 21* (1), 9-27.

Bashein, M.L., Marcus, M.L., & Riley, P. (1994). Business process reengineering: Preconditions for success and failure. *Informations Systems Management, 9,* 24-31.

Bell, S. (2007). Deep-level composition variables as predictors of team performance: A meta-analysis. *Journal of Applied Psychology, 92* (3), 595-615.

Berman, B. (producer) and Wachowski, A. & Wachowski, L. (directors). (1999). *The matrix.* Film. United States: Warner Brothers: Burbank, CA.

Bodner, S. (1997). Experiential training: A stepping stone for work teams. Center for the Study of Work Teams, University of North Texas: Denton, TX.

Bohm, D. (1996). *On dialogue.* New York: Routledge.

Campion, M.A., Medsker, G.J., & Higgs, A.C. (1993). Relations between work group characteristics and effectiveness: Implications for designing effective work groups. *Personnel Psychology, 46,* 823-850.

Campion, M.A., Papper, E.M., & Medsker, G.J. (1996). Relations between work team characteristics and effectiveness: A replication and extension. *Personnel Psychology, 49,* 429-452.

Collins, J., & Porras, J. (1994). *Built to last.* New York: HarperBusiness.

Cowan, D.A. (1995). Rhythms of learning: Patterns that bridge individuals and organizations. *Journal of Management Inquiry, 4* (3), 222-237.

Cusumano, M.A. (1997). How Microsoft makes large teams work like small teams. *Sloan Management Review,* Fall, 9-20.

De Dreu, C.K., & Weingart, L.R. (2003). Task versus relationship conflict, team performance, and team member satisfaction: A meta-analysis. *Journal of Applied Psychology, 88* (4), 741-749.

Driskell, J.E., Hogan, R., & Salas, E. (1987). Personality and group performance. In C. Hendrick (Ed.), *Group processes and intergroup relations: Review of personality and social psychology* (vol. 9, pp. 91-112). Newbury Park, CA: Sage.

Friedman, E. (1999). *A failure of nerve: Leadership in the age of the quick fix.* Bethesda, MD: The Edwin Friedman Estate and Trust.

Garvin, D.A., & Roberto, M.A. (2001). What you don't know about making decisions. *Harvard Business Review, 79* (8), 108-116.

Goleman, D. (1998). *Working with emotional intelligence.* New York: Bantam Books.

Hackman, J.R. (1987). The design of work teams. In J. Lorsch (Ed.), *Handbook of organizational behavior* (pp. 315-342). Englewood Cliffs, NJ: Prentice Hall.

Hansen, M.T. (2009). *Collaboration.* Boston: Harvard Business Press.

Isaacs, W. (1999). *Dialogue and the art of thinking together.* New York: Currency/Doubleday.

Jehn, K. (1994). Enhancing effectiveness: An investigation of advantages and disadvantages of value-based intragroup conflict. *International Journal of Conflict Management, 5,* 223-238.

Jehn, K. (1995). A multimethod examination of the benefits and detriments of intragroup conflict. *Administrative Science Quarterly, 40,* 256-282.

Jehn, K. (1997). Affective and cognitive conflict in work groups: Increasing performance through value-based intragroup conflict. In C.K.W. De Dreu & E. Van de Vliert (Eds.), *Using conflict in organizations* (pp. 87–100). London: Sage.

Jordan, M. (1998). *For the love of the game.* New York: Crown.

Kahane, A. (2004). *Solving tough problems.* San Francisco: Berrett-Koehler.

Kotter, J.P. (1996). *Leading change.* Boston: Harvard Business School Press.

Kozlowski, S.W.J., & Ilgen, D.R. (2006). Enhancing the effectiveness of work groups and teams. *Psychological Science in the Public Interest, 7* (3), 77-124.

Lencioni, P. (2002). *The five dysfunctions of a team.* San Francisco: Jossey-Bass.

Lowney, C. (2003). *Heroic leadership.* Chicago: Loyola Press.

Martin, A. (2007). The changing nature of leadership. Center for Creative Leadership, www.ccl.org/leadership/pdf/research/NatureLeadership.pdf.

McCrae, R.R., & Costa, P.T. (1987). Validation of the five-factor model of personality across instruments and observers. *Journal of Personality and Social Psychology, 52,* 81-90.

Miner, T., & Priest, S. (2000). *Experiential quotes.* Lakebay, WA: eXperientia Publications.

Nieva, V.F., Fleishman, E.A., & Reick, A. (1985). Team dimensions: Their identity, their measurement, and their relationships. Research note 85-12. Washington, DC: U.S. Army, Research Institute for the Behavioral and Social Sciences.

Peck, M.S. (1987). *The different drum: Community making and peace.* New York: Touchstone.

Priest, S. (1998). The effect of program setting and duration on corporate team development. *Journal of Experiential Education, 21* (2), 111-112.

Priest, S., & Gass, M. (1997). *Effective leadership in adventure programming.* Champaign, IL: Human Kinetics.

Revans, R.W. (1991). Action learning—Its origins and practice. In M. Pedler (Ed.), *Action learning in practice* (2nd ed.). New York: Gower.

Robinson, G. (2003). The anatomy of a successful learning based change initiative. *OD Practitioner, 35* (2), 33-37.

Robinson, G. (2005, April). Action learning. *Research and Practice, 2* (1), 79-88.

Robinson, G., & Rose, M. (2004). *A leadership paradox: Influencing others by defining yourself.* Bloomington, IN: AuthorHouse.

Robinson, G., & Rose, M. (2006). *A leadership paradox: Influencing others by defining yourself.* (rev. ed.). Bloomington, IN: AuthorHouse.

Robinson, G., & Rose, M. (2007). *Teams for a new generation: A facilitator's field guide.* Bloomington, IN: AuthorHouse.

San Martin-Rodriguez, L., Dominque-Beaulieu, M., D'Amour, D., & Ferrada-Videla, M. (2005, May). The determinants of successful collaboration: A review of theoretical and empirical studies. *Journal of Interprofessional Care, 1,* 132-147.

Schein, E. (1996). *Organization culture and leadership.* San Francisco: Jossey-Bass.

Senge, P. (1990). *The fifth discipline.* New York: Doubleday.

Senge, P., Ross, R., Smith, B., Roberts, C., & Kleiner, A. (1994). *The fifth discipline fieldbook.* New York: Doubleday.

Simons, T., & Peterson, R. (2000). Task conflict and relationship conflict in top management teams: The pivotal role of intragroup trust. *Journal of Applied Psychology, 85,* 102-111.

Thomas, K.W. (2000). *Intrinsic motivation at work.* San Francisco: Berrett-Koehler.

Tuckman, B., & Jensen, M. (1977). Stages of small-group development revisited. *Group Organization Management, 2,* 419-427.

Chapter **11**

Risk Management in Leadership

Robert Kauffman

" *To look is one thing. To see what you look at is another. To understand what you see is another. To learn from what you understand is something else. But to act on what you learn is really all that matters.* "

Winston Churchill

On May 9, 1992, on a high water trip on the New River, Scott Hill, an experienced river raft guide, entered the Upper Keeney Rapids, a class IV/V rapid on the International Scale of River Difficulty. He missed the move on the wave in the Upper Keeney Rapids. He needed to move the raft toward river left behind Whale Rock (visible on the right side of the photo in figure 11.1). Rather, the raft flushed into a large wave called a Hawaii Five-O, where four of the six passengers were ejected from the raft. Scott rescued two of the victims in Middle Keeney and nearly rescued Linda and Cheryl Taylor. To his credit, he did a herculean job of nearly rescuing everyone given the circumstances. Linda flushed through a chute (not shown) and was subsequently rescued. Cheryl either washed onto Flint Rock (not shown) or purposely swam to it in an effort to self-rescue and get out of the ferocious water. She died on the Flint Rock strainer.

The estate of Cheryl Taylor sued the raft company, which was found in a jury trial not to have been negligent. In his deposition, Scott Hill testified that after lunch he had decided on his own, and without seeking the guidance of the trip leader, to be the first raft through the Keeneys. The testimony of others indicated that he was out in front of the rest of the group, that they could not see him and he could not see the group, that they did not see him run the rapids, and that they did not see the incident occur. At the trial it was generally agreed that he was roughly 10 to 15 boat lengths in front of the next boat on the trip.

From a leadership perspective, the question is, Why was Scott Hill 15 boat lengths ahead of everyone else on the trip while the other rafts were clearly in a tight formation as they went around Whale Rock? Also, had he been in tight formation with the rest of the group, had he not been out of sight of everyone else, and had he not been 15 boat lengths in front of the nearest boat, would it have made a difference in the rescue of Linda and Cheryl? From a leadership perspective, what, if anything, could Scott Hill and the other guides have done to prevent the accident?

Figure 11.1 The normal route is to run river left (right side of photo) behind Whale Rock. Scott missed the move and ran into a large wave where he ejected four of his six passengers into the water. Note the tight formation of two of the rafts grouped together next to Whale Rock. A third raft is just out of sight but still in a tight formation.

This still photo was captured from a video taken by the videographer (Exhibit-8). Estate of Cheryl A. Taylor v. Class VI River Runners, Inc., et. al (1995). Exhibit-8, Circuit Court of Fayette County, West Virginia. Civil Action No. 94-C-0124. The routes and the text overlays were added by the author.

Learning Outcomes

At the conclusion of this chapter, students will be able to:

▶ Describe the 2×2 risk matrix.

▶ Explain the adventure experience paradigm (AEP).

▶ Describe the accident process including the domino model and barrier analysis.

▶ List the four components of negligence and explain how they relate to leadership.

▶ Outline the four risk management strategies.

Those in the business of providing leisure and recreation activities must have a strategy for reducing risk. Such a strategy should include an examination of the outdoor program planning and leadership process to make activities safer while at the same time embracing risk. Preventing accidents also reduces the likelihood of negligence lawsuits.

Negligence Considerations

Recreation leaders and programmers in Western countries live in an increasingly litigious society. For example, in the United States, the proportion of lawyers in the workforce has nearly doubled from 1970 to 2000, and it seems as though everyone is suing everyone else over everything and anything (Will, 2009). It was no different for the estate of Cheryl Taylor. Many people have a fear of being sued, and no book can keep this from happening. That is the choice of the plaintiff, the injured party. This section introduces the concept of **negligence** and describes the four components (duty; breach of duty; proximate cause; and injury, damage, or loss) necessary for it to occur. It provides strategies to prevent injury, damage, or loss (accidents)—obviously, *no accident* most likely means *no lawsuit* (a later section explores accident prevention). Recreation professionals need to know the common practices of their activities and their industry and then follow those practices. If they are sued, normal leadership and program planning skills may protect them.

A tort of negligence is an injury that occurs between two parties. The **plaintiff** is the injured party, and the **defendant** is the party who has allegedly committed the harm. The following four components are necessary for negligence:

1. Duty
2. Breach of duty
3. Proximate cause
4. Injury, damage, or loss

These four components are both necessary and sufficient for negligence to be deemed to have occurred. If any one of the components is absent, legally, the situation cannot be considered one of negligence. It is a causal relationship in the classic sense.

Consider each component of negligence as a window. All four windows must be kept open for the plaintiff, or the injured party who is bringing the suit, to win. Shutting any one of the windows removes one of the elements necessary for negligence and ends the case. The plaintiff's attorney seeks to keep the windows open. In contrast, the defendant's attorney seeks to close any one of the four windows.

To determine negligence, a recreation leader first has to have a **duty**, or obligation, to the participant. The question is, What is that duty? (This will be discussed shortly.) Next, a **breach of duty** needs to have occurred. Generally, there are two types of breaches. **Omission** refers to not doing something one was supposed to do. **Commission** refers to doing something one was supposed to do, but incorrectly, or doing something one should not have done. The third component of negligence is **proximate cause**, which means that a reasonable relationship must connect the breach of duty with the **injury, damage, or loss**. Finally, the plaintiff must be able to show that injury, damage, or loss actually occurred.

Standard of Care

The **standard of care** is normally defined as what a reasonable and prudent person would do in a similar situation (Kaiser, 1986). Professionals in the recreation and parks field are expected to know and follow the **common practices** of the activity or industry. It is a component of the duty owed by a recreation professional. This does not refer to a low level of knowledge and skill, but training in the common practices of the activity or industry. In discussing the standard of care, van der Smissen (1975) expanded the concept of a reasonable and prudent person to suggest that a recreation professional needs to be a reasonable and prudent *professional*. This means that recreation professionals need to know and follow the common practices, or **industry standards**, of their activities.

How do recreation leaders or programmers become familiar with the common practices, or industry standards, for their activities, disciplines, or industry? Accrediting agencies include the Commission for Accreditation of Park and Recreation Agencies (CAPRA), the Canadian Camping Association (CCA), the Association for Experiential Education (AEE), the New Zealand Rivers Association (NZRA), and the Association of Mountaineering Instructors (AMI) in the UK and Ireland. These organizations and others like them promulgate standards and regulations for their particular activities. Although some organizations may not

Best Practices From the Field

There is a reason the Adventuresports Institute at Garrett College in Maryland, USA, is one of the premier academic programs in adventure sport. Mike Logsdon, the academic director of the program, notes that its purpose is to prepare professionals for the adventure sport industry. He summarizes this purpose by noting that "Their challenge is to take individuals who are consumers of adventure and teach them to be providers of adventure activities."

The Adventuresports Institute has always been at the forefront of the adventure sport industry. The program dates back to the 1989 Whitewater World Championships and the 1992 US Canoe and Kayak Whitewater Team Olympic Trials held on the nearby Savage River. Garrett College was actively involved in promoting the events, which brought international recognition to the local area. They saw a need to develop leaders and professionals in the adventure sport and recreation industries, and they have pursued that mission. They even originated the term *adventuresports.* In 2014, the program came full circle with its involvement with the 2014 ICF Canoe Slalom World Championships, held on one of the first artificially recirculating whitewater courses in the United States at Adventure Sports Center International in McHenry, Maryland.

In preparing professional providers of adventure activities, the program has four main thrusts: climbing, whitewater, snow or winter, and backcountry living. To help students transition from consumers to providers of adventure activities, teachers expose them to nationally recognized standards and programs, and they become instructor educators using those standards.

In terms of **risk management**, Logsdon notes that the program seeks to "manage risks and teach students to make good judgments." Managing risks and making good judgments complement each other. In a risk-rich environment, students and professionals need to exercise good leadership and programming skills to enable them to manage the risks at an appropriate level.

The Adventuresports Institute at Garrett College is recognized by many as a leader in the adventure sport industry. The organization has gained an enviable reputation because of its leadership culture and its continuous leadership in the field (among other things), and so is a fitting example of best practices in 21st-century leadership in the field of recreation and leisure services.

---

need to become accredited, they may want to consider complying in principle and practice with the standards and practices of their industry. For example, if the standard suggests a ratio of staff to participants of 1:6, it might be prudent to incorporate this ratio, regardless of accreditation status.

Joining a trade organization is another way to ensure adherence to best practices. Often, general professional organizations such as the NRPA (National Recreation and Park Association) in the United States, or state or provincial organizations, provide information about what others are doing in the activity area. However, more specialized trade organizations, such as PPA (Professional Paddlesports Association) in the United States, provide recreation professionals with specific information regarding their activities (Kauffman & Councill, 2005). In addition, professionals can consider attending professional conferences, becoming certified, and attending workshops and in-service trainings.

Recreation professionals are held to a standard of care that represents the commonly accepted

practices, or industry standards, for the activities they conduct. Therefore, they need to know what these common practices are. Essentially, these practices are generally the leadership and programming techniques learned in standard recreation and parks courses and curricula. Following graduation, professionals should maintain professional development in their areas of expertise and professional interest. There may be no better argument for continued professional development than this.

Risk Management Strategies

In the risk management literature there are traditionally four methods to address risks (Campfire Girls, 1993; Herman, 2009; Kaiser, 1986; van der Smissen, Moiseichik, & Hartenburg, 2005): reduction, avoidance, transfer, and retention. Reduction refers to seeking to reduce the likelihood of an accident or incident occurring. Avoidance is eliminating or not doing the activity. It can include eliminating the activity in its entirety or it can be the temporary closing of the activity due to ephemeral conditions. Transfer and retention are cost-reduction approaches and do not reduce the likelihood of an incident; rather, they indicate who pays for the loss. For those in the business of providing a service, the two most viable risk management approaches are reduction and avoidance.

As its name suggests, **reduction** involves steps that an agency takes to reduce the likelihood of an accident. If there is no accident, there is no injury, damage, or loss and, most likely, no lawsuit. The issue is how to keep an accident from happening. Consider the question from the opening scenario of why Scott Hill was 15 boat lengths in front of the rest of the group and out of sight of the rafts behind him. Had he been in the tight formation with the rest of the group, the other rafts may have assisted in the rescue by picking up Linda and Cheryl. This is a leadership issue that will be discussed in more detail later in the chapter. In terms of this discussion, the simple answer is that soft barriers (i.e., administrative policies) should have been implemented and followed, which would have reduced the likelihood of this tragedy.

Avoidance is the elimination or discontinuation of the activity. Most people believe that avoidance means the total elimination of the activity. However, it could include the temporary suspension of an activity. The New River was a high water run. The videographer happily stated so at the beginning of his video documentary of the trip for resale. The plaintiff's attorneys noted the high water condition as a contributing factor. They cited evidence from the trip's videographer at the lunch stop showing that the river was overflowing its banks and into the permanent vegetation along the side of the river. Although this may have been a contributing factor to the accident, it was generally concluded that the river was below the cutoff point for ceasing rafting activity and that numerous spring runs were run at this level (i.e., avoidance). In addition, most raft guides were familiar with this water level on the river. Although the plaintiff pressed this point, the general consensus was that this water level was not abnormal for the river and for the raft guides.

Transfer involves transferring the program or the cost of the program to someone else. This is generally done in one of three ways: (1) transferring the cost to someone else, usually an insurance company; (2) contractually transferring

responsibility or some of the duty to the participant through waivers; or (3) subcontracting the activity to someone else, who assumes the duty.

Although waivers are necessary tools, they do not prevent lawsuits. Cheryl Taylor signed a **waiver** before participating on the raft trip. She did so freely and without coercion. The raft company (the defendant) argued that she understood the inherent risks associated with white-water rafting. Essentially, they argued that certain dangers are associated with white water because it is white water and that she knew of these dangers. They argued that Cheryl Taylor had signed a waiver containing an indemnification and hold harmless clause, in which she agreed not to sue even if the raft company screwed up and was negligent. Also, they noted that Cheryl was of legal age when she signed the waiver. They argued that the waiver should be upheld and the case dismissed.

The plaintiff (the estate of Cheryl Taylor) acknowledged the preceding points. There was some banting about on some of the issues, but for the most part there was little disagreement. They argued that the actions of the raft company were reckless and constituted gross negligence, and that the raft company was not following the common practices of the industry. They noted that Scott Hill's raft was separated by 15 boat lengths from the rest of the group and that he was out of sight of the next raft on the trip. By their own admission, the other guides on the trip were unaware that Scott Hill was off track, that he had lost four passengers from his raft, and that Cheryl Taylor was pinned on Flint Rock until after they had passed Flint Rock. Also, the plaintiff's attorney noted that this violated the common practice, or industry standard, of keeping the rafts in front and behind in visual contact. They argued that because the negligence was so bad, the waiver should not be enforced and the lawsuit should continue.

Essentially, the judge ruled that the jury should decide whether the incident constituted ordinary negligence and was covered by the waiver (the defense's position) or whether it was gross negligence and the case should continue (the plaintiff's position). The case moved forward toward trial. The point here is that in today's litigious society, waivers are important and need to be taken seriously. As in this case, they are often a bump in the road for both sides on the way to trial. However,

Leisure Leaders

C.C. Williams

MY PREPARATION

- BSc in Recreation and Parks Management with concentration in Adventure Sports—Frostburg State University, Frostburg, MD

- MEd in Education—Frostburg State University, Frostburg, MD

MY CAREER

I am the outdoor education coordinator for the Parks, Recreation, and Tourism Department of Rock Hill, South Carolina, where I use risk management principles in the delivery of outdoor education programs. In addition, I teach beginning climbing and kayaking courses part-time at Winthrop University. My professional goal is to introduce others to the outdoors and help them to live a full life using adventure as a catalyst for personal growth.

I am responsible for educating the general public using local public outdoor resources. Our number one goal is the safety of the participants and staff. Facilitating safety requires good communication. It is more than requiring people to wear life jackets; it involves communicating safety throughout the experience in brochures, promotional materials, websites, and other sources of information. Good communications helps to reduce "push-back" from participants if, for example, we need to cancel a kayaking trip because of high water or other safety issues.

Photo courtesy of C.C. Williams.

My responsibilities also include training the trainers. This involves a monthly staff training in which we cover topics such as environmental education, river safety and training, and first aid and CPR. I am also responsible for teaching swiftwater rescue to the local fire department.

I attempt to integrate the use of the underlying factors in the Domino Accident Model seamlessly into the design and implementation of all programs. No checklist is necessary. The seamless application of these factors in the design process results in safer programs. On occasion, I use the domino model to explain the accident process and the safety measures we are taking. The model is easily understood and empowers parents by providing the tools they need to participate in outdoor activities safely with their families.

MY ADVICE TO YOU

My favorite leadership quote to inspire students interested in entering the field is from well-known mountaineer Paul Petzoldt: "I have three rules for leaders in the outdoors: You have to know where the people you're leading are coming from. You have to know what you want to do with them, and you have to love them." I encourage you to make it your goal to practice these three rules in your personal leadership and in your career.

---

if not taken seriously, the judge could easily dismiss the case by concluding that the negligence is ordinary and covered by the waiver.

The fourth strategy is **retention**. Generally, the organization pays for expenses out of pocket or creates an internal fund in place of insurance. The deductible portion of insurance is an example of retention.

In summary, recreation professionals need to understand the principles of negligence. Waivers are also important. However, the two strategies that reduce accidents are reduction and temporary avoidance. The focus should be on what can be done to prevent accidents in the first place. Before addressing risk reduction strategies and managing for safety, we discuss the design of activities that include risks as integral parts of the experience.

Designing the Experience

The recreation and parks field, and in particular the outdoor adventure area, has embraced risks as a necessary component of the outdoor experience. Rather than eliminating them, leaders in the field often view risks as an integral part of the activity or program, especially in the outdoors. For the activity leader and programmer, the issue is managing the risks to create the desired experience.

In contrast, the legal liability, risk management, accident causation, and safety management literature suggests that the role of the safety manager in an organization is to reduce or eliminate all risks if possible. Risks are equated with hazards, and both are considered bad. Couple this with the fact that risks can result in lawsuits, and it is easy to understand that any risk is a bad risk.

For outdoor and recreation leaders and programmers, this situation can be confusing. Should risks be included as part of the activity? How can they design outdoor activities to provide the desired outdoor experience safely? It is important to frame the issue of risks and risk management in terms of the experience the leader is trying to create. Recreation leaders and programmers seek to create an experience through their activities, and risk may be an integral component of that experience. The issue they have to address is how to manage risk to provide the desired experience while avoiding accidents and lawsuits.

2×2 Risk Matrix: Perceived Versus Actual Risks

The **2×2 risk matrix** expresses a relationship between perceived risks and actual risks (see figure 11.2). The model evolved out of research on the Potomac River for the Maryland Department of Natural Resources. The model was developed from a survey of Potomac River users that related their perceptions of how dangerous they viewed their river experience versus their experience as measured by a specialization index (Kauffman, 1991; Kauffman, Taylor, & Price, 1991). Although resource managers can apply the model to the outdoor experiences they offer, it can easily be generalized to general recreation also.

The Potomac River study found that most fatalities occurred at moderate water levels. They did not occur at flood level, nor did they occur at the normal low flows found during the summer. Intuitively, this may not make sense; however, upon closer inspection, it does. In doing so, the management of the Potomac River directly relates to three of the categories in the 2×2 risk matrix. Although originating from a resource management issue, the paradigm can easily be expanded to include traditional programming situations. The relationship of the three water level conditions (flood, moderate level, and summer low flow) to the 2×2 risk matrix can be used to introduce the categories in the following sections.

The focus of the paradigm is on the recreation provider (resource manager, leader, or programmer) who is providing the recreation experience. The

		Perceived risk	
		Low	High
Actual risk	High	**Drowning trap** The user perceives the risks to be low while they are actually high. This is a potentially dangerous situation.	**Upper Yough River** There are high actual risks present and the user perceives the risks as high.
	Low	**Lazy river** The actual risks involved are low and the user perceives these risks to be low also.	**Roller coaster** The user perceives the risk to be high while they are actually low.

Figure 11.2 From the perspective of the recreation provider (resource manager, leader, or programmer), the 2×2 risk matrix compares the perceived risks with the actual risks present for participants.
Reprinted, by permission, from Kauffman, 2013, *Integrated risk management for leisure services* (Champaign, IL: Human Kinetics), 132.

provider must assess the actual risks of the experience in terms of the participants' perception of the risks involved. The assessment helps to determine the risk management approach of the recreation provider. This matrix complements the adventure experience paradigm discussed later in the chapter.

High Actual Risks and High Perceived Risks

In this category, participants recognize the high risks as such. For the leader or programmer, the task for this category is straightforward: to provide the appropriate knowledge, skills, and abilities to help participants handle the situation. In contrast with the high actual risk and low perceived risk situation, participants tend to be more receptive to the needs of the situation because they recognize the risks involved in the activity. In addition, for those seeking mastery, actual risks become an integral part of the activity. In addition, the leader or programmer needs to provide the usual support including staff, equipment, preplanning, and activity selection. Designing experiences in this category complements the adventure experience paradigm in the next section.

In Figure 11.2, the **Upper Yough category** is exemplified by the Upper Yough river. It is a class IV/V white-water river that drops 150 to 170 feet per mile. Its high gradient creates high actual risks. Also, most participants correctly perceive the risks as high. Their perception is consistent with the actual risks. It is difficult for the raft guide to reduce the actual risks on a natural river; the issue is managing the risks in an effort to reduce them. The guides run the river under known conditions and have designated routes through the rapids. They set up safety at the bottom of the major rapids and go through the rapids single file. The owner, who also serves as safety, critiques the run of the rafts through the rapids. The guides are well trained. By managing the risks, they create a safer environment for participants. The task of the leader or programmer is to provide the support services necessary for performing safely in a high-risk environment.

The Keeney Rapids on the New River were a similar example of a situation with high actual risk and high perceived risk. In her deposition, the trip leader suggested a rather casual leadership approach to the trip through the Keeney Rapids. Her description of her role as trip leader provides a glimpse of her leadership style on the trip (see

figure 11.3). In her defense, it should be noted that she was under considerable pressure by the plaintiff's attorney, who was trying to determine negligence in the form of inadequate supervision on her part, and she was trying to avoid saying anything that might be incriminating.

Low Actual Risks and Low Perceived Risks

The lazy river ride at a water park exemplifies this category (figure 11.2). As its name suggests, the lazy river is designed as a float trip during which participants can get a good suntan. Other than getting sunburned, the lazy river is an example of a situation with low perceived and low actual risks for participants. Many recreational activities fall into the **lazy river category**. Watching movies, driving for pleasure, taking a walk in the park, and birthday parties are examples of activities that would most likely fall into this category.

Leaders and programmers of activities in this category must continually assess them to ensure that the risks remain low and that the situations don't inadvertently creep into the high actual and low perceived risk category. Professionals experienced in the activity and who have the knowledge, skills, and abilities to run the activity need to recognize changes that might transform their activities into high actual and low perceived risk situations.

High Actual Risks and Low Perceived Risks

The high actual risk, low perceived risk category is called the **drowning trap category** because, like a trap, it catches unsuspecting people (Kauffman 1992, 2002). Extended backcountry trips in which participants are two or three days from medical help, such as the Everglades trip shown in figure 11.4, fall into this category. A minor medical incident in the frontcountry that is within an hour of a trauma center can often be life threatening in the backcountry. Playing on certain playground equipment is a classic example of a situation with a high actual risk and low perceived risk of head entrapment (National Playground Institute, 1994). On challenge courses, the electric fence was discontinued after a long-term study indicated that many people fell while being passed over the fence and sprained or broke an ankle. Because the wire was relatively low (fence), people didn't perceive

Spacing Between Rafts on the Trip

The following is a description of Joy Marr's testimony on the spacing between rafts on the trip. Joy Marr was the trip leader. Read this from a supervisory perspective of a leader who may or may not be in control of her trip. In this passage, she acknowledges three things. First, she is not responsible for maintaining spacing. Second, spacing is important for rescue purposes, and third, order of the rafts on a trip is unimportant. Particularly in a high actual risk or high perceived risk situation, is this an appropriate leadership style that will lead to a safer experience? As a footnote, it was acknowledged on page 126 that a spacing of three to four boat lengths was the normal spacing for going through the Keeneys.

Taylor vs. Class VI, et. al - Deposition of Joy Lynn Marr on March 17, 1997
Mr. Hill – Examination

Page 99

20 21	Q	As trip leader, are you responsible for the spacing of rafts going down the rapids?
22	A	No, I'm not directly responsible.
23	Q	Spacing is an important safety concern?

Page 100

1	A	Yes.
2 3	Q	You don't want to be too close and you don't want to be too far?
4	A	Correct.
5 6	Q	If you are too far away, you cannot be there to effectively assist in a rescue, correct?
7	A	Correct.
8 9	Q	If the trip leader is not responsible, who is responsible?
10 11 12	A	We are collectively, as a trip, responsible for each other and ourselves. Each guide to be able to monitor the flow.
13 14 15 16 17	Q	The spacing that we just saw between the rafts in this particular Class VI going through the Keeneys, is it your testimony, if I understood it correctly, that you did not breach any standard in the industry regarding the spacing of the rafts?
18	A	That is correct.
19 20	Q	It is your opinion that the rafts were not too far apart at any point in time?
21	A	No.
22 23	Q	If Scott Hill was either the least experienced or the next to least experienced of the guides

Page 101

01 02 03 04		on this particular trip, do you still think it was appropriate – given the individuals in his raft, do you still think it was appropriate for him to go first down the Keeney Rapids?
05	A	Yes.

Figure 11.3 Trip leader Joy Marr's description of the spacing and order of rafts on the New River trip.

Estate of Cheryl A. Taylor v Class VI River Runners, Inc., et. al (1995). Deposition of Joy Lynn Marr, Circuit Court of Fayette County, West Virginia. Civil Action No. 94-C-0124. pp. 99-101.

the danger associated with passing someone over it. The large number of injuries associated with this activity suggested a low perceived risk and high actual risk situation (Collard, 2001; Project Adventure, 1995).

Low Actual Risks and High Perceived Risks

This category offers the most programming opportunities for recreation providers. The **roller coaster category** refers to low actual risks and high perceived risks. The amusement park (recreation provider) seeks to create thrills and chills without any injuries. The ride is designed to maximize perceived risk for its riders while minimizing actual risk. The high ropes course is another good example. Because the participant is always belayed into the system and there is adequate vertical distance to catch a fall, there is little chance of actually hitting the ground (low actual risk). It could be argued that the roller coaster approach is a viable strategy for most activities.

Categorically, this situation of providing challenge while minimizing actual risk is the safest. In describing the role of the facilitator on an initiatives course, Collard (2001, p. 67) wrote, "In an ideal adventure program, an experienced facilita-

tor will design a program/activity which aims to keep the 'perceived risk' as high as possible (to heighten the challenge, interaction, and tension), while managing the actual risk to be as low as possible." In essence, he is describing the roller coaster experience.

Many recreation activities fall into this category. With the exception of those creating activities seeking mastery (Ellis, 1973) or that require challenge as an integral part of the experience (e.g., the adventure experience paradigm), recreation providers should consider this category as the norm. In terms of the accident process and negligence, the leader's strategy is to reduce or manage the human, environmental, and equipment factors to reduce the likelihood of a severe incident or accident. Again, the activity or program is like a roller coaster ride, full of thrills and chills but low on real risks.

Adventure Experience Paradigm

In the outdoor adventure field, Priest and Gass (1997) developed the **adventure experience paradigm (AEP)**. The paradigm builds on the previous works of Martin and Priest (1986), on Ellis' (1973) optimal arousal theory of play based on the

© Robert Kauffman.

Figure 11.4 Many backcountry trips exemplify the high actual risk, low perceived risk category. This Everglades trip in Florida is two days into the backcountry and one to two days from rescue if an emergency occurs. Participants don't perceive the risks among the beautiful and dense mangroves.

inverted-U curve, and on the flow concept developed by Csikszentmihalyi (1975). The main focus of the adventure experience paradigm is creating the appropriate experience for the participant. The paradigm complements the earlier discussion of the 2×2 risk matrix.

The foundation of the adventure experience paradigm is seeking optimal arousal, or a flow experience. Ellis (1973) suggested that people seek optimal arousal in their play as well as in their normal activities. He used the inverted-U curve to illustrate the concept of seeking optimal arousal.

The flow model developed by Csikszentmihalyi (1975) relates the skill level or competence of the participant to the challenges present. Csikszentmihalyi suggested that when skills (action capabilities) match the challenges (action opportunities), a flow experience can result. The flow experience is characterized by a merging of action and awareness, a loss of a sense of time, and a total focus on or immersion in the activity. As odd as it may seem, participants know they are experiencing flow when they are not thinking about how they might be experiencing flow.

In developing the adventure experience paradigm, Priest and Gass (1997) superimposed a participant topology based on risk and competence on the flow model (see figure 11.5). In their model, they translated the flow model's skills and challenges into competence and risk. If the risks far exceed the competence level of the participant, **devastation and disaster** result. The category title is self-explanatory in terms of the participant's experience. If the competence level of the participant is only slightly exceeded, a **misadventure** results, which includes some anxiety and some mishap. If competence far exceeds the risks, the participant experiences **exploration and experimentation**. If competence exceeds the risks, an **adventure** occurs. In essence, participants aren't pushing themselves appropriately or in terms of optimal arousal because they are not fully challenged and therefore not totally engaged (i.e., they aren't typing or texting at their optimal speed). Finally, a **peak adventure** results when the risks match the competency of the participants. It corresponds to the potential for creating a flow state as described by Csikszentmihalyi (1975).

Next, the adventure experience paradigm juxtaposes the perceived risks and competence of the participant with the real risks and competence. The expected outcome is what participants perceive or

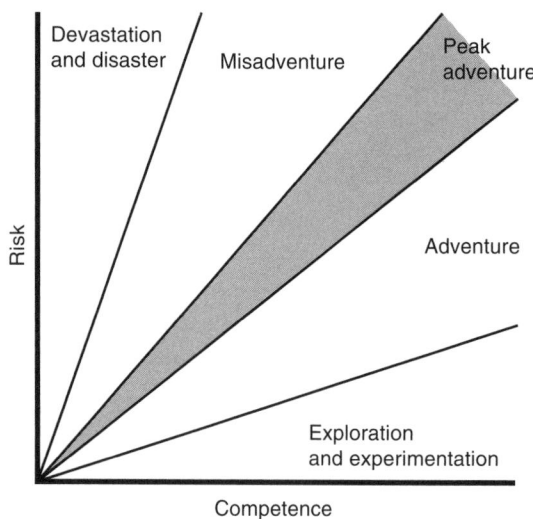

Figure 11.5 The adventure experience paradigm uses the flow model to create five adventure situations.
Reprinted, by permission, from R. Kauffman, 2013, *Integrated risk management for leisure services* (Champaign, IL: Human Kinetics), 136.

expect based on their perceptions of their skills and the risks involved. The resultant outcome is the result of the real risks and actual competence while the participant is engaged in the activity. The model analyzes the discrepancy between the expected outcome and the resultant outcome, which it calls adaptive dissonance. In addition, the model can be viewed from the perspective of both the participants' and the leader's expectations.

Consider a participant who signs up for a rafting trip on a moderately difficult river. He has some previous experience rafting, and his perception is that he should have a peak adventure. He perceives that his skill level, or competence, matches what he perceives to be the challenges or risks associated with the rafting trip (see figure 11.6).

However, this participant finds that the actual trip is different from what he expected. There are high water conditions, and the risks or challenges of the experience exceed his actual competence or skills. The actual experience is in the misadventure range rather than the peak adventure range. Thus, a discrepancy occurs between what the participant expected on the raft trip and what he actually experienced. In this case, his experience may not be optimal. However, it may also result in pushing him to develop new skills or to moderate his challenges in the future. If the situation is not handled correctly by the guides on the trip,

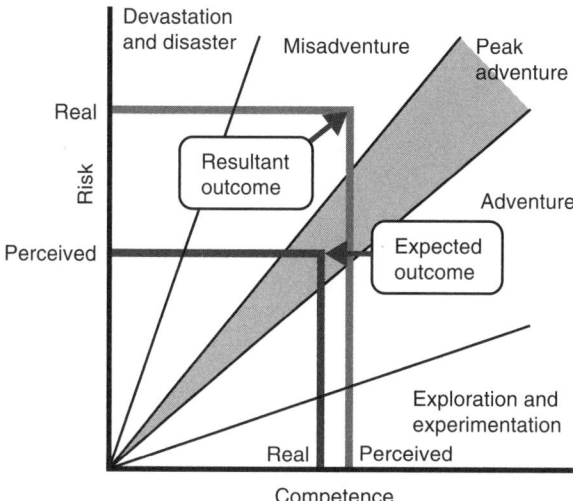

Figure 11.6 In this model, perceived risks and competency lead to the expected outcome. This is compared with the actual risks encountered and the actual competency of the participant.

Reprinted, by permission, from R. Kauffman, 2013, *Integrated risk management for leisure services* (Champaign, IL: Human Kinetics), 136.

the participant may experience anxiety and not participate in the activity again.

In terms of the AEP, Scott Hill's raft trip was most likely perceived as providing a peak adventure and not a devastation and disaster experience. The people on the trip expected a high water trip with big waves and large rapids. They may not have fully appreciated the implications of class IV/V white water, but they were having the experience they expected and wanted. Examination of the videotape revealed that people on the trip were generally enjoying themselves. They were all smiles at the lunch stop. Of course, the videographer is not going to film someone moping around and looking depressed. However, in terms of the AEP, there is every suggestion that Scott Hill and the rest of the guides on the trip were providing an experience that the participants in their boats were expecting. There was congruence between the expected outcome and the resultant outcome.

The X-axis of the adventure experience paradigm relates to the competency of Scott Hill and the participants in the raft. Except for one caveat, Scott Hill was an experienced raft guide who knew the New River. The caveat is that this was his first commercial trip for the year at this water level. Although there is no reason he shouldn't have guided on this high water trip, there is a

question about whether he should have been the first raft through the first class IV/V rapids on the New River. Normally, trip leaders place their rafts in the middle of the group. Regardless, in terms of the AEP model, Scott Hill and his participants possessed the competency to negotiate the river. Again, in terms of the AEP model, the participants were receiving what could be termed a peak experience. The focus now shifts to whether they were running a safe trip. This is a leadership question.

Accident Causation and Safety Management

Accident causation focuses on the causes of an accident, whereas safety management focuses on developing practices and procedures that reduce the likelihood of an accident. They are interrelated and complement each other. The end product of both accident causation and negligence is injury, damage, or loss. However, they have different purposes. In contrast to a lawsuit, which determines negligence and guilt, accident causation seeks to determine the causes that resulted in an accident in an effort to make the activity safer. The analysis of the New River incident in this chapter is an example of a post-incident analysis designed to make future raft trips safer. People and organizations operating in accordance with the common practices of their industries will most likely not be found negligent. However, an accident investigation may determine that procedures and practices that are common practices of the industry should be changed or modified to make the activity safer. Making administrative changes is not necessarily an indication that previous practices were negligent. It may be an indication of merely improving and honing procedures and practices that already are consistent with the common practices of the industry or activity.

A common thread or theme in most of the safety management literature is the dictum that safety needs to be integrated into the basic fabric of the organization. Heinrich, Peterson, and Roos (1980) and their successors, Bird and Germain (1985), referred to this as "loss of control." Actually, it is the obvious. Reason (2008) referred to this base level as "organizational factors." For recreation professionals, the base level or the basic fabric of the organization refers to how the activities and programs are conducted. It is the culture of the organization and how the organization performs its tasks. For example, if an automobile smashes through a guardrail and crashes into a tree, it may be easy to determine that the cause of the accident was that the driver fell asleep at the wheel. The assessment is correct but misses the underlying cause. From a management perspective, the real question is, Why did the driver fall asleep at the wheel? Was she working double shifts resulting in increased stress and fatigue? And, did this increased stress and fatigue result in her falling asleep at the wheel? If so, management may need to address the policy on working double shifts. From this simple example, it is easy to see how safety management permeates the entire culture of the organization at the base level. To increase safety, the organization really needs to be focusing on its double shift policy or how it conducts its business.

In outdoor leadership, the need to manage the organizational structure may not always be obvious. Figure 11.7 shows a portion of a legal deposition in which Thomas Mills, the leader of a raft trip on the Lehigh River, describes rendering first aid to Mr. Percheski, who suffered damage to his knee while on the trip. Most important, on lines 17 and 18 of page 65, Mills indicates that he didn't find out what happened with Mr. Percheski until the end of the trip. Is this appropriate supervision? Is this Thomas Mills' fault or the fault of management, which set him up for failure (lack of supervision) by having only three raft guides on a trip of roughly 70 people in 15 rafts. Like most people, Thomas Mills wants to do the right thing. There is every indication that he desired to be a competent guide and act responsibly. Reading between the lines of his deposition reveals that his inability to supervise the entire trip may really be management's fault. Management needs to consider hiring more guides or providing better communications between guides, or reexamine how trip leaders position themselves throughout the trip. Conceptually, Thomas Mills' inability to supervise the entire trip is similar to the employee's inability to stay awake at the wheel of her car; working double shifts was the underlying cause of the accident, just as Mills' problem was the result of poor management. The example points out the importance of creating a work environment that facilitates safety as well as productivity.

Traditional Outdoor Models

The outdoor adventure field has long had an interest in accident models. The accident models developed in the outdoor field tend to be leader focused because the field relies heavily on leaders in the field to deliver and facilitate experiences. With slight modifications, these models are easily applied to the general recreation field. This section starts with a quick review of these models and then focuses on the domino accident model. Additional models and concepts from the general safety management field are also addressed, most notably the concepts of energy transfer and barrier analysis.

The early outdoor models were outlined and discussed in Priest and Gass (1997) and Jillings (2005). These models include those of Hale (1983), Raffan (1984), Priest and Gass (1997), and Meyer and Williamson (2008). Two recent outdoor models were articulated by Curtis (2005) and Kauffman (2004, 2005, 2007). Conceptually, the Curtis and Kauffman models have a lot of similarities. Both use human, environmental, and equipment factors. Most of the models are metaphorical in that they relate accidents to the balancing of a scale or the falling of dominos. The Curtis model uses the concept of a scale in which the human, environmental, and equipment factors that can create unsafe acts are balanced with, or offset by, safety factors and protocols.

Domino Model

In contrast to the Curtis model, the **domino model** developed by Kauffman envisions unsafe acts and unsafe conditions as a series of dominos (see figure 11.8). An unsafe act places a metaphorical domino on the table, and a safe act removes one. The dominos are grouped into the traditional human, environmental, and equipment factors. The factors were derived from the personal and job factors developed by Bird and Germain (1985), and the domino metaphor was borrowed from the classic model developed by Heinrich, Peterson, and Roos (1980) from the 1920s through the 1940s. Usually, an incident occurs with a transfer of energy, and the dominos fall. In general, the more dominos that are present, the more likely serious injury, damage, or loss will be. Conversely, by addressing these factors and reducing their impact, or by eliminating their presence, a leader removes dominos and makes the activity safer.

The strategy of a recreation leader using the domino model is threefold. The first strategy is to identify as many of the dominos that affect the activity as possible. Once they are identified, the

Supervision: Whose Fault Is It? Percheski Case

Setup: In this portion of the deposition, the plaintiff's lawyer, Mr. Lombardi, is seeking to determine what the common practices on the Lehigh River are regarding handling an injury. As is noted in this passage, John Percheski engaged in a water battle with other passengers and dislocated his knee. Thomas Mills is the trip leader for the raft trip that is being questioned by Mr. Lombardi.

The primary reason for including this passage is that it shows how the plaintiff lawyer is seeking to determine the common practices or industry standards in dealing with injuries on the Lehigh River (see the questioning on page 65, lines 22-24). It is evident that his line of questioning seeks to determine these common practices so he can compare and contrast the actions taken against the standards.

The secondary reason for including this passage is that it raises an interesting philosophical question for future recreation and parks professionals. Think about the situation for the trip leader and the two guides on the trip. The raft trip has 70 guests in 15 to 20 rafts. There are three guides for the entire trip. This is a ratio of 1:23 guides to guests. Some in the adventure experience industry believe that there should be a 1:5 or 1:6 ratio. Read the passage carefully, does the trip leader really have *general supervision* of this trip, let alone *specific supervision* of the injury once it occurred? Did management set Thomas Mills up for failure in terms of supervision and was his inability to supervise the entire trip really the fault of management?

The issue for the future professional in the recreation and parks field to consider is whether the company put the trip leader and the guides in a compromised position because of their administrative practices and policies. Do they really have adequate supervision on the trip to handle this, or for that matter, any situation? The trip leader certainly doesn't sound like he is very professional or that he knew what was going on during his trip. However, is the problem really structural rather than the fault of the trip leader or guide?

Q: Mr. Lombardi (plaintiff's lawyer)
A: Thomas Mills (trip leader)

Page 65

12	Q	Did you ask Mr. Percheski what happened
13		to him?
14	A	I did not have an opportunity to talk to Mr.
15		Percheski at all. He was removed from the river by my
16		guides and I believe some of his friends that were on
17		the trip. I had gained this information upon the end
18		of the trip, talking to my guides. I never saw Mr.
19		Percheski at all from the accident. I remained with
20		the rest of the trip and he was removed from the
21		gorge.
22	Q	Is that standard operating procedure,
23		that when an accident occurs on the river one of the
24		guides is to remain with the group?
25	A	Yes, you would have to, absolutely.

Page 66

1	Q	In this case, the trip leader?
2	A	Yes. Which was myself.

continued

Figure 11.7 Examine Thomas Mills' deposition from the perspective of whether he could provide general and specific supervision of his raft trip. Is this really a management issue that set him up for failure?

Reprinted, by permission, from R. Kauffman, 2013, *Integrated risk management for leisure services* (Champaign, IL: Human Kinetics), 16-17; Thomas Mills, John M. Percheski and Fern C. Percheski, his spouse, per quod, versus Lehigh River Rafting, LTD. Et al., Superior Court of New Jersey Law Division – Middlesex County Docket No. W-001468-89, January 18, p.65-67.

Supervision: Whose Fault Is It? Percheski Case *(continued)*

Q: Mr. Lombardi (plaintiff's lawyer)
A: Thomas Mills (trip leader)

3 4	Q	The guides on the Romanowski group, to my understanding, were George Munro and Marylou Mylett?
5	A	That is correct.
6-20		[deleted section on where they currently lived]
21 22 23 24	Q	After the incident occurred, Tom, did you have an opportunity to speak with either or both Marylou and George Munro as to what happened to Mr. Percheski?
25	A	I did eventually have an opportunity to discuss

Page 67

1		the specifics with them at the end of the trip.
2	Q	What do you recall?
3 4 5 6 7 8 9 10 11 12	A	From my understanding, what had happened was Mr. Percheski was standing up in the raft, threw a bucket of water and dislocated his knee. At that point Marylou and George administered first aid, put the gentleman in a splint and I believe George after they hauled him up the bank, George ran down to Rockport, which is our designated take out spot, and notified DER. [Dept of Environmental Resources] I know he was removed, I'm not sure if it was by ambulance or by a DER truck. I don't recall.
13 14	Q	Your investigation of the accident occurred after the rafting trip?
15	A	Yes.
16 17 18	Q	Again, the reason why you did not remain with Mr. Percheski was as a trip leader your responsibility was to the remainder of the group?
19 20 21	A	That is correct. I knew I had qualified guides who were certified in CPR and my responsibility was the safety for the rest of the trip.

Figure 11.7 *(continued)*

task becomes to reduce or manage their impact. The second strategy is to identify invisible dominos and make them visible. Not all factors are visible to a leader before the incident occurs. Leaders who have a good understanding of the accident process are trained to identify many of the dominos. Regardless, a leader cannot be expected to recognize all of the potential dominos. Usually, hindsight after an incident is when all the dominos become visible and can be identified. Third, to be meaningful, the **underlying factors** need to be integrated directly into the planning process of the activity. These factors can become a checklist to use to improve operations.

As previously noted, the underlying factors, or the dominos, can be applied to Scott Hill's rafting trip. For example, his decision to run first down the Keeney Rapids because "I like running first" (see figure 11.9) suggests both poor decision making and poor judgment (mental and psychological).

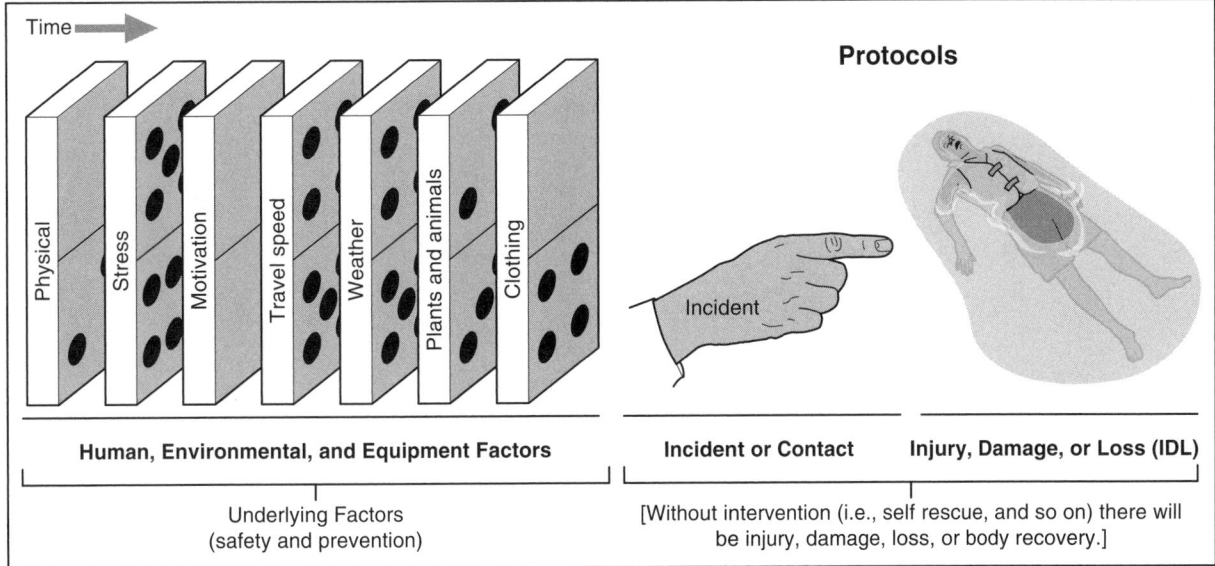

Human Factors

Physical or physiological capabilities or stress
(conditioning, restricted range of motion,
age-related issues, vision or hearing deficiencies,
disabilities, allergies, coordination, prior injuries,
illness, fatigue due to sensory overload, exposure
to temperature extremes
[hypothermia/hyperthermia], oxygen deficiency,
inadequate food intake, drugs, and so on)

Mental or psychological capabilities or stress
(fears or phobias, poor judgment, poor decisions,
inexperience, emotional overload, extreme
judgment/decision demands, extreme
concentration/perception demands, confusing
directions, conflicting demands, preoccupation
with problems, frustration, and so on)

Knowledge (lack of experience, inadequate
orientation, inadequate training [initial and
updates], not knowing the accident process, and so
on)

Skill (inadequate initial instruction, inadequate
practice, infrequent performance of activity, lack of
coaching, and so on)

Motivation (improper attempt to save time or
effort, improper attempt to avoid discomfort, peer
pressure, aggressive behavior, passive behavior,
cultural norms like high achievement, and so on)

Leadership and group dynamics
(miscommunications, inappropriate leadership
style, cultural norms, organizational norms, lack of
experience, lack of experience in similar setting,
inappropriate goals, trying to adhere to a schedule,
and so on)

Preplanning (inadequate or no risk management
plan; inadequate trip planning for any of the
human, environmental, and equipment factors)

Unsafe travel speed (travel too fast, travel too
slow, and so on)

Environmental Factors

Weather (rain, snow, fog, sun, lightning, and so on)

Change in weather conditions (change in any of
the above weather conditions [it begins to rain],
change in intensity of the weather conditions
[drizzle to pouring rain], and so on)

Terrain conditions (open water, restricted water
passage, waves, whitecaps, hydraulics, eddies,
strainers, tidal effects, current, desert,
mountainous, hilly, avalanche prone, and so on)

Change in terrain conditions (change in any of
the above terrain conditions, change in intensity of
the terrain conditions [increase of the wave size],
and so on)

Animals or plants (jellyfish, sharks, poison ivy, and
so on)

Equipment

Inadequate or inappropriate clothing (not using
wetsuit/drysuit or other cold weather/water
protection when needed, inadequate protection
from elements, and so on)

Inadequate or inappropriate equipment (not
using a sprayskirt when needed, use of
canoe/kayak in an environment for which it was
not designed, use of equipment in ways for which
it was not designed, navigational equipment, and
so on)

Inadequate maintenance or wear and tear (use
of old or worn out equipment, material fatigue, and
so on)

Figure 11.8 The domino model likens the accident process to a series of dominos. Unsafe acts add dominos, and safe acts remove them. When an incident occurs (i.e., when the dominos are pushed over), its severity and whether injury, damage, or loss occur depend in part on the number of dominos present. Reducing unsafe acts reduces the likelihood or severity of an accident.

Reprinted, by permission, from R. Kauffman and M. Moiseichik, 2013, *Integrated risk management in recreation and parks* (Champaign, IL: Human Kinetics), 126.

Scott Hill's Decision to Go First

The following is a description of Scott Hill's testimony on why he decided to go first down the Keeney Rapids on the New River. The group stopped at the lunch stop on shore, located just above the Keeney Rapids. They launched after lunch and dropped fairly quickly into Upper Keeney rapid. This testimony is related to their launch after lunch.

Taylor vs. Class VI, et. al - Deposition of Eric Scott Hill, Vol I on 8/1/95
Mr. Hill – Examination

Page 115

8	Q	Who made the decision, if you can answer
9		this, that you would be the first raft through Keeney
10		rapids?

| 11 | A | There was no verbal decision. |

| 12 | Q | How was the determination made that you |
| 13 | | would be the first raft through Keeney rapids? |

| 14 | A | I guess I was the first ready to go. I |
| 15 | | like running first. |

Page 123

15	Q	And do I understand correctly that it was
16		not Joy Whelan that made the decision that you be the first
17		going down the Keeney rapids, but rather you made that
18		decision on your own to be the first raft down the Keeney
19		rapids?

20	A	As I said earlier, there was really no
21		decision. I was - - We were ready. We were in the
22		current, and we went with it.

| 23 | Q | Joy didn't say - - Joy Whelan didn't say |

Page 124

| 1 | | as trip leader, give you a signal or tell you in any way, |
| 2 | | shape or form to be first? |

| 3 | A | No. |

| 4 | Q | Just so I understand, you made that |
| 5 | | decision on your own? |

| 6 | A | Yes. |

| 7 | Q | Was that common practice at that time? |

| 8 | A | Yes. |

9	Q	Upon approaching each rapid on the trip
10		down the Lower New River, was it the custom and practice
11		of any one of the guides to make a decision on their own
12		to go first?

13	A	If the trip leader does not want a
14		certain person up there, they will make it known;
15		otherwise, it flip-flops around.

16	Q	You didn't get any signal from Joy Whelan
17		not to go first when you made the decision to go first
18		down the Keeney rapids then?

| 19 | A | No, sir. |

Figure 11.9 Scott Hill's testimony on why he decided to go first. Compare it with the trip leader's testimony in figure 11.3.

Estate of Cheryl A. Taylor v Class VI River Runners, Inc., et. al (1995). Deposition of Scott Hill, Circuit Court of Fayette County, West Virginia. Civil Action No. 94-C-0124. pp. 115, 123, 124.

Several leadership and group dynamic factors were at play in the New River raft trip scenario. The trip leader wasn't really leading, which indicates an inappropriate leadership style. The loose organizational structure of the trip suggests that cultural norms may have affected group behavior or organizational norms. Overall, the guides had considerable prior experience on the New River. Their experience in similar settings might remove dominos. However, because this was Scott Hill's first high water commercial trip down the river for the year, it could be argued that he might have a lack of experience.

The fact that it was a high water trip adds another domino in the category of environmental factors (i.e., terrain conditions and changes in terrain conditions). The fact that everyone wore life jackets and appropriate clothing removes dominos, under the category of equipment factors.

Normally, an incident occurs as a result of an energy transfer; the dominos are pushed over resulting in the potential for injury, damage, or loss to occur. When Scott Hill hit the wave, the kinetic energy of the wave dumped four of his six passengers into the water. Cheryl floated into the strainer on Flint Rock and drowned.

The underlying factors can be used in an accident investigation to help determine the factors that led to the accident. More important, they can be used in the planning process to make the activity safer. The planner uses these factors to ask questions about the activity. In summary, the underlying factors used with the domino model can easily be adapted to most of the other traditional outdoor models. In addition, the factors can be modified and adapted to meet the changing needs of the activity.

Barrier Analysis

In the 1970s, the accident causation and safety management field developed new models of accident causation. Developed for the U.S. Department of Energy by William Johnson, the management oversight and risk tree (MORT) emphasized the development of fault tree analysis and analyzed accidents as series of events (Johnson, 1973). It is representative of a school of thought that sought to examine from an organizational perspective complex organizations and events in areas such as nuclear power, the space program, and strategic air command. From a leadership perspective, barrier analysis, which was built on Haddon's (1973)

concept of energy transfer, has direct applicability to the recreation and parks field and leadership. In addition, it can easily be retrofitted into the domino and other accident models that are leadership oriented.

Barrier analysis has become a conceptual cornerstone in the field of accident causation and accident prevention (Trost & Nertney, 1995). Although it is an important component within MORT, it is a stand-alone analysis that is useful in the area of accident process and accident prevention. Because barrier analysis identifies barriers prior to the occurrence of an accident, it is a useful tool in accident prevention and in leadership models.

The concept of **barrier analysis** is not difficult to understand. As its name suggests, the object is to place barriers between the target (i.e., people or objects) and the potential hazard to prevent the transfer of unwanted energy (see figure 11.10). When there is a **less than adequate (LTA) barrier**, there is the potential for an unwanted energy transfer and the occurrence of an incident or accident. It is important to note that an energy transfer does not necessarily occur just because a LTA barrier exists.

Some of the traditional energy forms are kinetic, chemical, biological, thermal, electrical, and ionizing and nonionizing radiation (Haddon, 1973). Although not always initially intuitive in the field of recreation and parks, energy transfers are fairly commonplace. Examples of kinetic energy transfers include falls from playground equipment, bicycles, or gymnastics equipment. Chemical energy transfers may result from the use of chlorine in swimming pools and herbicides and insecticides in park management. Heat exhaustion, dehydration, and hypothermia may result from thermal exchanges. Lightning from a thunderstorm striking a tree on the golf course is an example of electrical energy transfer.

Energy transfer is normally divided into two types: wanted (controlled) and unwanted (uncontrolled). Usually, wanted flow is associated with the work being performed and is necessary to accomplish the work. Generally, unwanted energy transfer is not desired and can lead to a mishap. Consider a camper who uses a gas stove to boil a pot of water. The energy transfer involved in boiling the water is controlled and it is desired. It is wanted. Accidentally, the camper knocks over the stove and the pot of boiling water. An unwanted energy transfer occurs as the boiling water spills

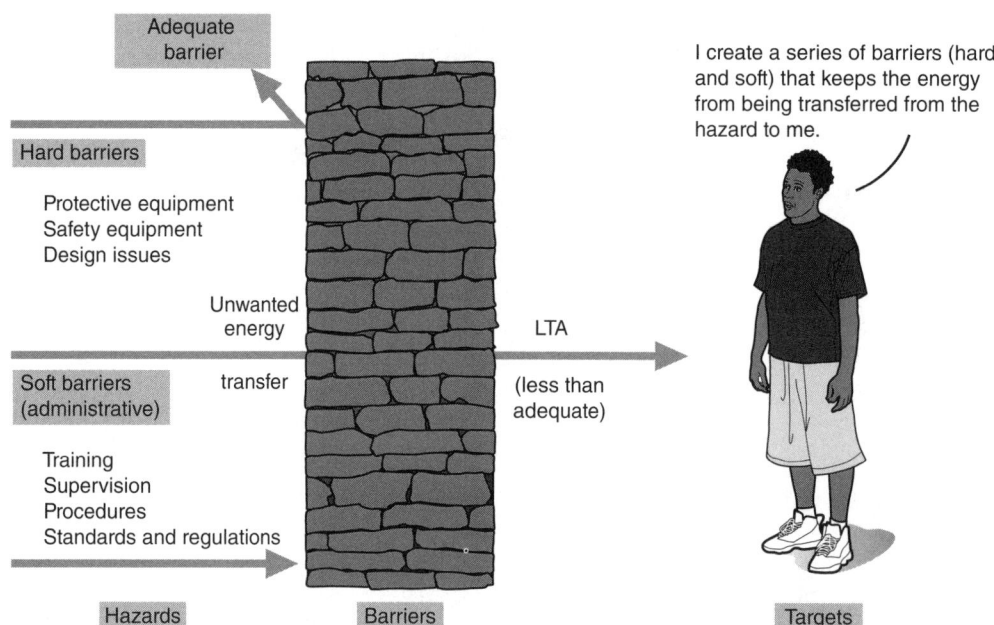

Figure 11.10 The leader or programmer facilitates safety by placing **hard barriers** (physical) and **soft barriers** (administrative) between the target (participant) and the hazard. If the barrier is less than adequate (LTA), injury, damage, or loss can occur to the target.
Reprinted, by permission, from R. Kauffman and M. Moiseichik, 2013, *Integrated risk management in recreation and parks* (Champaign, IL: Human Kinetics), 87.

over objects and people. It is unwanted. Also, an unwanted energy transfer can result from the open flame from the stove. If the water hits the earth harmlessly, it is a harmless incident; if it burns the cook, injury, damage, or loss occurs.

Scott Hill's raft hit the large wave in the Upper Keeney Rapids on the New River. His account of the incident is provided in figure 11.11. His account seems reasonable and is most likely accurate. A small misalignment of the raft on his part most likely resulted in his going right rather than left. Because of his misalignment, the kinetic energy of the wave forced him right instead of left. The force of the wave created an unwanted energy transfer. However, had he gone to the left, it would have been a wanted energy transfer. Subsequently, his new course through the rapid forced him into the large standing wave called Hawaii Five-O, where he lost four of the six passengers out of his raft, including Cheryl Taylor. That wave too resulted in an unwanted energy transfer.

The concept of barrier analysis is foundational and can easily be retrofitted to older models including the domino model and most of the other traditional outdoor accident models. For leaders and program planners using the domino model, it is easy to examine the activity and program using the underlying factors as part of the normal program planning process. Examination of the activity or program using the underlying factors becomes triggers or a checklist for identifying potential unwanted energy transfers that could lead to an accident.

Leaders using these models are affected by the protocols developed by their agencies or organizations in the form of administrative and policy modifications. In terms of the barrier analysis, these are equivalent to soft barriers. For example, requiring the development of an emergency action plan (EAP) for each off-site activity, requiring staff-to-participant ratios consistent with industry standards, and requiring minimal levels of first aid training and certificates are examples of administrative policies (protocols) that directly affect the leaders conducting the programs. In addition, the utilization of these protocols reduces the likelihood of creating unwanted energy transfers.

To be effective, barrier analysis needs to be operationalized into the organization as part of its planning process. Figure 11.12 provides a working table for identifying potential hazards, targets, barriers and controls, and purposes. The last step in the process is determining the practicality or the limitations of the barrier.

Scott Hill's Description of the Incident

The following is Scott Hill's description of the incident, in which four of his six passengers were dumped into the New River just below Upper Keeney Rapid. Consult figure 11.1 also. Whale Rock is in the upper right of the photo.

Taylor vs. Class VI, et. al - Deposition of Eric Scott Hill, Vol I on 8/1/95

Page 152

10	Q	Well, am I correct that the boat, the
11		raft, did not go where you wanted it to go at that point?
12	A	No, it didn't.
13	Q	And it was because the raft did not go
14		where you wanted it to go that you did not eddy out behind
15		Whale Rock?
16	A	Yes.
17	Q	The best you can tell me, why did the
18		boat not go where you wanted it to go at that point?
19	A	Because we hit a wave that crashed right
20		as we hit it; it stood the boat up, and instead of sliding
21		to the left, it slid [us] to the right. It slid us over two
22		feet to the right.

Page 154

1	A	Once we came off that wave, the only
2		thing left to do was just straighten the boat up.
3	Q	Did that occur?
4	A	Yes.
5	Q	Where to when in relation to hitting that
6		wave did you lose four passengers?
7	A	A rough estimate? 25 yards from that
8		wave.
9	Q	From that wave to the point that you lost
10		your passengers, approximately 25 yards, what happened in
11		that 25 yards? What happened to the raft?
12	A	I went from being sideways to straight
13		down the river.
14	Q	What caused the four passengers to come
15		out of your raft?
16	A	A large standing wave.
17	Q	Does that large standing wave have a
18		name?
19	A	We call it the Hawaii Five-O Wave.

Figure 11.11   Scott Hill's description of the incident in which he dumped four of his six passengers into the New River just below Upper Keeney Rapids. See figure 11.1 also. Whale Rock is in the upper right of the photo.

Estate of Cheryl A. Taylor v Class VI River Runners, Inc., et. al (1995). Deposition of Scott Hill, Circuit Court of Fayette County, West Virginia. Civil Action No. 94-C-0124. pp. 152, 154.

Barrier Identification Table: Activity or Program—Scott Hill's Rafting Trip

Energy Flow (Hazard) Harmful agent, adverse environment condition	Target Vulnerable person or thing	Barrier & Controls To separate energy and target	Purpose/Prevention	Limitations
Keeney Rapids on the New River	Raft participants	Place more people in the raft	The purpose is to increase the weight and inertia of the raft helping it to plow through large waves.	This may break up groups who want to travel together into separate rafts. It requires someone to break up the groups.
	Raft participants	Place less experienced rafts in the center of trip [1]	The purpose of placing less experienced rafts in the center of the trip is that if a mishap happens, the other rafts will be able to assist in rescue.	In terms of rescue, the measure is less of a barrier to the initial incident than it is a measure to focus on the rescue after an incident occurs. On most rivers, it is a standard procedure. A limitation is if all rafts are inexperienced.
	Raft participants	Place less experienced rafts in the center of trip [2]	A second purpose of placing inexperience rafts in the center of the trip is to help them to avoid the hazards (wave) by keeping them on track through the rapids.	This is a common practice on raft trips. A limitation is if all rafts are inexperienced.
	Raft participants	Use kayak safeties for rescue	The purpose of using kayakers as rescue safeties is that they can more quickly affect a rescue than another raft.	The measure is less of a barrier to the initial incident than it is a measure to focus on rescue after an incident occurs.
	Raft participants	Use a designated lead and/or sweep boat	The purpose is to place the two most competent boats at the two most vulnerable trip locations, the beginning and end of the trip.	The lead and sweep are the most competent rafts and least likely to have an incident. Also, the lead sets the course for others to follow. This is a common practice on many rivers.
	Raft participants	Wear life jackets	The purpose is to float the participant if they enter the water.	To meet the carriage requirements, Type V life jackets are required by law to be worn while in the raft.

Directions:

1. Identify the activity or program. This identifies the system level.

2. In column one, list all the potential hazards that can affect the program.

3. In column three, list the potential barriers or controls for each hazard. Consider the following barriers: equipment and facility, physical barriers, warning devices, procedures/work/protocols, knowledge and skills, attitude and culture, and supervision. (Conceptually, the flow is from column one through three. Most people will address the barriers and controls second, in response to the hazard.)

4. In column two, identify the target or the vulnerable person or thing.

5. In column four, indicate whether the barrier will prevent, control, or minimize the hazard. Indicate how.

6. In column five, indicate any limitations to placing the barrier (e.g. cost, feasibility, administrative feasibility, etc).

Figure 11.12 A simple barrier analysis performed for rafting the Keeney Rapids on the New River.

Adapted from J. Kingston et al., 2009, *NRI MORT user's manual—For use with the management oversight and risk tree analytical logic diagram* (AG Delft, Netherlands: The Noordwijk Risk Initiative Foundation), xx; Oakley 2003.

To illustrate how barrier analysis can be used to increase operational safety, an analysis was performed for the Keeney Rapids on the New River. One alternative is to place the less-experienced rafts in the center of the trip. This would help in the rescue of any passengers that fall out of the raft. It would have directly affected the rescue of the four passengers who fell out of Scott Hill's raft. Also, it is a common practice in rafting.

Summary

This chapter advanced the thesis that accident prevention can reduce the likelihood of a negligence lawsuit. The chapter examined the accident process in terms of preventing injury, damage, and loss. It underlined how the accident process and the use of underlying factors can be integrated into the design of activities and programs to make them safer. It discussed designing the experience in terms of risks. It presented the 2×2 risk matrix and the AEP paradigm. Accident prevention coupled with good program design reduces the likelihood of injury, damage, or loss and the likelihood of being sued.

The chapter used the example of the Cheryl Taylor incident as a unifying thread. In terms of risk management and the accident process, it questioned why Scott Hill's raft was 15 boat lengths ahead of the other rafts. The simple answer is that he chose to be the first raft through the Keeneys. He testified, "I like running first." His comment sheds light on the trip leader's leadership style and most likely the management culture of the raft company. His situation is similar to that of an employee who works double shifts and then falls asleep behind the wheel of her car. Of equal importance is the management approach of the trip leader who allowed Scott Hill to make the decision to go first. Given his level of experience, normal practice would have placed him in the middle of the group where the others could have assisted him in case of mishap. This is where risk management and safety come full circle and return to the issue of good leadership and program planning practices.

Returning to Churchill's quote at the beginning of the chapter, a purpose of this chapter is to provide the reader with a new perspective with which "to look" at and "to understand" their activities and programs. Providing good staff training, developing good habits, and defining the role and responsibility of the trip leader are normal steps that can be implemented to help prevent accidents. Leaders and managers should constantly assess their operations and work to improve them. They should examine their operations through the prism of the underlying factors and barrier analysis. Even with proper planning, accidents can still occur. Even if the rafting company discussed in this chapter improved their operations, the New River incident may still have occurred. Remember, there was an unwanted energy transfer that moved Scott Hill's raft right rather than left. However, had his raft been in the middle of the group of rafts on the trip, other guides on the trip would have been in a better position to react to the incident and effect a rescue.

Negligence was the first issue addressed in the chapter because it is normally first in most people's minds. Was the outfitter for the New River trip negligent? This is a moot issue because a jury trial found that the outfitter was not negligent. Regardless, the trial cost thousands of dollars, affected many lives, and affected the raft company and the local economy of Fayette County in West Virginia. Even though one side technically won, in the end, everyone lost something. Recreation professionals can use the tools outlined in this chapter to prevent lawsuits by preventing accidents. However, these tools are useful only if the recreation professional focuses on risk reduction and safety. Also, the overall management culture must do the same. In applying Churchill's quote, it truly is looking, seeing, understanding, and then acting that creates a safe program environment. Therein lies the answer to why Scott Hill was 15 boat lengths in front of the rest of the group.

Questions for Reflection and Discussion

1. Imagine that you are taking a first-time group of youth on a three-day hike on the Appalachian Trail. Using the domino model, how would you manipulate the factors to provide both a safe and peak adventure for the youth group? Be sure to address at least four factors.

2. For the three-day hike on the Appalachian Trail addressed in question 1, create a simple barrier analysis table (see table 11.12). Use the following column titles: Potential sources of energy flow (hazards) (column 1), Targets (column 2), Barriers and controls to separate the energy and target (column 3), Purpose/prevention (column 4), and Limitations (column 5). Once you have completed the table, discuss whether the measures in the limitations column will contribute to, detract from, or have little or no effect on making this trip a peak adventure. Be sure to include at least three energy flow sources and at least one barrier and control for each.

3. Defend or refute this proposition: The safety management principles discussed in this chapter will eliminate all of the fun from recreational activities.

Key Terms and Definitions

2×2 risk matrix—A matrix that expresses a relationship between perceived risks and actual risks for an activity. It contains four quadrants: lazy river, drowning trap, Upper Yough, and roller coaster. (See also *drowning trap category, lazy river category, roller coaster category,* and *Upper Yough category.*)

adventure—In the adventure experience paradigm, a situation in which participants' competencies exceed the risks of the activity. (See also *adventure experience paradigm.*)

adventure experience paradigm (AEP)—A paradigm based on seeking optimal arousal, or a flow experience. The five experiences identified in the model are devastation and disaster, misadventure, peak adventure, adventure, and exploration and experimentation. (See also *adventure, devastation and disaster, exploration and experimentation, misadventure,* and *peak adventure.*)

avoidance—A risk management strategy that focuses on the elimination or discontinuation of the activity or the temporary suspension of the activity. (See also *risk management.*)

barrier analysis—An accident causation and accident prevention analysis in which hard (physical) and soft (administrative) barriers are placed between potential hazards and the target (people or objects). If the barrier is less than adequate (LTA), there is the potential for an unwanted energy transfer and for an inci-

dent or accident to occur. (See also *less than adequate [LTA] barrier.*)

breach of duty—The second component that determines negligence; the two types of breaches are omission and commission. (See also *commission, negligence,* and *omission.*)

commission—The act of doing something one is supposed to do, but incorrectly, or doing something one should not have done. (See also *negligence* and *omission.*)

common practices—High-level practices recreation professionals are expected to know and follow. (See also *industry standard.*)

defendant—In a lawsuit, the party who has allegedly committed the harm. (See also *plaintiff.*)

devastation and disaster—In the adventure experience paradigm, the situation in which the risks of the activity far exceed the competencies of the participants. (See also *adventure experience paradigm.*)

domino model—A model that metaphorically envisions unsafe acts and conditions as a series of dominos. The dominos are grouped into the underlying categories of human, environmental, and equipment factors. (See also *underlying factors.*)

drowning trap category—In the 2×2 risk matrix, the high actual and low perceived risk category. (See also *2×2 risk matrix.*)

duty—An obligation to a participant, and the

first component that determines negligence. (See also *negligence.*)

energy transfer—A term to describe an incident or accident; it is normally divided into wanted (controlled) and unwanted (uncontrolled).

exploration and experimentation—In the adventure experience paradigm, the situation in which participant competencies far exceed the risks of the activity. (See also *adventure experience paradigm.*)

hard barriers—In barrier analysis, hard barriers are physical restraints such as guardrails and railings that are designed to reduce the likelihood of an accident occurring. (See also *soft barriers.*)

industry standard—Formalized common practices. (See also *common practices* and *standard of care.*)

injury, damage, or loss—The fourth component that determines negligence; the plaintiff must be able to show that injury, damage, or loss actually occurred. (See also *negligence.*)

lazy river category—In the 2×2 risk matrix, the low actual and low perceived risk category. (See also *2×2 risk matrix.*)

less than adequate (LTA) barrier—In barrier analysis, when the barrier is less than adequate, there is the potential for an unwanted energy transfer and an incident or accident to occur. (See also *barrier analysis.*)

misadventure—In the adventure experience paradigm, the situation in which the risks exceed the competencies of the participants. (See also *adventure experience paradigm.*)

negligence—A failure to exercise a standard of care that results in injury, damage, or loss. Four components are necessary to determine negligence: duty; breach of duty; proximate cause; and injury, damage, or loss.

omission—Not doing something one was supposed to do. (See also *commission* and *negligence.*)

peak adventure—In the adventure experience paradigm, the situation in which the risks match the competencies of the participants. (See also *adventure experience paradigm.*)

plaintiff—In a lawsuit, the injured party. (See also *defendant.*)

proximate cause—The third component that determines negligence; a reasonable relationship must connect the breach of duty with the injury, damage, or loss. (See also *negligence.*)

reduction—A risk management strategy that seeks to reduce the likelihood of an accident or incident occurring. (See also *risk management.*)

retention—A risk management strategy in which the organization pays for expenses out of pocket or creates an internal fund in place of insurance. (See also *risk management.*)

risk management—The use of one or more of four strategies to lessen the likelihood of an accident or injury: reduction, avoidance, transfer, and retention. (See also *avoidance, reduction, retention,* and *transfer.*)

roller coaster category—In the 2×2 risk matrix, the low actual and high perceived risk category. (See also *2×2 risk matrix.*)

soft barriers—In barrier analysis, soft barriers are the administrative procedures and protocols designed to reduce the likelihood of an accident occurring. (See also *hard barriers.*)

standard of care—What a reasonable and prudent person would do in a similar situation. For parks and recreation professionals, it is knowing the common practices, or industry standards, for the activity or program and following them. (See also *common practices* and *industry standard.*)

transfer—A risk management strategy that involves transferring the cost of the injury to someone else. Generally, there are three approaches: insurance, subcontracting, and waivers. (See also *risk management* and *waiver.*)

underlying factors—In the domino and other models, the factors (human, environmental, or equipment) that led to the incident.

Upper Yough category—In the 2×2 risk matrix, the high actual and high perceived risk category. (See also *2×2 risk matrix.*)

waiver—A risk management strategy of transfer in the form of a document participants sign to assume the cost of any injury, damage, or loss even if the provider of the service is negligent.

Bibliography

Bird, F., & Germain, G. (1985). *Practical loss control leadership*. Loganville, GA: Institute Publishing.

Campfire Girls. (1993). *Management of risks and emergencies, A workbook for administrators*. Kansas City, MO: Camp Fire Inc.

Csikszentmihalyi, M. (1975). *Beyond boredom and anxiety*. San Francisco: Jossey-Bass.

Collard, M. (2001). The "reasonable man" test: Or how do we know what you did was safe? *Australian Journal of Outdoor Education*, July, 67-69.

Curtis, R. (2005). *The backpacker's field manual*. New York: Three Rivers Press.

Ellis, M. (1973). *Why people play*. Englewood Cliffs, NJ: Prentice Hall.Estate of Cheryl A. Taylor v. Class VI River Runners, Inc., et al. (1995). Deposition of Joy Lynn Marr, Circuit Court of Fayette County, West Virginia. Civil Action No. 94-C-0124.

Estate of Cheryl A. Taylor v. Class VI River Runners, Inc., et al. (1995). Deposition of Scott Hill, Circuit Court of Fayette County, West Virginia. Civil Action No. 94-C-0124.

Estate of Cheryl A. Taylor v. Class VI River Runners, Inc., et al. (1995). Exhibit-8, Circuit Court of Fayette County, West Virginia. Civil Action No. 94-C-0124.

Haddon, W. (1973). Energy damage and the ten counter-measure strategies. *Human Factors Journal*, August, 355-366.

Hale, A. (1983). *Safety management for outdoor program leaders*. Unpublished manuscript.

Heinrich, H., Peterson, D., & Roos, N. (1980). *Industrial accident prevention: A safety management approach*. New York: McGraw-Hill.

Herman, M. (2009). *Ready ... or not —A risk management guide for nonprofit executives*. Leesburg, VA: Nonprofit Risk Management Center.

Jillings, A. (2005). *What's new in accident theory?* Presentation at the AEE International Conference, Tuscan, AZ. November 5-7.

Johnson, W. (1973). *MORT: The management oversight and risk tree*. Washington, DC: U.S. Atomic Energy Commission.

Kaiser, R. (1986). *Liability and law in recreation, parks, and sports*. Englewood Cliffs, NJ: Prentice Hall.

Kauffman, R. (1991). *Potomac River on-site survey*. Annapolis, MD: Department of Natural Resources, Boating Administration.

Kauffman, R. (1992). The drowning trap: On the Potomac River most people drown well below flood level. *Trends Magazine*, March, 10-12.

Kauffman, R. (2002, April 28-May 1). The drowning trap. The International Boating and Water Safety Summit, Daytona Beach, FL.

Kauffman, R. (2004). A new use for the movie *Cold, Wet and Alive*. Norfolk, VA: Association of Experiential Education.

Kauffman, R. (2005, August 1-2). The accident process: How to effectively use the video *Cold, Wet and Alive* to teach risk management and the accident process. Quantico, VA: Paddlesport Leadership School and Encampment.

Kauffman, R. (2007, March 4-6). Depicting the accident process with the new ACA sea kayak video. International Boating and Water Safety Summit, San Antonio, TX.

Kauffman, R., & Councill, E. (2005). Working with paddlesports rental businesses: Safety and contracting issues. *Parks and Recreation Magazine*, May.

Kauffman, R., & Moiseichik, M. (2013). *Integrated risk management in recreation and parks*. Champaign, IL: Human Kinetics.

Kauffman, R., Taylor, S., & Price, R. (1991). *A recreational gauging and information system to alert Potomac River users of dangerous water levels*. Annapolis, MD: U.S. Department of Natural Resources, Boating Administration.

Martin, P., & Priest, S. (1986). Understanding the adventure experience. *Journal of Adventure Education, 3* (1), 18-21.

Meyer, D., & Williamson, J. (2008). Potential causes of accidents in outdoor pursuits. www.nols.edu/nolspro/pdf/accident_matrix.pdf.

National Playground Institute. (1994). *The dirty dozen: Are they hiding on your playground?* Ashburn, VA: National Playground Institute.

Oakley, J. (2003). Accident investigation techniques. Des Plaines, IL: American Society of Safety Engineers, p. 23.

Priest, S., & Gass, M. (1997). *Effective leadership in adventure programming*. Champaign, IL: Human Kinetics.

Project Adventure Inc. (1995). *Twenty year safety study*, Hamilton, MA: Project Adventure Inc.

Raffan, J. (1984). Images for crisis management. *The Journal of AEE, 7* (3), 6-10.

Reason, J. (1980). *Managing the risks of organizational accidents.* Hants, UK: Ashgate Publishing Limited.

Trost, W., & Nertney, R. (1995). *Barrier analysis.* Idaho Falls, ID: Technical Research and Analysis Center, SCIEN-TECH, Inc.

van der Smissen, B. (1975). Legal aspects of adventure activities. *Journal of Outdoor Education, 10* (1), 20-22.

van der Smissen, B., Moiseichik, M, & Hartenburg, V. (2005). *Management of park and recreation agencies.* Ashburn, VA: National Recreation and Park Association.

Will, G. (2009). Litigation nation. *The Washington Post.* Available:

http://www.washingtonpost.com/wp-dyn/content/article/2009/01/09/AR2009010902353.html

Part III

Organizational Leadership

Part III takes a look at leadership from an organizational perspective. These chapters address how a leadership professional might contextualize the concepts and practices of leadership on a broader level, with a view beyond leading participants in a specific program or group. Part III seeks to prepare leaders to move into roles that require varying levels of visionary engagement to support, enhance, and change the direction of organizations, or even the larger field of recreation and leisure itself.

In chapter 12, Amy Hurd combines the disciplines of leadership and human resources to make the case for sustained organizational renewal and personnel training. In a discussion of succession planning (the practice of mentoring and grooming staff for long-term career advancement in positions key to the organization), she demonstrates that healthy, vibrant organizations connect job satisfaction, performance quality, and employee commitment to the agency's vision and mission. She lays out detailed strategies for identifying and training promising candidates for succession planning, discussing how effective assessment and development plans focus on the targeted individuals.

In chapter 13, Dale Larsen discusses the importance of external organizational leadership. Drawing on case studies, he demonstrates how recreation and leisure professionals are influenced by individuals and groups that exist outside the professionals' organizations. Engaging these people is necessary for participating in and influencing the direction recreation and leisure policies take locally, regionally, and nationally. Chapter 13 not only provides insight into institutions such as governing bodies in the field of leisure services, but also describes skill sets for leaders who see the benefits of going beyond the boundaries of their own organizations to interact with others who have vested interests in shaping the field of recreation and leisure services.

Concluding part III, as well as the book, is Jane Adams and Elaine Schilling's chapter, Leading in the Profession. They assert that leaders who want to maintain their relevance must accept and embrace change. They point out that social trends will inevitably affect organizations and the programs they offer, and note that judicious students of trends will position themselves to take advantage of developments as societies change. Using currently developing trends such as childhood obesity, they demonstrate how park managers and organizational leaders can capitalize on other trends such as social media to encourage participation in healthy lifestyles. Adams and Schilling also discuss recent global economic pressures and the potential impact on recreation and leisure services providers. They conclude by calling on recreation and leisure leaders to drive the changes they observe, and provide practical competencies and examples of how others have created opportunities from the changes they encountered.

Chapter 12

Internal Organizational Leadership and Professional Development

Amy Hurd

" *The educated person needs to bring knowledge to bear on the present, not to mention molding the future.* "

—Peter Drucker, *Post-Capitalist Society*

The executive director of the agency calls a meeting for the department heads and their direct staff. She announces that she has done a review of all the staff in the agency and realizes that 35 percent of the employees could retire within the next five years.

This comes as quite a surprise to many people in the room. Although most have an idea of how old their coworkers are, they have never considered who would be retiring soon.

The executive director asks the staff to come up with ideas for dealing with the attrition in the staff and the consequent loss of institutional knowledge. She has estimated that over 125 years of experience will be lost, and believes that some of these people are the only ones who know how to do their jobs.

In a discussion after the meeting, a few upper-level managers expressed their concerns about how many senior leaders would be leaving and the fact that many middle managers were not ready to assume higher-level positions and more responsibility. From this conversation, each of the managers was determined to come up with ideas for building skills in their middle managers and how they themselves could further develop as leaders so that upper- and middle-level managers could uphold the strong reputation the agency has in the community.

What ideas might the managers come up with to maintain a quality agency and deal with the loss of institutional knowledge and staff talent? How can they develop their own skills?

Learning Outcomes

At the conclusion of this chapter, students will be able to:

▶ Differentiate between replacement plans and succession plans.

▶ Define competencies and explain their role in training and development.

▶ Understand the job analysis process.

▶ Assess individual competencies.

▶ Describe the steps within an individual development plan.

For decades, scholars have debated whether organizations succeed because of those who lead them or because of something inherent to the organization itself (e.g., marketing, visioning, product quality). The answer most likely lies in both; however, solid leadership certainly strengthens organizations. The more competent the staff is, the more efficient and effective the organization will most likely be. Staff members who do well at their current jobs and are prepared for future career development and advancement benefit the entire organization.

Leadership knowledge and staff development come from two academic disciplines—leadership and human resources management. Recent research has merged these two disciplines and created what is now called performance management leadership (PML). PML "encompasses broad and proactive leader behaviors that serve to motivate, direct, support, modify, assist, monitor and reinforce employees in pursuit of goal accomplishment" ("Performance management," 2006). This leadership and development concept focuses on supporting and coaching, communicating using approachability and feedback, providing positive consequences for quality work, providing feedback on performance, setting goals, and establishing and monitoring performance expectations. Although the concept of PML sounds good in theory, its value is in the practical application to leaders. **Training** and **development** often receive verbal priority within agencies, but both are often cut from budgets in lean economic times. However, training and development need not cost a lot of money. Careful planning can help even the most cash-strapped agencies develop their staff.

A micro-level approach to training and development, which tailors a development plan to meet the needs of individuals, can enhance the entire organization. A comprehensive way to do this is through succession planning. Succession planning focuses on management and leadership development in a systematic manner that is often affordable even for small agencies. It uses the elements of PML while remaining rooted in the agency's values, vision, mission, and goals.

This chapter focuses on the three-step process of succession planning, which requires agencies and individual staff members to examine their current and future needs and the current status of staff skills. Succession plans are customized to the agency and not a cookie-cutter approach to

staff development. Rather, the underlying purpose of succession planning is enhancing current staff and developing their skills for the future.

Establishing a quality and systematic staff development program can be challenging. However, recent emphasis in parks and recreation and other fields has been on succession planning. Because of this trend, which is predicted to become the professional norm, we have chosen to expand on traditional training and development and ensconce it within the succession planning process to create a more long-term approach to developing quality employees and future leaders.

Throughout the discussion on succession planning, two agencies—the Virginia Beach Parks and Recreation Department (VBPRD) and the Champaign Park District (CPD)—will be used as examples. VBPRD has been immersed in succession planning for several years with much success. CPD is new to the process and has a strong foundation established within the agency. These two agencies provide real examples of how two agencies used two different methods of training and development to achieve their goals and prepare their staff for the future.

Succession Planning

Succession planning is a systematic process that identifies people within an organization who are capable of filling key positions. The process evaluates current talent within the agency and develops that talent to meet future organizational needs. A common misunderstanding and inaccurate assessment of succession planning is that it establishes an heir apparent or a replacement for someone who retires or leaves an organization. Replacement planning is short term; succession planning is long term (see table 12.1). Succession planning provides a much more stable environment because of its longevity and forward thinking and planning in terms of staff development.

Succession planning, although greatly underused, has received much attention in the business world and has been specifically designed for large-scale organizations. Unfortunately, many organizations do not implement succession plans because of a number of factors. First, it is a time-intensive process that requires a great deal of organizational commitment. Second, although the process is seen as important, companies generally sweep it under the rug because immediate

Table 12.1 Replacement Plans Versus Succession Plans

Replacement plans	Succession plans
Short term (0-12 months)	Long term (12-36+ months)
Focus on immediate needs of organizations	Focus on future needs of organizations
Develop backup staff for key positions	Develop staff able to fill several positions within organizations
Focus on one or two people per position	Focus on several people capable of filling a position

results are not evident (e.g., some employees are not ready for higher-level positions for at least two years). Third, some organizations view their employees as short term. Accordingly, they consider investing in employee training and development a waste of resources, especially when results are not immediately forthcoming. Finally, some managers may be threatened by the idea of developing staff who could later assume their positions and those of others at a similar level within the organization.

So, the bigger question is, Why plan for succession? First, leaders and potential leaders want to work for a solid company dedicated to enhancing its employees. Succession planning shows agency commitment to staff by committing resources to making the staff better. Second, the agency is able to identify future leaders and develop them for advancement. Third, investing in training and development makes for a stronger organization that can adapt to change and respond quickly using ideas and solutions outside the normal realm of thinking. Lastly, succession planning builds a strong organizational core; the more talented the staff is, the more solid the organization will be and the greater its ability to function will be.

Leisure services agencies typically do not have large staffs (i.e., 10 people or more who can be developed for positions within the organization). Fortunately, succession planning can be adapted to fit any size agency. The succession plan is a simple three-step process:

1. Understand agency development needs.
2. Assess job demands, competencies, and bench strength.
3. Build the talent pool.

The first two steps involve information gathering; step 3 uses that information to create and implement a plan to build individual talent within the organization.

Step 1: Understand Agency Development Needs

The first step in succession planning identifies the purposes behind undertaking this extensive process and develops a framework for what the succession plan will achieve. The process is often initiated by leaders of the organization; thus, their reasons for adopting this process will drive what the plan ultimately looks like. For example, a chief executive officer may recognize that major shifts will be occurring in the agency in the next several years as department heads and the CEO approach retirement. This movement of employees can cause major vacancies that could potentially be filled with properly skilled internal candidates. Another purpose of the succession plan may be to establish a structured development process for employees. Employee development is more successful when it is purposeful and systematic. With limited staff training and development budgets, a structured development plan can dictate how to spend those dollars and even justify additional allocations to the training and development line item within the budget.

Succession planning can also be done by agencies that want to become learning organizations. **Learning organizations** place a high priority on continual learning to enhance the individual and, ultimately, the organization. Establishing a learning environment allows the organization to respond quickly to change, remain competitive in the workforce, and transform itself as needed. Without emphasis on learning, an organization becomes rigid and entrenched in thinking and acting as it has always done. Learning allows staff to think outside the box and look at things from various perspectives, even if it means deviating from organizational norms (Senge, 2006).

Once the organization establishes the purpose for the succession plan, it can develop the framework for the program and determine how it will develop employees. At this point, agency leaders conceptualize how many people will be selected for the development program, how they will be selected, and whether there will be one program for all employees or multiple programs based on the structure of the organization. For example, the Virginia Beach Parks and Recreation Department established five departmental learning tracks—landscape management, management, administrative support, programming, and operations. This structure allowed for the development of personnel in administration, recreation programming, and landscape and maintenance operations. The Champaign Park District (CPD) chose to focus on organizational levels within the organization as well as departmental areas. For example, the agency is divided into operations (maintenance and landscape), recreation, and administration (finance, marketing, and human resources). CPD selected the following tracks around which to develop its succession plan:

▶ Director Track—Recreation & Administration: Includes the executive director, recreation and administrative department heads, and other director level employees; Operations: Includes operations department heads and other director-level employees (i.e., planners)

▶ Coordinator/Manager Track—Recreation & Administration: Includes managers and coordinators within recreation and administration

▶ Supervisor/Specialist Track—Operations: Includes supervisors and operations specialists within operations

To determine what tracks or levels to select, agency heads need to examine the agency structure. Key positions can be identified by looking at the decisions, responsibilities, activities, and services that would be diminished with their vacancy. Jobs should be examined in terms of their overall impact on agency efficiency and effectiveness and any unique aspects performed in this position and in others (Rothwell, 2005). Those positions deemed key are labeled as high priority and become the focus of the succession plan. Large agencies, such as VBPRD and CPD, may have many tracks, whereas smaller agencies may be better served with fewer tracks.

In addition to establishing the tracks for succession planning, the number of participants to accept into the succession planning program is a key issue to address. Although turning someone down is difficult, the agency may not have the resources to accept all interested parties at once. It may be in the best interest of the agency and participants

Best Practices From the Field

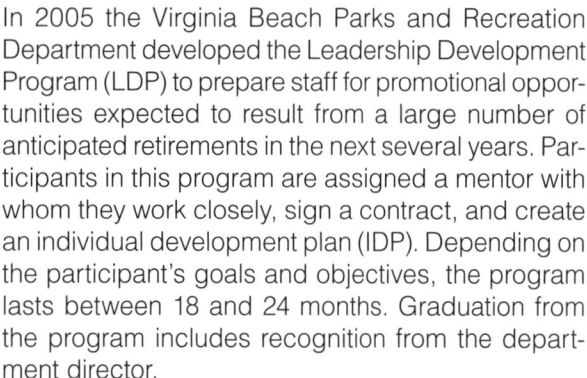

In 2005 the Virginia Beach Parks and Recreation Department developed the Leadership Development Program (LDP) to prepare staff for promotional opportunities expected to result from a large number of anticipated retirements in the next several years. Participants in this program are assigned a mentor with whom they work closely, sign a contract, and create an individual development plan (IDP). Depending on the participant's goals and objectives, the program lasts between 18 and 24 months. Graduation from the program includes recognition from the department director.

Open enrollment in the program is held every other March; interested people complete applications and answer three essay questions. Additional steps for entry into the program may include input from the applicant's direct supervisor and a personal interview with the applicant. An average of 30 applicants are selected for participation during each enrollment period; to date, 30 have completed the program. The

participant, the mentors, and the organization have benefited from improved job performance, greater marketability within the department and the city, and increased success.

Outcomes of the program include the following:

• Internal promotions for staff at all levels of the department, including from part-time to full-time

• Lateral movement into new challenges and work units within the department, including new opportunities recently created by a strategic realignment

• Promotions to other departments within the city

• Promotions to agencies outside the city

• Increased confidence levels in existing positions

• Sharing and retention of institutional knowledge

to accept a certain number of participants each year. The number an agency can accept will vary based on monetary resources, mentors available to guide participants, and other resources.

Because succession planning focuses on high-performance employees with high potential, not all employees will be, or will even want to be, part of the plan. These people should not be excluded from development opportunities, however. Agencies will need to determine how to provide professional development opportunities to those not participating in the succession planning program. Denying professional development opportunities can cause a decline in employee morale because some staff members may believe the agency does not care about them.

The first step in the succession planning process is the learning and information-gathering phase. Reasons for doing the plan, and the structure it takes on, ultimately drive the entire process for the agency. Because of this, agencies should spend ample time establishing a strong foundation for succession planning and creating a solid process to follow.

Step 2: Assess Job Demands, Competencies, and Bench Strength

The second step in the succession planning process can be quite labor intensive, but the knowledge gained from this process is invaluable to all employees, and not just those involved in succession planning. This step involves three processes:

job analysis, competency profile development, and bench strength assessment. These three processes can be completed simultaneously and provide a lucid picture of where the agency is now and where it needs to be in the future.

Job Analysis

Whether undertaking the succession planning process or not, agencies should periodically undergo a job analysis. A **job analysis** is a process used to ascertain the competencies required for top job performance. **Competencies** are the skills, knowledge, abilities, and characteristics needed to be successful in a position. These four elements are defined as follows (Hurd, Barcelona & Meldrum, 2008, p. 5):

▸ Skills—Physical or psychomotor aptitudes required to perform the particular tasks and actions of a job

▸ Knowledge—Understanding of information required for the position

▸ Abilities—Aptitudes for a position, or what and how well a person is able to perform certain tasks or behaviors

▸ Characteristics—Distinguishing qualities, attitudes, or traits needed by the person in the position

A job analysis requires an in-depth look at the true functions of a job. It requires examining a broad spectrum of the job areas (see table 12.2).

The data for the job analysis can come from interviews, questionnaires, structured checklists,

Table 12.2 Elements of a Job Analysis

Job areas	Descriptions
Educational requirements	Degrees, training, and certifications
Equipment used	Equipment and tools used such as mowers and blade sharpeners at an ice rink
Working conditions	Weather, indoors/outdoors, travel, schedule
Supervisory and management responsibilities	Full-time and part-time employees and volunteers managed
Interpersonal communication skills	Levels and types of communication used, including internal and external contacts; phone, e-mail, or written communication; and frequency of communication
Agency contacts	People within the agency the employee comes into contact with to complete tasks
External contacts	People outside the agency the employee comes into contact with to complete tasks
KSAOCs	Knowledge, skills, abilities, and other characteristics (competencies) needed to complete job tasks

Data from Hurd & Anderson 2011.

observations, diaries or logs, or a combination of methods. Many agencies have employees track their behaviors for a certain period of time and then complete questionnaires about their jobs. Using multiple methods to collect job information strengthens the quality of the job analysis. The result of the job analysis is a complete profile of the requirements of the job and an updated job description. Updated and accurate job descriptions justify competencies and provide an understanding of competency progression for various levels of employment in the profession.

Competency Profile Development

The job analysis provides information about what is currently happening in the agency. The competency profile moves beyond internal functions and gathers competency information externally as well. This profile is created using the job description, research in the field, and a thorough understanding of employee development. Some may question why it is not enough to use a job description and simply prepare an employee for one internal position. This goes back to the difference between replacement and succession plans. If the agency is training for a specific position, the one source for competencies is sufficient. However, succession planning is designed to prepare people for multiple positions within the agency and, sometimes, to take skills to other agencies. Although the latter is not ideal, it is a reality. When an employee who moves to another agency is highly skilled and productive, it is a positive reflection on the previous employer.

In addition to the job description, the second resource for creating a competency profile is outside sources. Research on a wide variety of jobs within the parks and recreation industry is available. For example, competencies are known in the public sector for **entry-level employees** (Hurd, 2005), chief executive officers (CEOs) (Busser & Bannon, 1987; Hurd & McLean, 2004), and board members (Fokken, 2003; Hurd, 2004). They have also been established in campus recreation (Barcelona & Ross, 2004; Jamieson, 1987), for therapeutic recreation professionals working with at-risk youth (Sprouse, 2004), for CEOs in nonprofit organizations (e.g., YMCAs, Boys & Girls Clubs) (Hurd & Buschbom, 2010), and for commercial recreation professionals (Hammersley & Tynon, 1998). Such

sources can be used to identify profession-wide standards.

The third element needed for a competency profile is an understanding of competency progressions. It is not enough to have a list of competencies; true value comes from fully understanding competency progressions and how people develop throughout their careers at various levels within the organization. There are several ways to look at this. One is to examine hard skills (job expertise) and soft skills (personal characteristics). Soft skills include such things as being a self-starter, having patience, and being creative and innovative. Hard skills, on the other hand, include such things as developing and staying within a budget, establishing priorities, writing goals and objectives, and program planning.

The balance of the use of hard and soft skills changes as an employee progresses within the organization. Entry-level employees rely more strongly on their hard skills and less on their soft skills (see figure 12.1). Typically, universities teach hard skills through classes such as programming, finance, and management, which lead to increased ability in the areas of problem solving, conflict resolution, and critical thinking. Soft skills, or personal characteristics, are derived from a person's personality traits and experience. This is not to say that agencies hiring entry-level employees are not interested in candidates' characteristics, but they will not initially be an overwhelming part of the job requirements.

As the employee moves up to higher-level positions, such as department head or CEO, soft skills

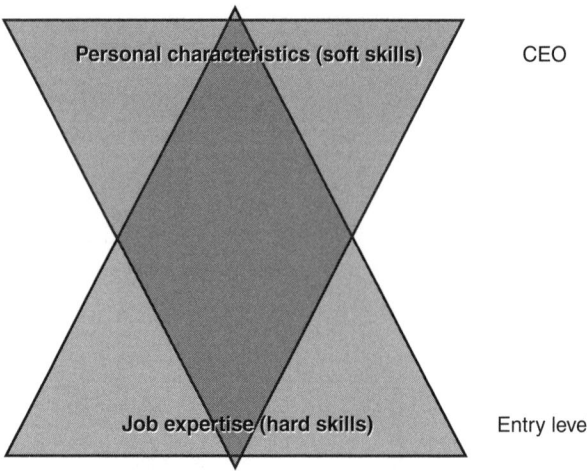

Figure 12.1 Competency progression.
Used with permission from Daniel D. McLean, PhD.

become more desirable and necessary. A person who is diplomatic can easily supersede a person without these qualities who has worked in all aspects of the agency. Just because higher-level employees use more soft than hard skills does not mean that hard skills are unnecessary. Hard skills help with decision making, problem solving, and developing relationships with lower-level employees, and they provide a better understanding of the big picture, just to name a few benefits.

The job description and competency research are used simultaneously to examine competency progression during the development of a competency profile for each level within the organization. For example, entry-level and CEO-level competencies in public parks and recreation share 25 common competences, including these:

▶ Communication

▶ Comprehensive knowledge of the field

▶ Creativity and innovation

▶ Customer service

▶ Flexibility and adaptability

▶ Leadership and management principles

▶ Multitasking and time management

▶ Networking

▶ Problem solving and decision making

As a result of **career progression**, how competencies are used vary as employees work within each level of the organization. Competency progression can be subtle or extreme as an employee progresses through the ranks and responsibilities change. For example, financial management initially requires the ability to develop a program budget; at higher levels, however, employees need a thorough understanding of the

entire financial management process (see table 12.3). Customer service skills evolve based on the groups the employee has contact with. An entry level employee will work directly with participants and other customers, whereas the CEO may deal with board members, donors, and influential community members.

The competency profile is created using the external job description competency data and understanding competency progressions. For example, the Virginia Beach Parks and Recreation Department has a competency profile for each track in the succession plan that reflects the current job analysis and the competencies for the profession as a whole (see figure 12.2).

Bench Strength

In addition to assessing job demands and competencies, the second step in the succession planning process requires agencies to assess their bench strength. **Bench strength** is essentially a depth chart at each key position within the organization. The readiness of current staff to assume identified jobs in the organization is documented in one-year increments. For example, the Champaign Park District used three time periods: ready immediately, ready in one to two years, and ready in two to five years (see table 12.4).

Ideally, this chart would have names in all cells to ensure that the agency is ready for changes in personnel. The reality, however, is that most agencies have gaps. Some show that no one is ready for another two years or more, someone is ready now, or no one will be ready even in five years. In this example, the most glaring problem is with the superintendent of recreation position, for which no one will be ready for two to five years.

Table 12.3 Sample Competency Progression

Competency	Entry level	Middle level	Upper level
Agency mission	Understand what the mission of the agency is	Possess working knowledge of the agency mission	Operate according to the agency mission
Partnerships	Build program partnerships	Build department-wide partnerships	Build agency-wide partnerships
Supervision	Supervise part-time staff	Supervise full-time entry-level staff and part-time staff	Supervise department heads or midlevel managers who also supervise staff
Hiring	Understand the hiring process	Possess knowledge of effective and legal hiring practices	Understand personnel law

Programming

- Planning
- Evaluation
- Marketing/promotion of programs

Core Requirements

- Communication
- Coaching
- Supervision
- Leadership
- Conflict resolution

Track-Specific Requirements

Basics of Event Planning

- Understanding budget needs for program
- Utilizing timelines and checklists (using points of contact, building rapport)
- Program evaluation (were programs goals and objectives met, did participants and staff enjoy program, what are the recommendations to improve program next time?)
- Universal program standards
- Utilizing the citywide parks and recreation activities calendar

Programming

- Utilization of current trends and community demographics to determine programming needs
- Establish program goals and objectives (measurable/clear and concise)
- Program planning worksheet and pricing tool
- Gap analysis
- Developmental assets for youth programs

Marketing/Research/Trend Analysis

- Learn how to complete a request for marketing services
- Schedule time with marketing staff
- Schedule time with sponsorship/partnership manager
- Create program flyers, posters, ads, etc., in conjunction with marketing unit
- Catalog training
- Research sponsorship/partnership opportunities
- E-marketing

Specific Suggested Trainings for Programming Track

- Dealing with difficult people
- Inclusion (service standards training)
- Generational differences
- Time management
- Effective communication
- Customer services
- Team building
- Coaching

Figure 12.2 VBPRD programming core competencies.

Virginia Beach Parks & Recreation Department.

Gaps such as this one demonstrate the need for a succession plan. While it is not suggested that all jobs be filled internally, it is suggested that people with the proper skill set step in temporarily until a search is conducted to hire the most qualified person. A skilled person in a job will keep the organization.

Step 2 in the succession planning process is labor intensive and time consuming; however, it is key to understanding the type of skilled employees needed in the organization. It also identifies gaps in skills so employees understand their own weaknesses and can address them to better meet future career goals.

Table 12.4 Bench Strength

Position	Current staff	SUCCESSION CANDIDATES		
		Ready immediately	Ready in one to two years	Ready in two to five years
Superintendent of recreation	Carlos Colon	—	—	Jordan Allen Ali Ahmed
Superintendent of maintenance	Tom Po	Felix Rodriquez	Steve Hem	—
CEO	Susan Smith	Carlos Colon	—	Tom Po

Step 3: Build the Talent Pool

The key to a quality organization is having quality, well-trained staff. This step in the succession planning process involves building the **talent pool** within the organization. Typical succession planning requires selecting a core group of high-potential employees who exhibit high performance. These people have been nicknamed HiPos (pronounced "hippos") and are generally the strongest employees within the agency. HiPos traditionally meet four criteria:

1. They are capable of advancing two or three more levels within the organization unless they are a department head with the capability to become the CEO.

2. They have not reached a career plateau.

3. They currently exceed minimum job expectations.

4. They are committed to improving, and desire to improve, themselves professionally.

Assessment

Once HiPos have been identified, they must be assessed to determine their current competency levels. With a long-term staff development process like this one, several assessment strategies may be involved. Some may already be in place within the organization, and others may be new. Assessments can include past performance appraisals, 360-degree performance appraisals, work portfolios, assessment centers, and supervisor assessments and self-assessments.

Past performance appraisals can be used to determine the HiPos' strengths and weaknesses over time and should already be in the person's personnel file. These evaluations show the level at which the employee has consistently performed over time.

Some organizations use a 360-degree performance appraisal system that provides the perspective of peers, supervisors, and subordinates. Each group or individual completes the same evaluation, and the results are compared. The 360-degree evaluation gives multiple perspectives and often provides new insight into the person's performance.

The next assessment method is the work portfolio. Staff can compile and present work portfolios that contain the best examples of their work. These portfolios should be competency and outcome based. Once completed, the portfolio can be submitted for review or presented to those responsible for assessment. Following are items to include in a work portfolio ("How to Create," n.d.):

▶ Writing samples

▶ Finished products

▶ Testimonials from program evaluations or customers (or both)

▶ Positive performance reviews

▶ Examples of problems or issues solved

▶ Examples of leadership of others

▶ A list of activities the person can currently do, can do with little training, and wants to achieve over the long term

Assessment centers are job-related tests, exercises, and simulations that emulate the job tasks. Reviewers evaluate the person's responses to the tasks given during the assessment center to ascertain his competencies for a job. Assessment centers are traditionally used in the hiring process, but can also be used to assess staff behaviors.

Assessment centers can feature role playing, leaderless group discussions, paper and pencil tests, and other written activities (Pynes, 2009). Although assessment centers allow reviewers to see how the person would perform higher-level tasks or in high-level situations, they have declined in use because they are time consuming to create and subjective to assess. Moreover, people analyzing the results are often not trained to do so. Agencies can opt to use external assessors, but they are usually cost prohibitive. Despite this, the Virginia Beach Parks and Recreation Department successfully uses the assessment center by creating scenarios faced by upper-level managers. The person being assessed addresses the case study, and his responses are subsequently analyzed.

The last assessment is the supervisor assessment and self-assessment. This assessment requires the supervisor and the employee to rate the employee on select competencies derived from the competency profile in step 2. This assessment is much like the 360-degree assessment without the input of peers and subordinates.

Several types of assessments can be used as long as at least one tool measures competencies. Because the needed competencies for higher levels were determined in the previous step, they should be used as the foundation to establish individual competency gaps. To illustrate, the Champaign Park District uses a four-part assessment instrument. Part 1 is a competency assessment completed by the supervisor (see figure 12.3) that lists the competencies developed in the job analysis phase of the plan. It is often beneficial to remind the employee being assessed that these are competencies for higher-level positions and they will not always rate highly on them. The rater needs to also keep this in mind and not overinflate ratings. This is not an appraisal form, but a means to create a long-term development plan for the employee.

The remaining sections of the assessment instrument (see figure 12.4), based on the work of Norman Carter (1986), evaluate overall current performance and potential. The second part of the assessment is an overall measurement of the employee's performance to date (see figure 12.4). This rating should reflect the result of past performance appraisals. Part 3 is a rating of the person's potential to advance to higher levels in the organization or profession.

Part 4 assesses when the person is ready for the next higher level. If the supervisor also completed the bench strength form, this part of the assessment should be very similar, depending on the scale used on the bench strength instrument. When combined, these assessments should provide

Part I: Competency Assessment

Please rate the candidate on the following competencies:

Competency	Excellent	Good	Fair	Poor	Unable to rate
Ability to manage projects	4	3	2	1	NR
Ability to manage contracts	4	3	2	1	NR
Ability to prepare specifications for bid documents	4	3	2	1	NR
Ability to develop and administer a budget	4	3	2	1	NR
Knowledge of financial management	4	3	2	1	NR
Knowledge of human resources management	4	3	2	1	NR
Fair and respectful treatment of people	4	3	2	1	NR
Public speaking skills	4	3	2	1	NR
Written and verbal communication skills	4	3	2	1	NR

Figure 12.3 Competency assessment sample from Champaign Park District.

Part 2: Performance Rating

1 = Unsatisfactory results and performance

2 = Marginal—Does not meet requirements of position; remedial actions needed

3 = Satisfactory—Generally meets job requirements but room for improvement

4 = Above average—Surpasses overall job requirements but lacks strength in some areas

5 = Superior—Some elements of performance may rate as exceptional, but overall performance falls below an exceptional rating

6 = Exceptional—General all-around excellence in quality/quantity of work, initiative, self-development, new ideas, and attitude

Part 3: Potential to Advance

1 = Outstanding—Can advance two levels above present position

2 = Considerable—Can advance at least one level above present position and/or assume substantial added responsibility at present level

3 = Some—Can assume added responsibilities at present level

4 = Limited—At or near capacity in present position

5 = Key capacity in current position—Vital technical knowledge precludes movement

Part 4: Readiness to Advance to Next Level

1 = Qualified to move now

2 = Within one to two years

3 = Within two to four years

4 = Current level appropriate

Figure 12.4 Performance and advancement assessment.

"Guaranteeing Management's Future through Succession Planning," Norman H. Carter, *Journal of Information Systems Management* (Summer 1986), 20. Reprinted by permission of the publisher Taylor and Francis Ltd., http://tandf.co.uk/journals.

a clear picture of the strengths, weaknesses, and potential of the employee.

Development Plans

The result of this extensive competency assessment is the development plan. A **development plan** is a written document that details learning goals, strategies to reach these goals, development opportunities, and tracking criteria to ensure that the employee will achieve desired outcomes. The development plan is the driving force behind enhancing the competencies of the employee. All of the previous steps in succession planning result in a document containing the development process.

The employee follows the seven-part process (outlined later in this chapter) and is assigned a mentor who helps enhance her skill set. This mentor may be either within the organization or external to the agency if the needed expertise cannot be found within the agency. A mentor does not necessarily need to be the person's direct supervisor; she can be someone with knowledge of the position desired by the mentee. Because selecting the right mentor can be key to the HiPo's achieving her learning goals, this step needs to be completed before beginning the development plan process.

Mentoring

A mentor, someone with more experience than the mentee, guides the mentee through the learning process. Traditional mentoring programs pair a seasoned employee and a new employee so the mentor can teach the mentee about the organization and the job and how to build skills to advance in the profession. This definition of the mentor relationship sounds as though only the mentee benefits. However, a true mentorship also enhances the mentor, who should reflect on how and why she does the things she does and on her own abilities, and learn to facilitate experiences for her mentee.

A quality mentoring relationship is based on the following assumptions (Zachary, 2000):

▶ Mentoring is about engagement and connection between the mentor and mentee. Mentorship is most successful when both parties collaborate and are committed to reaching the same goals.

▶ Mentorship requires preparation and dedication. The mentor must take the time to create positive interactions, experiences, and learning opportunities for the mentee. The mentor should not assume that these will happen without planning.

▶ Mentorship focuses on the learner, the learning process, and the learning.

Leisure Leaders

Jennifer Bruggeman, CPRP

MY PREPARATION

- BS in park and recreation administration and commercial recreation—Illinois State University, Normal, IL

- MS in management and organizational behavior—Benedictine University, Lisle, IL

- Certified Park and Recreation Professional (CPRP)

Photo courtesy of Gregg Bruggeman.

MY CAREER

The Batavia (Illinois) Park District is a local government agency that offers the residents of Batavia (population 26,000) 40 parks over 350 acres in addition to two community centers, a historical depot museum, a dance hall, a swimming quarry, a performing arts pavilion and center, a riverwalk recreation area, a boat house, and a dog park. Serving over 100,000 visitors to the facility annually, we operate under a $3.5 million budget and have 31 full-time employees and 140 part-time employees (during the peak season). The District's mission statement is: Committed to providing fun, save, and innovative open space and recreational opportunities that will enrich the quality of life for our residents.

As the human resources and risk manager, I coordinate recruitment, professional development, succession planning, employee benefits and wellness, and safety training. My enthusiasm and strategic thinking allow me to serve an important role on the leadership team, which is responsible for developing and implementing organizational initiatives and change.

My career path has included part-time and seasonal employment with park districts close to home. An internship extended into part-time work. In my first full-time job with a small park district, I was responsible for a fitness facility and classes, and for youth and adult athletics. Before working with the Batavia Park District, I moved to the Wheaton Park District to become involved in cultural arts and teen programming. Through that job, I gained responsibility for many employee-focused initiatives, such as all-staff team building events, annual in-service trainings, and recognition and wellness programs.

One of my favorite parts of my job is hearing success stories after having coached managers on how to deal with difficult employee situations. Also, I enjoy providing employees with opportunities to recreate, which makes work more fun and reminds us all why we chose this field.

Situational leadership is a key to success for anyone at any level. To be great at it, I must first know what drives me and what I am great at. Second, I must understand the motivations and strengths of those around me. With that knowledge, I am as equipped to lead project teams comprised of upper management as I am to delegate customer service items among part-time instructors.

MY ADVICE TO YOU

Never miss an opportunity to grow professionally. Volunteer inside and outside your organization. Work as many part-time jobs in the parks and recreation field as you can. There is no excuse for having no experience in this field. A large responsibility of this industry is to prepare youth for the work force.

If you choose this field, you get to go to work every day knowing that those around you saw similar perks. Long hours, full weekends, and complaints are dealt with while enjoying time with your work family, down in the trenches.

Mentoring relationships can take on many structures including one-on-one, peer, supervisory, group, and distance mentoring.

The traditional one-on-one relationship pairs one mentee and one mentor. In this situation, the mentor may be tempted to teach everything he knows. A better approach is to determine what the mentee needs to learn and then determine how best to facilitate this learning.

In peer mentoring, people at the same level within or external to the organization mentor each other. This method usually serves as a sounding board for both parties on how best to develop their careers. For example, the Indiana Park and Recreation Association has a Young Professionals Group that convenes periodically so entry-level and early midlevel employees can discuss issues they are facing.

A supervisory mentoring relationship in which an employee's boss is his mentor is an obvious scenario. Although this can be helpful because supervisors are well versed on the skills their supervisees need to build, they are still their supervisors. The supervisor–employee mentor relationship can be prohibitive in some situations. For example, if the relationship is strained, the mentee would be unlikely to share difficulties or issues of concern with the mentor. The fact that the mentee reports to the supervisor may diminish objectivity in some situations. Furthermore, a mentee who is considering other jobs would be unlikely to talk to a mentor who is a direct supervisor. In most cases, the supervisor mentorship role is informal and just naturally occurs.

In group mentoring, one mentor works with several mentees in a group setting. This has been done with learning communities (i.e., groups of people who have similar goals or experiences and want to further develop their competencies in a profession). The mentor serves as the facilitator, and the group decides the learning agenda and how to accomplish it.

Distance mentoring is growing as technological communication advances. Mentors and mentees no longer have to be in the same agency or the same community. Technology now allows for face-to-face interactions without being in the same location (e.g., via Skype or videoconference). Discussion boards and e-mail are other ways to connect.

As with any development opportunity, a mentoring program should be created with the needs of the mentee at the forefront. The mentor should then facilitate meeting these needs so that both parties benefit.

Once the mentor is selected, the development plan can be implemented. The employee and the mentor work together to accomplish the goals outlined. Theoretically, accomplishing the goals in the plan will close the competency gap and prepare the employee for the desired job level. The development plan requires using the information collected through the succession planning process, outlining a plan, and having a candid discussion about the person's career aspirations and abilities. The development plan has seven parts (see figure 12.5), which will be discussed next.

Part 1: Identify the Job(s) or Job Level(s) the Employee Desires

A discussion between the mentor and the employee identifies the job and job level the employee ultimately desires. The identified job and job level dictates the required competencies. For example, a current midlevel manager may set a goal to be a CEO. The next logical step in career progression may be a department head position prior to moving to the top position in the organization. The initial development plan will most likely focus on the department head position before moving to CEO-level competencies.

Part 2: Discuss the Competency Gap

A **competency gap** is the difference between the competencies the person currently has and the competencies the person needs to obtain the desired level within the organization. This step requires a comparison of the person's competency assessment and the competency profile developed, which will show strengths and development areas. The areas that need to be developed, the competency gaps, are the focus of the development plan. Once these gaps are closed, the person is ready for the next level.

Part 3: Discuss the Time Line

An honest discussion between the mentor and the HiPo will establish a realistic time line for achieving the desired goals and job levels. In the example in part 1, it is fairly unlikely that a middle manager would be a CEO in a year unless the agency is quite small. The job of the mentor is to help the HiPo set

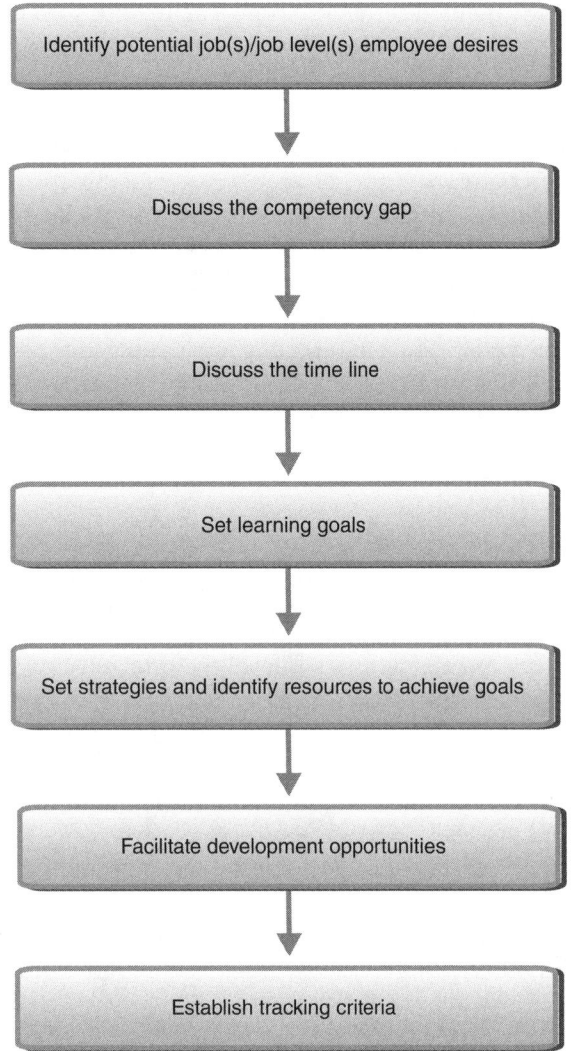

Figure 12.5 Development plan.

a realistic time line for achieving the established goal. At this point in the process, the results of the bench strength exercise can be shared. Mentors should keep in mind that a time line may be a year or much longer or shorter. The length depends on the results of the competency assessment; people with more competencies progress faster than those who need to acquire more skills.

Part 4: Set Learning Goals

The competency gaps are the basis for the learning goals. Because the development plan is long term, learning goals will cover one or more years. Following are examples of learning goals:

1. Enhance understanding of financial management and revenue generation.
2. Gain experience in aquatics management.

It is not necessary to establish all learning goals at once. Because this is a long-term plan, goals may be set biannually, annually, or longer term. They can also be modified as needed to close competency gaps.

Part 5: Set Strategies and Identify Resources to Achieve Goals

The strategies are the specifics for achieving goals. They are concrete tactics that must be accomplished to gain the experience necessary to close the competency gap. Along with these strategies, an assessment of necessary resources is required (e.g., people, money, time, equipment, and facilities). The resources needed will vary from strategy to strategy. Some require very little; others require a major commitment from the agency (see table 12.5).

Part 6: Facilitate Development Opportunities

The development plan calls for many growth opportunities for the HiPo as established in the goals and strategies step. Before establishing what these opportunities are, the person's learning style must be assessed. Much discussion is going on in the business world about generations, their learning styles, management styles, and overall organizational behavior. These generations bring an added complexity to training and development. For example, a baby boomer employee may prefer open discussions at workshops and conferences where she can share her experiences and learn from the experience of others. Someone who is in generation X or Y could possibly reject this approach for something quicker and more hands-on. Finding the right development opportunity to meet the person's learning style requires open dialogue and flexibility. However, mentors should keep in mind that people do not all strictly adhere to their generation's **learning styles** (see table 12.6), because these descriptions are generalities. Regardless of which generation the HiPo is in, he will likely subscribe to a type of learning that best suits him. This knowledge is key in helping him use his preferences to build skills in a positive way.

Once the employee's development preferences are established, any number of trainings can be used. Adopting a variety of methods may be the best approach to meet the diverse needs within the organization. Development opportunities can be classified as either informal or formal.

Table 12.5 Development Plan Strategies and Resource Needs

GOAL: ENHANCE UNDERSTANDING OF FINANCIAL MANAGEMENT AND REVENUE GENERATION.		
Strategy	**Time line to complete**	**Resources needed (other than time)**
1. Attend revenue management school	Spring 2015	$1,500
2. Meet weekly with chief financial officer to discuss financial issues	Begin immediately	None
3. Work with superintendent of recreation to establish a Friends of Parks and Recreation nonprofit group	Spring 2016	Access to legal counsel for filing of paperwork
GOAL: GAIN EXPERIENCE IN AQUATICS MANAGEMENT.		
1. Work with the current aquatics supervisor to manage the seasonal aquatics operations	Summer 2015	None
2. Participate in summer lifeguard and manager staff training	Summer 2015	None
3. Obtain Aquatic Facility Operator certification	Spring 2016	$500

Table 12.6 Generations, Learning Styles, and Training Preferences

Generation	Ages	Attributes	Learning styles	Training preferences
Silent	Born before 1946	• Like hierarchy and structure • Are dedicated and hard workers • Like rules and order • Place duty before leisure • Are good team players • Respect authority • Are least embracing of diversity	• Auditory/lectures • Want data to back up what is said	• Face-to-face direct communication • Classroom • Formal trainings • Go to traditional conferences and workshops
Baby boomers	1946-1964	• Are work oriented, started the concept of workaholism • Are team oriented • Value personal growth in jobs • Are competitive and self-driven	• Visual learners • Prefer dialogue, discussion • Detail oriented	• Roundtable discussions • Relaxed atmosphere • Open forums for discussion
Generation X	1965-1976	• Want a work/life balance • Appreciate diversity • Think globally • Want a fun workplace • Like informal workplace • Don't like to be micromanaged	• Hands-on • Access to a lot of information in a straightforward manner • Stories and examples • Don't necessarily need face-to-face interaction	• Fun, informal environment • Specific and practical outcomes with efficient delivery • Access to information and resources
Generation Y/ millennials	1977-1990	• Are tech savvy • Are very confident • Value achievement • Appreciate and embrace diversity • Are optimistic about the future	• Hands-on • Access to a lot of information very quickly • Autonomous learning • Like to find resources to help with solutions and learning	• Informal, fun, fast, interactive • Use of technology • Being given information and allowed to try it out • Open to learning on their own

Data from: www.uiowa.edu/~nrcfcp/training/documents/Participant%20Packet%20Intergen%20Dynamics.pdf

Informal learning opportunities are casual and incidental with little structure. These opportunities are often not required but provided as a chance to learn. Informal settings do not have specific goals, objectives, or outcomes associated with them. Despite this, they can be a tremendous asset to those desiring to build their competencies.

A popular informal learning opportunity is a discussion group. Informal groups may meet periodically to discuss a topic of relevance to the agency, such as risk management or trends in the field. These types of discussions can be led by either employees or nonemployees. Discussion groups have also been formed to discuss a book that everyone in the group reads or to evaluate a magazine or journal article relevant to the profession. Some agencies have established Lunch and Learn or Brown Bag programs, during which a monthly topic, book, or article is discussed over the lunch hour.

For succession planning, formal development is more common than informal training. Formal development is structured; has specific goals, objectives, and outcomes; and uses systematic methods to facilitate learning. The traditional formal development opportunities include conferences and workshops at the local, state, or national levels. Many agencies also provide in-service training to full-time staff. An in-service training is much like a workshop, but it is done internally for the agency's staff. Trainings can be facilitated by internal or external trainers. For example, the Wheaton Park District hosts an annual **in-service staff training** facilitated through the human resources department on topics such as violence in the workplace, interviewing and hiring, harassment, agency values, and business plan creation. The Urbana Park District uses an outside source, Parkland College Business Training, to facilitate trainings on such topics as workplace relationships, productive practices, project planning, and customer service.

Less common formal development opportunities include apprenticeships, job rotations, and job swapping. An apprenticeship is a rigorous system of learning designed for those with existing aptitude to enhance their skills under the supervision of a higher level employee (Charan, 2008). People are placed in apprenticeships for long periods of time, generally from six months to a year or longer. Apprenticeships immerse the person in the realities of the position to gain the necessary experience and competencies to be successful in that position.

Job rotation systems are short-term apprenticeships. The person is moved to two or more jobs for a shorter period of time in which he is exposed to the intricacies of the position and gains new skills along the way. Job rotation is not as intensive as an apprenticeship and may not lead to the person being ready to assume that job after just a short period of time. The development opportunity has breadth as its focus rather than gaining in-depth experience. Job rotation has been successful in enhancing employee understanding of how other departments function and their interrelatedness within the organization.

Job swapping is trading jobs with another person, either within an organization or with another organization. Each person takes over the responsibilities of the other person's job for a period of time. Job swapping ensures that no position goes unfilled as the current employee takes over a different job. Most often, job swapping occurs within the same agency. However, it can cross over to other agencies when agencies trade employees for a period of time. The logistics of a job swap may be extensive, but the benefits of learning a new job and learning about a new agency could be immeasurable.

This step in the succession planning process ensures that learning styles are matched to development opportunities. If they do not match, the time spent conducting the assessment and creating the development plan is wasted. Facilitating quality development opportunities builds skills, closes competency gaps, and allows HiPos to achieve their desired goals.

Part 7: Establish Tracking Criteria

The seventh and final step in the succession planning process is arguably the most important for achieving the goals and objectives of the entire program. The development plan will only be successful if the accomplishments are tracked and evaluated. The employee and the mentor need to be held accountable for the progress made on the development plan. Some strategies are easier and faster to accomplish than others. Some have very defined start and completion dates; others need to be adjusted for various reasons. The development plan is a working document and may be altered to meet the needs of the employee. To ensure success, mentors must establish review dates and adhere to them (see table 12.7).

Table 12.7 Development Plan With Development Opportunities and Tracking Criteria

GOAL: ENHANCE UNDERSTANDING OF FINANCIAL MANAGEMENT AND REVENUE GENERATION.				
Strategy	Time line to complete	Resources needed (other than time)	Development opportunity or method	Tracking criteria
1. Attend revenue management school	Spring 2015	$1,500	Small hands-on annual conference	Review third quarter 2012
2. Meet weekly with chief financial officer to discuss financial issues	Begin immediately	None	One-on-one meetings	Review each quarter
3. Work with superintendent of recreation to establish a Friends of Parks and Recreation nonprofit group	Spring 2016	Access to legal counsel for filing of paperwork	One-on-one meetings; complete *The Nonprofit Center's Starting a Nonprofit Organization* either in person or online	Review fourth quarter 2012; review again third quarter 2013
GOAL: GAIN EXPERIENCE IN AQUATICS MANAGEMENT.				
1. Work with the current aquatics supervisor to manage the seasonal aquatics operations	Summer 2015	None	One-on-one meetings; hands-on experience with special projects	Review third quarter 2012
2. Participate in summer lifeguard and manager staff training	Summer 2015	None	One-on-one meetings; hands-on experience with entire process	Review third quarter 2012
3. Obtain Aquatic Facility Operator certification	Spring 2016	$500	Pass exam by completing the AFO course in person or as a webinar through NRPA	Review third quarter 2013

Negatives of Succession Planning

Succession planning is beneficial to the agency because it prepares staff to take over vacated positions, strengthens the knowledge base of the staff, and enhances the overall ability of the agency to respond to change. However, succession planning has some negative aspects, such as the following:

▶ It is time consuming to establish and can require extensive resources—of both time and money.

▶ It can set HiPos up to think they are heirs apparent when, in actuality, that should not be an expectation.

▶ Some people within the agency will not be selected as HiPos or will have no interest in the process. These people need special consideration and attention to keep morale up within the organization.

For the preceding reasons, not all agencies can undertake an extensive process such as succession planning. Another option is to implement pieces of the process to build bench strength. Starting small, with a few pieces of the succession plan, can yield results and enhance staff performance. A full succession plan enhances bench strength and better prepares staff for the future. Regardless of the degree of staff development, building leadership skills is never a waste of resources and only strengthens individuals and agencies.

Summary

Regardless of whether a parks and recreation agency is in the public, nonprofit, or commercial sector, it is always competing for people's time and money. Customers gravitate to outstanding agencies that provide good services for the best value. To meet the needs of customers, agencies must position themselves to deliver quality products. An effective way to do this is through training and development.

This chapter introduced performance management leadership (PML), a process in which employees are mentored, given feedback, rewarded, and helped to set goals for high performance. This chapter framed PML around succession planning.

Succession planning and the staff development process presented here strongly adhere to this philosophy by structuring development to meet organizational and individual needs, and to design a systematic process to improve performance.

In succession planning, competencies are developed for staff members' current positions and long-term career advancement. Succession planning requires that high-level managers understand the agency's current and future needs in terms of staff and talent. They assess job demands, competencies, and bench strength to gain a lucid picture of the agency's strengths and weaknesses as well as the strengths and weaknesses of its staff. From here

they build the agency's talent pool by helping staff develop in a systematic and productive manner. Staff development, which includes such things as mentoring, job rotation, and workshops, is structured to best adhere to each person's learning style.

Succession planning takes a very individualistic approach to training and development, but the agency ultimately benefits, because any agency is only as strong as its staff. A strong staff results in an agency that is well equipped to address trends and issues in the community, change when needed, stay competitive in the marketplace, and provide quality services to its customers.

Questions for Reflection and Discussion

1. From your own perspective, what type of training would you find most beneficial to enhance your own skills? Why did you choose that one?

2. Your agency has completed an assessment of its bench strength. Would you share this with all staff members so they can see where they are in the organization? Why or why not?

3. Define hard and soft skills. Which one is easier to teach? Why?

4. What methods would you use to teach soft skills and hard skills? How do training methods differ?

5. Do you believe that mentoring is a good method to train and develop staff? Why or why not? What type of mentoring would be most beneficial to you?

Key Terms and Definitions

bench strength—The number of people capable of stepping in to do a job successfully.

career progression—The upward movement of employees within a particular profession.

competencies—The skills, knowledge, abilities, and characteristics needed to be successful in a job.

competency gap—The difference between the competencies a person currently has and the competencies needed to obtain the desired level within the organization.

development—Competencies gained to enhance job performance in the workplace.

development plan—A written document that details learning goals, strategies to reach these goals, development opportunities, and tracking criteria to ensure that the employee will achieve desired outcomes.

entry-level employees—Front-line, full-time employees who need no more than five years of experience to be qualified for a higher position.

in-service staff training—Training held by an organization for its employees.

job analysis—A process used to determine the competencies required for successful job performance.

learning organization—An organization that prioritizes continual learning to enhance employees' competencies, which in turn strengthens the organization.

learning styles—The patterns or processes people use to acquire information.

succession planning—A process for identifying and preparing quality, talented employees for career growth.

talent pool—A collection of skilled workers with the potential to fill positions within an organization.

training—The acquisition of competencies resulting from organized educational opportunities such as conferences and workshops.

Bibliography

Barcelona, B., & Ross, C.M. (2004). An analysis of perceived competencies recreational sports administrators. *Journal of Park & Recreation Administration, 22*, 25-42.

Busser, J.A., & Bannon, J.J. (1987). Work activities performed by management personnel in public leisure service organizations. *Journal of Park and Recreation Administration, 5* (1), 1-16.

Carter, N.H. (1986, Summer). Guaranteeing management's future through succession planning. *Journal of Information Systems Management*, 20.

Charan, R. (2008). *Leadership at all levels.* San Francisco: Jossey-Bass.

Fokken, P. (2003). *Construction and validation for competencies of Board Self-Assessment Questionnaire (BSAQ) for park and recreation board members: A model development.* Unpublished doctoral dissertation, Indiana University, Bloomington.

Generational differences chart. (n.d.). West Midland Family Center. http://www.wmfc.org/uploads/GenerationalDifferencesChart.pdf

Hammersley, C.H., & Tynon, J.F. (1998). Job competencies of entry level resort and commercial recreation professionals. *Journal of Applied Recreation Research, 23* (3), 225-241.

How to create an awesome work portfolio. (n.d.). Manifest Your Potential. www.manifestyourpotential.com/work/take_up_life_work/8_get_hired/how_to_create_awesome_work_portfolio.htm.

Hurd, A.R. (2004). Competency development for board members in public parks and recreation agencies. *Journal of Park and Recreation Administration, 22*, 43-61.

Hurd, A.R. (2005). Competency development for entry level public park and recreation professionals. *Journal of Park and Recreation Administration, 23*, 45-62.

Hurd, A.R., & Anderson, D.M. (2011). *The park and recreation professionals handbook.* Champaign, IL: Human Kinetics.

Hurd, A.R., Barcelona, R., & Meldrum, J.T. (2008). *Leisure services management.* Champaign, IL: Human Kinetics.

Hurd, A.R., & Buschbom, T. (2010). Competency development for chief executive officers in YMCAs. *Managing Leisure, 15* (1), 96-110.

Hurd, A.R., & McLean, D.D. (2004). An analysis of perceived competencies of CEOs in public parks and recreation agencies. *Managing Leisure, 9*, 96-110.

Jamieson, L.M. (1987). Competency-based approaches to sport management. *Journal of Sport Management, 1m*(1), 48-56.

Performance management leadership: 'Blocking and tackling' of the CEO playing field. (2006, January 28). W.P. Carey School of Business, Arizona State University. http://knowledge.wpcarey.asu.edu/article.cfm?articleid=1168#.

Pynes, J.E. (2009). *Human resources management for public and nonprofit organizations* (3rd ed.). San Francisco: Jossey-Bass.

Rothwell, W.J. (2005). *Effective succession planning* (3rd ed.). New York: AMACOM.

Senge, P.M. (2006). *The fifth discipline: The art & practice of the learning organization.* New York: Currency Doubleday.

Sprouse, J.K.S. (2004). Key competencies for entry level therapeutic recreation professionals working with youth at risk populations. Unpublished master's thesis, Illinois State University, Normal, IL.

Zachary, J. (2000). *The mentor's guide.* San Francisco: Jossey-Bass.

Chapter 13

External Community and Organizational Leadership

Dale Larsen

"*Never doubt that a small group of thoughtful, committed people can change the world. Indeed, it's the only thing that ever has.*"

—Margaret Mead

I was the 1960s and 1970s, and a group of dedicated women—Dorothy, Maxine, Penny, and Ruth—were not happy with Phoenix, Arizona, City Hall. This isn't surprising for this time in our history, because social unrest and dissatisfaction with government were widespread. But these women were different. They weren't the classic "flower power" children of this era. They were neighborhood people who cherished the beauty of the natural geography. These were nonpolitical community-minded people who were upset that lavish homes were being built on the slopes of the most beautiful iconic mountain in the middle of the city. Weren't there any laws or ordinances prohibiting residential development and disturbing the public's views and appreciation of the signature mountain of the city?

This group of women banded together and formed a volunteer organization based on conservation and preservation. They recruited other seemingly nonpolitical community members who also had a deep appreciation for the protection of desert mountains. "Save Our Mountains" became their theme. As a result of their grassroots campaign to prevent development and preserve precious mountain slopes, major local legislation was passed supporting their efforts.

These women all went on to serve terms on the parks and recreation board. They were a political force without ever thinking of themselves that way. Over the course of 50 years, these women, known affectionately as the Matriarchs of the Mountains, became a leadership power rarely observed before. Their efforts birthed similar preservation campaigns across the region. Indeed, just as Margaret Mead suggested in the quote that opened this chapter, a small group of thoughtful, committed people can change the world.

Learning Outcomes

At the conclusion of this chapter, students will be able to:

▶ Identify the differences between internal and external organizational leaders.

▶ Understand the concepts of external community leadership and external organizational leadership as components of external leadership.

▶ Identify the skills and knowledge necessary for becoming external leaders in multi-organizational groups.

▶ Identify unique community-based skill sets required to become an external leader.

▶ Understand the distinctions and relationships between formal and informal agency authority and how these affect external community leadership experiences.

▶ Give specific examples of external organizational leadership structures and their positive impact on public service and the public good.

▶ Understand the powerful influences external organizational leaders have on the development of effective public policy.

Leadership is one of the most studied subjects in any industry—public, private, nonprofit, or a combination of these. Particularly during times of massive change, leadership often comes under scrutiny as one of the guiding forces in remedying community problems and providing direction. Regardless of the specific leadership theory, most researchers now agree that leadership is a combination of traits and learned skill sets. The ability to lead is based on one's own self-expression as well as on one's community and surrounding environment.

In this chapter, **external leadership** refers to the behaviors that are employed to reach goals when multiple individuals or agencies (or both) come together around an issue. The chapter distinguishes two types of external leadership: **external community leadership**, which is exerted by community members (usually laypeople who become involved out of a desire to improve their communities), and **external organizational leadership**, which is demonstrated by those who work for a particular organization and find themselves working with individuals and representatives from other organizations in the pursuit of common goals. As someone working in leisure services and recreation, you can expect to encounter both types of external leadership. Collaborative work with external community leaders can have powerful effects on public policy and the public good. Working with external organizational leaders can be fruitful as well, but it can be much more complex because it includes a diversity of missions and agendas, some of which may be in direct conflict.

Organizations that provide recreation and leisure services are affected by constant change from external forces. Declining financial resources and revenue support are forcing organizations to change strategically. The competition for traditional financial resources (e.g., tax revenues, bond support, fees and charges, private sponsorships, philanthropic contributions) has always existed. However, the extent to which serious budget reductions, especially those affecting municipal parks and recreation agencies and educational institutions, have resulted in organizational changes such as layoffs, consolidations, and even agency eliminations has been profound. Therefore, organizational change is vital as a response.

Organizational change is traditionally directed through normal internal hierarchical channels as agencies undertake budget reviews, organizational reviews, and strategic plan reviews. Internal organizational leaders are fairly easy to identify because they are acknowledged in the structures of the organizations they represent; they include city and town managers, regional executives, mayors, committee chairs, and department heads. Often, their powers are described in formal policy documents such as charters, ordinances, and local laws. This chapter does not address common internal organizational leadership, although it is important to acknowledge its influence.

This chapter addresses the leadership knowledge, skills, and abilities that lie outside traditional organizational charts and titles. As other chapters in this book have pointed out, the very nature of leadership and its structures are in the midst of change. Working groups are more diverse, leadership structures are becoming flatter, and processes are becoming less defined.

Students who understand how multiorganizational groups are created, and who have the capacity to work well with groups comprising a diverse array of workplace cultures, will better understand the leadership competencies needed for succeeding in fast-paced, ever-changing communities. Students who care about their communities and are willing to work to bring organized and unorganized coalitions together to create better communities will learn firsthand the leadership skills necessary to support community organizations.

External Community Leaders

External community leaders are generally dedicated citizens who work behind the scenes on boards, commissions, and councils and in neighborhoods and groups. They represent the spirit of stated agency mission, vision, and value statements that ultimately define the agency's formal authority. Agency administrators depend on external community leaders to represent the mission, vision, and values of the organization. External community leaders often carry great community influence in the establishment of policy and practices. This chapter provides several external community leadership examples, people and outcomes. Following is a simple formula for how external community leaders create change.

▶ Create a sense of urgency
▶ Pull together a team of people who can achieve results

▶ Create a clear and inspiring vision

▶ Practice effective communication

▶ Become empowered both formally and informally

▶ Strive for short-term wins that build into long-term, sustained practices

▶ Never give up

▶ Create a new sustainable community culture

External community leaders are the myriad leaders in the fields of leisure services and conservation who work with others outside the halls of the established organizations and agencies; together they represent multiple agencies and individual interests. Their stories are unique because they find their way with less clearly defined processes than those who work in more traditional organizations. The work cultures, practices, mission statements, visions, and expectations of external community leaders must all be at least accounted for. In many community projects, grassroots groups, neighbors, and community-minded citizens are all added to the mix. Such groups contain emotionally involved people who advocate for public parks, recreation, and conservation or, conversely, corporate and development interests. Leaders of such groups must have the ability to facilitate open, honest communication, find common ground, and steer their groups toward the goal of improving the community's well-being. Community leaders are often genuine, sincere people with little interest in proving themselves, but a powerful interest in expressing their opinions on important community issues.

Leadership from the inside is clear. Professionals and practitioners working in their fields of expertise are generally financially compensated for advancing the vision and values of their organizations. However, they should never underestimate

Best Practices From the Field

Voluntary leadership and civic engagement are two of the most powerful community-based practices that citizens can experience. Mother Nature affords citizens of all demographics an array of meaningful volunteer leadership experiences. My Phoenix My Park is an excellent best-practice example developed as a result of reductions in maintenance budgets in community outdoor park and mountain preserves in Phoenix, Arizona.

With 188 city parks totaling over 4,700 developed acres and more than 38,000 acres of natural desert mountain parks and preserves, Phoenix has one of the largest city park systems in the United States. Major reductions in personnel budgets, largely accomplished by not filling and eliminating vacant positions, negatively affected day-to-day maintenance operations. Parks around the country for decades have sponsored Adopt a Park programs, where citizens volunteer for park clean-ups.

Phoenix took this traditional concept to a new level by promoting and branding an enhanced volunteer leadership effort aptly named My Phoenix My Park. MPMP actively recruits, reinforces, recognizes, and retains (4 Rs) neighborhood volunteers, corporations, partners, and civic groups into volunteer leadership experiences. In 2012, more than two dozen parks were formally adopted by community groups, 66,000 hours of volunteer sweat and labor were generated, and 7,500 individual volunteers were registered as MPMP engaged leaders. National voluntary financial impact standards support the calculation of $1.5 million of human capital value used in MPMP in 2013.

In addition to neighborhoods, civic groups, and corporations, MPMP has created new leadership partnerships with AmeriCorps VISTA, Bureau of Land Management America's Great Outdoor Project, National Public Lands Day, Keep Phoenix Beautiful, and Hands On Greater Phoenix. The status and credibility of MPMP have grown in recent years. The downside of severe budget limitations has created an upside in community civic engagement and **empowerment**, all for the goal of improved parks and preserves.

The lead-in description of the chapter External Leadership offers a powerful example of community engagement detailing the "matriarchs of the mountains" and their commitment to saving Phoenix mountains. My Phoenix My Parks takes the community lessons learned from this significant part of public park history and transforms it into a current best practice.

For more information on My Phoenix My Park, go to www.phoenix.gov/parks/index.html (link to Volunteer in the Parks and get the latest on My Phoenix My Parks).

the influence and power of community leaders. The challenge for internal leaders is to maximize the potential and effectiveness of external groups and to develop the leadership potential of the people who make up these groups.

Opportunities to serve abound in all communities—student councils, PTAs, faith-based councils, youth sports club boards, alumni associations, Girl or Boy Scout Councils, petition campaigns, parks and recreation boards, town boards, youth agency boards or committees, bond committees, nature organization commissions, and school boards. For many, these grassroots opportunities are their first experiences of exerting their influence on important public policy matters. Even college students can become engaged in policy-making opportunities on boards, councils, or commissions. Experiencing a clear, hands-on, personal view of how policy-making groups work is an excellent first step in gaining a rich understanding of external leadership skills.

Practical experience with decision-making bodies is crucial for gaining knowledge of one's chosen field. However, many students studying leisure management and leadership have never attended a public policy board or committee meeting, unless they were assigned to do so. College students who join campus-based advisory or policy groups that help shape decisions affecting tuition, student status, residency, and other important student issues receive important leadership training and exposure.

This chapter focuses on several examples of external leadership outcomes and provides a foundation of knowledge, skills, and abilities. A key premise is that leadership is a learned behavior resulting from rewarding personal experiences. People become leaders through the personal discovery that results from rich community experiences.

The groups that come together to work on leisure services projects and policies range from legally authorized policy groups to advisory groups, foundations, stakeholder groups, **stewardship** organizations, and less formal general community volunteers. The following sections describe the nature of these groups.

Formal Agency and Authority

In the United States, hardly a month goes by without some kind of national or global emergency taking place. We see on television the horrific aftermath of some enormous storm, earthquake, fire, flood, or war. One of the first relief groups on the scene in the aftermath is often the American Red Cross. The importance of the Red Cross seems obvious: it is an organization that helps people in emergencies. The history of this iconic organization began in the same way most local organizations started: as a mission in response to critical emergencies. Over time, the American Red Cross has come to serve as a guiding example of thousands of volunteers serving in leadership capacities.

Following is the mission of the American Red Cross: "The American Red Cross, a humanitarian organization led by volunteers and guided by its **Congressional Charter** and the Fundamental Principles of the International Red Cross Movement, will provide relief to victims of disasters and help people prevent, prepare for, and respond to emergencies." The fundamental principles referred to in this mission statement are humanity, impartiality, neutrality, independence, voluntary service, unity, and universality.

The often-heard term *International Red Cross* is actually a misnomer, because no official organization bears that name. In reality, the movement consists of several organizations that are legally independent from each other, but are united through common basic principles (Wikipedia, 2014). The formal authority of the organization helps volunteers (external leaders) understand their role in the decision-making process of this influential organization.

The American Red Cross was founded by Clara Barton in 1882 following her travels in Europe after the Civil War. She discovered the noble efforts of the International Committee of the Red Cross (ICRC), a private humanitarian institution founded in 1863 in Geneva, Switzerland. The U.S. Congress approved the American Red Cross charter, the original in 1900 and a second in 1905. Therefore, the American Red Cross, a private, nonprofit charitable organization, derives its power and authority from the U.S. Congress (American Red Cross.org – Museum and History). The basis of legitimacy, in this case, is congressional approval.

The authority of a public agency has to be set forth in a legal document. Most public agency authority is derived by state statute, local charter, city ordinance, or a special designated district code. Most nonprofit organizations, because of their tax-exempt charter status with the Internal Revenue Service, derive their authority from the federal IRS and the **articles of incorporation** on file with their respective states. Most private or corporate organizations have their source of authority placed on file as a state and/or national commercial business license.

Why do external leaders need to understand **formal agency authority**? Many volunteer organizations, unless they file articles of incorporation with their states or the IRS, have no formal source of authority; rather, they exist on the basis of personal leadership and public opinion. Such informal groups often need to attain more formal status to sustain their missions; otherwise, people may lose interest and the group may fall apart.

Public Policy Board Authority

The Commission for Accreditation of Park and Recreation Agencies (CAPRA) defines public policy boards as follows:

The policy-making entity is legally, ultimately responsible for the operation of the recreation and parks department; it has the power to accomplish without recourse. It may be the city council or commission, an elected board of citizens, established and elected body. This entity usually has taxing power and must approve the budget; it holds title to property. It also serves an important function in interpreting the programs, services, and facilities and in exerting influence throughout the community to improve and expand park and recreation programs, services, and facilities (National Standards, fourth edition, revised April 2009, sponsored by the National Recreation and Park Association, Public Authority/Policy Body commentary).

When the policy-making entity is not an elected independent board specifically for parks and recreation, the governing entity may appoint a parks and recreation board, which is delegated authority for operating policies and general administrative practices. This body would be considered a semi-independent board, since it would depend upon city council or county commission for ultimate policy approval, in addition to approval

and allocation of its funds. The board would be an integral part of city or county government or other local entity; and, the park and recreation board itself. The parks and recreation executive should be responsible to both. When the operating policy-making body is a citizen's board, it should hold regular meetings, duly publicized, with the actions of the board and reports of the administrator officially recorded and available. Board members should be representative of the total community and serve with staggered terms (CAPRA 1.1.1).

In other words, the minimal standard of compliance for a formal policy-making authority directly related to government is as follows: "The organizational authority structure should provide for one public authority responsible for policy-making functions" (CAPRA 1.1.1).

Further, CAPRA standards go on to state that "there should be citizen advisory boards/committees." Following is a description of these groups: "Advisory boards may serve an entire local governmental area, but also may serve a specific neighborhood, function, activity, center, or a particular site. The board(s) may be appointed by the mayor and the city council and/or the county commissioners, or may be elected. They may have delegated authority or responsibility for policy or administration. These types of boards may be composed of a relatively large body of representatives from all interested factions of the locality. In addition to those members appointed by officials of the city or county, interested civic groups may select representatives. The advisory board(s) engages the community and serves as advocate(s) for the advancement of programs, facilities, and services (CAPRA 1.1.2).

Formal Policy Groups vs. Advisory Groups

Unlike federal and state governments, which operate under the legal authority of a constitution, local governments operate under charters, enabling legislation, or special district or city or county code books and ordinances. Local governments operate as public jurisdictions under the auspices of state and federal governments; in other words, a local government is established via the approval of a state government, which in turn is established

Leisure Leaders

Jessica Voss

MY PREPARATION

- BS in parks and recreation management (therapeutic recreation)—Arizona State University, College of Public Programs, School of Community Resources and Development, Phoenix, AZ

- Red Cross First Aid and CPR

- Red Cross Cat and Dog First Aid and CPR

- Certified therapeutic recreation specialist

- Instructor, 4-H Green Team Dog

- Member, Arizona State Therapeutic Recreation Association

- Member, Sierra Club

- 2013 Arizona State Therapeutic Recreation Association Student Recognition Award

- President, Arizona State Therapeutic Recreation Association (ASTRA) Student Club

- President, Parks and Recreation Student Association (PRSA) at ASU

- PRSA and ASTRA Student Club Leadership Award

- Student chair, Arizona Parks and Recreation Association 2013 Conference Committee

MY CAREER

I work as a therapeutic recreation specialist for River of Dreams, a small nonprofit organization in Phoenix, Arizona, that provides adaptive outdoor recreation and wilderness adventure experiences to teenagers and adults with disabilities or significant life challenges. The mission of River of Dreams is to improve the quality of life for people with disabilities through the power of outdoor recreation. The organization began as part of the adaptive recreation services offered by the city of Phoenix. In 2009, the city cut its adaptive rec programming due to their budget

Photo courtesy of Arizona State University. Photographer: Felipe Ruiz

crisis. This nonprofit organization is the product of a resilient and driven group of volunteers who are passionate about what this program has to offer. It now consists of two paid part-time staff and several volunteers, and it will grow as resources allow. River of Dreams has partnered with the Virginia G. Piper Sports and Fitness Center and Arizona Bridge to Independent Living while still maintaining a partnership with the city, which owns the equipment.

As a contracted therapeutic recreation specialist, my job is to jump in wherever needed, whether it's office work or assisting a person up a mountain who wouldn't have had the opportunity without adaptation or assistance. Ultimately, it is my responsibility to ensure that programs are safe, effective, and fun. I attained the unique knowledge and skills necessary for this job through education in therapeutic recreation; leadership experiences with academic and state professional organizations; community volunteer experiences with a variety of populations in diverse settings; professional development, learning, and networking at national conferences and local events; and running my own pet-sitting business. My job not only allows me to participate in activities that I enjoy, but it's completely fulfilling as well. I am awed and thankful that I am getting paid to do what I love. I have strong values regarding the right to leisure, autonomy, accessibility, and the therapeutic capacity of nature, and I have a job that actively supports those values.

MY ADVICE TO YOU

To truly be satisfied with one's job is to live a rich life. If you love your job, you'll never work a day in your life. Why waste half or more of your life doing something you don't enjoy? You have only one life. Decide how you want to live, and go for it. Don't revolve your life around someone else's definition or expectation of success. Define *yours*, make a plan, and follow it. Don't be afraid to change course. Make sure that you are paying attention to how you may be changing in terms of your values, ideals, morals, desires, aspirations, and needs. The plan you made three years ago may no longer match your ideal plan today. Embrace the change and remain adaptable. Always keep your goal or dream in mind. When you feel frustrated or discouraged, take a step back from the situation and look at the big picture. Recognize how far you've come and how much you've accomplished when you've had the choice to quit. Focus on who you are, who you want to be, and how you want to get there. Always ask why along the way, and never let anyone define your limits. You are the only one with that power.

Sometimes you need to take small steps to prove to yourself that you are capable of achieving more than you or others expected. Set your priorities and take action to show it. If school is your first priority, make financial arrangements so that you can focus on your studies instead of work. Explain to your friends that you won't be able to hang out if you have responsibilities with classes. Organize your time, and stick to an agenda. If you make a commitment, especially to yourself, stick to it as much as possible. No one is perfect, but be honest with yourself when making decisions and reflecting on the past. If you don't learn from your mistakes by analyzing the truth, those experiences will remain mistakes and you won't improve. The more you show yourself what you're made of, the more empowered you can become!

via the approval of the federal government. Why and where this is important is explained later in a case study. For now, it is enough to note that many positions of responsibility and decision making are occupied by people who are appointed or elected to seats on policy and advisory boards.

Generally, policy and advisory board members (i.e., external community leaders) serve without compensation. They volunteer their time to serve in an otherwise statutory environment. Board members come from all walks of life and varying neighborhoods, businesses, schools, and professions. They are soccer moms, lawyers, neighborhood activists, students, business owners, teachers, nonprofit leaders, nature lovers, athletes, religious leaders, doctors, dentists, nurses, professionals, musicians, youth leaders, parents, grandparents, and blue-collar workers. Why do they serve? In addition to the obvious reason of being chosen by an elected official, they usually have a passion for public parks and recreation services. Their qualifications generally include a love of and loyalty to public service, a willingness to serve, and the time to attend many meetings. External leaders on formal policy-making boards serve under the pressure of public scrutiny. They also serve for the pleasure and pride of seeing children, youth, and families benefit from the quality of life that parks and recreation services brings to their community.

Strong, formal policy-making groups (boards, commissions, and councils) often appoint, delegate, or designate an **advisory committee** to maximize outreach to the community regarding the issue at hand. In some instances, an advisory committee must include specific **stakeholders** who have vested interests or **claims** (hence, the term *stakeholder*) related to the issue. This requirement is ordinarily spelled out in the formal motion approving the creation of the committee. An advisory committee may also have a time line in which its work must be accomplished. **Ad hoc/task force committee** is another name for an advisory group convened to generate a recommendation to a formal policy group. Whatever they are called, advisory groups advise on policy issues; formal policy groups approve policy.

What kinds of external community leaders serve on advisory committees, and what kinds serve in formal policy groups? In most instances, the same kinds of people serve on both. The difference is that a formal policy group requires legislative approval and scrutiny. Often, members of advisory groups ascend to formal policy appointments or elections based on the experience and qualifications they received while serving on their advisory groups. External community leaders who are novices to the more formal policy-making environment of politics and public scrutiny either "retire" from their short-term experience once it is completed or choose to participate in a formal policy group because they desire more power in the decision-making process. Boards, commissions, and councils are filled with inexperienced citizen volunteers who later ascended to more powerful policy-making groups having "cut their teeth" in less formal community groups.

Case Study: Dog Park in Phoenix

The relationship between formal and advisory policy-making groups is demonstrated in the recent public conversation about a proposed downtown dog park in Phoenix, Arizona. Off-leash parks, commonly known as dog parks, usually receive serious community attention. Depending on the neighborhood, there may be as many people objecting to a dog park as there are supporting it. Without getting into the formal debate of why there should or should not be public dog parks, this example is interesting because the idea for a dog park was generated by people residing in downtown Phoenix. Urban dwellers often have pet dogs. Phoenix does not have a downtown off-leash park. Although the parks and recreation department operates five formal dog parks in the city, none are within walking distance of downtown.

The issue of the need for a downtown dog park was advanced by the mayor and city council— a legislative, formal policy-making group. The creation of an advisory/task force committee was recommended and approved by the city council. However, instead of limiting the committee to a certain number of citizens, the formal action stated that all interested people could participate, as long as they applied online by a designated date. More than 70 citizens, the majority of whom lived or worked in the downtown area, requested membership on the committee. The chairman of the committee was a representative from the parks and recreation board—a policy-making board created by city charter with powers that even the city council could not override, except on financial issues. The committee consisted of business representatives, downtown workers and residents, pet advocates, and university students. Many supported the concept of a downtown dog park, and, of course, some did not.

Certain conditions were placed on the establishment of the committee. In addition to the condition that anyone could apply to be a committee member, a deadline was established for the committee's work to be accomplished. The committee structure would cease at the conclusion of this public process, no public funds could be used to construct the park, and a boundary in the downtown area was established for the proposed facility.

A recommended site for an off-leash dog park was eventually identified in a nearby downtown area park. The final details of design and operation were shared and discussed with interested members of the park conservancy, which was composed of park constituents, neighborhood groups, and so-called stakeholders in the park. The dog park is not without its critics, which is true of most proposed public policy initiatives. However, without the influence and collaboration of external community leaders working with formal agency representatives, the creation of a downtown public dog park would likely not have been realized. In this case, external community leadership was crucial for a successful outcome.

The committee's final recommendation to the parks and recreation board and the city council brought this public policy debate to a conclusion. The advisory committee was immediately disbanded (commonly referred to as "sunset"). The dynamic relationship of two formal policy-making groups (the city council and parks board) and an advisory/task force citizen's committee, and the ultimate decision of a proposed and somewhat controversial public dog park, hung in the balance. Without the benefit of significant external community leadership in the form of a large group of citizens, this public policy proposal would likely have been doomed from the beginning.

Empowerment of Community Leaders

Empowerment is a term often used in leadership and management circles, literature, and organizational applications. The assumption is that people who are empowered also receive the authority to implement and evaluate their actions. The difference between being an external leader on a formal policy-making group and being one on an advisory/task force group is often the difference between being empowered and not being empowered. Because advisory groups *advise,* the empowerment factor is usually not discernible. However, a strongly organized advisory group can influence the actions of a formal policy-making group by being strong community advocates, supporters, and external leaders.

Open Public Meetings

Another important distinction between external formal public policy groups and advisory/task force groups is the degree to which they must adhere

Courtesy of Ann Wheat, City of Phoenix

The creation of a beautiful dog park to serve the citizens of downtown Phoenix would not have happened without collaboration between external community leaders and formal agencies.

to strict public open meeting law procedures. Good public policy requires a high degree of trust and confidence among formal public policy makers, management, citizenry, and the external community leaders charged with the responsibility of seeing that change or advocacy happens. External community leaders need to be aware of and actively practice **open public meeting** procedures. Numerous state and local laws require that meetings of public policy groups be open to the public and that public records (minutes, recordings) be made available to the public for inspection and review, which often takes the form of the media.

Procedures for public policy groups such as parks and recreation boards may differ from one jurisdiction to another, but the fact remains that open government gives the public confidence that services are being performed properly and without ethical violations. Matters of public policy, whether generated by formal or advisory groups and organizations, must be conducted openly. A simple e-mail communication among citizen members of a public policy group may be in violation of open meeting laws if it is interpreted that public business is being conducted. A special public

community event that brings together a group of external citizen leaders who serve on a particular board or committee needs to be posted—even if business is not being conducted—to protect the leaders from public criticism. External community leaders need to be trained and coached on all aspects of open meeting law applications to avoid ethical violations including conflict of interest. This requirement alone may deter some people from serving on formal or informal policy groups, if they are unable to meet such high public standards.

Friends Groups and Foundations

The previous sections paint a rather formal and sometimes stressful picture of what it takes for external citizen leaders to provide policy-making community leadership and service. So for those citizens who do not have the desire to serve on a formal policy-making group, what options are there? Seemingly one of the most efficient and, from a personal point of view, satisfying forms of external leadership is volunteering to serve on parks, recreation, and conservation–based **foundations**, or what are commonly referred to as **friends groups**.

These private nonprofit groups are formed to provide the following essential community functions:

- ▶ Act as IRS-authorized fiduciary organizations eligible to accept and administer tax-free donations.
- ▶ Raise private funds and apply for grants.
- ▶ Recruit and train volunteers to perform significant community service.
- ▶ Promote and campaign on behalf of people rallying support for capital improvement projects, bond elections, and operational budget support.
- ▶ Serve as recognized land trusts, thereby giving governmental agencies the opportunity to acquire or manage open spaces outside of the traditional governmental acquisition process.

The external community leaders involved in foundations come from every area of community organizations and neighborhoods. These grassroots leaders include students, philanthropists, retirees, business leaders, environmentalists, political advocates, religious leaders, tourists, nonprofit staff members, government staff members, police officers, firefighters, teachers, and civic leaders.

Private nonprofit and charitable foundations can operate outside of the highly scrutinized public open meeting law environment of government. This is not to say that they do not have to maintain high ethical and legal standards. Clearly, they do. There are numerous examples of nonprofit organizations (e.g., in youth services) whose ethical and procedural lapses have been publicized in the media and needed to be resolved in formal judicial court proceedings. Stories abound of youth sport coaches and their "winning at all costs" style of leadership, of volunteer treasurers of nonprofit clubs using funds for their own purposes, and of organizations failing to file tax returns or violating their tax-exempt charters. Such stories often get front-page attention. However, the majority of positive stories of how volunteer "friends" have filled gaps in operational budget cuts by providing hundreds of hours of maintenance and park clean-up work often get relegated to back-page community news sections of the media.

One example of a friends group is the Phoenix Parks and Conservation Foundation, founded in 1979 through the efforts of the Junior League of Phoenix as its anchor community service project. The foundation's mission statement is as follows: "The City of Phoenix Parks and Conservation Foundation facilitates the private sector and community participation in the development of Phoenix parks and programs, and the preservation and restoration of natural resources." Members pay a small membership fee and generally get their information via website links, Facebook, and Twitter.

The Austin (Texas) Parks Foundation has been the voice of the Austin Parks and Recreation Department since 1992. The foundation staff and hundreds of members work with several recognized community groups, local businesses, and concerned citizens to adopt and improve parks through direct action, advocacy, fund-raising, and programming. The Austin Parks Foundation joins forces with other organizations to speak up for bonds and legislation that protect and expand precious open space.

The Philadelphia Parks Alliance was formed to provide community support for the famous Fairmount Park and other recreation and park facilities. A recent community-led park reform movement raised significant public awareness of the condition of Philadelphia's parks and recreational facilities. Each year thousands of citizen volunteers contribute millions of dollars of "sweat equity" by working on park grounds and at park facilities. An Alliance newsletter reported: "Fairmount Park's future depends on its ability to work with lots of people. It will never get all the support it needs from dedicated and overburdened park staff. It will always depend on partnerships and teamwork."

One of the most intriguing and best examples of external leadership is the story of Elizabeth (Betsy) Barlow Rogers. Rogers studied art history at Wellesley College and city planning at Yale University in the 1960s and then moved to New York City. She developed an interest first in parks and then in Frederick Law Olmsted, the pioneer and father of modern landscape architecture, publishing books and articles about both. Outraged at the demise of Central Park in the mid-1970s, Rogers began to raise private funds and organize volunteer labor. In 1976, while urging a private solution to the park's problems, Rogers declared, "New York can no longer afford its parks, not even Central Park." Thus, before her appointment as the newly created Central Park Conservancy administrator by then-Mayor Ed Koch, Rogers had been prominent in the private sector and quite determined to save Central Park during New York's fiscal crisis.

Rogers' extraordinary fund-raising success rested in part on Central Park's status as a cultural and artistic treasure. She convinced New Yorkers that the park deserved the same financial support as the city's museums, libraries, and symphony orchestras, arguing that the park was also a cultural institution and a more urgent candidate for assistance. Following her tenure in 1996 as the Central Park Conservancy administrator, the Conservancy had raised more than $150 million and spent most of it on rehabilitation of the park.

After leaving the Conservancy in 1996, Rogers formed the Cityscape Institute, a nonprofit organization dedicated to assisting residents and elected officials in the improvement of public places. In 2007 Betsy Rogers was recognized by the American Academy for Park and Recreation Administration in association with the National Park Foundation as the recipient of the prestigious Honorable Cornelius Amory Pugsley Award.

Stewardship and Watchdog Groups

Another kind of external community-based advocacy group that is largely informal but carries tremendous influence in the public policy process is the **stewardship group**, or so-called **watchdog group**. Similar to friends and foundation groups, stewardship groups are often organized around specific causes or issues. They may or may not be organized as charitable, nonprofit, tax-exempt organizations; in some instances they are volunteer groups that choose not to maneuver through the complex process of registering and reporting articles of incorporation or bylaws. A stewardship group may exist as a short-term advocacy group to address a specific issue such as a campaign election or a public initiative. Generally speaking, the reason a stewardship group chooses to become a charitable nonprofit organization is to receive and collect tax-exempt donations.

For the purposes of this discussion on external organizational leadership, the term *stewardship*

Photo from http://www.loc.gov/pictures/item/ny1586/

The leadership of Betsy Rogers was crucial in the effort to preserve Central Park, a cultural and artistic treasure of the New York City community.

refers to the responsibility to take care of something owned by the public. Stewardship is an environmental ethic that embodies planning and managing protected natural resources or facilities. Citizen leaders actively engage in the preservation of environmental resources and strive to promote long-term sustainability. The term *watchdog* is used in the description of these kinds of groups by the media and often by professional managers themselves. These external leaders regularly and routinely attend public meetings, review public meeting agendas and proceedings, take positions on policy items of public interest, lobby formal public policy officials, and campaign on behalf of or against issues of public interest. Such groups may not be formally registered lobby groups with their legislative government jurisdictions. However, their lobbying efforts consist of making telephone calls, meeting with public officials, being interviewed by the media, and promoting general community interest in the issue.

Although professional managers and practitioners need to gain the support of stewardship groups, in general, universal agreement does not always occur. The term "tree huggers" has been unfortunately coined by some professionals who believe that "preservation only" stewards do not support a reasonable balance of preservation and recreational uses. Good governance requires the cooperation and collaboration of so-called watchdog groups and park managers. Name-calling tends to cast a poor light on professional practitioners.

An example of an effective stewardship group is the Phoenix Mountains Preservation Council (PMPC). The opening scenario of this chapter describes the external leadership and volunteer work of four inspiring women: the Matriarchs of the Mountains. These women developed a grassroots organization to educate and protect precious environmental natural resources. The Phoenix Mountains Preservation Council grew out of that grassroots movement of the late 1960s and early 1970s. The preservation of the desert Mountain became a cause in which ordinary people were deeply and emotionally involved.

Efforts by individuals to save the mountains from development within the city limits of Phoenix began when the PMPC was founded in August 1970. The Council stated its objective as "setting aside the Phoenix Mountains as a unique wilderness park." To accomplish this objective, the Council agreed to "enlist the enthusiastic support of all persons who want to preserve the natural beauty of this mountain range." Members began circulating petitions and gathered several thousand signatures (Phoenix Mountains Preservation Council, http://phoenixmountains.org/AboutUs.htm). In the decades following the success of its initial campaign to save the mountains, PMPC has campaigned for and against sensitive environmental issues affecting Phoenix's preserved desert mountain. Its signature legislative success was the approval in the 1980s by the voters of Phoenix to pass Chapter 26 of the Phoenix City Code—City of Phoenix Mountains Preserve. A key element of this local law is this statement: "In no event shall any real property within the City Mountain Preserve be sold, traded or otherwise alienated, redesignated or deleted from the Mountain Preserve except by approval of the electors voting thereon . . . ." This legislative effort was motivated in large part by an approved land swap of a portion of mountains preserve property and adjacent land owned by a well-known resort developer. Over the ensuing years, parks professional management has worked hard to promote a positive partnership with PMPC.

The Phoenix Mountains Preservation Council grew out of a volunteer citizens led grassroots movement headed by the "Matriarchs of the Mountain" in the 1960s, and coalesced in the 1970s with the formal establishment of the PMPC, Inc. Today, PMPC continues to be an active community leadership public force. A state-authorized freeway that would cut a swath through another Phoenix iconic desert mountain (South Mountain Park) has been met with great resistance. The proposed freeway, approved before Chapter 26 was legally authorized, also includes the participation of a Native American Tribal Council. PMPC continues to play a vital role in influencing public policy with environmental issues affecting the preservation of Phoenix's desert mountains.

Community Volunteers

The least organized and sometimes most underappreciated form of external community leadership is the service provided by thousands, perhaps millions, of citizens who donate countless hours of volunteer service and leadership to parks, recreation, and conservation agencies. Especially during this era of extreme economic constraints affecting the budgets and personnel of public service departments, volunteerism is flourishing as never before. Literally every community around the country organizes volunteer efforts and campaigns to clean up parks, teach classes, coach youth sports, respond to public emergencies, provide customer service, promote legislative campaigns and issues, donate financial support, serve on boards and commissions, and perform the hundreds of tasks that are key to the survival of parks, recreation, and conservation agencies. I use the term *underappreciated* hesitantly, because the recognition of volunteerism is increasingly becoming the norm in public agencies.

The keys to sustaining external volunteer leadership lies in ongoing and organized efforts to recruit, train, retain, and recognize volunteers for their incredible community leadership. University students represent a significant pool of external volunteer leaders. Volunteer leadership experiences are excellent resume builders and career network builders. Over the years, I have invited many professional managers and leaders into my classes to describe the education and experiences that led to their successful careers. Invariably, they mention the importance of volunteer experiences and the contacts they have made through them.

As a result, volunteerism is an important part of their lives.

The value of volunteerism and its relationship to external organizational leadership can never be overstated or overvalued. It is difficult to accept, but undoubtedly true, that the most common reason people do not volunteer is that they are not asked.

External Organizational Leadership

Professionals in the field are finding that multiorganizational working groups are more common than they used to be. As resources become scarce, and as policy makers realize that multiple stakeholders have vested interests in social issues, groups form to solve problems or offer services that may not be easily offered by single organizations. Resolving land use conflicts, dealing with increased competition among service providers, overseeing industry standards, and outlining guidelines all involve a cooperative effort from a number of organizations and agencies. Interested individuals and organizational representatives come together for a variety

Photo courtesy of Brent Cuthbertson.

When you recruit university students as volunteers, you get energetic young leadership and they get valuable experience to build their resumes and prepare them for their careers.

of reasons, sometimes voluntarily for a recognized opportunity and sometimes as a working group mandated by a higher authority. Nonetheless, multiorganizational groups form, reshape themselves, and disband constantly to address needs within the public sphere.

An understanding of the benefits as well as the drawbacks of multiorganizational groups is now essential to anyone in a profession that is engaged with shared public interests. This places the leisure services professional smack in the middle of a trend that is likely to continue. This section examines the formation and structure of multiorganizational groups, the benefits and successes of some groups, the dangers and failures of other groups, and some overall suggestions for leisure services professionals participating in such groups.

Formation and Structure of External Organizational Groups

Multiorganizational groups form for a variety of reasons. Recognizing an opportunity for competitive advantage by becoming part of a coalition is one reason. A macro example is the European Union (EU). However flawed the result and process may have been in setting up the EU, the intent was to create a bloc of countries that would benefit from a freer flow of people and trade across their borders. Spy agencies from politically aligned countries have arrangements to share information and periodically cooperate with each other on missions. Companies in the same line of business create professional associations to assist each other with information and networking opportunities. Political authorities set up roundtables to facilitate agreement among diverse stakeholder groups.

The glue that binds genuine multiorganizational groups together is the recognition that some goals and anticipated outcomes cannot be achieved by any one agency or organization alone. Leisure services organizations, in their function of serving public needs, increasingly find themselves part of these groups. As a professional in your particular field, you will almost certainly be asked at one point to serve in some capacity as a representative of your organization. The success of these collaborative groups is more elusive than that of teams or working groups that form in-house, however. The need to manage greater variability in the group's structure, diverse organizational cultures, an increased likelihood of competing interests and

values, and different decision-making processes can all make progress toward a goal, even a shared goal, difficult and awkward.

Irandoust and Benaskeur (2008), in presenting a typology of multiorganizational coalitions, defined what they called **multiorganizational structures (MOS)** simply as "new organizations or arrangements that result from the partnership of two or more organizations" (p. 1). Their typology provides six features that distinguish MOS:

- ▶ **Purpose of partnership.** The purpose of partnership is the reason for the existence of the group. What will be achieved (or is hoped to be achieved) by its formation? The purpose of the group sets the tone for all other features of the MOS.

- ▶ **Functioning mechanism.** A functioning mechanism outlines the way the MOS interacts with the host organizations. Most often, a new MOS is set up as a separate entity to which the host organizations designate representatives. Those representatives engage each other and report back to their host organizations. Over the life of the MOS, a feedback loop exists among the MOS and the host organizations. Partner organizations may also communicate directly with each other without setting up separate working groups, particularly if the purpose is simply information sharing. However, when discussion and decisions are required, inevitably separate groups are formed.

- ▶ **Collaborative processes.** The style of collaboration that might exist in an MOS ranges from information sharing to the coordination of activities (e.g., offering joint programs) to resource sharing. Of course, an arrangement among the host organizations could witness two or all of these collaboration types happening in combination as part of the group's mandate.

- ▶ **Dynamics of membership.** This spells out the conditions of membership (e.g., open to all interested parties, appointed by someone in authority, or invited by founding members). Membership is largely influenced by the purpose of the MOS.

- ▶ **Life span.** The life span of an MOS may be long term or short term. If the goals are concrete and readily attainable, the MOS will most likely be a short-term entity. On the other hand, if the issues to be addressed are complex, involve multiple stakeholders with divergent initial agendas, or are only vaguely definable, the group may require a more permanent status.

▶ **Control architecture.** Control architecture refers to how the MOS operates in terms of control and accountability. Is the structure hierarchical or heterarchical? The former indicates a classic model of control as centralized and top-down, whereas the latter implies an egalitarian coalition of equals. Heterarchical models are more common in multiorganizational groups that form among industry peers or in situations in which all voices are considered equally important. Figure 13.1 illustrates models of hierarchical and heterarchical structures.

Now that we have a basic understanding of multiorganizational groups and their structures, a question that still needs an answer is, What are they? The response arises from an understanding of their benefits and successes—in other words, what they are capable of doing, and what they have done, for others.

Benefits and Successes of Multiorganizational Groups

The benefits of multiorganizational collaboration are very much aligned with the gestalt perspective that the whole is greater than the sum of its parts. The reasons organizations engage other organizations in cooperative arrangements is that the goal can be reached—or at least realized more fully—if a collaborative effort is mobilized. The benefits of collaboration among organizations are often reported as synergy, enhanced learning and problem solving, the formation of a consensus on potentially divisive issues (i.e., inclusivity in decision making), decreased costs as a result of resource pooling, and heightened legitimacy for agreements reached.

There are good reasons for the proliferation of multiorganizational collaborations. Examples abound in which the decision making that arises from an earnest collaboration has benefitted the groups involved as well as society at large. The Mackenzie Valley Pipeline Inquiry, a landmark environmental impact assessment in northern Canada in the 1970s, sought input from a diverse range of stakeholders. The commission's review of the proposed project, headed by Justice Thomas Berger, is still held up as one of the most comprehensive, and the decision rendered is widely regarded as one of the wisest made in the context of environmental impact assessments. That process was under national scrutiny and proved to be a watershed event for future assessments of projects with potential environmental effects. The outcome was a decision in 1977 to impose a 10-year moratorium on pipeline development in the far north. Thirty-five years later, experts agree that the original decision to defer development until critical issues in natural and cultural sustainability could be addressed was indeed sound.

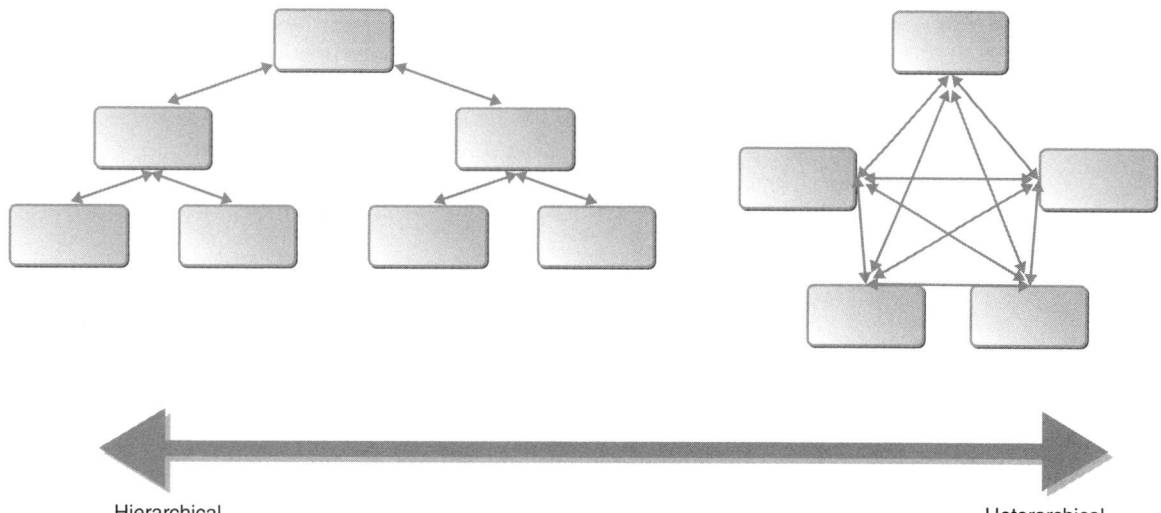

Hierarchical

Heterarchical

Figure 13.1 Sample models of hierarchical and heterarchical structures.

From business initiatives to public roundtables to improved health care standards to land use policy development, the momentum for multiorganizational collaboration builds steadily as the benefits and successes of these efforts are realized. However, success tends to also breed increased expectations. Although there have undoubtedly been positive results, both large and small, there is a need for caution in the implementation of multiorganizational collaborative groups and in what we should expect from them.

Dangers and Failures of Multiorganizational Groups

The benefits of multiorganizational groups are not always equal, and the result may not even benefit all members. Trust among members is not a given, even when organizations are willing participants, and in fact, at times not all members participate for the right reasons. Recently, researchers have concluded that unless clear collaborative outcomes and processes can be envisioned and articulated, practitioners should steer clear of these types of endeavors (Huxham, 2003; McGuire, 2006).

Limited successes and outright failures are more common than the literature tends to acknowledge (McGuire, 2006), and they can lead to greater negative outcomes than if collaboration had not been attempted in the first place. In an analysis of how multiorganizational groups negotiate their purposes, Eden and Huxham (2001) identified behaviors that were destructive to progress, both intentional (e.g., spying while withholding information or resources) and unintentional (e.g., bonding and creating agreement within the group even though the agreement is counter to the interests of the member's host organization). In the latter example, the collaborative group member may well have intended to make the process work, but in poorly representing his own organization, trust between the host organization and the collaborative group was eroded, eventually undermining the overall effort.

A case study in British Columbia involved a roundtable of representatives from 14 sectors of the public and private domains. Although the provincial government initiated the formation of the multistakeholder group that was to advise the government on land use policy of protected lands, it was not able to provide critical information that the group needed to address its mandate. This contributed to the creation of confusion and power plays to fill in the gaps (Wilson, Roseland, & Day, 1996). Factions developed within the group, and one of the more powerful member organizations pressured another to adopt a particular position. In the end, competing reports were submitted to the commission overseeing the process, one of which was never agreed to by the group as a whole.

Clearly, in some instances more damage than good can be done by collaborative groups when they are not prepared for the challenges of managing people who represent divergent interests and wildly different work cultures, some of whom may have grandiose expectations despite limited resources. Following are common reasons for the failure of collaborative groups:

▶ Lack of agreement on the purpose of the group (i.e., its reason for existing)

▶ Insufficient buy-in or support from group members, host organizations, or an initiating authority

▶ Inappropriate expectations

▶ Too many or too few members or organizations represented

▶ Complex issues to be resolved with inadequate time or resources, or both

▶ Lack of agreement on decision-making processes

Suggestions for Professionals in the Field

Despite the dangers embedded in multiorganizational collaboration, there are two reasons to learn how to work with them. First, the practice is ubiquitous. Collaborative groups are becoming common enough among leisure services providers that it is entirely likely that you will be part of one, whether you want to be or not. Second, there are significant benefits to pooling diverse talents. When they operate well, these groups can and do produce wonderful results.

Eden and Huxham (2001) suggested that success is more often experienced by collaborative groups that "have small numbers (two or three) of member organizations, a well defined goal and a high level of resource" (p. 385). Given this observation, one piece of advice would be to ask if it's reasonable for your group to mirror these conditions. However, streamlining the numbers, goal, and process to manageable levels is not always possible. Besides, these groups often form precisely *because* the path to success is not always clear. Even though there is no universally appropriate recipe for success (each group and each situation is unique), the trick is to find the right approach. Here are some principles to follow that will help:

▶ **Negotiate a solid understanding of purpose.** It is difficult to overemphasize the importance of this principle. Without knowing the reason for your group's existence, it is quite possible that you will feel directionless and disconnected as a group. Even if you believe the purpose is straightforward or self-evident, take the time to articulate it and get agreement from all group members. Make sure this is written down and shared with everyone. Encourage (or even require) all members to take the purpose statement back to their host organizations for comment and ratification if needed. This step will serve you well as your group moves on to more practical tasks. It provides a touchstone to return to in difficult or tense conversations, and it makes it less likely that someone or a small group within the larger coalition will be able to divert the group's purpose at a later point. During the process of setting out your group's purpose, solicit contributions from everyone. Impress upon your new group members the value of combining everyone's visions. To create a truly inclusive group with a purpose that everyone can support (as well as their host organizations), you need to ensure that all voices are heard.

▶ **Understand your control architecture.** What powers do you have as individuals and as a group? Will all decisions your group reaches have to be independently approved by the host organizations? Are you an advisory or a decision-making body? How much autonomy and flexibility exists? It may be useful to sketch out a model or diagram that visually describes your relationship with each other and the group's relationship with the host organizations. How will you make decisions within the group? In other words, what is the *internal* structure of your *external* group? Will you operate using consensus, or will you vote? If you vote, will all organizations commit to the outcome? If not, you will need to revisit your architecture.

▶ **Develop a plan.** Outline the tasks you will need to tackle to accomplish your primary goal(s). In addition to the tasks you identify as a group, make a list of resources that you anticipate needing. Who—or what entity—will supply those resources? With this knowledge, set out a rough time line for accomplishing each task and then your final goal(s). Make sure your group's estimates are reasonable; avoid the temptation to be overly optimistic in your initial enthusiasm. Remember that tasks usually take more time than you originally estimated. Spell out individual roles and subgroup divisions if you anticipate splitting up some of the work.

▶ **Develop a communication plan.** A communication plan may be controversial because it asks members to agree on how to communicate with each other during the life of the group. You will need to use your judgment when deciding how far to push for this component. Nonetheless, even sketching out some basic principles of open, honest, and transparent communication can help. If there is a willingness among group members, further development is advisable. Agreements on what constitutes acceptable and unacceptable communication, appropriate reactions to ideas presented by members, and how to handle tense discussions can be helpful in a communication plan. More detailed strategies can be found within this text or in other reputable sources. Do a little reading before you meet with your group, and decide when it might be appropriate to broach the topic. In some extreme cases, it may be advisable to develop a communication contract, a document that all members sign to indicate their commitment to certain communication behaviors.

Summary

External leadership is a form of leadership practiced by those outside of traditional organizations. External leaders are characterized as either community or organizational leaders. Community leaders often take part in grassroots advocacy to improve their local communities and the quality of life of their citizens. External organizational leaders work to bring together disparate organizations with their diverse interests, agendas, and organizational cultures. As a result of massive and compelling change in our communities and in our world, external leaders are sometimes recruited without much knowledge of the political environments in which they will be working. They are called to serve, not because of their formal ranking and power in the community or organization, but because of their attention to needs requiring addressing in their communities or professions.

This chapter examined the issue of authority in public, nonprofit, and private organizations, as well as standards of compliance, charter-based organizations, stewardship organizations, and informal volunteer groups. Without an understanding of authority, external community leaders are powerless in their quest to improve community well-being and public service. In addition, external organizational leaders must understand the complex interactions that occur in multiorganizational groups.

The decisions—both formal and informal—of external leaders influence public policy and serve the public good. External leadership is a powerful force in our communities and professions because of the scope of these decisions.

Questions for Reflection and Discussion

1. What skills, knowledge, and abilities are necessary for becoming an effective external community leader?

2. What is the differences between internal and external leaders?

3. Why is it important for external community leaders to understand agency authority?

4. What is the significance of grassroots advocacty to external community leadership?

5. Some say that without external leaders, managers would be unable to perform the functions of their agencies. Do you agree or disagree? Why?

6. Why do mission-based organizations such as the American Red Cross depend on the skill sets of external volunteer leaders?

7. Why is it important to define the policy-making authority of an organization?

8. Think about a situation in which you have worked with a diverse group of people to meet a common goal. What event or events led to the success or failure of the group? Why?

9. What types of people become external community leaders?

Key Terms and Definitions

advisory committee (or ad hoc/task force committee)—Usually an appointed group of citizens that is authorized to advise a formal policy organization. Advisory groups do not have formal authority; however, they can meet in public, collect information and data, and advise or make recommendations to the group who authorized them. Sometimes referred to as an ad hoc committee.

articles of incorporation—These are the primary rules that govern the management of a corporation. These are kept on file in the corporations' respective states.

claims—The vested interests made by stakeholders.

community stakeholders—Community members or organizations having a vested interest or "stake" in a community issue.

Congressional Charter—A law passed by the U.S. Congress that grants authority to a group's mission and activities. The American Red Cross received a charter from the U.S. Congress.

empowerment—The granting of formal authority to act.

external community leadership—Lay community people, often volunteers, who become involved out of a desire to improve their communities.

external leadership—Behaviors employed to reach goals when multiple individuals or agencies (or both) come together around an issue.

external organizational leadership—Organization practitioners who professionally work for or volunteer for a specific organization and find themselves working with representatives of other organizations in the pursuit of community goals.

formal agency authority—Legal basis and formal written documentation that identifies the purpose and responsibilities of the agency or organization and its makeup and responsibilities.

foundations—501-c-3 or 6 non-profit, charitable, or tax-exempt organizations approved under IRS guidelines and rules.

friends groups—Nonprofit groups formed to provide essential community functions.

multiorganizational structures (MOS)—New organizations or arrangements that result from the partnership of two or more organizations.

open public meeting—A meeting open to the public that is based on clearly defined rules and procedures approved by each state. Such meetings also describe parliamentary procedures, conflicts of interests, and ethics guidelines.

stakeholders—These are members of an advisory committee who have claims, or vested interests.

stewardship—Responsibility to take care of a feature or service owned by the public or government. In this chapter, stewardship is described in environmental and ethical contexts.

watchdog group—Organized around specific causes or issues, this is an external community-based advocacy group that influences the public policy process.

Bibliography

AARPA (n.d.). Retrieved from: www.aapra.org/pugsley-bios/elizabeth-betsy-barlow-rogers.

Eden, C. & Huxham, C. (2001). The negotiation of purpose in multi-organizational collaborative groups. *Journal of Management Studies, 38* (3), 373-391.

Huxham, C. (2003). Theorizing collaboration practice. *Public Management Review, 5* (3): 401-423.

International Red Cross and Red Crescent. Retrieved from http://en.wikipedia.org/wiki/International_Red_Cross_and_Red_Crescent_Movement

Irandoust, H. & Benaskeur, A.R. (2008). Multi-organizational structures. Association for the Advancement of Artificial Intelligence, www.aaai.org.

McGuire, M. (2006). Collaborative public management: Assessing what we know and how we know it. *Public Administration Review,* Special Issue (December), 33-43.

Redcross.org. Retrieved from www.redcross.org/about-us/history/federal-charter#early-organization

Wilson, A., Roseland, M. & Day, J.C. (1996). Shared decision-making and public land planning: An evaluation of the Vancouver Island Regional CORE process. *Environments, 23* (2), 69-86.

Chapter 14

Leading in the Profession

Jane H. Adams and Elaine Schilling

> " *It is not the strongest of the species that survive, nor the most intelligent, but the one most responsive to change.* "
>
> —Author unknown

lice is a bit worried. As the new director of parks and recreation for the town of Happenstance, she is the new kid on the block; she was specifically hired to move the department into the 21st century. She is meeting all the department staff two days from now. The team has been together for many years; some even grew up in the department having attended day camps and worked part-time in the department during college. They were not in the recent meeting she had with the city manager, who raised several issues he wanted addressed or changed: the department's strategy to go it alone when addressing community-wide issues; the slow adoption of technology; no training in place to prepare new leaders; and an overall unwillingness to address the changing needs of the community.

As a member of both her state and national park and recreation associations, Alice is familiar with their resources. She has attended recent workshops on trends and she feels well connected with peers across the county, yet she is unsure about whether her leadership style will be accepted and how to introduce the changes desired by the city manager. She has heard that her style is different from that of her predecessor, but she has not been told in what way. Well, worried or not, the clock on her desk says get to work. It is time to prepare for the meeting with the team.

Learning Outcomes

At the conclusion of this chapter, students will be able to:

▶ Discuss strategies for leading the park and recreation profession into the future.

▶ Identify macro trends and explain their relationships to the parks and recreation profession.

▶ Describe two competencies essential for leading in the park and recreation profession: leading change and strategic thinking.

Binoculars are important if you are a birder, photographer, forest ranger, police officer, or zoologist because they allow you to see things that are far away in greater detail. They even bring into focus things you might completely miss with the naked eye. Think how exciting it would be if you, as a parks and recreation leader, were given a pair of binoculars that allowed you to see with 100 percent accuracy the future of the profession. With these parks and recreation "binos," you would have a clear vision of what will be important, who you will need to work with, who you will need to influence, and who will be the best people to hire. Your role as a leader would be easier knowing these things. Regretfully, such binos do not exist. However, with a clear understanding of the leader's role and the competencies needed for the future, you can learn how to create a vision, communicate that vision, lead others, and identify trends that will help you make decisions.

Leaders must be comfortable with change. Comfort, in this discussion, is not about ease but about accepting change. When you are comfortable with change, you won't panic when something does not happen exactly as planned or even hoped. Change is inevitable regardless of your position within a park and recreation agency. When you lead, you must learn to accept the inevitability of change and learn how to modify your goals, expectations, and outcomes. In one of the numerous books on understanding change, *Who Moved My Cheese* (1998), Spencer Johnson, introduces four characters: two mice named Sniff and Scurry and two "little people," Hem and Haw, who are all confronted with the need to change. How the characters address change mirrors what many of us do in the same circumstance: we do not pay attention to the signs indicating that change is coming; we refuse to acknowledge change even when confronted with it; we respond in our own ways to change; and if we see that embracing change is positive, we adapt and learn to "move the cheese".

In this chapter you will work alongside Alice, a new park and recreation director. This is Alice's first job as a director, and although she feels competent as a leader, she is nervous about the unknowns awaiting her. You will work with Alice as she prepares for her first meeting with her new team. You will examine trends that Alice believes are affecting the park and recreation field, look at the leadership traits and skills Alice brings to her

planning, and consider your own viewpoint on the leadership skills that are critical for the future of the profession.

Macro Trends Affecting Parks and Recreation

Our environment changes every day as a result of new information, fads and trends, new gadgets or technology, new leaders, and even new customers. To be successful in the future, you must become a savvy **trend watcher**; you must be able to communicate effectively, network in your community, and create and sustain partnerships (across disciplines and agencies).

Trend watching must be undertaken with open eyes and ears and an open mind-set. What may be viewed as a trend may in fact be a fad. Trends in this context are large influences that affect how we live, what we buy, and how and where we spend our time. Fads are things that are enthusiastically embraced by many but are short-lived. Examples of fads are mini-skirts, skinny ties, and the grapefruit diet. A trend, on the other hand, is a general tendency, movement, or direction that affects consumers' behaviors. A singer with one hit may be viewed as a fad, whereas rap started a trend in music.

Inactivity is a national trend in the United States; it is not a fad. In California, as an example, the Department of Public Health stated in 2010 that obesity rates had tripled among children and adolescents in the past 30 years and had remained high as more than 30 percent of California's low-income children were overweight or obese in that year. An outcome of inactivity is obesity and its subsequent health-related issues such as high blood pressure, heart disease, diabetes, asthma, and cancers. The business costs associated with obesity are as high as $147 billion annually (Finkelstein et al., 2009).

Researchers in both parks and recreation and public health are recognizing and identifying ways the built environment and programs affect people's health. Organizations such as the Robert Wood Johnson Active Living Research Center (http://activelivingresearch.org), the National Recreation and Park Association (www.nrpa.org), the Institute of Medicine (www.iom.edu), and the Prevention Institute (www.preventioninstitute.org) provide tools and resources the profession can use. In 2001 the California Park & Recreation Society (www.cprs.org) published one of the first strategy papers to focus on the role of parks and recreation in promoting health and wellness, *Leading to Promote Health & Wellness* (California Park & Recreation Society, 2001). Leaders in the parks and recreation profession must be knowledgeable about preventable diseases associated with obesity because the programs, services, parks, and facilities they manage can play a major role in addressing and even reversing this trend.

Sports and outdoor recreation are venues in which youth can be active. What are the trends in youth involvement in sports and outdoor recreation? The Outdoor Foundation, supported by the Outdoor Industry Association (n.d.), has published annual outdoor recreation participation reports since 2007 (http://outdoorfoundation.org/research.participation.html). These reports provide valuable insights into trends in recreation participation across the country and can help parks and recreation professionals understand the youth and outdoor markets. Figure 14.1 offers some trend-monitoring guidelines to use in your own agency.

Alice needs to capture all the thoughts that are running through her head. She pulls out a piece of paper and writes three columns: my thoughts, staff agenda items, and to-do items.

Alice watches (or studies) trends to see, for example, how people use their leisure time, what they buy, what events they attend, and what activities their children are involved in. She always attends trend sessions held at parks and recreation conferences because these give her insights into what is happening across the county. She believes these help her in discussions with her supervisor and her staff about current programs, special events, and when activities should be scheduled. Alice considers creating a trends task force with her staff so they can all become trend watchers. She knows she needs to be clear about the purpose of a trends task force, and she wants to energize her staff so that the research is exciting.

Alice makes the following short list of the initial tasks of the trends task force:

▶ Identify why we are doing the trends research.

▶ Identify where we could go to spot trends (e.g., blogs, e-newsletters, websites, magazines, authors).

▶ Decide what types of trends we will watch: consumer, children, seniors, physical activity, adult learning, the environment—the list is endless, but specifics are important.

▶ Give the task force a name.

▶ Decide how often to meet or make assignments.

Trend watching can be overwhelming in scope and complexity. Any one trend can have one or two anti-trends working against it. The general categories are **macro trends**, **consumer trends**, and **industry trends**. Industry trends, which are at the mercy of consumer and macro trends, can be followed by belonging to national or state professional organizations, reading industry publications, attending conferences, and surfing the Internet. Consumer trends can be followed using some of the resources listed at the end of the chapter. This chapter briefly describes three macro trends and their possible implications for the field of parks and recreation. The book *Creating Community in the 21st Century: An Action Plan for Parks & Recreation* (Adams, 2008) identified a number of trends and opportunities associated with them; three are updated and shared in this chapter.

Demographic Trends

Beginning January 1, 2011, American baby boomers (75 to 80 million born between the years of 1946 and 1964) started to turn age 65. Every day for the next 19 years, about 10,000 more boomers will cross that threshold. This generation of people will redefine the term *old* as they seek activity and wellness in today's economy. Many boomers will also hang on to their jobs, primarily as a way to satisfy the need for health benefits and to combat a decline in retirement benefits. Some communities are changing the names of their senior centers to "adult centers" or even the generic "community centers" because boomers do not want to be associated with the term *senior* (that phrase is for their parents—not them!).

Adults over 65 years of age constitute the fastest-growing age segment in the United States. In 2012, the U.S. Census Bureau stated that by 2060 there will be 92.5 million Americans over the age of 65—this is more than double this group's projected population of 40.2 million in 2010 (U.S. Census Bureau, 2012). Meanwhile, the majority of people aged 65 and older are living with a spouse or alone in their homes (National Aging in Place Council, n.d.). The National Aging in Place Council defines *aging in place* as seniors living in a place of their choice as they age. Many seniors wish to remain

Studying trends can be a full-time job, but it does not have to be. Here are ideas for starting your own trend-watching group from trendwatching.com:

- Know why you are trend watching. Trend watching is one way to gain inspiration, new ideas, programs, and services for (and with) your customers. Trend watching is about what is happening now, the major and the minor. Not everything applies to everyone, and each trend has its anti-trend (that doesn't "cash it out").

- Have a point of view about the world around you. Be curious and open-minded. Observe without judging. Look cross industry (e.g., read a random magazine each week, visit a new blog). Ask questions. Get rid of negativity, taboos, and prejudices. Challenge your own thinking.

- Identify places to spot trends such as websites, blogs, books, Google alerts, colleagues, competitors, universities, researchers, RSS feeds, and trend-watching firms.

- Create a common language for naming trends (if you find them). This will help your group refer to a project or a trend quickly. Faith Popcorn (one of the first trend watchers) named trends by choosing two or three words that described what she was seeing and then mixing them up. As an example, one trend is called transumers

(consumers in transition at airports). This was coined by Fitch, a global design and business company that helps companies sell their products. They noted that people at airports buy things while in transit (especially during "happy hour"). One option that has emerged as a result of identifying this trend is being able to buy a book at one airport and return it at another and get some of the purchase price back. [*Source:* www.trendwatching.com. Visit to subscribe to their free monthly trend briefing.]

- Trend watching can be intimidating both from a time and an expertise perspective. Try giving your group a fun or inviting name such as "P & R Watchers, Wanderers, and Wonderers."

- Set up weekly or monthly sessions. Find a location, provide refreshments, and distribute your findings, notes, etc., widely. Ask one person to talk for 20 minutes about a trend or finding; talk as a group for 30 minutes about what is driving this trend, and then spend 30 minutes talking about its impact on your agency or the profession.

What could you do with the transumer trend in your agency? What about a coffee cart where parents pick up their children from preschool or classes? What about a T-shirt exchange at a teen center?

Figure 14.1   Being a student of trends.

Reprinted, by permission, from Timothy Pitts. Available: www.trendwatching.com.

in their homes or downsize to smaller residences in the same community. Many trend watchers expect new groups of aging adults to emerge, such as extroverts with substantial incomes and good health who can be active and engaged and will not use services provided by local park and recreation agencies. Those with health issues, limited family members or friends, and limited incomes will likely access the health, wellness, nutrition, and financial services often offered at community senior centers.

The definition of the term *child* is also changing as children influence more of a family's decision making. Children may be viewed as older because of their responsibilities of caring for younger siblings or themselves as a result of working parents and caregivers. Young adults are slower to leave their parent(s) or caregiver(s) because of economic

issues, and others return home after leaving initially. The Annie E. Casey Foundation (2010) "Kids Count" report measured the well-being of children and highlighted several issues that had improved since 2000. Improvements were seen in infant mortality rate (decrease of 3 percent), child death rate (decrease of 14 percent), and teen birth rate (decrease of 10 percent). However, also noted were an increase in the number of children living in poverty, from 18 percent in 2008 to 24 percent in 2012, and an increase of 3 percent in the number of children living in single-parent families (Kids Count Data Center, 2014).

Ethnically, the United States is changing. According to the U.S. Census Bureau (2012), the population as a whole will become a plurality nation, with the non-Hispanic white population remaining the largest group, although no group in the majority.

© Human Kinetics

Meeting the needs of aging baby boomers will be a significant challenge for park and recreation organizations in developed countries in the 21st century.

▶ The non-Hispanic white population will peak in 2024, and unlike other population groups, is expected to slowly decrease.

▶ The Hispanic population is expected to more than double; by the end of 2060 nearly one in three U.S. residents will be Hispanic.

▶ The Asian population is projected to nearly double; this group's population will increase from 5.1 percent to 8.2 percent.

▶ The United States is projected to be a majority-minority nation for the first time by 2043, meaning no one group will make a majority.

▶ The black population is projected to increase, raising its share of the total population to 14.7 percent by 2060.

▶ In 2056, those aged 65 and older will outnumber the young (under age 18).

Certain areas of the United States are projected to grow in population more than others. Certain states in the Northeast have lost congressional representation, whereas states in the West are increasing in population. Currently, Americans are clustered in large urban centers close to coastlines or large bodies of water. Finding open space to accommodate growing populations will be challenging for these large urban areas.

Alice begins writing questions to determine who lives in the community. She quickly realizes that she needs to meet with other organizations, particularly those providing services to children, youth, and seniors. She writes these questions:

▶ Who will likely be consumers of the city's recreation programs in the next three to five years?

▶ Will they be younger, older, more diverse, active, inactive, family groups, singles? Are there any shifts in the diversity of the community? Is the number of residents over the age of 55 increasing or decreasing? Are there fewer or more children under the age of 12? Are there more Hispanic or Asian residents now than there were five years ago? Has the average household income risen or fallen? How many school districts are in the city—one or several? Who are the school superintendent(s)? What demographic changes have schools seen in the past five years, and what are they projecting for the next five years?

▶ What other youth-based organizations are in town, and what do they think? What programs and services are we offering to combat the general high level of inactivity among our residents? What is the obesity level in the community? Is it rising or falling? What is the obesity level of children in the school district(s)? Where can I find data on these issues?

▶ What are my staff members seeing in regard to participation in our youth programs? Are some programs being cancelled? Where are the gaps? Are there competing programs? Is there an age group no one is addressing? Who can the department partner with to maximize our resources and expand our reach?

▶ How many boomers live in the community? How many of them are beginning to turn 65? Does the department know the leisure interests of the community's boomers? Will they participate in our senior programs? If no, what needs to change to attract them? What other private or public providers in the community are offering recreation programs to boomers? Are there any designated senior neighborhoods or residential neighborhoods?

▶ What role can the department play in ensuring that adults over 65 remain in their homes and connected to the community? Should we expect an increase in attendance at the senior center? Should we rename the facility? Do our current programs and services meet the needs of our current *and* projected users?

▶ What values and expectations do Hispanic and Asian residents have about open space, parks, and recreation programs? Are they different from those of our Caucasian residents? Do our current parks and their amenities attract a culturally diverse group of users? Are there community organizations focused on those populations? Is there an Asian or Hispanic chamber of commerce? Where can I go to get more information on this?

Alice could do all this research by herself, but she needs her team to be involved. After all, they likely have varied interests because they read different magazines, blogs, and newspapers; watch different TV shows; and know different people in the community. She decides to introduce the trend-watching concept at her second staff meeting.

Using the questions she wrote down, Alice starts to make a plan for exploring demographic trends in her community. First, she looks at her notes (see figure 14.2; Alice uses three columns—My thoughts, Staff agenda items, and To-do items—for future reference because she has a lot to remember). Then, Alice pores over census data she gathered from the U.S. Census website. Looking at registration data, she identifies several zip codes in the community and starts pulling down the charts.

Alice notices that in the last 10 years there has been an increase in the number of adults over the age of 65 who live alone. She knows that fire personnel often are first responders to calls for help. She makes a note to talk to the fire department about any changes in the frequency of calls from homes occupied by adults over 65. Maybe they can give her insights into the issues facing that segment of the community. She needs to talk to staff about any changes they are noticing. Are the seniors who are coming to programs "elder seniors" or "boomer seniors"? She remembers from her previous position that boomer seniors did not come to the senior center.

She also makes a note to ask whether the school district has any data on the conditions of children. She wonders who else is caring for school-age children while their parents are working. She adds to the meeting agenda "Identification of resident types." She wants staff members to share their impressions of who their program participants are.

Technological Trends

According to the Pew Research Center (2010), Internet usage is up. Almost 80 percent of adults age 18 and over, both men and women, used the Internet in 2010. As shown in table 14.1, this almost doubled between 2000 and 2010. Older Americans are staking their online presence as well. Of adults ages 70 to 75, close to half (45 percent) now use the Internet. Among all adults age 65 and older, 41 percent go online. Income and education are strongly related to Internet penetration. Nearly all high-income (94 percent) and college-educated Americans (95 percent) are online, whereas only 57 percent of Americans earning less than $30,000 and roughly a third of those with less than a high school education use the Internet.

My thoughts	Staff agenda items
Look at census data for the community to see if there are any demographic trends.	What data are available on current program participants?
How adept is the department with social marketing? How comfortable is staff using computers?	What data are available on use of online registration versus in office or mail registration?
	Define social marketing and explain how to use it.
How can I informally assess staff's computer and mobile photo skills?	**To-do items**
	Schedule a meeting with the fire department to discuss incidents involving seniors at their homes.
	Register for a department class online.
	Schedule a meeting with IT department.

Figure 14.2 Alice's worksheet: demographic trends.

Paying attention to the household incomes of Internet users will be important to park and recreation agencies, which are increasingly relying on Internet access to register participants, reserve facilities, and promote activities and programs. Table 14.1 shows the steep increase in people who are connected wirelessly via smartphone or computers (0 percent in 2000 to close to 60 percent in 10 short years) as well as a dramatic increase in the use of social networking sites. The percentage of people with Internet access in their homes has also skyrocketed: more than 60 percent of people now have broadband service.

The effect of home computer use by children is newly chartered territory for researchers. Investigators have been looking at the effect computers have on children's physical, cognitive, and social development and are seeing both positive and negative effects. Initial research suggested that access to computers increases children's total screen time at the expense of other activities such as play and sports, which may influence the increase in childhood obesity. (Other factors affecting the increase in childhood obesity are the neighborhood in which children live, access to fresh fruits and vegetables, parents' sense of safety in the neighborhood, and access to parks.) Extended computer screen time by children is also resulting in seizures and hand injuries.

The American Academy of Pediatrics advises parents to limit the time their children spend on computers and emphasize activities such as play, sports, and exercise. Children may be spending more time alone (or even playing side by side with friends on computers), thereby reducing the time they spend in groups learning social and group skills. One area of research is the impact of violent computer games on children's behavior in other situations. New generations of computer games are increasingly more aggressive and violent. Teen

Table 14.1 Technological Trends in the United States

Percentage of adults	2000	2010
Using the Internet	46%	79%
With broadband at home	5%	64%
Engaged in social networking	0%	48%
Connected wirelessly	0%	59%

http://www.pewinternet.org/Static-Pages?About-Us/our-Research/Use-Policy.aspx. Reprinted by permission.

girls' use of computers is also increasing. Teen girls like using the Internet for communicating with friends, meeting new people, and joining groups.

The Internet and smartphones have changed how we access and share information. A smartphone is a mobile phone that offers more advanced computing ability and connectivity than a contemporary basic telephone. Smartphone manufacturers are in a race for market share, and the number of applications (apps) for these phones is escalating. In June 2009 there were 50,000 iPhone apps. One year later there were 225,000 apps, and the most recent statistic from January 2013 reveals over 775,000 iPhone apps (Apple Press Info, 2013). According to PC World ("Google, Apple," 2013), the increase in the number of Android apps is equally amazing. In September 2013, Google reported that it hosted 675,000 apps in its store.

How many apps are there for parks and recreation sites? A search of iPhone apps found hundreds that locate things such as RV parks, dog parks, national parks, state parks, amusement parks, hunting and fishing sites, skate parks, and kids play parks. There are apps to find parks, playgrounds, and tennis courts near your current location or where you expect to be. Many of these apps ask users to upload photos of and comment on the site (e.g., cleanliness, amenities). There are also applications for plants, landscaping, pests, turf, water, aquatics, and health care, providing technical advice, resources, and even best practices. The list is overwhelming and growing. Imagine how someone who is not familiar with parks and recreation might feel when confronted with these choices? We can only expect that the list is going to get longer.

Alice considers the trends in technology and can't help but wonder how many of the city's residents have smartphones or Internet access. One of her first assignments is to increase the use of technology in the parks and recreation department. To do this, she needs to know how savvy her staff members are with technology. Once she knows this, she can build a learning plan to bring them all to the same level. She writes four questions in her notes: (1) Who on staff is viewed as a smartphone wiz? (2) Who is on Facebook, Twitter, and LinkedIn? (3) What is the department's overall expertise with technology? and (4) What other city departments are using technology to reach residents?

Smartphones bring enormous amounts of information to our fingertips, and we can use them to communicate enormous amounts of information to others. We can quickly communicate our location, who we are with, and what the place looks like (by taking a picture or a video); post the photo or video on Facebook, Twitter, YouTube, or other sites; and write a review that in all likelihood the manager of that park or facility will never see! This access makes consumers more aware and more likely to communicate dissatisfaction with their experience. The old customer service adage is that unhappy customers tell 19 people that they are dissatisfied. Now with our smartphones we can tell hundreds (possibly thousands) of people that we are unhappy with a store, restaurant, park, or day camp program.

Another important technology trend is social networking, with sites such as Meetup and Yelp. People use Meetup to find others interested in the same sport or hobby by selecting an interest and typing in their zip code. Meetup circumvents having to seek out traditionally organized groups, pay a registration fee, and have a paid leader. People need only a computer to connect with hundreds (or possibly thousands) of individuals or groups in their own communities. Yelp, a social communications site, encourages people to post reviews of restaurants, stores, parks, and programs. Alice makes a note on her pad to go to Meetup.com to find groups that might be using the city's facilities or parks for their activities, such as hiking, tennis, yoga, walking, or canoeing.

In addition to the personal use of computers, technology is advancing how parks and recreation agencies are managed. Information technology can perform six basic tasks or functions:

1. Data collection
2. Communication (moving data from place to place)
3. Processing (transferring data from one form to another)
4. Storage (storing data for future use)
5. Retrieval (recalling data when needed)
6. Output (transforming data to a usable format for planning, evaluating, and forecasting) (Van der Smissen et al., 1999)

Some local park and recreation agencies are building their own apps to provide information to residents and visitors. One example is interactive maps that show where facilities, programs, trails, and so on, are located. Residents can use apps to register for classes; view seasonal brochures; or reserve campsites, picnic sites, or pavilions. One university updates hourly how busy its recreation facility is, which helps users decide when to visit the facility. Agencies can also solicit user feedback about such things as broken sprinkler heads, filled trash receptacles, and dirty restrooms. User comments can help determine the appropriate staffing to ensure that facilities are clean and safe.

Geographic information systems (GIS) can help park and recreation agencies with planning, inventory, scheduling, and user information; building a web presence; or creating presentations and promotions. The application of GIS in the state of California led to the development of GreenInfo Network, a nonprofit, tax-exempt organization that provides GIS and information technology to public organizations and agencies in California and throughout the United States. GreenInfo has developed a site (www.parkinfo.org) to help users find any park or open space in California. It uses 3D Google Earth or Bing to provide bird's-eye views of parks, trails, and open spaces.

The National Recreation and Park Association has introduced PRORAGIS, a national online database and management tool for parks and recreation agencies. Agencies can create accounts and enter data regarding their park acreage, facilities, personnel, budget, programs, and services. This online database provides benchmarking data that agencies can use to compare their performance with that of other agencies in similar population or budget categories.

Registration software allows people to register for classes from the comfort of their homes, during work breaks, or even on their smartphones. This software can also tell the customer whether a particular class if filled and whether there is a waiting list. Software is now used to monitor the moisture in sports fields, on turf, or in landscaped areas. It can be used to turn on or off irrigation systems, sports lights, and security systems, as well as to schedule meetings and assign staff to shifts or locations.

Recreation and park leaders should address the issue of technology by asking themselves the following questions:

▶ Has our agency invested in technology to make the department run efficiently and effectively?

▶ How skilled am I at using social media to inform, promote, and evaluate the agency's parks, facilities, programs, and services? Where can I go to learn what other parks and recreation professionals are doing and discussing?

▶ How can our agency use technology to connect with partners, policy makers, the media, and current and potential users?

▶ What role can the agency play in educating parents or caregivers about technology so they are informed about the drawbacks and positive effects?

As is her usual practice, Alice makes some notes on her pad to assess the department's use of technology (see figure 14.3 for her notes). She was on the department's website prior to the interview so she knows that it uses online registrations, but what other ways does it use technology? How widely is online registration promoted or embraced by users? Is it easy to register? She decides to register for a class so she can see for herself what residents are experiencing online.

Alice believes that social marketing opportunities such as Facebook, Yelp, and Twitter are exciting. She quickly looks up the agency name to see if it has a Facebook page. Regretfully, Alice finds that it doesn't. She wonders whether the city has a policy about social media. Is a Facebook page even allowed? She knows that some cities prohibit it and others embrace it as a means to connect with residents. She makes a mental note to see how many employees bring their mobile phones to the meeting—that might be an indicator. She also makes a note to check with the IT department. Where is the city overall on the IT scale? Alice quickly jots down her thoughts, what she will ask the staff about, and a list of action items to help her better understand how her department and community use technology (see figure 14.3).

Economic Trends

Many countries (e.g., Iceland, Mexico, Greece, Ireland, England, and Portugal) are experiencing a recession not seen since the Great Depression of the 1930s. In the United States, unemployment rates range from 9 to over 14 percent based on the state and even the region within a state. The housing crisis has cut into numerous industries and professions such as banking, mortgage lending, real estate, and construction and has affected tradespeople such as electricians, plumbers, heating and air conditioning specialists, and carpenters. The recession has also hit the public sector because public services are typically supported by a variety of taxes (property, income, sales), and these are not recession proof. The loss of property tax revenues coupled with the decline in sales tax has dealt a double blow to many recreation and park providers. In addition to having less revenue from tax sources, public agencies (state and local) are dealing with rising pension costs (as baby boomers reach retirement age and the value of the pension fund has decreased) and health benefit costs. Additionally, public agencies such as cities, counties, special districts, schools, and universities are furloughing or laying off part-time and full time staff.

Parks and recreation agencies in the United States, particularly state park systems, are facing dramatically reduced operating budgets. Arizona, New York, Missouri, and California are experiencing budget reductions that have forced the closure of some parks completely, the rolling closures of others, and most important, the halting of the maintenance and rehabilitation of aging facilities. The National Trust for Historic Preservation declared state parks and historic sites the "nation's most endangered historic places" (National Trust for Historic Preservation,

My thoughts	Staff agenda items
• Look at census data for the community to see if there are any demographic trends. • How adept is the department with social marketing? How comfortable are staff members with using computers? • How can I informally assess the staff's computer skills? Mobile phone skills?	What data are available on current program participants? What data are available on the use of online registration versus in-office or mail registration? Social marketing—what is it? How can we use it?
	To-do items
	• Schedule a meeting with the fire department to discuss incidents involving seniors at their homes. • Register for a department class online. • Schedule a meeting with the IT department.

Figure 14.3 Alice's worksheet: technological trends.

Leisure Leaders

Tom Hellmann

MY PREPARATION

- BS in recreation administration (emphasis in program management)—California State University, Sacramento
- National Recreation and Park Association (NRPA): certified park and recreation professional
- American Red Cross instructor trainer: Lifeguarding/CPR/AED/First Aid
- American Red Cross instructor: Bloodborne Pathogens, Oxygen Administration, Title 22 First Aid for Public Safety Personnel
- National Recreation and Park Association: Aquatic Facility Operator
- American Swim Coaches Association: Level II swimming and water polo coach
- Aquatics International: Next Generation Power 25 honoree, 2012
- California Park & Recreation Society (CPRS) Citation of Merit Professional Award, 2012
- CPRS District 2 J.R. Needy Professional Award, 2011
- Jeff Ellis & Associate International Aquatic Safety Gold Award, 2007
- CPRS Award of Achievement, 2002 and 2003
- California Park & Recreation Society
  - Aquatic Section
  - Administrators Section
- California Park & Recreation Society Aquatic Section president, 2011-2012
- California Park & Recreation Society, State Board of Directors, 2012-2014
- California Park & Recreation Society District 2 president, 2013-2014
- American Red Cross
  - Instructor Trainer: Lifeguarding/CPR/AED/First Aid
  - Instructor: Bloodborne Pathogens; Oxygen Administration; Title 22 First Aid for Public Safety Personnel
- Northern California Golf Association

Photo courtesy of Cosumnes Community Services District.

MY CAREER

The vision of the Cosumnes Community Services District, Parks & Recreation Department in Elk Grove, California (located in Sacramento County), is to "design and maintain parks and facilities that meet current and future needs; offering recreational programs that promote health, fun and lifelong learning; and providing exceptional service to our customers." Elk Grove is a diverse community that grew 125 percent from the early 2000s to reach the current population of 162,000. The Cosumnes Community Services District is a special district within the City of Elk Grove with a five-member elected board of directors and over 200 full-time employees in three departments (Parks, Administration, and Fire) that work together to offer all essential services to the community.

As recreation supervisor, I create a safe and fun environment in which youth, adults, and families can experience aquatic play and participate in learn-to-swim, fitness, and educational opportunities. I safely operate facilities in excess of $15 million with a $2 million program and facility budget. I offer employment to high school and college–age youth; the district is the largest employer of youth in Elk Grove. By adhering to county, state, and federal laws, I ensure the safety of staff, participants, and the facility.

My first job was as a lifeguard at age 15 at the Pleasant Hill Recreation & Park District (CA), where I grew up. I started swimming competitively at age

6, and the head swim coach was also the aquatic supervisor for the district. I was recruited at 15 to work as a lifeguard and swim instructor and did so for nine years—through high school and college.

When I realized that I could make aquatics a career, I decided to get a degree in recreation administration. I had a terrific professor at CSU Sacramento, Judy Quattrin, who pushed me to be the best I could be and helped pave the way for my first full-time job as a recreation supervisor just 10 months after graduation. I have had the pleasure of working for three special districts in Northern California ranging in population from 42,000 to 162,000, and every year I believe that I am becoming a stronger professional through my involvement in the California Park & Recreation Society (CPRS) and the industry.

I really enjoy my involvement as a CPRS leader at the district and section levels and aspire to serve on the state board. I have been a speaker at the CPRS annual conference for the past six years, and have also spoken nationally at the National Recreation and Park Association (NRPA) Congress for Parks & Recreation. I believe that I have made an impact on the park profession at a statewide level through my involvement and I enjoy the opportunity to enhance the profession and shape it for the future. I am a doer and want to be at the front leading others toward change that positively affects the profession and classifies parks and recreation as an essential service in every community. Simply put, I cannot imagine a community without access to local parks, athletic fields, swimming pools, recreation centers, youth classes, teen classes, and adult classes, to name just some of the things this field offers.

Leading from the front can be challenging when people do not agree with your views of the profession. Not everyone wants the load of ambassador of change on their shoulders. I grew up with a strong team sense, culled from playing many team sports at De La Salle High School in Concord, California. I learned the importance of being part of a strong, cohesive team and developed a strong sense of leadership that I use today to inspire and energize others.

Working for a municipal government has many good qualities and some that I have learned to understand and accept. The work I do enhances the lives of local families, and the best part of my job is seeing the smiles and laughter of par-ticipants visiting the complex. There is no better sign of a job well done than a smile. I am also rewarded by working with an awesome staff. I have had the privilege of working with hundreds of youth over my career, and many have moved on to professional careers of their own. Many have thanked me for the opportunity, training, and skills I provided that prepared them for their jobs. I feel like a school teacher as I see all those young adults mature into healthy and positive people who are making their profession better.

Unfortunately, the few things that can make my job stressful are mostly things that are out of my control. My creativity and imagination are often halted as a result of budgetary constraints. Currently, our profession is battling a difficult recession and tough economic times that can be draining and a challenge to overcome. I try hard not to let this negatively affect me. I believe that the economy will change, and I have to be prepared for this change so I can take full advantage of it immediately. I strive to view life through a "glass half full" rather than a "glass half empty" lens.

MY ADVICE TO YOU

I did not imagine that I would be where I am now when I was in college. So many opportunities presented themselves once I got into the profession, and I am extremely fortunate to have had them. I encourage you to recognize opportunities that arise and to run with them. College will give you the fundamental educational experience you need to be a recreation and parks professional, but you will need to continue your learning as a professional and search for opportunities that will enhance your skills and networks. I strongly believe that you get out of something what you put into it, and that you have a choice. You can do the minimum amount of work, or you can strive for excellence and celebrate working in a way that will forever enhance everyone you came in contact with. I am grateful that my involvement in CPRS has given me the opportunity to affect so many people.

I have the opportunity to do extraordinary things every day. The only thing that holds me back is my own level of creativity and drive. Following every feel-good moment I have, I try to identify why I felt so good. I then challenge myself to duplicate that feeling and celebrate the little victories to keep myself motivated to continue to lead and create for others.

2010). Proposition 21, a California initiative that sought to increase the vehicle registration license fee by $18 to create a permanent trust fund for state parks, failed to pass in November 2010.

To deal with reduced operating budgets, parks and recreation agencies are instituting new fees, raising existing fees, searching for grants or outside funding, and seeking sponsorships and partnerships. New operational models are needed as the direct provider role of parks and recreation agencies is reduced as a result of staff layoffs, furloughs, and retirements. Following are other roles parks and recreation agencies could consider (Stevens et al., 2010):

▶ Facilitator/broker—The agency provides the facility or space for the program, and another entity provides the direct leadership.

▶ Information/referral—The agency collects information from all the providers in the community and serves as resource central directing users to the appropriate agency or organization.

▶ Advocate—The agency communicates the need for the program and seeks others to provide the service.

In addition to considering new operating models, agencies need to prioritize their funding needs, a process that would involve a variety of stakeholders including employees, policy makers, partners, and the general public. In 2008 the California Park & Recreation Society undertook a public opinion research study to determine what the public valued and saw delivered by local parks and recreation agencies. This research revealed that the public valued certain services over others. The following services received high scores in terms of value and delivery:

▶ Provide places where children are free to play and be active.

▶ Provide parks, facilities, and trails for self-directed exercise and play.

▶ Preserve land in its original, natural state, and protect wildlife to ensure that they are there for future generations.

▶ Provide open spaces (greenbelts, flowers, landscapes) among the housing and commercial areas to beautify the community.

▶ Provide places and activities for children and teens during nonschool hours that are safe, healthy, and fun.

▶ Provide positive, alternative activities, life skill development, and an opportunity to meet role models during nonschool hours.

Tightly coupled with the recession are two general employment trends: (1) baby boomers are retiring and (2) baby boomers are continuing to work as a result of a decline in their retirement funds. As boomers retire, they are leaving a vacuum in agencies that may or may not be filled. The proliferation of layoffs has resulted in many believing that the unwritten agreement of working for one company for an entire career is broken. Remaining employees are nervous often in spite of being told that their jobs are secure. This results in a decline in employee loyalty.

Some American boomers who are retiring may be doing so with rancor. Factors that lead to their uncertain economic future include the uncertainty of Social Security as a stable retirement income, a lack of health care coverage until the age of 65, a lack of retirement savings, and extended longevity. These factors may mean the abandonment of retirement as older adults continue to work part-time, start new careers in which they can direct the amount of time they work, or use sabbaticals for personal or physical renewal.

Recreation and park leaders should address these trends by asking themselves these questions:

▶ How has the recession affected parks and recreation agencies in our region or state? How is employee morale?

▶ What roles should parks and recreation agencies consider in times of economic stress?

▶ How can a parks and recreation agency assess its priorities for funding?

Alice recognizes that taking over a department in tough economic times is very challenging. She knows that decisions will need to be made and that she may not have the historical knowledge to make decisions that will be viewed positively. She wonders what plans have already been approved. Is there a strategic plan? Is there a park master plan? She knows that staff will be watching her every move and decision, and that they will discuss them behind her back. She asks herself several questions, including: How can I make the staff feel comfortable so they can open up to me and share valuable information? She again pulls out her pad and writes down her thoughts, to-dos, and staff agenda ideas: How can I get background on topics to make informed and strategic decisions? Who should I talk to? What does the department control, and what does it not control?

Alice quickly jots down these questions, thoughts, and ideas. (See figure 14.4 for what she wrote down. Note that Alice adds her ideas to existing columns and doesn't start a new page for each new topic or idea. This helps her track the big picture of her department and community.) Alice's notes in figure 14.4 reveal that she decides that she needs to learn more about the department. What's the department's history? What milestones have occurred, and when did they occur? She believes that meeting one on one with each full-time employee could give her an overview of the department's history from a variety of perspectives. She could also ask questions about their future with the department—is anyone planning to retire in the next few years? What plans have been approved (e.g., strategic plans, master plans)? Are there funding priorities she needs to know about? Is the department's budget increasing or decreasing? As you can see from Alice's notes in figure 14.4, she believes that a meeting with the finance director is necessary; she wants to understand the city's overall financial picture and to learn the source of the department's revenues, its major expenses, and the costs it controls and does not control. What role does the department play with its partners—facilitator/broker,

information/referral, or advocate? Alice picks up the phone to schedule a meeting with the finance director first.

Competencies for the 21st-Century Parks and Recreation Leader

The trends described in the preceding section are changing the parks and recreation profession. As leaders, we need to ask ourselves a critical question: What competencies are needed to lead in the profession?

Alice has read about these trends and seen examples of them in the town of Happenstance. She has made notes on her worksheets about actions she will take to gauge where her agency stands in relationship to the trends. She plans to engage her staff in discussions about these trends and begin to develop their skills to move the department into the 21st century, her primary responsibility in her new role. But before she meets with her staff, she wants to reflect on the competencies she thinks a 21st-century leader needs to develop and master.

The trends, whether they are demographic, technological, or economic, have a common thread running through them, which is change. Trends define the changes that are occurring in our lives and reshaping our communities, agencies, and profession. To lead and influence responses to the trends, leaders must demonstrate competence in two areas: leading change and strategic thinking.

My thoughts	Staff agenda items
• Look at census data for the community to see if there are any demographic trends. • How adept is the department with social marketing? How comfortable are staff members with using computers? • How can I informally assess the staff's computer skills? Mobile phone skills? • Get familiar with the department's history—*fast*!	• What data are available on current program participants? • What data are available on the use of online registration versus in-office or mail registration? • Social marketing—what is it? How can we use it? • Sharing stories (part 1)—What's the most wonderful thing the department has done since it started?
	To-do items
	• Schedule a meeting with the fire department to discuss incidents involving seniors at their homes. • Register for a department class online. • Schedule a meeting with the IT department. • Schedule a meeting with the finance director. • Obtain a list of current agency partners.

Figure 14.4 Alice's worksheet: economic trends.

We will define and describe these two competencies and look at how Alice uses them in her role as a leader.

Leading Change

For recreation and parks professionals, leading change is no longer a choice. The real question is not whether to lead change, but how to go about doing so. Will you lead change by making informed and strategic decisions, or will you wait until change is forced on you? Were you told that your department was moving under the jurisdiction of the Public Works Department, or were you part of the planning process that came to that conclusion? Will how the change occurred affect your leadership style?

Leadership defines what the future should look like, aligns people with that vision, and inspires them to make it happen despite the obstacles.

—*John P. Kotter, author of Leading Change (1996)*

If you don't like change, you're going to like irrelevance even less.

—*General Eric Shinseki, U.S. Secretary of Veterans' Affairs*

How do leaders move their organizations and communities from trends to ideas to implementation in a situation that is constantly shifting? There are many approaches to leading change. This section focuses on leading change by empowering recreation and parks employees, which results in more engaged staff delivering more strategic and valued services.

Leaders need to understanding how people view and respond to change. It is widely believed that most people dislike and resist change. According to Bridges (2009), "It isn't the changes that do you in, it's the transitions" (p. 3). Typically, the way change is led, the way people are moved from the old to the new, creates resistance and negativity, which leads to the failure to change. Most organizations do not pay attention to the psychological aspects of change, the transitions that people must go through to implement change successfully. As a leader, you will likely see opportunities in changes before your staff sees them. You may feel a sense of urgency and might be in a hurry to make a change without adequate preparation. However,

making the transition smoother for staff will result in smoother implementation of the change. You can do this by doing the following:

- ▶ Acknowledge what is changing and describe what will be different as a result. Paint a picture with as much information as you have at the time. You are preparing people for the eventual outcomes.

- ▶ Acknowledge the emotional as well as the organizational effects of change. Expect that people will have a range of reactions. Be empathetic and continue to paint the new landscape as often as you need to. Be clear about what is ending and what is staying the same. Be clear that you still expect results.

- ▶ Give people the resources and support they need to make the transition. Acknowledge their discomfort and reassure them that they will be equipped with the training and structure needed to facilitate the process.

- ▶ Teach staff tools to assess and manage their situations. An effective tool adapted from Covey's *The 7 Habits of Highly Effective People* (2004) is called the CIO model; CIO stands for control, influence, and out of area of control.

Leaders can use the CIO model mentioned earlier with employees to illustrate that they do have control over some areas and that their actions can make a difference. If they address the areas they control, their influence grows. It is even possible to influence areas over which they thought they had no control.

For example, a nonprofit organization ran an after-school wellness and fitness program in partnership with a neighborhood elementary school. The school principal informed the nonprofit director and staff that their funding was going to be cut 50 percent in the next school year. The school's budget was being reduced, and cosponsoring the program at the current level was no longer feasible. Fortunately, they were still going to be able to use the school facilities for the program.

The director of the nonprofit and her staff were demoralized by the news; they felt as though they had no control over the situation. They were also aware that their program was unique and addressed one of the most prevalent trends related to their participants, childhood obesity. Each day they saw evidence of the negative effects of obesity on children in their program. They also knew that the program was the only provider of healthy food and fitness for the majority of the children who attended. The director decided that she had to be a proactive advocate for the after-school program. She was not willing to risk losing the program, which had positive effects on children. She thought about how they might influence the principal in the decision not to cosponsor the program. One of her first decisions was to empower her staff to become advocates by communicating the positive effects of the program on children. As shown in figure 14.5, the staff is one area of control the program director has at her disposal to try to expand their area of influence, which is the principal.

At the next staff meeting, the director taught the staff how to use the CIO model. She had chosen the CIO model because she wanted her staff to focus on the areas over which they have control. By doing so, they could convince and influence others to support their program. Through this influence, they could address areas over which they believed they had no control, such as the school district's budget. The goals of the session were to assess the situation and develop a strategy for keeping the program alive.

The director and her staff brainstormed the areas that they believed were out of their area of control, as depicted by the largest box in figure 14.5: the state's budget crisis, school district budget cuts, and a low priority for children's health and wellness issues on the part of the local government. By identifying these areas that seemed out of their control, they were able to focus on how they might influence the people who did have control.

Next, the director and the staff brainstormed the areas over which they had control and came up with the following list: connections with neighborhood businesspeople and interested community volunteers, experience teaching fitness classes, experience planning nutritious meals, knowledge of the effects of obesity on children, and a passionate commitment to the health and fitness of children. From this list, they brainstormed the following specific actions they could take:

▶ Work with volunteers to develop fact sheets on healthy eating and the dangers of childhood obesity.

▶ Translate the fact sheets into the three languages most commonly spoken in the neighborhood.

▶ Solicit local grocers and restaurants for contributions of healthy food.

▶ Partner with the community garden members to plant a vegetable garden in a corner of the schoolyard.

▶ Ask nearby fitness centers to cosponsor programs.

▶ Establish a Fit and Proud Club for children that the PTA could cosponsor.

As indicated by the arrows in figure 14.5, these actions could potentially expand their area of control as well as their area of influence with the principal.

The director set up a meeting with the principal in which the staff presented their proposals. With the principal's approval, they implemented their ideas within one month of the CIO session.

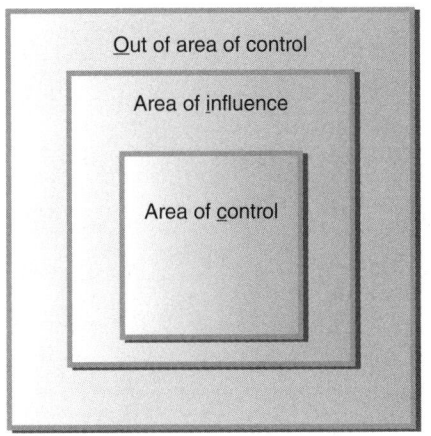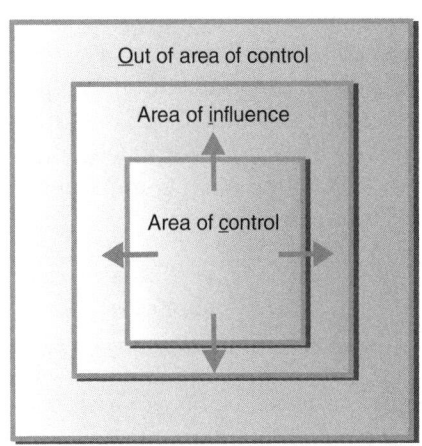

Figure 14.5 CIO model.

By taking control of the areas they could (represented by the small box in figure 14.5), they were able to influence the principal, get parents to care for the vegetable garden on weekends, get local businesses to provide T-shirts for the Fit and Proud Club, and gain the support of previously uninvolved families for their program (shown as the arrows in figure 14.5).

As a result of the efforts of the director and her staff, enrollment in the program increased. In addition, two powerful, unexpected results occurred. The first was a new sense of pride in the school and surrounding community. The second was that the nonprofit organization was seen by the community and colleagues as running a best practice wellness and fitness after-school program. The director of the nonprofit organization led the change by empowering her staff to act and teaching them an assessment tool (the CIO model) that led them to take action that influenced decision makers and stakeholders.

Recreation and park leaders should address the competency of leading change by asking themselves these questions:

- How do I respond to change? How would I like to respond change, and how can I get there?

- Do I understand the change and transition process and its effect on people?

- What do the changes mean for the team I lead? What competencies will they need to implement these changes?

- What leadership competencies do I need to develop to be able to lead change?

Strategic Thinking

Strategic thinking is the way leaders view, think about, and create the future for their organizations and professions. It is much more than reacting and responding to day-to-day and long-term challenges, opportunities, and trends. Strategic thinking is proactive, continuous, and focused on results. It requires discipline and a commitment to lead. And it always involves change.

The greatest danger in times of turbulence is not the turbulence; it is to act with yesterday's logic.

—*Peter Drucker*

As Alice thinks about leadership competencies, she finds herself picturing a former boss who was a leader in the profession and widely admired by those with whom she worked. Alice always admired her boss's strategic thinking competency. Following are the strategic thinking characteristics that her boss demonstrated and tried to develop in Alice and others:

- Developing and communicating a vision of what the future could look like based on trends, professional expertise, and a connection to a community or client base

- Being willing to think differently, explore new ideas, and take intelligent risks

- Understanding the need for both process and results, and recognizing that how an initiative moves forward is critical to achieving the desired results

- Being able to assess issues and put forward plans on many levels, such as strategic, operational, financial, human resources, and evaluation

- Investing in the long-term; being able to keep sight of the big picture and destination instead of just today's gain

Alice thinks about an analysis tool that the director used that taught her about strategic thinking: SWOT (strengths, weaknesses, opportunities, threats). The strengths and weaknesses sections refer to internal conditions such as staff competencies, program effectiveness, and talent management. The opportunities and threats sections refer to external conditions such as trends, customers, and competition.

Strengths are the characteristics of your organization that will help you achieve results. After you've identified them, ask: How can we take advantage of our strengths?

Weaknesses are the characteristics of your organization that will limit or preclude your ability to achieve results. After you've identified them, ask: How can we mitigate or eliminate the effects of our weaknesses?

Opportunities are factors in the external environment that could help you achieve results if you took advantage of them. After you've identified them, ask: How can we capitalize on our opportunities?

Threats are factors in the external environment that could negatively affect the ability to achieve results. After you've identified them, ask: How can we manage threats effectively?

Alice decides to lead her staff through a SWOT analysis. The objective of the analysis is to identify

Table 14.2 SWOT Technology Exercise

OBJECTIVE: TO IDENTIFY HOW HAPPENSTANCE RESIDENTS AND CUSTOMERS ARE USING OR NOT USING TECHNOLOGY TO FIND RECREATION OPPORTUNITIES AND PARKS	
Positive	**Negative**
Strengths • Online registrations are increasing • Leagues are using Facebook to notify players, referees, and coaches of game changes • Staff is excited about using social media	Weaknesses • City's website is dated and does not allow departments to change information • City leadership is not engaged in social media • IT blocks access to social media sites
Opportunities • Share websites of other cities with city leadership • Ask IT director to attend technology workshop on social media • Survey participants about their use of Facebook, Twitter, and other social media	Threats • Doing nothing will position the city and department as out of touch • Missing ongoing conversations about the department that are already occurring • Not reaching customers who use technology • Missing opportunities to expand customer base to teens and young adults

A SWOT analysis is a fundamental tool of strategic thinking that has these purposes: to assess the organization's position in relationship to a trend; to assess the organization's position in a specific market such as ecotourism; to analyze a new program idea; to assess potential new partnerships; to analyze a product or brand; and to craft a strategic plan. The analysis in table 14.2 considers both external and internal conditions and presents a picture of today's reality as well as directions in which to focus if Alice decides to move forward. A SWOT analysis is usually conducted by brainstorming with those closely involved in the topic and, often, stakeholders.

Now what? Once you've completed your SWOT analysis, stop before you launch into action around the factors you've identified during the process. Do you have a current strategic plan, business plan, or trend analysis? What SWOT factors are already being addressed by your current strategy? If you discover a factor from SWOT that is not being addressed anywhere else, decide whether you will revise your strategy to include it.

Alice thinks of the many issues facing her department and sees many areas in which structured strategic thinking would help her and her staff determine their future. She turns to her computer to plan how she would use leadership competencies in her role and to develop her staff.

At the end of a busy day, Alice sits at her desk and thinks about the competencies she needs to develop to lead her department into the 21st century—that is, leading change and strategic thinking. As you can see from Alice's notes in figure 14.6, she decides that she needs to assess her level of competence in each of these competencies

My thoughts	Staff agenda items
• The two critical competencies I need right now are leading change and strategic thinking. • Assess my competency to determine my own development plan. • What competencies does my staff need to develop? How can I assess their strengths and areas for development? • What tools and techniques can I teach the staff? • Who can I call on to support staff development and offer training? • Does the staff have individual development plans? • What training have the staff received?	• Department training—what training have they attended that was beneficial to them? • Invite a colleague from a professional society to introduce the topic of competencies and how they're used. • Discuss the top trends affecting the community. **To-do items** • Review employee files for staff development plans. • Involve the staff in using the CIO model and SWOT analysis after the trend discussion.

Figure 14.6 Alice's worksheet: leadership competencies.

to determine her development plan. Next, Alice thinks about assessing the staff's competencies and areas for development. She puts several items on the agenda for the next staff meeting, including talking about competencies and how they are used. Finally, her to-do items in figure 14.6 are to look at the staff's personnel files to see whether they have development plans and to involve the staff in using the CIO model and SWOT analysis.

Recreation and park leaders should address their strategic thinking competency by asking themselves these questions:

▶ What is my vision for my leadership in the profession?

▶ Am I future focused? What are examples of this?

▶ What strategic thinking characteristics do I possess? Which ones do I need to develop and master?

▶ How do I analyze trends and their implications for my community?

Summary

Being a leader in the parks and recreation profession during a period of ongoing and large-scale demographic, technological, and economic change requires adopting strategies to shape a clear vision of the future. Leaders must become savvy trend watchers who can engage employees and clients in discussions and planning related to these trends, and make strategic decisions about services, resources, partnerships, and staffing.

Leaders for the future need to be proficient in many competencies, including leading change and strategic thinking. Leading change by empowering recreation and park employees will result in more engaged staff delivering more strategic and valued services to customers. Strategic thinking includes assessing one's strengths and weaknesses as well as analyzing trend data to ensure that organizations and services meet the needs of clients, employees, and the profession.

Questions for Reflection and Discussion

1. What trends do you believe will affect the park and recreation profession?

2. Do you think you are knowledgeable about which societal trends will affect the parks and recreation profession in the next three to five years? Why do you feel that way?

3. What steps can you take to become a trend watcher? Who can you get to join you as a trend watcher?

4. What current leader do you admire? What competencies do you feel this leader exhibits?

5. Which leadership skills do you feel you currently have? Which skills do you need to develop?

6. How skilled are you at thinking strategically?

7. What competencies do you feel a park and recreation professional will need to develop in the next three to five years?

Key Terms and Definitions

consumer trends—Habits or behaviors of people when buying goods or services.

industry trends—What is happening in any industry (i.e., the field of parks and recreation is currently in a trend of restructuring, reduced fiscal resources, and expanding partnerships).

macro trend—A trend with a long life that is the result of many forces: demographic, economic, government, societal, and technological.

opportunities—Factors in the external environment that, if taken advantage of, can achieve results.

strategic thinking—The process of analyzing and evaluating information and situations to help with problem solving, decision-making, and conceptualizing.

strengths—Characteristics of an organization that achieve results.

threats—Factors in the external environment that negatively affect the achievement of results.

trend watchers—People who study trends and may try to predict the future based on those trends.

weaknesses—Characteristics of an organization that limit or preclude the achievement of results.

Bibliography

Apple Press Info. (2013). App store tops 40 billion downloads with almost half in 2012. https://www.apple.com/pr/library/2013/01/07App-Store-Tops-40-Billion-Downloads-with-Almost-Half-in-2012.html

Adams, J.H. (Ed.). (2008). *Creating community in the 21st century: Action plan for parks & recreation.* Urbana, IL: Sagamore.

Annie E. Casey Foundation. (2010). *Kids count* http://www.aecf.org/MajorInitiatives/kidscount.aspx

Bridges, W. (2009). *Managing transitions: Making the most of change* (3rd ed.). Philadelphia, PA: De Capo Press.

British Columbia Recreation & Park Association: https://www.bcrpa.bc.ca/

California Department of Public Health. (2010). *California obesity prevention plan: A vision for tomorrow, strategic action for today.* Sacramento: State of California.

California Park & Recreation Society. (2001). *Leading to promote health & wellness.* www.cprs.org

Center for Creative Leadership: www.ccl.org

Covey, S.R. (2004). *The 7 habits of highly effective people.* New York: Simon & Schuster.

Finkelstein, E.A., Trogdon, J.G., Cohen, J.W., & Dietz, W. (2009). Annual medical spending attributable to obesity: Payer- and service-specific estimates. *Health Affairs, 28*, 822-831.

Google, Apple, Microsoft app number wars heat up. (2013). *PC World.* www.pcworld.com/article/2023783/google-apple-microsoft-app-number-wars-heat-up.html.

Johnson, S. (1998). *Who moved my cheese?* New York: G.P. Putnam's Sons.

Kids Count Data Center (2014). http://datacenter.kidscount.org

National Aging in Place Council. (n.d.). Age in place, www.ageinplace.org.

National Trust for Historic Preservation (2010). *Explore America's 11 most endangered historic places.* www.preservationnation.org/issues/11-most-endangered/

Outdoor Industry Association. (n.d.). The Outdoor Foundation participation studies. http://outdoorfoundation.org/research.participation.html.

Pew Research Center. (2008). *The databank. Key data trends.* http://www.pewresearch.org/key-data-points/economy-pew-research-center-key-data-points/

Pew Research Center. (2010). Pew Internet and American Life Project, www.pewinternet.org.

Schlau, L., & Hiner, H. (2009). *Report on results of market research to support CPRS building the brand initiative.* Sacramento, CA: California Park & Recreation Society.

Stevens, C.A., Murphy, J.F., Allen, L.R., & Sheffield, E.A. (2010). *A career with meaning: Recreation, parks, sports management, hospitality, and tourism.* Urbana, IL: Sagamore.

Subrahmanyam, K., Kraut, R., Greenfield, P., & Gross, E. (2000). The impact of home computer use on children's activities and development. *Children and Computer Technology, 10*: 2.

TrendScan, Leisure Lifestyle Consulting, Glastonbury, CT: www.cprs.org/index.php?option=com_content&view=article&id=65&Itemid=84

Trendwatching.com: www.trendwatching.com

Trendwatching.com. (n.d.). 15 trend tips. http://trendwatching.com/tips/ www.trendwatching.com.

U.S. Census Bureau. (2010). *The next four decades: The older population in the United States: 2010 to 2050.* https://www.census.gov/prod/2010pubs/p25-1138.pdf

U.S. Census Bureau. (2012). *U.S. Census Bureau projections show a slower growing, older, more diverse nation a half century from now.* http://www.census.gov/newsroom/releases/archives/population/cb12-243.html

Van der Smissen, B., Moiseichik, M., Hartenburg. V., & Twardzik, L. (1999). *Management of park and recreation agencies.* Ashburn, VA: National Recreation & Park Association.

Workitect, www.workitect.com

Index

About the Editors

Photo courtesy of Janet Zanutto.

Timothy S. O'Connell, PhD, is a professor of recreation and leisure studies at Brock University in St. Catharines, Ontario. He has taught group dynamics since 1997 and has been a wilderness guide since 1991. A member of the National Recreation and Parks Association, the Society for Teaching and Learning in Higher Education, the Association for Experiential Education, and the Council of Outdoor Educators of Ontario, O'Connell has developed outdoor recreation curricula and coedited the Journal of Experiential Education. He has received many awards for his teaching. An avid outdoor recreationist, O'Connell enjoys rock climbing, sea kayaking, and home brewing in his spare time.

Photo courtesy of Kim Cuthbertson.

Brent Cuthbertson, PhD, is an associate professor of outdoor recreation, parks, and tourism at Lakehead University in Thunder Bay, Ontario. He has been a wilderness educator and guide for more than 25 years and coeditor of the Journal of Experiential Education. He has written book chapters, papers in refereed journals, and a variety of other refereed and nonrefereed contributions. Cuthbertson has received awards for his teaching excellence. In his leisure time he enjoys wilderness canoeing, sea kayaking, woodworking, and sailing.

Photo by Jeff Tiemann. Courtesy of Terilyn Goins.

Terilyn J. Goins, PhD, is an educational trainer and consultant and an adjunct professor at Regent University in Virginia Beach, Virginia. She has worked in the academy for more than 20 years at various institutions as a professor of communication studies and has also served administratively as department chair. Dr. Goins received the National Speaker's Association Outstanding Professor Award, was voted Professor of the Year at Christopher Newport University by the student body, and has published numerous articles for trade and academic journals related to personal and professional growth and development. Additionally, Goins is a vocalist, has recorded five CDs, and speaks and performs for conferences, retreats, and other professional venues.

About the Contributors

Jane Adams served as executive director of the California Park & Recreation Society in Sacramento from 1988 to 2014. CPRS provides education, networking, resources, and public advocacy for California's park and recreation professionals. In 2000 Jane led the implementation of the profession's first strategic plan, Creating Community in the 21st Century: The VIP Action Plan. She is editor of *Creating Community: An Action Plan,* a collegiate and professional text published by Human Kinetics. Jane led the creation of the nation's first research-based public awareness campaign, Parks Make Life Better!, in 2011. Forty-five percent of California's park and recreation agencies are campaign partners.

Lynn Anderson is a Distinguished Service Professor in the Recreation, Parks and Leisure Studies Department at State University of New York at Cortland, and director for the Inclusive Recreation Resource Center. She is an active teacher and scholar in therapeutic recreation, inclusion, and outdoor recreation, and has won numerous teaching, service, and research awards. She serves as associate editor or reviewer for several journals and has written two popular textbooks. Dr. Anderson has particular research interests in inclusion, accessibility and the strengths approach. She received her M.S. from the University of Oregon and her Ph.D. from the University of Minnesota.

Mary Breunig is an associate professor in the Department of Recreation and Leisure Studies at Brock University and director of the Brock University Social Justice Research Institute. She has worked in the field of experiential education for over 20 years and is past president of the Association for Experiential Education. Her research interests include outdoor and environmental education within the K-12 schools (Ontario), experiential education and social justice, critical pedagogy and Freirean praxis both in and out of the classroom, wilderness trips, and psychological sense of community. She is an educator, researcher, speaker, community activist, and wilderness trip guide.

Marilynn R. Glasser, Ed.D., CPRP, CPSI, has more than 35 years of both professional parks and recreation administration and college teaching experience. Her consulting firm, Parks and Pastimes, Inc., specializes in dog parks and playground safety consulting. Her recreation and parks degrees are from Springfield College and New York University and her professional memberships include the National Recreation and Park Association, the New York State Recreation and Park Society and the Westchester Recreation and Park Society. Dr. Glasser is the author of Human Kinetics' "Dog Park Design, Development, and Operation", the first dog park "how-to" book written by a parks and recreation professional. Her leisure interests are extensive: golf, fishing, antique collectibles, guitar, the 1950s, animals, nature, classic automobiles, art deco and outdoor events such as flea markets and concerts as well as spending time on Cape Cod and in Florida.

Amy Hurd, PhD, CPRE is the director of the graduate school and a professor in Recreation and Park Administration at Illinois State University. Her research focuses on competency development and succession planning. Prior to coming to Illinois State University, Amy was a visiting lecturer at Indiana University and worked for the Champaign Park District.

Dr. Hurd was a visiting scholar in Sustainable Tourism at Srinakharinwirot University in Bangkok, Thailand and traveled to Opole University of Technology in Poland and University of Cuyo in Argentina for a student–faculty cultural emersion experience.

Amy has coauthored numerous articles and textbooks, including Official Study Guide for the Certified Park and Recreation Professional Exam, Kraus' Recreation and Leisure in Modern Society, Parks and Recreation Professionals Handbook, and Leisure Services Management.

Robert B. Kauffman is a professor in the Recreation and Parks Management department at Frostburg State University in Frostburg, Maryland.

He has more than 30 years of experience in the boating safety field. In 2013, he co-authored the textbook *Integrated Risk Management for Leisure Services*. His boating safety videos include Cold, Wet, and Alive; Decide to Return; and Almost a Perfect Day. They earned three CINE Golden Eagle Awards (2012, 1994, and 1989). In 2014, Kauffman received a Regent's Award for public service. In 2005, he received the Citation Award from the Maryland Recreation and Parks Association for his lifetime achievement in recreation. Kauffman and his wife, Sally, reside in Frostburg, Maryland. In his free time, he enjoys canoeing, rafting, biking, and photography.

Dale Larsen, Professor of Practice and Director of Community Relations for the Arizona State University College of Public Programs, has been a manager in the parks and recreation field for 4 decades. Formerly the Director of the Phoenix, Arizona, Parks and Recreation Department, he was responsible for the executive administration of 1,000 full-time personnel. He teaches in management, leadership, civic engagement and community organization at Arizona State University (ASU). Dale is a Past - President of the American Academy for Parks and Recreation and has served as a Chair for the Commission for Parks and Recreation Accreditation. He is a member of the National Parks and Recreation Association, the Trust for Public Lands, City Parks Alliance, and serves on several Phoenix area committees. Dale has been married to his bride Christine for 43 years and is a proud father and grandparent who practices never growing up.

Greg Robinson is currently president of Challenge Quest, LLC in Pryor, Oklahoma, the managing member of Adventure Quest Recreation, LLC, and associate professor of Outdoor Leadership Ministries at John Brown University. Previous to coming to Challenge Quest, Robinson spent five years with Williams, a Fortune 500 energy company in Tulsa, Oklahoma as a managing organization development consultant. Robinson has a PhD in Organizational Behavior and Leadership from the Union Institute and University in Cincinnati, Ohio. He also has a masters degree in Counseling from John Brown University. His professional career has concentrated in the areas of experiential learning, team development, leadership development, facilitation, and consulting with organizational change efforts. He is the author of A Leadership Paradox:

Influencing Others by Defining Yourself, Teams for a New Generation: A Facilitator's Field Guide Adventure, and The Way of Jesus and Lessons of the Way: Using experiential activities to explore the way of Jesus. Robinson currently resides with his wife Jeannie, his daughter Keely, and his son Kobe in Pryor, Oklahoma.

Elaine Fukuhara Schilling, MPA, has held leadership and consultant roles in the public and non-profit sectors, higher education and corporations. She was previously director of training and development at UC Berkeley and at a large financial institution. She worked for the Department of Defense Recreation Services in Germany and with municipal recreation and community service agencies. She is on the faculty at San Francisco State University, where she teaches classes in organization development, supervision and human resources management for the Department of Recreation, Parks & Tourism, and the Department of Child & Adolescent Development. Elaine holds an MPA from Notre Dame de Namur University.

Michael Van Bussel is the chair of Language and Liberal Studies at Fanshawe College in London, Ontario, Canada. His research interests include leadership in sport, leisure, and recreation; communication in coaching; and conflict in sport executive committees. Michael is also an accomplished coach with over 20 years' coaching experience. He has a Masters of Education in Coaching and a Diploma in High Performance Coaching from the National Coaching Institute in Victoria, British Columbia. In 2003 and 2004 Michael was named the Ontario University Athletics (OUA) Coach of the Year for his work with the Western University Women's Soccer Program.

Brent Wolfe is an associate professor in Recreational Therapy at the college of Health and Human Sciences at Georgia Southern University in Statesboro, GA. He is a certified therapeutic recreation specialist and is on the board of directors for the American Therapeutic Recreation Association. Brent has spoken at numerous national and international conferences on the topic of facilitation and believes that the key to being a successful facilitator and a successful person is the same thing—listening. Brent spends all his free time with his wife, Becky, their two daughters, Austyn Grace and Taylor Faith, and their dog, Bella.

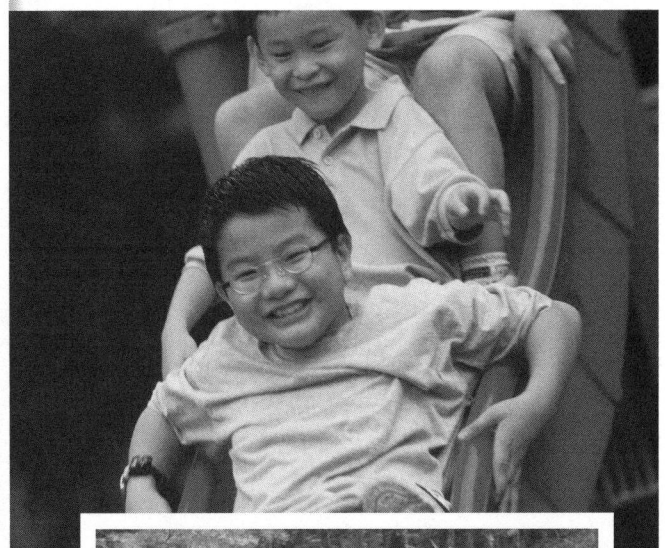